Reviewed by Amy Raines for Readers' Favorite

Behind Her Smile: The Adventures of a Tall Girl from WVA and Her Life as a Stewardess is written by Beverly Golden Cuevas. Beverly's younger years were pretty normal as she navigated through her life, trying to figure out where she fit in. She tried her hand at singing and playing instruments but quickly discovered that a career in music was not in her future. She made an attempt at writing, but that didn't work out the way she had hoped either. Thanks to a very dear friend, Beverly became a flight attendant. In spite of a traumatic event, she loved her job and the amazing people she got to meet through the years.

Behind Her Smile is an interesting memoir that reinforces the idea of how important it is not to give up on living your best life no matter what the circumstances might be. I enjoyed reading about the life Beverly Golden Cuevas led as a stewardess and the friendships she maintained along the way. I enjoyed learning about the difference between the way stewardesses handled a flight years ago versus the way things are taken care of onboard a plane now. I find it inspiring that she kept her focus on the future even during the dark and difficult times. I recommend Behind Her Smile to anyone who enjoys an autobiography that outlines the life choices and the lifestyle of an interesting career path that is rarely discussed. I hope that Cuevas decides to write more books that will inspire others to follow their hearts and chase their dreams while they can.

BEHIND HER SMILE

The Adventures of a Tall Girl from WVA and Her Life as a Stewardess

BEVERLY GOLDEN CUEVAS

Behind Her Smile

1603 Capitol Ave., Suite 310 Cheyenne, Wyoming USA 82001
1-888-980-6523 | admin@urlinkpublishing.com

URLink Print and Media is committed to excellence in the publishing industry.

Published in the United States of America

Library of Congress Control Number: 2023914329
ISBN 978-1-68486-483-6 (Paperback)
ISBN 978-1-68486-486-7 (Hardback)
ISBN 978-1-68486-488-1 (Digital)

10.11.23

ACKNOWLEDGEMENTS

Karen Hanna, my BFF since 1957. None of this would have happened if you hadn't made me go to those interviews.

Susan Nurre, my constant support and encouragement. "Evil 2" you are the BEST!

Erin Mc Donnell, you made my dream a reality. I'm still in awe of you!

Chris Harrison, my cover designer (Realistic Form). You made this book come to life.

Donald B. Johnson, my favorite Captain. (I should have listened to my Mom.) Thanks for all of those talks throughout the years "Father Don."

My Mississippi Family - Donnie, Tam, Dana, La Risa, Roy, Maeson, Beau, Deron and Michael. "Ya'll" have accepted and loved me from the very beginning. I love you all!

Rand, my EVERYTHING! My hubby of 43 years. I'm so glad you fell in love with me "at first sight."

Josh - (My Heart) and Kaleb- (My Joy) God couldn't have sent us better blessings than you, our sons!

Steph - (Josh's Mrs) and Katy- (Kaleb's wife and Eden's Mom) Thanks for making our sons so happy!

To my grandchildren Eden Jane, Elijah, Ellie, Logan and Holly - May my Lord bless you all.

NOTE FROM THE AUTHOR

Many times I've been told I should write a book about my life and career as a Stewardess. I have been extremely fortunate to experience some things in my life that I never imagined would be possible. So after conferring with both of my sons and my husband, I've decided to write this book. They all said that they would not read it, but they felt it was something I should do.

This book is the very heart and breath of me. It contains some of the happiest, and a few of the saddest, times of my life so far. There are people and situations I have written about in this book that are my opinion. There will be those who disagree and dispute my word. To those individuals I say, "These are the times as I remember them and have documented in personal diaries. It may be different from what you recollect, so I invite you to write your own version if you see fit to do so."

My life written in this book is BC, before finding Christ. My second book will be written AC, after finding Christ, when it became important to me to establish a relationship and commitment with my Lord. Some incidents and language may offend and surprise some of my friends and fellow Christians, but before December 7, 1980, I was not born again. The first part of my life was not lived as a Christian. My earnest prayer is that the remainder of it will be.

I would like to thank my Daddy, Raymond Golden, and my Mom, Helen, for the way they raised me. They told me, "Never give up and always believe in yourself." To the boys and men I have loved -- Terry, Jimmie, Alphie, Derek, Wendell, and Rand -- I would like to say, "You have all contributed to helping me understand the meaning of love in so many ways."

I hope I am able to establish in our sons, Joshua Aaron and Kaleb Micah, how to love and be loved. I wish them a happy, healthy, loving life, committed to family and friends, and most of all, to their Lord. For truly With God, all things are possible. (Luke 18:27)

CONTENTS

THAT "OH SO IMPORTANT" FIRST CHAPTER

Vicki Bennett, Charlotte Gibbons,
Me, Karen Hanna and Cindy Mackensen

I have so many mixed emotions going to this 50th High School Class Reunion. First, I find it hard to believe that my classmates and I graduated 50 years ago. Time truly has flown by, for me, in more ways than one. I'm still amazed that for nearly 35 of those 50 years, I was a Stewardess/Flight Attendant; me, the tallest, most flat-chested girl in our class. Never in my wildest dreams could I have imagined I'd have even the smallest chance to do what I did for a living. I must admit I have a great sense of pride and accomplishment to have been chosen for that job, especially with only a High School education. Yes, I had work experience; I had been working since age fourteen, to be exact. Being as tall as I was had some advantages. Everyone thought I was older than my true age, so I could get that job at Woolworth's without a Social Security number.

I am looking forward to spending time with Karen (Roth) Hanna, the woman responsible for dragging me to all of those Stewardess interviews. It will be so much fun to catch up with her. Yes, we've kept in touch for all these years but to actually have "girl time" with no husbands or boyfriends to force us to act mature is going to be so enjoyable...... I hope. I pray there is still some silliness left in us because I sure could use it. The last three years of my life have been a total nightmare!

Daddy died on May 14, 2001. On June 25, 2011, I lost my brother, Mike, after his two and a half year battle with Lung Cancer. Three months later, on November 1st, my Mom, Helen, my best friend throughout my life, died of a heart attack in my arms. She had lived with my husband, sons, and me for five years. Twenty days later, my beloved and adored dog, Dixie

Belle, passed away. To add to the shock of all of this, my younger sister, Charmaine, died from Creutzfeldt-Jakob disease (a degenerative brain disorder that affects one in a million people per year) less than two years after Mom passed. My whole entire family is gone. Now there is no one to talk with about memories of my childhood, my teenage years, my time growing up. No more questions will be answered by anyone from my past. There is no one to ask, "Remember the time we did this, or saw that, or went here or there?" It is an empty feeling. Thank the Lord I can still make memories with my husband, Rand, and our sons, Joshua and Kaleb (along with their wives Stephanie and Katy).

"Bev, we need to get to the airport. Are you ready?" asked my hubby.

"Yes, Rand, I'll be right out." I was in my bathroom putting the "finishing touches" on my makeup. Now, after being overwhelmed recalling the sadness that has plagued my life over the last three years, I needed to redo my mascara. "Pull yourself together, girl," I thought. "You are embarking upon three days of walking down Memory Lane." ("Memory Lane" - also the theme of my Senior Prom, which was a disaster!)

Rand kissed me and told me to have a good time. He did not want to go to this Reunion. In all honesty, I didn't want him to go either. Reunions are always miserable for the spouse of the classmate unless they attended the same school. Sometimes, though, that is even worse, especially if old boyfriends and girlfriends have unresolved issues from High School romances.

The only issue I brought was the one-sided love I had for the boy in my seventh-grade class; I was so crazy about him from the first time I laid eyes on him. I just could not wait to see Terry Kneisely again. It had been years! He had come to my Daddy's funeral viewing. We spent a small amount of time dancing and talking at our 30th Reunion. Where did another 20 years go? I did chat with him by phone whenever I was home in Ohio visiting the folks. Because he was an only child and, truthfully, because I wanted him to think about me for at least a few minutes, I sent him birthday and Christmas cards every year. Yes, it will be wonderful to see Terry again.

I dressed up to get on the plane because that is how we Stewardesses always traveled. Boy, was I surprised at the stares I got at the airport! The TSA guard said to me "WOW! You look fantastic! It is such a shock to see someone dressed up instead of looking like they just rolled out of bed and came to the airport in the clothes they just slept in."

"Well, thank you, kind sir," I replied. "Do you mind if I go back through security so I can hear you say that again?" He laughed and said it would be his pleasure.

When I checked in at the gate, the agents, two women and one man, seemed to step back and stare at me as if to get a better look at how I was dressed. It was a nice feeling to see their reaction to how I looked. The male agent reached for my ticket, "My you look so nice today" he said looking at my name on the ticket, "Miss Cuevas."

I checked his nametag, "Why thank you, John. I do believe you just made my day." He smiled and told me we would be boarding in about twenty minutes.

As I went to sit down, I decided to glance around me to observe the passengers in the lounge area. It had been a long time since I had flown, but I didn't realize just how much the traveling public had changed. Most men had on sport shirts and jeans or slacks. A few were wearing t-shirts. The women too, wore either slacks or jeans and t-shirts, some with their kid's pictures on them. The younger guys and gals had on shorts or jeans with t-shirts (AGAIN) with their college's names, silly sayings, or political references on them. I was surprised to see so many of the guys wearing flip-flops, which is foot attire I expect to see at the beach, not at the airport. Occasionally, I saw a girl in a nice skirt and blouse.

Things have definitely changed since I started my career back in 1966. Men wore suits, ties, and beautifully pressed button-up shirts. The few women there were "dressed to the nines" in suits and designer dresses with gorgeous shoes and purses. I must say I do not like the way people dress these days. Yes, it is true, everyone seems to go more for comfort than class, but all of these t-shirts were so unattractive. Sadly, I don't see people going back to dressing in the *Mad Men*-series style, but this attire is a shame.

John made a boarding announcement, and I knew I had to wait because I was traveling on a pass. Suddenly John called my name and handed me a First Class boarding pass. "Here, you so deserve this," he stated.

"Well thank you, John. that is so kind of you." I smiled at him as I made my way toward the jetbridge to the plane. I was looking forward to flying again, as I had only flown once since 9-11. I still had moments when I missed flying, but I, like a lot of Flight Attendants, no longer felt safe being in the sky with unknown people potentially hell-bent on killing you for no reason.

I was about to get an even greater surprise regarding the Flight Attendants working this trip. I was cordial to the man boarding the flight, and he was anything but. He may have been upset that the flight was full, and his demeanor certainly showed it. I sat down in the last First Class row by a man who I guessed to be in his forties (I'm terrible at guessing ages), and we began to chat. One of the Flight Attendants came forward from the coach cabin and stopped by the closet to hang coats. I nearly fell out of my seat! This woman - I had no idea how old she was - had absolutely no makeup on whatsoever, and her hair didn't appear to have seen a comb or hairbrush in days. I'm sure I had an astonished look on my face when I leaned back in my seat.

The man beside me looked at me and stated fairly loudly, "Do you believe her?!? Whatever happened to Flight Attendants who cared about how they looked? The ones without a smart-ass, excuse me, attitude? I fly several trips a month, sometimes three or four, and the cabin crews keep getting worse and worse. What happened?"

"Sir, I honestly don't know. Things are so different now than when I flew." "Are you a Flight Attendant? Sorry if I insulted you," he said quickly.

"No apology necessary. I was one but I got hurt and had to quit flying. I must admit, I am as astonished as you are." About that time, I noticed the third F/A (Flight Attendant) as she came up to the First Class galley. Once again I was taken aback by a crewmember. Her uniform blouse looked like she had slept in it for at least a week! Her skirt was a wrinkled mess!

My seat partner looked at me and said, "It just keeps getting worse!"

I was so sad to see this. In the process of lowering my head, my eyes caught sight of the seatback pocket in front of me. There were crumbs falling out of it and wrappers stuffed in along with newspapers and Kleenex. "Oh my," I said, in what I had hoped was under my breath. But it wasn't.

"I'm sorry, what did you say?" the passenger beside me asked.

"Nothing really, I am just amazed at the condition of this airplane too. The carpets are filthy!"

"Well, welcome to the new age of air travel," he stated, "Where no one gives a damn anymore."

"I feel like I should apologize to you," I said softly.

"No need. I can tell by your appearance that you never would have shown up for a flight looking like this."

I shook my head and exclaimed, "No sir, I never would have." I sat back and thought to myself how sad this is, how very, very sad.

Karen Roth Hanna

I got to the hotel and called Karen. We hugged and hugged. I was so happy to see her. That first night we went out to dinner with an old friend, Bill Van Gieson. I had contacted Bill, a fella we both knew in High School who was a few years ahead of us. Both Karen and I dated Bill, and we all came to the conclusion that we were better being friends than boyfriend and girlfriend. One particular date Bill and I had together was quite embarrassing. We had gone to see South Pacific at a small theater on the Ohio State Campus and passed by several fraternity houses walking home from the movie. A group of guys sat on the porch of one house, and the sight of 5'6" Bill and 5"9" me was entirely too much for them to witness without commenting. One of the guys yelled "Hey Buddy, where did you find that long, tall drink of water?" All of the other guys burst out laughing. Bill and I hurried down the street as fast as we could.

He entered the hotel lobby with a sign reading, "Yes, It's Bill Van Gieson. In case you didn't recognize me." We laughed at him with his silly nameplate, and it was like we had all been together yesterday. I actually introduced him to his first wife. We had a great time telling each other about what had been going on in our lives over the years. It was so good to see Bill again.

The first day of festivities was titled "North on the Fourth." Our High School was named North, home of the mighty Polar Bears. There was a huge crowd in the auditorium, and it was difficult greeting former classmates as there was a program planned. I figured we had three days to catch up with the people with whom we wanted to visit. The worst part was there was no air

Bill Van Glesom

conditioning. Funny we never noticed that when we went to school there. Eventually, it got pretty unbearable, so Karen and I were glad to leave.

Virgina

We went to visit Virginia Coffmon, the mother of my first boyfriend, Jimmie Dale. She happened to live a short distance from our school. I had kept in touch with Virginia and her family since I was 16 years old. We had a great visit catching up on her, her 12 children, and bunches of grandchildren and great-grandchildren! Jimmie, her first son, had passed away several years before, and she still deeply felt the loss. I noted particularly how wonderful she looked for a lady her age, and I hope I am as fortunate to look as lovely as she does when I get there.

Besides my gal pals there were a few guy friends I would be happy to see, including Tim Buel, Doug Rund, Dan Sagstetter, and Sam Smith. And one I was not happy to see, whose name I won't mention.

This particular classmate had "come on to me" at the 10th and 29h reunions, and now he was at it again. At the 25th, he actually followed me into the ladies' restroom after I shrugged off one of his advances. He yelled at me, "Terry Kneisely, Terry Kneisely; that's all you ever cared about! That was then, and this is now. You need to give me a chance." I reminded him where he was and told him to leave immediately. He was unfazed and continued ranting about wanting me to give him a chance. Well tonight he tried again and with his wife there. He hadn't changed a bit. He had backed me up against the wall. When Karen saw the look of terror on my face, she ran over, and grabbed me by the arm, and dragged me away. Thank you for the rescue, Karen. Some people never learn!

Tim Buel

I got to chat with Tim Buel for a while. He was one of the popular guys at our High

School, and I thought he was so handsome. He played several sports and dated mostly cheerleaders. Still, he was always nice to me. I appreciated the fact that he even knew my name. It was always good to visit with Tim and catch up with what had been going on in his world.

The evening ended much too soon. Still I was rather tired and figured we still had some events to enjoy in the next two days and people that we hoped to see; especially Terry Kneisley!

I told Karen I had been emailing with Charlotte (Baker) Gibbons and Cindy (McElligott) Mackensen for weeks about the Reunion. They, and about eight others, had worked incredibly hard to put this event together. I told Karen I wanted to take them and Vickie Bennett, our former classmate and friend, out for lunch the next day. It would be a small "thank you" for all of their time spent making the reunion possible.

It was a fun luncheon. We got caught up on the last ten or twelve years, and when we got back to the hotel, Charlotte teased me that tonight was the night the love of my life would arrive. I laughed, but inside I was so excited at the thought of seeing Terry.

That night was our cookout at the hotel. I waited and nearly hurt my neck constantly turning so I wouldn't miss Terry when he arrived. To my dismay, he never showed. He had paid his money for the cookout and dinner the next night, so no one knew why he wouldn't have come. I was heartbroken! But I decided I had to put my disappointment in the back of my mind and get through it by visiting with my former classmates.

I made a new friend that evening, a ruggedly handsome man with piercing blue eyes and silver grey hair named Dean Johnson, when he stopped by my table to chat. I don't think either one of us knew the other existed in High School. Now we seemed to have a lot in common and decided to become email friend so we could keep in touch.

Dean Johnson

Fortunately, Rand doesn't mind if I have male friends. He never seems to be jealous. I asked him about it one day and he said he trusts me; there was no need to be jealous. I think sometimes I kind of wish he were at least a little bit. He used to be extremely jealous, and I'm grateful he has grown from that, but it might be a little flattering if he showed the occasional sign of it.

Karen and I were taking pictures left and right, laughing a lot, and enjoying ourselves. A former classmate and fellow Girl Scout named Kay (Coffey) Walker arrived that afternoon. I saw her in the lobby, as Karen and I were about to go to her room have a bite to eat. Karen had visited the deli when she first arrived in Columbus and bought this deliciously stinky salami and hard French loaves.

Kay Coffey

We invited Kay to join us, and she was more than happy to share our smelly lunch and enjoy a cocktail. I didn't have one, but Karen and Kay were partaking. We told tales and laughed so hard. I think some of the stories I shared with Kay were shocking -- about some of the people I had met and some of the folks I had dated. I was definitely enjoying watching the looks on her face.

I had always thought Kay was so pretty in school and often wished we had stayed friends after Girl Scouts, but we had gone our separate ways. After the "Popular Table" incident (you'll hear that story later), I never spent any time with her. I was saddened that one day had terminated a friendship, but that incident was all it took. Kay was still as attractive as I remembered her. I looked forward to spending time with her during the next two days.

The last day, Karen and I ate breakfast and then took off to do some errands. We went by Indianola, our old Junior High School. We drove by her parents' home, then visited her parents' gravesite for a few minutes. I didn't want to go by my parents' former home because it was still too painful. Even though Mom had not lived there in a long time, I just wasn't ready to drive by all of those memories.

I had taken such pains to find the perfect outfit for tonight's dinner, but the dress I brought suddenly didn't seem as attractive as the one I had worn on the plane. I hoped I would get as positive a reaction to how I looked at the dinner as I had gotten at the airport. Before I dressed, I tried calling Terry. There was no answer. Maybe he would show up tonight. Oh, how I hoped he would. I put my royal blue dress on, glanced in the mirror before leaving, said a silent prayer that I looked good, and went to Karen's room.

At the dinner, each classmate was announced along with their home state. I turned to look around the room as Terry's name was called, but he still wasn't there. He was the one person I wanted to see above all the others, yet he didn't come that night either. I was so sad.

Doug Rund

Doug Rund, our class president approached me, and we hugged. "I have a question for you, Bev. Have you finished that book yet?"

I smiled and informed him I was almost done. "The hardest part of the whole book is the very first chapter. I have rewritten that one at least five times."

"Well I expect to get an autographed copy just as soon as it's published," he said flashing me his megawatt smile.

"2016 is the goal, Doug. God willing it'll hit your local bookshelf in 2016"

"I can't wait," he said as he went off to visit with someone else. I smiled to myself as Doug walked away. We were in Drama Class together our senior year. He had been in the play *Teahouse of the August Moon*. He played an Asian guy named Sakini and walked around the stage in the most peculiar way. Sort of hunched over and shuffling his feet; he was quite a sight. One day, our teacher, Mr. Dupree, picked Doug and me to play the male and female roles in *Barefoot in the Park*. I was being oh-so-serious, trying to engage in flirting with Doug as my leading man. Suddenly, half way through our skit, he turned into Sakini again. He was chasing me across the stage with that ridiculous walk. The entire class erupted in gales of laughter. Even our teacher had trouble trying to encourage Doug to get back into character and he never succeeded. It was such a sight, me trying to get away from my leading man. Those were fun times.

I saw a gal named Kathleen (Dalmy) Megown I had been with in Orchestra. I wanted to play the trumpet, but I couldn't make a sound when I tried to play it. So Mr. Dale gave me a cello. I nearly died! I was so embarrassed. Here I am, a giant, and now I have to put this huge instrument between my knees! I recalled having to carry it home to practice. I lived nearly fifteen blocks from the school and walked to and from school every day. Some guys drove by in a car and yelled to me, "Hey sweetie, got your boyfriend in there?" They burst out laughing and drove on. I was mortified. Fortunately, I developed an allergic reaction to the rosin you put on your bow to aid it in moving across the strings. I was elated! I could no longer touch the bow so I never had to "pretend" to play the cello again. I confessed to Kathy that I had never really learned to play the cello at all; I just mocked her movements. I said, "Well that's my confession from my orchestra experience." Kathy laughed and laughed; she'd had no idea.

I ran around taking more pictures with classmates and sharing "cliff note" versions of my life experiences thus far. Tom Crenshaw had become a policeman. Just on a whim, I asked him if he knew a guy named Alphie Di Guilio or his brothers, Jim and Gary. Tom said, "Alphie was in my class at the police academy. How do you know Alf?"

"I was engaged to him when I got accepted to be a Stewardess."

"WHAT? You and Alphie? NO WAY!!! I can't see that at all!" he practically shouted at me.

"Yes, Tom, we were going to get married in 1967. Instead, I left to become a Stewardess in '66. I fell in love with the job, and I felt like I just couldn't come back to Columbus to marry Alphie."

"I am beyond shocked!" Tom said as his wife approached to join in our conversation, and we ended up changing the subject.

Honestly, to this day, a part of me still feels guilty for leaving Alphie. He really was a great guy, and he truly loved me so much. Tom and I didn't mention Alphie again. He just kept looking at me with such a look of surprise at the thought of Alphie and me together.

Terry Kneisley

Terry popped into my thoughts again as I scanned our senior yearbook. I thought he was the handsomest guy in our class of nearly 350 students. I would have given almost anything to be his girlfriend, but in spite of several dates, I suppose he always thought of me as just a friend. Regardless, I wished he had come because we weren't getting any younger.

After the dinner, I thanked Karen for driving us around and for being my BFF (Best Friend Forever) for nearly 50 years. We always did have fun together. I reminded her again if it had not been for her, I never would have gone to those interviews and ended up with the best job ever. My one regret was that we didn't get to enjoy the job together since she had not been hired as well. Seriously, as crazy as we were, we might have been fired for being too silly. That would have been really sad.

I had to leave early the next morning, so we said our good-byes. It was time to get back to my life in Dallas. I have lived in Texas longer than any other state. I grew up in West Virginia and lived there until I was 11. I left Ohio at the age of 21 to become a Stewardess. New York was my home for almost five years, then I spent about the same amount of time in Oklahoma. I never dreamed I would live anywhere but Columbus, Ohio.

Rand was happy to see me when I returned, but he really didn't ask many questions about the reunion, which was fine with me. I did tell him a few stories about my escapes, but he didn't know anyone anyway, so I don't think he really cared too much. We had dinner with our oldest son, Josh. and his new wife Stephanie. He asked about my trip but, I think he was just being polite. Josh never knew anyone from Mom's High School days, although he had met Terry at his grandpa's viewing when he was very young.

After Rand left for work, I took my camera to CVS to get the pictures developed. I made extra copies to send to a few classmates and also to Terry. In the card I sent with the photo, I asked why he hadn't come to the Reunion. As was usual for Terry, I never received a response. The only time he ever responded to my cards or letters was when he was in Vietnam, so I really didn't expect a reply. I actually would have been surprised if he had written. He was so funny at times about me being married. Perhaps it had something to do with the way we were raised. Men and women couldn't be friends. I found out later from a friend of his that he really appreciated the pictures I had sent him.

"I thought it was only fair to embarrass myself
with my senior picture, too."

WE ARE FAMILY

Mom, Chairmaine, Dad,
Me and Mike. (1955)

Just like every other little girl, I grew up wanting to be a princess, but since my parents were far from being royalty that just wasn't gonna happen.

Instead, I set my dream on being a "hillbilly" singer. (Yes, that was what country music was called long before the term "country and western" was ever a thing.) Unfortunately, I couldn't carry a tune in a bucket. Yet, I remember swinging on the front porch swing at #4 Kenner Street in Parkersburg, West Virginia, singing at the top of my lungs. I would be out there practicing for hours. One day my little Granny Dickson, all 4' 11" of her, rushed out on the porch and asked me if I was alright. (Uh oh, that is not a good sign.) She said she heard some horrible squalling coming from the porch and thought she should see if I was okay. I needed a change of plans. So much for my singing career!

That's when I went into the kitchen, got out some paper and pencils, and decided to become a famous writer. I wrote tons of stories, mostly about princes and princesses. Then it dawned on me, I supposed there really wouldn't be much of a market for those stories once girls discovered boys; if only I could have foreseen movies like *Princess Diaries* 1 and 2.

Our family was probably considered lower middle class, but we didn't know any different. We had a cute little house with the coldest linoleum floors you had ever put your bare tootsies on, but it had a really cool screened-in back porch. The porch sat up high in the back of the house that was on a hill that sloped down into the backyard. The steps down the backside of the house led to the yard and the dreaded fruit cellar. I always hated having to go down there to get a jar of something that Mom and Granny had canned. (I still don't know why it was called "canned" when the food was actually in glass jars.) I just knew there was a copperhead snake waiting to bite me when I came in the door.

Me and Mike in a Kiddie Pool

My brother Mike and I always had fun together. Since there was only a two year difference in our ages, we were very close. We didn't have a lot of material possessions and toys, but we made the best of what we had and were constantly finding things to do outside. Daddy built us an airplane-shaped swing that hung from a tree. (Was that a premonition?) We had plenty of trees to climb, and our neighbor Mrs. Eagle, had the best cherry tree ever. We would climb up in it and eat cherries until we were about to pop. She almost never ran us off unless she had plans to bake pies that day. We also had a tent with an Indian on the side of it and an inflatable pool.

We didn't know we were poor. We felt like we had everything everyone else had.

I remember having my very first "gut feeling." Mom and I were folding clothes and I suddenly had a feeling Daddy was hurt. I turned to her to share what I was feeling with tears running down my cheeks. "Mom, Daddy's been hurt. He hurt his hand." "No Janie, he's fine he'll be home in about twenty minutes. Daddy walked through the door with his left hand all bandaged. He had cut it at work.

One of the most fun things we used to do at Christmas was make our own decorations. We used pictures out of coloring books and cotton balls for Santa's suit and beard, and we made our tree garland out of pieces of colored paper, glue, and glitter. After the holiday, Mike and I would scrounge the neighborhood for leftover trees and build a fort. There was always snow, so we were able to build tunnels between the trees.

We rode our bikes everywhere, and we even placed cardboard, attached with clothespins, to our spokes to make our bikes sound really loud. No one ever worried about us as long as we were home before dark. We had pet rabbits and chickens we had gotten for Easter, and Mom threw us great birthday parties.

I still shudder to think of one of the crazier things we did as kids. We crossed the road to the Corning Glass Plant's dump and played among all of the broken glass from old test tubes, bottles, and who-knows-what else. We didn't think a thing of it, but as a parent I would have gone bonkers thinking about letting my boys play on something so dangerous. It is a miracle we didn't get cut, or even worse, end up having children with four eyes, twelve toes, fangs, or something scarier with all of the chemicals we contacted.

Two things should have clued me in about the state of our financial situation. One time Mom, Mike, and I hid behind the sofa when the insurance man came to collect for a policy Mom and Dad had, and another time we would not have had Thanksgiving dinner but for the generosity of the Boy Scout Troop at a nearby church. They knocked on our door with a wooden clothes basket filled with a turkey and all the trimmings. Tears rolled down Mom's face, and Dad just turned and left the room. It was especially hard on him.

Dad was a hard worker, but he always seemed to get jobs with companies that depended on government contracts and when those contracts were filled, a bunch of guys would be laid off. Daddy was quite often the junior man, so he was the first to be let go. I know it hurt him to accept charity because Daddy had his pride, but I know in his heart he was so grateful for that meal, which Mom was able to stretch into several. Because of this, I will always have a special love for the Boy Scouts.

Parkersburg, West "My God" Virginia, as people liked to call it, was where my Daddy and his four brothers were raised. People called you "Hillbillies," "Ridge Runners," and of course, for those who made moonshine, they might be referred to as "Shiners." My Daddy and his brothers were the "Golden Brothers": Wilbert, Harry, Edgar, Raymond, and Arthur Golden.

Their mother, Julia Golden, known as Mamall Golden, was an unusual person. I only saw one picture of her in her younger days with her husband. She was a large woman, about 5'9" or 5'10" and not particularly feminine. She and Daddy's father lived apart more than together. Apparently he would leave her, get drunk, come home, and she would end up pregnant again. I don't know this as a fact, but I heard it from several relatives throughout the years. Mamall made her living as a cook, but she never made enough to keep the boys with her, so they all ended up in the Logan Children's Home except for Wilb.

Mamall Golden

Mamall was distant with me. She never seemed to like me; she just appeared to like my brother and my cousin Butch. If Mike and I were at her house and we got into an argument, it was always my fault no matter who started it. I found out later in life why I didn't think she cared for me, but at the time I just thought she didn't like girls.

I do remember that Mamall made the most wonderful Parker House Rolls, elderberry jelly, blackberry cobbler, and country butter in the world! I wish I had asked her to teach me how to make those rolls. They were awesome!

Dad's Football Picture

Sadly, Dad never finished High School. He was an awesome football player so I'm told, and he loved the game. It was a shame he didn't get to go to college and play. One of his teachers offered to help him get a scholarship but instead he signed up for the Army where he was a part of the Rainbow Division, serving under General McArthur. He never wanted to talk about the war but made an exception when my oldest son, Josh, had to do a project for history in the eighth grade. Dad actually went to Josh's school and talked to his class and teacher about the liberation of Auschwitz Concentration Camp. That was one of the most surprising things Dad ever did. He was not a talker and was not forthcoming about his memories of that time in his life, so he must have loved Joshua an awful lot to do that. The teacher, Mrs. Ferguson, was so excited about Daddy being there. She said it was like having a living piece of history right in her classroom.

Mom and Dad at Parkersburgh High School

Daddy had some books on the top shelf of his closet from World War 2 that we were not allowed to look at. Of course, when we got older, Mike and I got them down and looked through them, but I wish I hadn't. There were pictures of some of the atrocities the Nazis inflicted on people during the war, and the pictures could make you sick. (We only told Daddy we had seen them once we were adults.)

Daddy was engaged to another woman when he met my Mom, Helen Virginia Bryant, at a club called Leon's in Parkersburg. They were introduced to each other by a friend of

Mom's. Mom was engaged to a sailor named Ray Brinker. A petite little thing, about 5'3", weighing around 98 pounds, Mom had dark black hair and beautiful blue eyes. At first, Mom didn't care for Dad because she thought he was kind of cocky, but as the night wore on, they fell under each other's spell. Their love song was *"It Had to be You"* and for 56 years it was. They met on Friday October 20, 1944, and married on Wednesday, October 25. It was magic. Daddy had to return to the service, and Mom went to Ironton, Ohio to stay with her sister, Katherine.

Mom's background was similar to Daddy's. She had two brothers; the older one was Mardie Franklin and the younger one was Billy James. Her older sister was Katherine Belle.

Granny

Mom's mom, Violet Ann, was a pistol! Even though she was little, she never took any crap off anyone. Apparently when Violet was younger, after her husband died in an accident involving a team of horses, she enjoyed the company of several different men. One time she left my Mom, her brothers, and sister alone to fend for themselves. Violet hadn't left them enough food, and when they went to the neighbor to ask for some, the neighbor called Children's Aid, who took all the kids to the Davis Children's Shelter in Charleston, West Virginia.

Morn said the shelter was like a child labor facility. The kids were always sent out to do chores on different farms and kept with families until they didn't need them anymore, and then the kids would end up back at the shelter. It was a terrible life! Mom told stories of finding a few nice families that she would have loved to live with, but then Uncle Billy would act up because he always hoped that Violet Ann, who I called Granny Dickson, would come get them, so the kids would get sent back to the shelter.

Growing up in my day, it was a real event for relatives to visit one another. Having aunts, uncles, and cousins come for a good meal or a short visit was always special. Our families would bond over playing with toys or cards, riding bikes, and listening to records. As teenagers, my cousin, Aunt Kat's daughter, Sandy Kay, and I would spend the summer staying at each other's homes for a few weeks.

Me and Sandy

Mom would always make clothes for us so that we dressed like twins. Just one difference, though, since Sandy was built like Annette Funicello and I was more like Olive Oyl. When we were going to a movie one day Sandy looked over at me as I put on a sweater and said, "Janie, for heaven's sake, why don't you stuff your bra with Kleenex? That is, if you even own one. You look like a boy."

I was mortified. I stuffed my bra, but once we got to the movie, I felt so uncomfortable I went to the bathroom and removed all of the Kleenex. When I returned to my seat, Sandy rolled her eyes at me. She could be quite a stinker when she wanted to be, but we had a lot of fun times together.

My little sister, Charmaine, was born in Parkersburg, West Virginia, ten years after me. Any time Dad, Mom, Mike, Charmaine, and I spent together was special for us. In spite of the major age difference between us kids, Dad and Mom always tried to do things that everyone could enjoy.

Family was so important during my formative years. Whatever you had, you shared or you tried to help as much as you could financially because you would never consider letting someone in the family be in need.

Granny Dickson had her own room when she stayed with us, and we weren't supposed to touch her things. She loved chocolate-covered cherries. Mike spotted them on the dresser in her room one day as he walked down the hall and asked her for one. She told him no, so when she went downstairs to help Mom with supper, Mike and I snuck into her room and ate the whole box. Despite our later regret, the moment was pure victory. When Granny told Mom and Dad what we had done, they didn't know whether to spank us or laugh as they knew how stingy she could be with her things.

I do have fond memories of Granny Dickson braiding my hair when I was younger, only she called it "plaiting." She would brush my hair over and over until it felt like silk and then divide the hair down the middle and make a braid on each side. She would crisscross them and put bobby pins in to hold them down across the middle part of my hair. I felt so pretty.

When Granny Dickson wrote letters, she would hand me an envelope and say, "Back this envelope for me, Janie." What she meant was to address it for her. She didn't say envelope either it was pronounced "in veil up."

Granny made quilts, embroidered pillowcases, and crocheted doilies. She helped me earn some Girl Scout badges by teaching me different embroidery stitches, and I regret that I didn't learn how to quilt from her, but I'm honored to now have some of the quilts she made.

I rarely saw my grandmas, Mamall Golden and Granny Dickson, together. However, Mom said they were both with her when my sister Charmaine was born. She recalled a funny story about her trip to the hospital. Mamall Golden was afraid of elevators and never rode in cars, but Granny Dickson didn't seem to fear anything or anyone. The differences in their height and build, Mamall Golden being almost 5'9" and Granny Violet being about 4'11", made these personality differences even more humorous.

Granny didn't drive, and Mamall wouldn't ride in a car anyway, so the grandmas caught a bus to rush my laboring Mom to the hospital, then bolted through the front door with Mom dragging between them. Granny headed for the elevator. Mamall Golden put on the brakes, digging her heels into the floor with such determination that Granny nearly jerked Mom's arm off.

"Come on, Julia!" Granny yelled. "Helen is in labor and we've got no time to waste."

"No, Violet, I am not going in that elevator!" replied Mamall.

"Damn it, this is no time to be acting pigheaded. The baby will be here any minute. Now come on," Said Violet.

"I am not going in there, Violet!" insisted Julia.

Mom laughed hysterically at the sight of tiny Granny trying to coax the taller Mamall into the elevator, then she gasped and grabbed her belly. "I'm going up the stairs!" Mom managed to say between bouts of laughter.

Both grannies grabbed Mom and half-pushed, half-dragged her up three flights of stairs. As they arrived, a nurse ran towards them with a wheelchair. "My God, woman, sit down!" commanded the nurse, "or you are going to have that baby right here in the hallway!" The nurse yelled for the two spatting grannies to clear the way as she rushed Mom into the delivery room. They were still yelling at each other as the nurse rolled Mom away.

During labor and delivery, the grandmothers sat together, awaiting Mom and the baby's arrival. Charmaine was such a pretty little girl with big blue eyes and reddish hair. Her middle name was Ann after both grandmothers. I always loved her name, Charmaine, and of course she said she hated it. (I offered to trade her one day, but she admitted she liked her name better than mine.)

Mom asked Violet if she and Julia had made peace with each other. Granny flashed those sparkling blue eyes at Mom and said, "Shit, Helen, it's a wonder you made it in here in time. Who is afraid of elevators, for crying out loud?" Mamall just sat there. Mom tried not to laugh because it hurt too much, but she made note of the fact that Granny had actually lost a battle, a rare occurrence.

I cried a million tears when Mom told me that we had to leave West Virginia for Ohio because Daddy had found a job there. I recall sitting in school, looking out the window, where I could see my Daddy going from business to business trying to find work. I felt so sad for him. I was glad he had found a job, but why did it have to be in another state? I was devastated. Worst of all, we were told we couldn't bring our dog, Krinkles, with us to the half-double that Daddy had found for our home.

I remember the day Daddy brought home this little brown and white fuzz ball. He was a Cocker Spaniel, and Daddy had paid a fortune for him -fifty dollars, I think. We didn't want to be obvious and name him Freckles, due to the many brown spots on his white nose, so instead we settled on the name Krinkles.

One day, Krinkles was tied up by a bush in the shade and Charmaine wandered down to pet him. He started barking and growling like a crazy dog. Daddy ran down there with full intentions of kicking him in the butt because he thought he was growling at Sis. When Daddy got there, he stopped dead in his tracks, then scooped up Charmaine and ran in the opposite direction. Curled up underneath the bush near Krinkles was a copperhead snake.

Daddy hated snakes more than anything in the world. He was in Panama during a portion of his military service and was constantly encountering snakes. They were in the trees, crawled in your bed and boots, and he was petrified of them, which must be where I inherited my fear of them.

By the time Daddy got a shovel and was back to dismember the snake, it had crawled away. Daddy gave Krinkles a piece of chicken for supper. Even though we didn't have a whole lot for ourselves, he felt that Krinkles earned it that day.

When we left for Ohio, our dog remained with friends. Eventually, the landlord decided that it was okay to bring Krinkles to live with us, and even Daddy fought back the tears as we drove to pick up the dog and found out the sad news. Krinkles had escaped from the friend's house, returned to our hold house, and got hit by a car.

Other than losing Krinkles, the only bad memory I have of West Virginia is that Mike was sick so much. Mike was so cute, but he was a frail little guy with the bluest eyes you had ever seen, kind of like the penetrating blue eyes of Paul Newman. Sadly, he was never very strong and had constant bouts of bronchitis. I can still see those "tents" Mom used to make out of sheets to put him in with the vaporizer blowing that awful smell all around the room. She would crawl in there with Mike and hold him until he fell asleep. When Mom came out from under the tent, she was dripping wet from the heat inside. I cringe recalling the horrible smell of the stuff Mom had to put on Mike's chest. I think she called it a "mustard plaster" or some ridiculous name. Phew, did it stink!

My only health emergency as a child was waking up one night burning up with fever and pain in my right side. Daddy got this old Army blanket and put it around me - it was scratchy and hot - and pulled me up into his arms and ran to the neighbor, Mrs. Eagle, so she could rush me to the hospital. I had appendicitis, and it would have burst if they hadn't gotten me there as quickly as they did. I shudder that I can remember to this day the doctor putting that awful ether mask over my face to be put to sleep. Because it was around Christmastime, there was a photographer taking pictures of kids in the hospital, so I got my picture in the paper with Santa and a new doll, so it wasn't all bad.

Mom and Dad smooching

We had a good life in West Virginia and enjoyed our time together as a family. Going downtown to look in the store windows of Lazarus Department Store was a big thrill at Christmas time, and seeing a movie was the most incredible event in the world. We walked everywhere we went because Daddy didn't have a driver's license. We didn't have a lot of material things, but we had each other and a lot of love. This is one of my favorite pictures of Mom and Dad. It reminds me that the love in our family started with them and passed on to the three of us. I didn't want to move to Ohio, but we didn't have a choice.

SCHOOL DAYS, SCHOOL DAYS. WEINLAND PARK ELEMENTARY

Mike, Chairmaine, & Me

The move to Ohio brought with it a brand new experience. In West Virginia, the black and white folks lived in separate areas of the city, but we were integrated in Ohio. We were told that we would be going to school with "colored" kids. Mike and I weren't exactly sure what that meant; we joked about red and green kids, and then we'd snicker. Finally, Mom told us they were actually brown or black. She said we had to be nice to them but to stay away from them because they were from Africa, and some of them were cannibals. Dear Lord, we were petrified! Off we went on my first day of fifth grade and Mike's first day of third grade to see what it was like to go to school with colored kids.

Three days later, I came skipping down the street holding hands with a beautiful black girl named Marilyn Sammons, with Mike tagging along behind us. When my Mom saw us, she nearly fell off the front porch, where she would sit and wait for us to come home for lunch. I proudly told Mom that Marilyn had come home to eat lunch with us and that she was just like me; she had never eaten anyone. Mom turned beet red, nearly dropping Charmaine out of her lap as she gathered herself up out of the swing and told us to come inside for lunch.

I never thought anything of having a black friend. A lot of the other kids didn't think it was very cool, but I didn't care. I was a new kid, and she was the first person to treat me kindly. I was incredibly unhappy with the kids in Ohio. They continuously asked me if all the girls in West Virginia were as tall as me. They told me I had an accent and made fun of the way I talked. Not long after school started, the principal sent a note home to

Mom and asked her to come to the office. He told her I was so far ahead of the other students in the fifth grade, that he wanted me to skip a grade and go on to sixth. Isn't that ironic? Wouldn't you think a kid from West Virginia would have been further behind than a kid from Ohio? I did.

Mom thought about it for a while and decided against it. I was already new and she didn't want me to have to start all over again with another group of students from the sixth grade. I think Mom thought the school might be trying to discourage my friendship with Marilyn. If so, it didn't work. We stayed friends until she moved.

It was at Weinland Park that I was no longer allowed to be called Janie. The teachers insisted on calling me Beverly because you were supposed to be addressed by your first name, not your middle name. I did not like that one bit, because I loved being called Janie, but the teachers wouldn't hear of it.

Even worse, there was a fast food drive-in called The Big Bev, which only increased how much I was teased in Junior High School. I never heard the end of that. I was teased about owning it and was asked if my parents named it after me because I was so big? This was just what I didn't need in adolescence - made to feel even more self-conscious.

I made it through fifth grade and got promoted to sixth, where I had a wonderful teacher named Mr. Charles Crisler. He was understanding, patient, and soft-spoken. He was everything I thought a teacher should be. I even thought that maybe one day I might want to be a teacher too, just like him. Everything was going well until Mr. Crisler noticed that I dotted my "I's" with a circle. He tried everything he could to get me to quit, and I honestly tried to be more aware of it, but it was a habit I just couldn't break.

When grade cards were issued after first six weeks, I couldn't believe mine. I had gotten all As, but an F in writing! I was in shock! I ran home and threw myself on the couch in tears, heartbroken. When Mom came in, she asked why I was crying so hard, and I showed her my grade card. She was truly surprised too because Mr. Crisler had told her what a wonderful student I was and how he wished he had more like me. Mom grabbed her coat, and stormed off to the school. (This must be where I learned to get so involved in my own kids' school lives - a blessing and a curse.) On Monday, when I got to school, Mr. Crisler said he would give me a week to quit putting circles over my "I's," and then he would change my grade. I tried, but I just couldn't stop. Mr. Crisler relented and gave me an A anyway because he recognized the effort I made. To this day, I still put circles over my "I's," as does my son, Josh.

Scouting was the "All American" thing to do in the late fifties. I was very active in Girl Scouts Troop #262 and had the second most merit badges in the state of Ohio. I think I missed having the most by two badges. Mrs. Snider was my first leader, and Mom took over the second year.

Mom did so many neat things with and for us gals. We danced at the State Fair, took modeling lessons at Lazarus, our biggest and swankiest department store, had meetings that included activities with the Boy Scouts, and even learned to sing "Yes, Sir, That's My Baby" in Italian, which I later taught my sons. Of course, we sold lots of cookies and went to camp.

I felt so left out when we went to camp and everyone except me got poison ivy, that I found some poison ivy plants and rubbed them all over my arms and legs so I would be covered in pink calamine lotion when we got home. Despite the effort, I never got poison ivy. I was embarrassed about rubbing myself in poisonous plants, and of course I had no idea how dangerous it could have been to do it; I just didn't want to be different.

During one of our joint meetings with the Boy Scouts, one boy in particular caught my fancy. He was s-o-o-o-o cute! His name was Paul C. Wright, and I found out later that he lived across the street from me. After we had "tied knots" together at Scouts, he asked if he could come over to our house sometime so we could listen to records together. I was so pleased. I hadn't had a crush on a boy since Tommy Lucas in West Virginia, and that was because Tommy was the tallest boy in class.

Paul and I listened to records, laughed, and had a great time together. Then Paul asked my Mom and Dad if he could take me to the movies. "My parents will be driving us and picking us up right after the movie" he said.

Mom and Dad agreed. In case Paul "got fresh," Mom gave me a dime to put in my purse to call her. I wasn't exactly sure what "getting fresh" meant, and I didn't want to ask Mom. Paul did try to put his arm around me. I thought maybe that was what "getting fresh" meant. Each time he tried, I made a trip to the ladies' room -- I must have gone four times. Paul probably thought I had the weakest bladder in the world. At age 14, I wasn't ready to have a boy put his arm around me in a movie.

Needless to say, Paul and I never became a couple. We'd just wave at each other across the street when we saw each other outside.

Being shy, naive, and different were not things that you ever wanted to be! I was so tall that I stood out heads above everyone else.

Colleen, Sharon, Me, Kay and Denise

I had several close friends back then: Colleen and Sharon, Kay Coffey, Sandy Snider, and the twins, Mickey and Vicky Gustafson. We had a great time having "girly" parties. (You are going to get some real laughs out of the way we dressed for a party back then. So enjoy yourself.) We were so much more immature then girls that age are today. We blushed, played with dolls, giggled like crazy, didn't know any cuss words, and would never think of doing anything naughty. Mercy no!

INDIANOLA JUNIOR HIGH AND "PUPPY LOVE!"

Indianola Junior High

Indianola Junior High School opened on July 6, 1909. It was the first Junior High School in the United States.

Entering Indianola Junior High the first time was so terrifying! I had hope, hope, and more hope that maybe, just maybe, there would be some boys there taller than me, and I wouldn't have to spend the rest of my life feeling like a freak. I was tired of being "String Bean," "Long Tall Sally," or even, as Daddy called me, "Lanky" (although I liked that.). There may have been a few tall boys, but most of them were unattractive.

Terry Kneisley

Then one day, November 21, 1957 as I was going to my locker between classes, I turned to see this awesomely tall guy. He must have been six feet tall, with the waviest dark hair, brown eyes, and a beautiful smile he flashed my way when he caught me looking at him. My heart skipped a beat! I could hardly breathe.

I couldn't quit staring at him. Finally, I got some level of control over myself, caught my breath, took a book from my locker, and declared to myself, "I am officially in love!" As this gorgeous guy walked away from me, I peeked around my locker door and made note of his broad shoulders and slender waist, with long legs. He was dressed "Ivy League" or "preppy" as the kids today would say.

What more could a girl ask for? I found out his name was Terry Kneisley, and he was in the same grade I was. Although we didn't have any classes together, and never would over the next five years, I would still find myself running up three flights of stairs just to watch him walk down the hall. I know that was pitiful, but it was worth the effort to see him.

Occasionally, Terry would look my way and smile, making it even more worthwhile. Ah, one-sided, unrequited "Young Love."

At home, we had been able to get a television and a phone, and we really thought we were "uptown." Of course there weren't many channels or programs to choose from, but it was hip to watch *American Bandstand* with your friends and drool over the guys, learn new dances, and see what the "cool kids" were wearing.

I loved watching *Father Knows Best*, *Leave it to Beaver*, and *Ozzie and Harriet.* Ricky Nelson was such a nice looking young man that he was almost pretty. He wasn't a very good actor but definitely fun to watch.

I wished so many times I had a relationship with my Dad the way these TV families did, especially the one between Robert Young and his daughters, but my Dad was not ever going to be that way. I loved him to bits, but to sit down and have a one-on-one conversation about anything with Daddy was just never something we did. Part of the problem was that he worked nights and slept during the day. Although Daddy was home during the day on the weekend there was always work to be done. It was sad, but that's the way it was. If you've ever heard Reba McEntire's song, "The Greatest Man I Never Knew," that was Daddy and me.

It was such a "rich person" thing to have acquired a telephone, so we were all pretty excited. Even though only a few other folks had phones, we still had fun with it. At first, our phone was a party line, and we loved to listen in on other people's conversations. It never took long for them to realize we were on the line, though; our giggling would give us away, especially if it was a guy and a girl saying "mushy stuff."

Radene

Godee

Laura

If you are a fan of the movie *Grease*, and I really am, you can picture my three friends. Their names were Radene Robinson, Gloria "Godee" Brooks, and Laura Griggs.

Godee was "Frenchy," petite with curly brown hair and blue eyes, and very bubbly! She had two brothers, Larry and Gary, who used to delight in making our lives absolutely miserable.

Radene was Stockard Channing's character, "Rizzo." She was built like crazy!! She had a figure that could stop traffic. Radene did something so wild in eighth grade that everyone was in shock: she bleached her hair platinum and cut it really, really short! Most girls never could have pulled it off, but Radene made it look good. She always seemed to fall for the wrong boys, though. She liked the "bad boys," the ones with the tough guy reputations. We worried so much about the guys Radene chose to date. That is until she met her future husband, Frank Legg, an Army guy, who she married when she was only about 16.

Laura was the Pink Lady named "Jan." She was always the "true blue" friend who was by your side through thick and thin, and tears and joy.

We didn't really have a "Marty" in our little group, and I suppose I was "Sandy," Olivia Newton-John's character. I was definitely "Miss Goody Two-Shoes" as my brother Mike delighted in calling me.

We certainly had our share of adventures. Radene, Godee, and I all lived close to each other; so I spent more time with them than with Laura who lived further away. On any given weekend, we could be found at each other's homes listening to records, going to dances, bowling, roller skating, horseback riding, or walking to the drugstore for a coke and fawning over movie magazines. This was our entertainment "back in the day," as my younger son, Kaleb, says.

We always had something going on, but I think our favorite activity was slumber parties at each other's houses. We would stay up all night, giggling and calling the radio stations, making requests for our favorite song dedicated to the boy we happened to have a crush on that week. None of us had much money, but we were always willing to share with each other.

We had our spats and our "two against one" moments like the time I was accused of being responsible for Radene, Godee, and me getting into a car with two boys. +

We were walking down the street close to the pizza shop and these two boys drove by. Then they turned the car around and came back and asked us if we wanted to go for a ride. Radene had gone out with the driver, Jeff, once before, and Godee knew his buddy, Ted, so they wanted to go. We weren't supposed to get into cars with boys, especially in my case with boys I didn't know at all, but we did. We rode around for a little while with Radene and Jeff in the front and Ted, Godee and me in the back.

We girls decided we wanted to go to Godee's house to listen to records, but the guys wanted the two girls to go out so they ended up in an argument. Radene finally got bossy and demanded to be taken to Godee's, but we had them drop us off a few blocks from her house. Little did we know, but Godee's brothers, Larry and Gary, just happened to be walking down the other side of the street and saw the boys drop us off. They ran to the house ahead of us and told Mrs. Brooks. When we got there, she told Radene and me to go home and that she had already called our moms who were waiting to talk to us. We knew our goose was cooked.

Radene went home to face her Mom, and I went home to face my parents. Mom was waiting; fortunately, Daddy was lying down before he had to head to work. She asked me why I disobeyed her rule about getting into a car with boys I didn't know, so I told her that Radene and Godee knew the boys. Mom seemed surprised because she told me that Mrs. Brooks had called her again and told her it was my idea to get in the car. Then Mrs. Robinson called and told Mom that Radene had told her that I was the one who wanted to ride with those boys.

I cried and told Mom that was not the truth. I explained again that Radene and Godee knew the boys. Why would I want to get into the car with boys I didn't know? Mom took up for me and called Mrs. Brooks and Mrs. Robinson back, suggesting they get the truth out of their daughters and quit blaming me for a decision one of them made. Godee and Radene got in trouble, and we weren't allowed to get together for a week. When we did it was like nothing ever happened. We went right back to being buddies. Although we grew apart over the years and made new friends, we remained close for most of our Junior High School years.

Before I go on, I must share the unique bond I had with Mom. We were more like girlfriends than mother and daughter at times. Because Daddy worked late at night, I would often go into Mom's bedroom and sit on her bed to share what happened in school, such as who was dating or breaking up, when dances were coining up, or who was having a party. Since she had been our Scout leader, Mom knew all of my girlfriends, and it was fun keeping her up on all of the latest gossip.

I remember telling her all about Terry and how wonderful I thought he was. If you have ever seen the television series *The Guns of Will Sonnett*, then you've seen Terry. He looked similar to the young actor, Dack Rambo. For those of you who haven't seen the show, you'll just have to enjoy the pictures of Terry I've included here.

Mom called Terry my "dreamboat." She even wrote it above his head on a picture in our yearbook, and I turned nine shades of red for fear one of my friends would see it and tell him. I couldn't hide my enthusiasm over finding a boy taller than me! Mom was happy for me because she understood how difficult it had been to be the new kid in fifth grade, having a West Virginia accent, and being taller than everyone in my classes. We had such a wonderful time. Those times, sitting on her bed sharing, are ones I treasure to this day.

Without further ado, here is my story about Terry. At a dance in seventh grade, as I sat in the auditorium with my three friends, I looked up on the stage where we held our dances and saw a line of girls a mile long waiting to cut in to dance with Terry. I felt so sorry for him. Most guys would have loved that, but not Terry - he was shy and overwhelmed by all of the attention. Terry looked like he wanted to bolt out of the auditorium and never come back, but instead of figuring out a way to help the poor guy, I got up like a robot to get in line with the others and wait my turn for ten seconds to touch Terry.

I was shaking so hard when my left hand went to touch Terry's shoulder that I nearly missed it. My right hand was soaking wet when I put it into his. I could only manage to choke out a very soft sounding, "Hi." He looked down at me (God, what a wonderful feeling, a guy looking DOWN at ME!) with those soft brown eyes filled with so much pain and just smiled. Before I could say another word, I felt a tap on my shoulder and turned around to see Radene cutting in. How dare she do this! I was so shocked that my friend would do this to me when she knew Terry was mine. I walked back to my seat feeling so sorry for Terry and a little sorry for myself. It was obvious how uncomfortable he was and how he wanted this "never-ending song" to end so he could leave. As soon as the song was over, Terry left for the night.

Terry came to my first boy-girl party, the day before my thirteenth birthday on May 4, 1958. It was fun but awkward with about twelve kids there. We had just gotten a movie camera, a "rich person" thing to do, and my Dad filmed about five minutes of my precious party. (I have the film to this day.)

Looking back, it is amazing to remember most of the boys dressed in suits or dress slacks with jackets and ties and the girls all wearing dresses, which is a contrast to the way kids dress for social functions these days. We all looked so good, but that was the way you were expected to dress for parties.

I am sure the party was extremely boring, but Terry was there with me and, that was all that mattered. I don't know if we exchanged more than ten words the whole time he was there, but he sat beside me when we played this silly game called Slap, Kiss, or Hug. You stood behind a person in a chair and gestured by putting your hand to your cheek, asking "Who do you want to do this to?" (this gesture meant to slap someone). The person in the chair would say the name of someone at the party and then you would touch your lips and ask the same question, referencing a kiss. The last question was about hugging. You would wrap your arms around yourself meaning a hug. It was a lot of fun and pretty risqué for our day, if I do say so myself. Sadly, I only got to hug Terry, I never got to kiss him. Darn it!

After school let out for the summer, the greatest thrill was hanging out at our local swimming pool, The Olympic. We couldn't afford a season ticket but we got to go fairly often. One particular day, June 26, 1958, I was there and Terry showed up with his friend Dick Henderson, and Terry actually paid attention to me. We sat near each other on towels, but not too near. Well, Terry actually sat with his buddy, and I sat with some girls, but our towels touched. Swoon!

We played stupid games in and out of the water together, and Terry delighted in flipping me with the wet end of his towel, doing what I think were called "rat tails." It hurt when the towel hit your arm or leg and left a red mark for several minutes. As long as Terry was paying attention to me, I didn't mind a little pain. We had a wonderful time there together, but not really together because boys and girls kept their distance from each other during that time. I have pictures of him from that time, which I treasured for years and still have.

The pictures were kept pressed between the pages of my diary. Mom had given me my first diary for my twelfth birthday, and for years, I kept a daily diary. Then eventually I started skipping days, then months, then actually gave it up altogether in 1982. The reason for the lapse in time was the birth of our first son, Josh. I only wish I had kept the diaries as faithfully as I had from 1957 through 1963. It wouldn't be quite so hard to recall some memories.

On January 9, 1959, my friend Karen Roth (maybe she was our "Marty" from *Grease*?) had a party at her house. On a whim, I asked Terry to go, and he actually accepted. It was better than at my thirteenth birthday party, but not by much. There were several kids there, and we ate pizza and danced a little. At one point, Terry sat down beside me on the couch and put his arm around my shoulder, inadvertently pinning my hair under his arm. I tried to brush my hair out from under his arm, and Terry must have thought I wanted him to move his arm, so he did. I tried to figure out how to get him to put his arm back around me, but I couldn't make a move because that would have been too forward to mention.

Karen's Dad was so strict he actually scared me sometimes. At about 9:30 p.m., he started telling everyone it was about time to head home. I was spending the night with Karen, but I wanted to ride in the car with her Dad when he took Terry and the other kids home. Karen stayed home to spend a few extra minutes with her date, Bill Ewen, who was old enough to drive himself to her party.

In the car, Terry made "the big move" and kissed me. It wasn't my first official kiss with Terry though. That had happened at another party in the seventh grade. The party was about to end, and I was supposed to kiss Terry in the Slap, Kiss, or Hug game. Just as I was kissing him, his Dad appeared at the door to take him home. Terry's Dad calmly said, "When you're finished here, son, I'll be in the car." I thought I would die a thousand deaths. That kiss was my very first kiss, and I couldn't think of anyone I would rather have it with than Terry. It was short but sweet. Still it was a kiss.

I never dreamed that Karen's Dad was watching in the rearview mirror when Terry kissed me, so I was surprised when we got back to Karen's house, and her Dad made quite a point of saying how much I had enjoyed taking Terry home. I could have died! It was one thing for Mom Roth maybe to have seen Terry kiss me, but not Karen's Dad!

Mr. Roth couldn't wait to tell Karen about the incident he observed in the car. "Hey Karen, I know someone who really enjoyed the ride to take the kids home tonight. Got any idea who I am talking about, Bev?" he teased.

I turned bright red and ran giggling into Karen's room. "What happened?" Karen asked as she ran excitedly behind me.

I was in heaven, but my face was crimson. This kiss was so much better than the first one at the seventh-grade party. Kissing me tonight had been all Terry's idea, and it had lasted for at least a minute, I was sure.

I had actually experienced my first "real" kiss, and it sure beat kissing the mirror or your pillow! One girlfriend confessed once that she practiced kissing by kissing her own hand. Oh, brother, were we naïve!

The kiss is all Karen and I could talk about — how it felt, if it was good, how long it lasted, if I would want to do it again, etc. This was such an important event for a teenager. As I said, I was just so glad that Terry had been the one to kiss me. I foolishly thought we might actually date after that party, but it never came to be. Karen had been kissing for years; it was old hat to her, but to me it was a whole new life experience, and I definitely liked it.

This was not my only embarrassing moment concerning Terry. He was a basketball player, so I tried to see as many home games as I could. At one particular game, when Terry was running down the court, his teammate threw the ball in his direction. The ball was coming down right on top of Terry's head, so I yelled for him to look out Terry looked up, as requested, and the ball slammed right in his face. I wanted to crawl under the bleachers. Although I don't think Terry ever knew who had yelled, I felt like such a fool.

Another time, as I was going up the stairs with an armful of books, (running those three flights of stairs to see Terry!), this crazy guy named Sam Smith bellowed out the words to "Duke of Earl" at the top of his lungs right behind me. "Duke, Duke, Duke, Duke of Earl!" he yelled. He scared me so badly I screamed and dropped all of my books.

Who was behind Sam? Terry. He tried not to laugh, but I had screamed so loudly, and I must have looked like a one-armed juggler trying to recover my books. No wonder the guy never asked me out.

My one-sided romance with Terry continued on through High School. Although I dated several other boys, my heart always belonged to Terry, whether he wanted it or not, because he was my "Danny Zucko." I couldn't believe that for all of those years, the very sight of him set my heart into overdrive, and he never really knew I was alive.

MY FIRST LOVE

Jimmie Dale and Me

It was August 15, 1960, and we had moved from our half-double on Hamlet Street to a duplex on Hudson Street not too far from North High School. One day I spotted this nice-looking guy walking down the street, but he didn't see me sitting in the swing. He wasn't all that tall, maybe 5'10", and he had the most beautiful blonde hair. I snickered a little because he appeared to walk kind of bow-legged, but still he was cute.

I had made friends with Barbara Wiley, the girl next door, and I happened to mention to her about the cute boy I saw walking down the street. She laughed when I mentioned his bow-leggedness and said, "It must be Coffmon."

I looked at her rather oddly. What kind of a name was that I wondered? Actually, his real name was Jimmie Dale Coffmon, and Barb knew him. "So ya wanna meet him?" she asked. "Yes, I think I would like to. Is there anything I should know about him?" I asked.

Barb told me Jimmie was one of about ten kids or so — it would turn out to be twelve kids — and that she had gone to school with him. She said Jimmie was a "rebel," that he didn't really have a group that he ran with, and was more or less a loner. Barb also told me that Jimmie had done "IT" with several girls.

I was puzzled by what "IT" meant, and Barb burst out laughing after I asked her. When she told me what she meant, I was shocked!

In spite of being scared about Jimmie's reputation, I was still intrigued. I guess it was that "bad boy" thing that some good girls, like Radene, find dangerous yet appealing.

I met Jimmie on August 17 and invited him over to my house on August 20. I was pretty ticked off when he showed up an hour and a half late. It was so late I told him he had better come another day. Jimmie was surprised that I sent him home but interested enough to come over the next day. He came up on the porch, all cocky, and plopped down beside me on the swing. "So tell me about yourself, kid."

I felt very awkward, and I didn't like being called "kid." After all, I was fifteen! There didn't seem to be much to tell, but I told him about my family, my Mom, Dad, brother, and sister. I told Jimmie I loved Frankie Avalon. We just chatted for about an hour, and then it was, "I'll see ya later, kid." Why did he have to keep calling me that?

Suddenly, Jimmie leaned forward and kissed me, and I was too stunned to move or respond to him. I didn't even know if I had enjoyed the kiss because it had happened so quickly. He stood up and left, while I just sat there on the swing. I really didn't expect to see Jimmie again. I figured I had bored him to tears with trivial information about myself. Why would he want to come back?

Surprisingly, Jimmie started stopping by and would stay for as little as ten minutes or as long as a few hours. He was not like any guy I had ever met; he was so confident and sure of himself. Not only did Jimmie have beautiful hair, he had the most mischievous smile I had ever seen. It was like a little boy who got caught with his hand in the cookie jar. He was funny and made me laugh. He fascinated and terrified me all at once.

On our first real date, we doubled with Barb and her boyfriend, Jim Lepps. We went out to a movie, *The House of Usher*. I didn't like the movie very much, but it was fun being with Jimmie. He kissed me a bunch, which was a new experience for me. We went to the Ohio State Fair and had a ball, laughing and cutting up. Still, I always felt guarded. I never really felt sure of myself with Jimmie. I liked him a great deal, but I was also afraid of him and didn't really know why.

In spite of those feelings, Jimmie and I became close really quickly. I met his parents on September 4, 1960. They were nice, especially his Mom, Virginia. She was so easy to talk to and had a quick laugh. I liked her immediately. His Dad, Jim, was a little intimidating because he was so strict, but I imagined that with so many kids, you had to rule with an iron fist.

We spent many evenings at Jimmie's house or mine, just being together, talking, sitting on the porch, and kissing. Then on September 11, 1960, he asked me to go "steady."

This relationship was different. I was experiencing all sorts of funny feelings I had never felt before. Jimmie must have sensed that I was very inexperienced in relationships because he broke up with me only eleven days later, leaving me devastated! Even though we weren't going together, he continued coming over nearly every night. Jimmie kept me spinning in circles, and I didn't know if I was coming or going.

Jimmie asked me to go to Homecoming with him, so we went and had a great time. Around that time, I bought him a sweater for his birthday since I thought we might be getting back together. Then I caught him flirting with my friend, Sharon Prince, and he completely ignored me. Jimmie would say he was coming over and then he wouldn't. Then he would show up out of the blue and act like there was nothing wrong between us. He would see me at the grocery store one day and speak to me, and the next time, he would walk right by me.

I just didn't know how to act. Jimmie started dating Elsie Warren a girl at school with a really bad reputation. Barb said, "I told you Jimmie was a rebel and not to hang your heart on him." I was so sad at school when I would see him with his new girlfriend. Then Barb started going on double-dates with them. She said it was to find out how Jimmie really felt about Elsie, and Barb dutifully reported that it wasn't going to last and that Jimmie was interested in only one thing. Dumb me, I actually asked, "What?"

Barb's boyfriend just about busted a gut laughing and nearly fell over the porch railing at my house. "Is she for real?" he asked Barb.

"I'm afraid she is," Barb replied.

I started spending more time with my friends, Alice Moore and Dayle Mapes, two gals who lived in the neighborhood. Occasionally, I went out with other boys, but no one was like Jimmie. The boys were more like me, inexperienced and awkward. Jimmie finally came to his senses and stopped dating Elsie a few months later. Elsie actually wrote me a note and told me what a good girl Jimmie said I was. I just wanted to die. I was so mortified that they would be talking about me, especially like that.

Jimmie came back to me and asked me to the movies with his friend, Pat Bradshaw, and his date. We had a wonderful time, but after we got back to my house, Pat took me aside and told me something that nearly made me want to die. He said, "Jimmie said he wants to teach you how to kiss." I could not believe my ears! Pat told me that Jimmie told him that sometimes I kissed him too hard.

I wanted to vomit. How embarrassing! Nevertheless, I wanted so much to please Jimmie that when he got ready to leave, I kissed him so softly that I threw him off guard. Jimmie immediately put his arm around my waist and pulled me so close to him that I could barely breathe. I thought to myself, "Ok, Coffmon, so ya wanna teach me how to kiss? Well boy, here's you r chance." And he did. We sure had a lot of fun practicing.

For months after we had an on-again, off-again romance. Jimmie kept turning me upside down. Looking back, I think he was afraid to give in to how he really felt about me because of my age and because I was totally different from some of the girls he dated. I dated different fellows, all the while wishing Jimmie would make up his mind.

Jimmie showed up at my house on New Year's Eve 1961, drunk out of his mind. Daddy was furious! He sent him scooting, while I ran upstairs to my room crying my heart out. For Jimmie to show up at my house drunk was so disrespectful to my family and me. I just couldn't believe he would do that.

That was the only time Daddy ever came into my room and sat on my bed to talk to me about a boy or anything else for that matter. Daddy just didn"t talk much to me or any of us kids. Daddy told me that I was too good for Jimmie, that he was a "hood" (kind of like the "Fonz," only a bad boy.) He told me that I could do so much better than Jimmie, and he didn't want him to come around me ever again.

Jimmie's Dad showed up looking for him, and my Dad went down to tell him what Jimmie had done. He assured my Dad that Jimmie would never do that again. Still I was so upset, hurt, and embarrassed.

Jimmie stayed away for several weeks. He would write me notes in school and get his sister, Janet, to deliver them to me. Finally he got up the nerve to come to our house. Jimmie talked to Dad and Mom and promised to behave and not come near me when he was drinking ever again. Mom liked Jimmie and was willing to give him another chance. Dad didn't accept him as quickly as Mom did, but he let him stay.

I forgave Jimmie and let him back into my house and heart. We dated for about ten days, then he decided to become a hermit (yeah right), and then a week later he was back asking me to go steady.

Jimmie actually told me he loved me. He was the first boy to ever do that. I was caught off guard and didn't quite know how to respond. I knew I had deep feelings for him, feelings that I had never felt for any guy ever before, but these feelings scared me. When Jimmie would kiss me, I got what felt like gigantic butterflies flapping in my stomach. I had trouble breathing and didn't know how to react to such intense emotion.

Once again, after a necking session, he told me that we weren't working out, and he didn't want to go steady anymore. It felt like my heart physically shattered on the floor. I couldn't understand why Jimmie kept doing this to me. I sat there with tears streaming down my face as he walked out the front door. If only I had known more about sex, I might have understood what he was going through, but honestly I didn't really have any idea.

Jimmie ended up dating and going steady with some girl named Sharon Van Drummomd, and I thought my world had come to an end. I would see him at school, at the grocery store, walking down the street, and at the shopping center, but this time he stayed away. I had become close to his sister, Janet, during our on-and-off romantic periods, and she would keep me updated on news about Jimmie. I nearly went crazy in June when I heard he was engaged to Sharon. Then I heard he "had to" marry her because she was pregnant. I cried and cried. This just couldn't be happening to me.

To make matters even worse, we moved to far north Columbus in April 1961. Dad and Mom were finally able to make one of their dreams of owning their own house come true. We were going to have a home that was all ours.

Selfishly, I didn't want to go. I had already lost Jimmie, and now I had to move far away where I couldn't see him. Maybe I would even have to go to another school leaving all of the kids I had known since I moved to Ohio. This was one of the worst things in the world that could be happening to me, but I knew Mom and Dad wanted this so much. Besides, what could I do to change their minds? It wasn't fair to them; they were so happy. I don't think Mike or Charmaine cared one way or the other.

Without Jimmie, I felt like half a person. With him, I had experienced so many emotions that were all new to me. I fought with myself over what I was feeling. Part of me wanted to do things I knew were wrong, but I couldn't bring myself to do them with Jimmie or any other boy. Actually I never wanted to do anything with anyone but Jimmie, but I couldn't understand him. He just turned me every which way but loose, then break up and come back, stay a while, and leave again. Now Jimmie was getting married because he got some girl pregnant? How could he do this to me, and to himself, for that matter?

I didn't have very many happy days with the move and all. I hated hearing about Jimmie when I would talk to Barb or Janet. I wanted to hear it, but it was painful. I spent a lot of time in my room crying and listening to heart-breaking Roy Orbison songs. I listened to "Crying" so many times that the record almost broke. It was a miracle the record continued playing. Lordy, I didn't need to torture myself with Roy's gut-wrenching, brokenhearted ballads, yet I listened and cried for weeks on end.

Dad drove me every day so I wouldn't have to change schools when we moved to the other side of Columbus. Thank God, he had finally gotten his license at the age of 32. Before that, he would hitchhike to work all the time. Then one day, a neighbor sold Mom a 1950 Studebaker for $40. Dad taught himself how to drive by going down the alleys behind our old house. We all laughed at the sound of clanging trashcans as he ran them over, but Daddy was so proud of himself when he got his license. That Studebaker looked like a rocket ship. It was green and white with the heaviest doors in the world.

We had that car for years until we got our gorgeous turquoise and white 1956 Chevy - what a beauty! It was so much cooler to be driven to school in that car than the old Studebaker. Daddy would take me to school after he got off working all night, go home to rest, and then be there to pick me up after class, which he did for nearly two years. I was so grateful to him for doing it because he must have been exhausted, but Daddy never complained. I don't know if I ever told him how much it meant to me not to have to change schools, but I think he knew, and he was so wonderful to do this for me.

Mom was managing a dress shop called the Darling Shop. She always looked so nice when she went to work, all dressed up, never a hair out of place, and always, always in high heels. I just didn't know how she stayed on her feet like that all day long. One thing for sure, Mom always looked good no matter how much pain her feet endured.

Oh my stars, then Jimmie found out where we had moved. He showed up at my house in August and started turning my world upside down again. He had broken up with Sharon. I guess she wasn't pregnant or it was a false alarm; I never asked. I just couldn't believe Jimmie was there. It's amazing that I didn't fall flat on my face when I opened the door and saw him standing on the front porch. I was shaking so hard when he walked in and sat down on the couch. After he had been there for a while, Jimmie looked over at me, put his arm around me, kissed me tenderly, and asked, "Now that you've got me back, do you think you can put up with me?" I didn't know what to do or say. I just kissed him back and thought to myself, "Oh Lordy, here I go again."

Our dating consisted of going to each other's houses to watch TV or going to the drive-in movie. He accompanied our family to Port Clinton once and to Parkersburg, West Virginia another time. The night before we left for West Virginia, I remember I was in my room with my little sister almost asleep when the door opened and Jimmie stood there with a glass of water in his hand. I sat up and looked at him rather oddly. He just grinned that shit-eating grin of his and said, "Here's the water you asked me to bring you," as he leaned over the bed to kiss me good night. "I love you baby," he said.

"I love you too, Jimmie. Now get out of here before my Dad or Mom wakes up." He was a mess! Boys just didn't go into girls' bedrooms in the 60's. That was just too much temptation.

Once again, thank goodness for Daddy and our old video camera. He really wasn't very good with it, but one time Jimmie had come to our house all dressed up and looking gorgeous, and Daddy came out with the camera and took a few minutes of film of him. Jimmie was just standing there looking so handsome but couldn't be content with just being still. He got onto my little sister's tricycle, put his legs over the handlebars and rode it towards Daddy with me poised on the back. A few minutes later, we were standing beside each other as Daddy was filming when Mom yelled, "Come on! I've seen you two much closer than that; how about a hug?"As embarrassed as I was to hug Jimmie in front of my Dad, we put our arms around each other and smiled into the camera. (I treasure that few minutes of video.)

I felt so happy and still couldn't believe Jimmie was there with me. Even though I was constantly guarded and expected him to walk out the door and out of my life any second, Jimmie didn't do it. We dated all the rest of the year until he joined the Air Force on November 9, 1961. Jimmie was the perfect boyfriend during that time. He never broke up with me, although we had our share of fights over intimacy issues. He kept telling me how much he loved me and how much it would have meant to him for me to make love with him, but I couldn't.

Jimmie was so confusing. He seemed to put me on a pedestal at times and acted like I was so precious, and other times he would attack me. When I first heard about French kissing, I wanted to see what it felt like, so I kissed him that way. Jimmie smacked me on my behind and told me to never, ever kiss him like that again. What's a girl to do? I couldn't seem to win.

Jimmie Dale

Mom had always told me, "You can lie to me, but you can't lie to yourself. Always be a lady and never do anything that you would be ashamed of." I loved Jimmie as much as any sixteen-year-old could possibly love someone, but I couldn't go "all the way" with him.

Jimmie even wrote in my diary when he went off to the Air Force — he had taken to calling me Janie like my folks often did: "My darling Janie! I'm hoping from the bottom of my heart that nothing comes between us while I'm away. Maybe when I'm gone, you will realize how serious I am and how much it would have meant. You'll probably kick yourself for not loving me when I needed you most. I hope that someday in the near future, things will be the way we both want them to be. I want you to know you mean so much to me. Until we are together for always, I'll say bye-bye for now. From the only guy that will be true. With all my love, Your Jim."

I felt terrible, but even after his sweet words, I still couldn't do "IT." I loved Jimmie with all of my heart, but I guess I just wasn't emotionally mature enough to do something like that. He even asked me to run away and marry him. When he asked my parents, Mom told him I was getting my High School diploma no matter what else I did in my life. This was so important to both of my parents because neither one of them had graduated from High School. She said that if Jimmie waited, I could go across the stage, get that diploma in one hand, and meet the preacher at the other end to say "I do." But I would graduate! He accepted what she said.

We wrote and called and cried and tried our best to hold onto each other for the time Jimmie was in the service. He trusted me enough that he told me to date and enjoy my junior and senior years. I didn't want to, but he was so far away, and I knew Jimmie too well to know that he wouldn't be alone. He just wasn't the kind of guy who could be without a lady in his life, but as long as I didn't know about it, it didn't hurt. As long as he was coining back to me, I was okay with it.

Jimmie came home on leave on May 18, 1962. I was so excited to see him that I thought I was going to burst. That day he picked me up at school and brought me home. We were so happy together and spent every moment we could with each other. I was trying to learn to drive and Jimmie let me drive his folks' old station wagon. He acted like he got a big kick out of showing me how to navigate that monster on the road. We went on picnics, to the movies, and he took me wherever I had to go. It was so wonderful being near him - to see him, to smell him, to be "Jimmie's girl" again. He kept telling me how much he missed me, how much he loved me, and he just couldn't wait for us to get married. One night Jimmie was particularly insistent that we think about getting married before he went back to base. I looked into his big brown eyes and mouthed the word "S-C-H-O-O-L!!!!" He looked at me so hurt. I begged him to understand that it would only be a little over a year and a half before I would graduate. All we had to do was wait, and then we could be husband and wife like we always wanted.

Jimmie leaned over and put his arm around me and looked directly into my eyes and asked, "Janie, please wait for me, please." I told him that I would. Tears started to fall down Jimmie's cheeks. I was so touched because I had never seen a guy cry, except for my little brother but I didn't count that. Those tears made me feel much more confident that maybe, just maybe, we truly were in love and somehow we actually would get married after I graduated. I wasn't sure how I was going to feel about being an Air Force wife because Jimmie really liked the military and planned to make a career out of it, but I would have done anything for him except, well, you know. I supposed I would adjust, but I was afraid of leaving my family and going off to wherever Jimmie would be stationed. I still had time to see what happened between us. Time would tell.

Jimmie was different when he was home, specifically in that he didn't push me to have sex with him. It was like he had grown up in the time he spent at Lackland Air Force Base. Maybe he actually understood I had every intention of waiting until we got married, and he seemed to have accepted it. Jimmie told me he had heard a Roy Orbison song, (seems like so many of his songs were appropriate in our relationship) titled "Young and Innocent," which reminded him of me. He was glad he didn't have to worry about me while he was gone because he knew I was going to be a good girl until we got married.

Jimmie had to leave on May 30. My mom allowed me to go with him and his family to the bus. I might get in trouble because I was going to miss school, but it didn't matter to me, because I wanted to spend as much time with Jimmie as possible. I promised him I wouldn't cry, but I did because I felt like my heart was shattering inside my body. His mom was so understanding as I cried quietly in the back seat of the car staring out the window.

Jimmie Dale and Me in Late 70's

I honestly thought that even if I did date other folks while Jimmie was gone, somehow we would still be together after I graduated. I was wrong. On May 29, 1963, Jimmie wrote to tell me he had met someone in Germany, and they were getting married. Oh, I was devastated! I could hear "It's Over" by Roy Orbison (yep, him again and his broken-hearted melodies) playing in my head.

I wasn't surprised, yet it all seemed so unreal. I had loved Jimmie for so long, but I knew in my heart, I suppose I'd always known, that in spite of how much we cared for each other, this would happen. Still, I never forgot him; he always had a special place in my heart. For the longest time, I would hold onto those memories of what I thought real love was.

MY JUNIOR AND SENIOR YEARS

NORTH HIGH SCHOOL
Graduation Picture

Adjusting to life without Jimmie was hard. I got a temporary job at W. T. Grant Company's Grand Opening in July, as the S & H Green Stamp girl. I was embarrassed because I had to wear a green cape and a beret! I prayed no one I knew would come into the store and see me dressed like that. It was my job to greet people at the door of the store, welcome them, and hand them a booklet to keep the stamps in that they got from their purchases. After you saved so many of these books of stamps, you could get gifts out of a catalog.

After the Grand Opening, I heard that some of the girls were getting called back for other jobs. I showed up and told the woman who was placing the girls that I was supposed to be a cashier. She said she didn't remember asking me to come back, but I assured her that she did. So now I had a job at Grant's.

It wasn't my first job. I had worked at Woolworth's downtown on Saturdays since I was fourteen, and then I worked at another branch at the Northern Lights Shopping Center a few doors down from where my mom managed the Darling Shop. I wasn't too crazy about either job, but it gave me a few nickels to call my own. My motivation for getting a job occurred when I asked my Dad for 50 cents to buy a Blackberry Sundae at the Dairy Queen (yes, a sundae really only cost 50 cents!). He said if I wanted money, I should get a job; so I did. That was the last time I ever recall having to ask my folks for money.

At Grant's I did all sorts of jobs. I was a cashier, but I also worked in the candy department decorating Easter candy. I worked in toys and in ladies' dresses, anywhere they needed me really, because I was happy to just keep my job. The only thing I didn't do was work at the food counter, which never appealed to me anyway. I became close with my manager, Mr. Votsis, and his family. I babysat his children a few times, and anytime they came into the store, they made a beeline for me with their arms outstretched, which made me feel so good. They always seemed so happy to see me and hug my neck. I always loved kids.

I enjoyed meeting a wide array of people while working there. I dated several fellows, like Ben Reynolds, who helped teach me how to parallel-park his gigantic Lincoln Continental. We dated and had fun together but it wasn't a serious romance.

Laura set me up on a date with a lifeguard named Eddie Phillips. At the party we attended, all of the kids were playing "kissy face" because most of them were going steady, so I sat and blew bubbles with my bubble gum most of the night. I didn't want to go to a party with a guy I had just met and kiss him all night. Eddie tried to make me kiss him, and I gently, but firmly, pushed him onto the floor from the couch. He was shocked! I could tell Eddie wasn't used to being treated that way by any girl, so maybe that was what he liked about me. We decided we were better as friends than a couple.

Still, it was a miracle we stayed friends. We went out a few more times after running into each other at the pool or the shopping center. Eddie even went to my Junior Prom with me and caused quite a fuss with all of my classmates because he really was an all-American, clean-cut, nice-looking guy. All of the girls wanted to know where I had been hiding him and why they hadn't seen us together before. Eddie and I always had fun when we went out together, but for some reason we just had a good friendship that never developed into anything else. I recently found an old clipping from the Columbus Dispatch newspaper among my souvenirs, and there was a picture of Eddie on it. He really was a cutie.

Of all of the boys I spent a few dates with, no one ever had the effect on me that Jimmie did, but I did find myself taking yet another look at Terry.

Terry and I were actually together at a party at my house on November 11, 1962 during my junior year. It was a "girl asks boy" party, of course, in our basement.

Christiane Graham

My friend Chris Graham helped me plan it. We were supposed to all dress like hillbillies, which meant jeans and flannel shirts, straw hats, overalls, and the like.

When I went to pick Terry up, he was dressed like he just stepped out of a men's magazine. I felt sorry for him and embarrassed for myself because I was dressed in line with the theme - blue jeans, a baggy shirt with hillbilly drawings all over it, and sneakers. I just knew that Mrs. Kneisley had said no son of hers was going to go to a party looking all "jakey" in jeans, God forbid! Terry Kneisley just didn't do that!

When we got to my house and Terry saw all of the other folks dressed in costume, he looked at me and lowered his head. I could tell he felt uncomfortable, so I asked him if he would like to wear one of my Dad's flannel shirts. His eyes lifted, and he smiled from ear to ear and said, "Yes, that would be great!"

Terry and I had so much fun that night. We played games like Honest Judge, where you asked the person sitting in a chair in front of you a question that was preceded with the statement, "I am an honest judge, this is an honest court, and I want honesty as an answer." Then you would ask the person what color something was, and he would answer with the correct color, only to be told he was incorrect and to remove something he was wearing. It was hysterical to see the look on the boys' faces. Only one guy was allowed in the basement while the others waited their turn upstairs. We girls giggled and giggled. Of course we never let any boy go beyond removing shoes, shirts, and t-shirts; although one of the girl's dates started to remove his jeans. As each boy finished his turn, he would be allowed to sit and watch the other guys as long as he promised not to reveal the fact that what we wanted all along was the word "honesty" as the answer to whatever question we asked. This was a pretty risqué game for our era.

We did the Limbo and had races with cotton balls on spoons. We went on a Scavenger Hunt where you are given a list with a bunch of random objects to obtain with a set amount of time to find them before returning to the party with your treasures. Whoever got the most items won a record. Terry and I laughed and held hands. I thought we were the perfect couple.

Terry and I danced, and he really kissed me. My bratty brother snuck downstairs with a camera and took a picture at exactly the perfect moment; thank you, Michael! I pretended to be angry, but I was so glad Michael had taken that photo, one which I treasured and carried with me until my first marriage. We had the most wonderful time together, yet Terry never asked me to go out with him.

I also have a few minutes of video of this party, thanks again to Mike for sneaking down into the basement. All of the guys were blindfolded, and girls alternated dancing with guys other than the one they had brought to the party. The guys were supposed to guess who you were by asking questions. Then it was the girls' turn to be blindfolded. Well, the jerky guys went upstairs and waited while Mike filmed us standing there waiting for some guy to dance with us. The guys thought it was a riot to pull this prank on us. We do look pretty stupid standing in the basement all in line with our blindfolds on waiting for something to happen. Although the video isn't very good, I still smile at the memory from the party.

About a month after the party, I asked Terry to come over to my house. He didn't have a car, so I picked him up in my Dad's first-ever, brand-new Chevy II. We went back to our house and listened to records, danced, and kissed. Kissing Terry was great. Although I thoroughly enjoyed it, it was never as intense as it had been with Jimmie, which was probably a good thing.

I was taking Terry back home when I felt that he was a little uncomfortable with me driving him, so I pulled over and asked if he wanted to drive. Of course he did; what senior boy wouldn't want to drive a brand-new car? We hadn't gone even two blocks when a car in front of us made a quick turn to the left. The car had a Christmas tree sticking out of the trunk so Terry didn't see the driver signal for the turn (if he even did signal). There was snow on the street, so when Terry tried to stop, we couldn't, and we slid into the back of the car. I thought I was going to faint on the spot — my Daddy's new car! What in the world was I going to say to my Dad? I became pretty hysterical.

Now there was no car for Daddy to use to drive me to school. What was so sad was neither Terry nor his parents even offered to help get me to school, yet they needed me to go to court to say that Terry didn't see the turn signal or brake light on the car because of the Christmas tree sticking out of the trunk. I had to get rides from other kids' parents or Daddy had to borrow a neighbor's car. Years later, the car incident became a joke between Daddy and Terry when we got together after Terry came home from Vietnam. They got a good laugh out of it, even though down deep I think Terry was still embarrassed about the whole event.

I never understood why Terry and I would have such a good time together, yet he would never ask me out. To this day I can't figure that out. He broke my heart so many times my mom actually christened my room "Lake Terry" for all the tears I shed over him my junior and senior years of High School, but this was not the end of Terry in my life.

My senior year was work, work, and more work. I became a manager of the Ladies' Department at Grant's. I managed to have some fun times with a new gal at school, Chris Graham, who was a gorgeous Army brat and had become my very best friend. We were constantly together and spent hours on the phone after school every day talking about boys. We met some college boys from Otterbein College and had some wild and crazy experiences with them. We went to frat parties, double-dated, and drove up for visits. It was quite the thing to brag about to our friends, right up until the frat boys found out we were just seniors in High School, and they dropped us like hot rocks. It was fun while it lasted!

I was so proud the day I graduated, June 5, 1963. I thought of Jimmie a lot that night and wondered how his marriage was going. I felt a deep emptiness inside me when I thought about how I had intended to graduate and then get married to Jimmie.

It was a day of mixed emotions, and I had no idea what I was going to do with my life. There was no way I could go to college because my folks couldn't afford it, and I didn't feel like I was smart enough to go to college anyway. Although I still had a place in my heart for teaching, I just didn't see any way I could ever get a degree. I knew I didn't want to work for Grant's the rest of my life, but I wasn't sure about what to do instead. It was a very scary feeling.

I called Jimmie's house, and his Dad answered. He could tell I was upset and immediately went to get Virginia. She could tell I had been crying and listened to me as I cried in between words. Bless her, she was so understanding. Jimmie's mom kept saying she was sorry things hadn't worked out with Jimmie and me and assured me that they all loved me very much and wished nothing but the best for me in my future and to stay in touch with them. Although what she said was so sweet, it didn't ease my sadness.

My Uncle Mardie, Aunt Jean, Uncle Billy, and Aunt Gloria came to my graduation. It was really wonderful to have family there. Aunt Kat and Uncle Bill couldn't make the trip, and Granny Dickson was still in Port Clinton with them, so she didn't come. I don't remember why Mamall Golden wasn't there. Daddy and Mom were so proud of me.

I was also proud of myself but was worried about what I was going to do with myself. Karen was going to nursing school, Godee and Laura were working, and Radene was married and had a baby. I was supposed to be getting married to Jimmie after graduation, and that wasn't going to happen. I had no idea what was next.

MY ITALIAN TEDDY BEAR

Alphie Di Guilio

On July 6, 1963, I had gone bowling with some friends, and I met a guy named Alphie Di Guilio. His real name was Norman Francis, but NO ONE ever dared call him that, except for me, of course, much later in our relationship when we were pretending to be angry with each other.

Of the "tall, dark, and handsome," Alphie wasn't very tall, but he had the dark and handsome. He had jet black hair and brown eyes, a dark olive complexion, and was basically "rough around the edges," to say the least. He was dressed like a bum, wearing Bermuda shorts, a football jersey, and high-top tennis shoes. I don't for the life of me know why I found this guy attractive, but I did.

Alphie and his buddies, Vic Vangle and Jim Burleson, started talking to me. Vic asked for my phone number and for some strange reason, I gave it to him. Vic called me a few days later when Alphie was with him. Vic told me that both he and Alphie wanted to date me, and I had to choose which one I wanted. I didn't know either one of them so I flippantly tossed a penny in the air and said, "Heads, I date Alphie; tails, I date you." It was heads.

Alphie and I made plans to get together that Friday and go to a drive-in. When Alphie came to our door, my Dad took one look at him and asked to see me in the kitchen. He said, "No way, you are not going out with that guy." I didn't want to openly defy my Dad, but I was eighteen years old, and I kind of liked Alphie and I couldn't see what all the fuss was about.

Daddy didn't like the way Alphie dressed or looked, and he even seemed upset that Alphie was Italian. Most Italians were Catholic, and that alone was completely foreign to my Methodist family. Daddy just couldn't understand why I wanted to be with a guy like Alphie. I think even Mom was surprised. Alphie just wasn't like anyone I had ever dated, since I usually went for the clean-cut type. Mom and Dad usually liked the guys I dated and agreed with my choices, so this was a whole new world for us, being on opposite sides of my dating preference choices. In spite of their feelings, they reluctantly agreed to let me go out with him. I suppose Mom and Dad figured I would find out for myself that Alphie wasn't right for me eventually.

I was pretty nervous being with Alphie at first. We went to see a ridiculous movie at the drive-in starring Bob Hope titled *Call me Bwana.* I suspected it was a movie that Alphie had no intentions of actually watching. I knew deep inside that I probably wouldn't be paying too much attention to the movie either. This Italian guy really fascinated me. I wanted to get to know him better, so we made small talk and tried to "break the ice."

After we had eaten some popcorn and drank a coke, we both got quiet. I heard him move in his driver's seat towards me and then he put his arm around me, pulled me toward him, and kissed me. Uh-oh, Alphie French-kissed! I had never been kissed that way in my life! Whew, I didn't know quite how I felt about someone putting his tongue in my mouth. I must have looked at Alphie with a weird expression on my face after he finished kissing me because he asked me if I was okay. I was trying to figure out how I did feel and finally told him I was fine.

I didn't really want Alphie to know that no one had ever kissed me like that before. I wasn't sure if I liked it or not but I wanted to find out, so we did a bunch of kissing. I could feel those butterflies flying around in the pit of my stomach just like they had when I fell in love with Jimmie. Something told me this was going to be a totally different relationship than I had ever experienced before. I wanted to see what would happen, but I was also pretty scared.

Alphie started calling me after our first date, so we double-dated with Vic and some other girls. I really liked Alphie although I wasn't sure why. We had fun together, but he was pretty antisocial and quite shy. He wasn't shy around me when we were alone, but Alphie didn't like meeting new people or going to parties - he just wanted to be with me. And Alphie made me laugh. While he tried to appear to be a tough guy on the outside, deep down he was a teddy bear.

On our second date, Alphie told me he loved me. I was floored! He said that he had never ever said that to anyone before. I stared at him in disbelief, but I didn't say it back because I didn't feel the same way. Alphie said, "You don't have to say it back to me now, but one day you will." After that, we started spending all of our time together.

I met Alphie's oldest brother, Jim, who looked like a taller, more clean-cut version of Alphie. Jim was married to Sylvia when I met him, and they were the most darling couple ever. I always admired Sylvia because she seemed to know so much, and she was married! Then there was Gary, who wasn't dark like Jim and Alf with their dark olive complexions. Gary had light brown hair and green eyes. He was so handsome and conceited, but in a funny way, honestly thinking he was God's gift to the female population. Alphie's mom, Mary, was incredibly friendly and seemed to always be smiling or laughing about something. His Dad's name was James but everyone called him "Kaki." Kaki stole my heart! There was something about him that I loved immediately.

Alphie and I spent almost every single evening together after I got off work. We were either at his house, his Grandma Jean's house, or my house, or we were going to the movies, double dating with Jackie Mac Donald and Bob Russell, or just going to the Submarine Races. The "Submarine Races" was any parking spot. Needless to say, there were no submarines. It was Just an excuse to make out.

I had finally met a guy I enjoyed kissing as much as I had Jimmie Dale. The only difference was Alphie liked the way I kissed, obviously, and didn't want to teach me. Or maybe I had learned how to kiss really well. Sometimes Alphie would get frustrated with me, though, and it's a wonder he put up with me. It had to be hard on him (no pun intended) because I was not going to have sex until I got married, and that was just final! Alphie didn't pressure me the way Jimmie had, but I am sure there were times he wasn't sure he could make it. Alphie was a good Catholic boy and understood we were not going to have sex while we were dating. Period!

We got engaged at Christmas time, 1964, with the marquise diamond I had always wanted. My Granny Dickson was there when Alphie threw the ring into my lap. How romantic! He said, "You already know what this is." Of course I did because we had gone together to pick out the ring, but he was definitely lacking in the romance department with the approach to our engagement. That was Alf.

Granny said, "Janie, you don't need to accept that. You are too young to get married." She said it right in front of Alphie. I looked up at him, and he just shrugged his shoulders.

We were so different. Alphie was dark, and I was fair. He was moody and didn't necessarily like to be around people, and I loved to socialize. He was always happiest when it was just the two of us, and he was especially uncomfortable with my Dad. They never had negative words or anything, but Daddy didn't warm up to Alphie for a very long time. Daddy wasn't too pleased that I had gotten engaged, but as usual, he never said much of anything to me about who I was dating or what I was doing.

As I mentioned, I had always hoped Daddy and I would have the same kind of relationship that Robert Young had with his daughter in *Father Knows Best*, but that wasn't going to happen. Daddy had a cold mother who didn't show much emotion, and I honestly don't think Daddy knew how to show his love in words or actions. Granted, he always made sure we had clothes, food, some extras, like records, and he did drive me to school for two years with little or no sleep. I guess that was Daddy's way of showing me he loved me without actually saying it or doing anything openly to express it. I wish Daddy had told me what his reservations were about Alphie, but he never did. Finally, after over a year or so Daddy must have decided Alphie wasn't going anywhere and that we were really going to get married.

Of course, Daddy didn't say a word when I put the ring on my finger. I had so hoped that everyone would be happy for us. I knew Kaki, Mary, and Grandma Jean would be delighted, so I would just revel in their happiness and the fact that Alphie and I were excited about our future together.

I wished at times Alphie would have made more of an effort to get close to my family and been a little more outgoing when it came to my friends. The only friend I think he felt comfortable with was Jackie, and that was because she and Bob were with us so much. Jackie just accepted Alphie for the way he was. On the other hand, I never met a stranger, and loved being with people and going new places. I always felt there was a new experience right around the corner, and I wanted in on it.

Yet I was so content with Alphie. He genuinely loved me and never hesitated to tell me or try to show me in his own way. He made me feel special! Alphie knew that I loved him and we would be together no matter who liked it and who didn't. We planned on getting married in July, 1966.

Kaki

Mary

Alphie's Dad and mom seemed to adore me. Kaki reminded me of Errol Flynn with the dark hair, mustache, and blazing eyes. He was shorter and stockier than Flynn was, but there was definitely a "swashbuckler" inside Kaki just waiting to get out. Although he had a tough exterior, Kaki was really a softy at heart. One thing that always amazed me about Kaki was his hands. His fingers were huge! Alphie used to say his Dad could balance full orange crates on his little fingers. I believed it.

His Mom, Mary, was one of the sweetest people I had ever met. She was a little taller than Kaki, with auburn hair and the happiest dark brown eyes I had ever seen. Her eyes just seemed to sparkle and dance when she laughed. She had a warm, natural smile and a laugh that generally ended up in near convulsions as tears rolled down her cheeks.

I provided the Di Guilio family with a lot of reasons to laugh. Once Gary told us he was bringing a girl named Cheryl home for dinner, and all of our eyes bugged out. Gary just didn't do that sort of thing, so this must be serious, and Gary wanted Kaki to fix something really special on Friday night. I was supposed to work, but I got one of the girls to trade with me because I wasn't about to miss this. We were all on our best behavior, and Kaki and Mary prepared a delicious meal.

I was a little nervous about meeting Cheryl because she was everything I wasn't. She was tiny, very feminine, and had dark hair. She was "cheerleader" cute too, the kind of girl all of the guys wanted to date.

Midway through dinner, Mary passed me a plate filled with raw vegetables, and I started taking some off to put on my plate. Right then, she went into one of her laughing jags. I was dumbfounded - what in the world could be so funny about me taking veggies off a plate? Gary gave her "the look" that Kaki had mastered (I think it meant "enough foolishness, this is serious, straighten up!"), so she tried to calm down. Mary leaned toward Kaki and pointed to the plate I had just passed back to her. He smiled a big smile.

We chatted and managed to finish our meal without more hysteria. After Gary and Cheryl left, I looked over at Mary and asked, "What in the world was so funny at dinner?" She started up again.

I shook my head and looked over at Alphie. Kaki started laughing too. "Okay now you're starting," I said to Kaki. "I still don't understand what I did that you two think was so hysterical? Please tell me."

Apparently, the veggie plate Mary had handed me was not a veggie plate but was Kaki's dinner plate, and I was taking food off of it and putting it on mine. "Well, good Lord," I said, "I hope Gary never brings another girl here again. I don't like having to watch everything I'm doing." Then

I leaned over, grabbed a radish off Kaki's plate, and popped it into my mouth. They all burst out laughing, even Alf.

We had all been so surprised that Gary had actually brought a girl home. He was the Romeo of all Romeos and had more girls chasing after him than you could imagine. Gary was always conning me into doing something for him, usually ironing a shirt or a pair of slacks right before one of his big dates. He always promised to pay me fifty cents (I never saw a penny all those years), or Gary would promise us the use of his beautiful 1966 Chevy since Alphie didn't have a car.

One night Gary totally forgot he had promised us the car, and he was trying to get me to iron a shirt before he went out. Alphie and I reminded Gary that we had a double-date with some friends, and he had told us we could have the car. He quickly objected because he had important plans too. As Gary was trying to convince us that he hadn't promised us the car, Kaki appeared and reminded him that he had indeed made us that promise and that he would be keeping it.

"But Kak, I have a date!" Gary declared.

"Fine, son, you can take your mother's car." Gary was furious. He had to use his mom's old Ford Galaxy while we took off in his gorgeous '66 Chevy convertible. I learned quickly that Kaki was the law - whatever he said is what happened, no questions asked.

Alphie told me about a time when he, Jim, and Gary decided to take on the "old man." Gary and Jim were taunting Kaki, smacking at him and sort of throwing punches, and Alphie waited for the moment to run in for the kill. Kaki put up with this foolishness for as long as he could, then he asked the boys to stop, but they didn't. They kept feeling more and more confident that they could really show Dad who was boss. Once more Kaki asked them to quit because he was getting angry and this little game wasn't funny anymore. They persisted; they really weren't hitting him hard, they were annoying him more than anything.

In one swift movement, Kaki grabbed Jim and Gary by the backs of their necks with those huge hands, bumped their heads together, and let them drop to the floor. Then he looked over at Alf, "How about you son, you want to take ole Dad on?" he asked.

"No sir," Alphie replied, "I'm just here to pick up Jim and Gary." They all eventually had a good laugh over it, but the sons never tried that again.

Another time I had been teasing Alphie in the car about something silly, like the way his buddy, Slagle, cut Alf's hair. I hated it when Slagle would square it off in the back instead of following Alf's hairline, because it made Alf look even more "gangster-ish." I don't think Alf took it badly that I didn't like the way his hair was cut, but it gave him an excuse to act angry with me so that we could make up later. I know we probably acted immature, but we pretended to be upset with each other over the dumbest things, like he wouldn't kiss me or I wouldn't kiss him. It was silly, but we were young and innocent. Anyway, Alphie was acting like he was angry with me and was going to make me pay for it. I don't really know how he would make me pay for it but we were just enjoying teasing one another.

I opened the car door and ran into the house to find Kaki, who was in his favorite chair reading a racing form, which was his favorite thing to do besides play Pinochle. There he sat with the ever-present cigarette hanging from his lip. I grinned at him and asked, "What's for dinner Kaki?"

"I think you just might find some of that nasty chicken and rice soup that you love so much on the stove, Honey," he answered.

"Yippee!" I yelled. Kaki knew I loved his soup. I don't know what he did to it that made it taste so good, but it was delicious!

"Want some, Alf?" I asked as he came into the room, still pretending to be upset with me.

"NO! I had some earlier," Alphie barked at me, trying to stay in character.

Kaki's eyes shot upwards from the racing form because nobody messed with me or was mean to me when "my Kaki" was around. He gave Alphie the "that's about enough" look. Alphie smiled a really stupid smile and walked out of Kaki's reach, following me as I made a beeline for the kitchen.

I was warming soup when Gary came into the kitchen with a shirt in his hand. "Oh no, how did you know I was here? Were you looking out the window when we came in?" I asked.

"Now is that any way to talk to ole Gar? You know you like me better than Alf," Gary was grinning his most charming grin.

"Here, then you stir the soup while I iron your shirt. You are so spoiled." I said. "Want some soup?"

"Christ, no; every time Kaki makes this stuff he makes enough to feed a damn army," Gary responded. "This crap stays around here so long that you feel like you are eating a friend." I was just about to crack up when Kaki walked into the kitchen.

"Is that so, Gary? Any time that you don't like eating here, you just let me know. I'll rent your room to someone who appreciates the food and shelter that I provide for you." Kaki said.

"Ah, Kaki, I was only teasing Bev. I know she loves this shit....er, uh, I mean delicious soup." Gary turned and winked at me. Kaki could barely keep from laughing himself.

Gary could talk his way out of a hanging, even if he was sitting on the horse he had just stolen. I handed Gary the shirt and held out my hand for the fifty cents. "Put it on my tab. I don't get paid until Friday," he said as he kissed me on the cheek. I just loved my crazy Italian family.

Right after graduation, I had tried to get a job at Ohio Bell, but when I told them I wanted to try and go to college to be a teacher, they seemed to chill up on me in the interview. I didn't get the job, so I went to work at W. T. Grant's where I was making $1.20 an hour. After six months, I decided my chances of going to college were slim to none, so I wanted a better job with more money and benefits.

In September, I went back to Ohio Bell and told them I really had a desire to be a Long Distance Operator. To my shock, they gave me a test, hired me on the spot, and I reported for training in October. Although the two weeks of training was pretty interesting, I knew in my heart that I wouldn't be there very long.

Some of the best-laid plans don't always come out the way you expect. On February 17, 1965, Alphie got his draft papers. He showed up at the phone company to pick me up. When I came downstairs, he was standing outside of the car, which was unusual for him to do. Alphie grabbed me by the hand and asked me if I loved him. I looked into his eyes trying to read what was going on, but I couldn't. "Of course I love you, Alphie. Why?"

Then he told me that he had been drafted. I thought I was going to faint right there on the pavement. "What are we going to do?" I asked him with tears in my eyes.

"Let me work on something, okay?" he replied. The next day, Alphie tried unsuccessfully to join any branch of the reserves. We were beside ourselves. The following day, he went to the Ohio National Guard, and they told him that they could help him and let him join on the spot. Alphie still had to leave for six weeks and then serve once a month for four years but that was far better than being drafted.

Alphie and I became closer than ever, if that was possible. I guess the thought of losing him like I had lost Jimmie was in the back of my mind, and I did not want to go through that again.

Alphie went off and did his training, and I missed him like crazy. He would call me and ask me to come down to Kentucky and marry him on the spot. I just couldn't do that, though; I wanted to have a real wedding. Even if it was going to be small, I still wanted one.

Alphie and Me on
New Year's Eve 1964

When Alphie returned, we fell back into our routine of going to each other's houses, double-dating, and watching his adorable niece Stephanie and nephew JD. We were blissfully happy thinking our lives were set. Gary married Cheryl, and she asked me to be in her wedding. It was unbelievable that someone had landed ole Gar, and he was really going to make a commitment to one woman instead of the hundreds he used to date. We were all surprised but had the feeling this was going to be forever because Gary had enjoyed being a bachelor far too much.

It would just be a matter of time before Alf and I got married...or so I thought.

AN AIRLINE STEWARDESS! ME?

Chrismas Before
Stewardess School

After graduation, everyone promises to stay friends and never lose touch. Baloney! The only girl I stayed friends with was Karen Roth, the one I said was probably like "Marty" in *Grease*, except she was built like Annette Funicello. I always envied Karen's big bosom, since I had none. We were always doing crazy stuff to each other, all in fun, and sometimes on some of our double-dates. Karen went through a little period of thinking she was better than me because she went to nursing school (although she ended up dropping out), but we finally worked it out and were as close as ever, maybe even more so, than we had been at North High. Karen was still in love with Nathan Hanna, as she had been all through school.

Karen and I did a few double-dates, most of which turned out to be disasters.

That was the kind of stuff Karen and I did to each other during our High School years. To this day, we keep in touch when we can. I call her "Boobs" and, she calls me "Wings," pet names we gave each other after I became a Stewardess.

After Karen and Nate broke up for the millionth time, she decided she wanted to be a Stewardess because she was tired of working as an insurance agent.

I hated working at the phone company. It was the worst place imaginable, with nothing but women, most of them old maids with those awful "Wedgies" shoes that only old ladies wore. I remember my supervisor, Rosemary Forsythe, watching me like a hawk when I was being trained.

I was a good operator, although occasionally I did get into a little mischief. My favorite calls were "Camp Calls." That was when a gal was trying to find her boyfriend at boot camp in some branch of the service, and she wasn't exactly sure how to contact him because she only had his mailing address. It was like playing detective. You had to keep calling different sections of the camp trying to track down the boyfriend, but in the meantime, you got to flirt with all the guys who answered the phone. We had these timecards where we had to write down everything we did on a call to prove how we had spent our time. Rosemary felt these camp calls could be handled in a matter of minutes, so I quite often got lectures about spending my time more wisely.

We had six cords to pull into six holes when they lit up and six other cords to connect them to the called party. One night, I was bored beyond belief, so I filled up my board, leaned over to the empty board beside me and filled it up too.

I suddenly heard those "Wedgies" clip-clopping behind me as Rosemary beat a path to my seat. She plugged her headset into my board and asked me what in the world I was doing. "You can't do that!" she yelled in my ear.

"Do what?" I asked, in the most insipid voice I could muster.

"You cannot answer and direct more than six calls at any one time. It is strictly forbidden. Do not take any more calls. I want to see you immediately in my office." I waited and unplugged the calls as they finished, then found Rosemary waiting for me at the punishment desk. All of the other operators' eyes followed me as I went into her little cubby in the middle of the room to get my ass chewed out I was so ready to get out of there.

"I am going to interview with Delta Airlines to be a Stewardess, and you are going with me!" declared Karen.

"What? I asked. "Are you nuts? I am going to walk into that interview and they are going to say, 'Sorry, we are not hiring Amazons this week.' No way, Karen. Why would I subject myself to that kind of rejection?"

"You hate your job, right? You are miserable there. Why wouldn't you go?"

"Obviously, you weren't present on Career Day at North High when Chris Graham and I went to listen to some guy talk about the requirements needed to be a TWA Stewardess," I countered.

"No, but what has that got to do with anything?"

"Well, this is how it went. 'You must be this weight in proportion to your height. You can't be taller than 5'8" at the very most. It is preferred that you speak one or more foreign languages, and you better not have a single zit on your face,'" I explained.

"Oh, he didn't really say that about zits, did he?' Karen asked.

"Karen, you aren't listening! I am too tall at 5'10" in my stocking feet. I don't need to do this to myself."

Karen shrugged. "Ok, I am going with or without you. The least you could do is come along with me and give me moral support." I reluctantly agreed to accompany her.

This is where I owe Karen a very special "thank you" because she is the reason I became a Stewardess. If she hadn't encouraged (or badgered) me into going to those interviews, I would not have had the wonderful thirty-five year career I had.

When we arrived, the gentleman conducting the Delta interview put an application in front of me. I wanted to say, "Hello, can't you see that I am at least three feet taller than you? What are you doing?"

Karen glared at me and said, "Just fill the damn thing out." Karen interviewed first, and then she practically shoved me into the room.

The gentleman from Delta looked over the application, asked me a few questions, and then stated the obvious. "I'm sorry, but you are too tall to be a Stewardess for Delta, and I can see that is what you want to do." This was hysterical, since I was only there to accompany Karen and already knew I was too tall. Being a stewardess was the furthest thing from my mind, or so I thought.

He continued, "I'll make you a deal. If you don't get hired by one of the other airlines, although I am sure you will, I will see to it that you get hired as an agent or something else. Maybe our height limits will raise, and you can be a Stewardess at a later date." I was so surprised that it's a wonder my chin didn't hit the desk when he said that. He hadn't made me feel self-conscious or ugly; he actually gave me a boost.

I came out and told Karen what he had said. "See, your fears were for nothing." she said. "You actually might be able to do this." Suddenly, I had the Stewardess bug.

Next we set up an interview with TWA. Unfortunately, Karen got sick, so I went by myself. When I walked into the room, I was amazed; this woman had on enough makeup for two people. She raised her eyes to get the full view of me. She curtly said, "Walk across the room and sit down here." I swallowed hard and tried to walk straight even though I felt like this was the first step I had ever taken. When I got close enough to the seat, I nearly jumped over the arm to hurry up and sit down.

The TWA woman looked into my eyes, introduced herself, "I'm Priscilla Weston," and asked. "How many different colors have you had your hair in the last six months?"

My eyes must have been as big as golf balls! I gulped and squeaked out, "I just had my hair frosted a week ago."

She straightened up in her seat and spit out the question, "You did that to your hair on purpose!?!"

Nervousness and embarrassment made me almost stutter as I replied "Er, uh, uh, yes, ma'am I did."

Then came the next bullet to the heart, "What is the largest dress size that you have ever worn? Now tell me the truth," this evil woman asked.

"A twelve," I replied.

"Now come on, dear, let's at least be honest with each other."

"Seriously, the largest dress size I have ever worn is a twelve." Dear God, what am I doing here? I asked myself. This woman is tearing me apart.

"Stand up and walk across the room, then back to me," she commanded. I could feel her piercing eyes watching my every move. I made it across the room and back but I don't know how. "Dye your hair brown, and come back to see me in a month, and you had better be in a size 10 or less."

I don't know why I thanked her for her time, when, in reality I wanted to beat her profusely about the head and shoulders. Yeah, you'll see me in a month! Ha! Not in a lifetime, sister!

Later I told Karen to stuff her Stewardess crap where the sun didn't shine. She advised me to calm down and that we would talk about it before our interview with American Airlines. "Are you nuts!?! Forget it, Karen! I have had my ego shattered enough for the rest of my life. I am not going to any more interviews. Period!" I practically yelled at her.

After this, I had a couple of fun days at the phone company. One day I was so fed up with the daily routine that I pulled into two empty outlets and called both Terry Kneisley and Richie Irion at the same time. They each answered and thought the other one had called. We weren't supposed to listen in on conversations past the first exchange of words, but once in while we all did. At one point, I softly said, "Terry" into my headset. Richie immediately jumped on it and asked Terry who was with him. Of course, Terry denied anyone was there and accused Richie of playing a trick on him. I snickered to myself as they continued their squabble until they finally hung up thinking each one had played a trick on the other. That was fun!

Another time I received a collect call from a guy named Francis Flutter. This was a call to, so help me, his fiancée Parnella Foulfetcher. I could not believe my ears. I asked him a second time to be sure I had the correct names. He assured me that I did. When she answered, I got out the "I have a collect call for Parnella....." and I lost it. I burst into laughter, trying to hide it by covering my mouthpiece. She got awfully pissed off and said, "Yes, it's me, and I will accept the call, damn it!" Can you imagine her name would be Parnella Foulfetcher Flutter if they did get married? Dear lord, poor woman. Later on, once I became a Stewardess, when I was feeling silly as we introduced ourselves to the crew members, I would sometimes say my name was Parnella Foulfetcher just to see the looks on their faces. It was hysterical, because they just never knew if I was serious or not.

Luckily for Karen, when it came time for the interview scheduled at American Airlines, I had just experienced a hellish few days at Ohio Bell. Nothing I did was right, according to Rosemary. I think the old biddy was just jealous that we were young girls and that we knew how to work AND have fun. We could enjoy ourselves and still do a good job, but she wasn't the type to think there was anything else in the world but work. For Rosemary, that might have been true, but not for me.

Rosemary really lost it one day when a repairman came to fix one of the broken boards. He had squatted down on the floor by my station right beside me, and I looked down at him and said in my smart-mouth way, "Just what I've always wanted, men at my feet." The repairman started laughing so loudly that all of the gals in my area turned to look at me. I put my finger up to my lips in the sh-h-h motion, but I was too late. Rosemary was on her way, and I had another visit to the cubby desk in the middle of the room.

When Karen reminded me of our interview the next day, I quickly replied, "Count me in."

For the American Airlines interview, we walked into a hotel room and saw some seats in a semi-circle. A well-dressed man in a suit handed us each an application to fill out and said he would be right back. As I looked around the room, I felt like I just might throw up. There sat those perfect little cheerleader types, all prim and proper, and the girls from "the table" back in High School.

Here, at long last, is the story about "the table." All the popular kids sat at one table in the middle of the lunchroom at Indianola Junior High. I know that was so all of us less-than-popular kids could admire them daily. One day,

I was sitting with my dear friend, Wanda Ball, discussing boys, clothes, and life in general. We always had a good time together. Wanda was sweet and had the challenging ordeal of teaching me how to dance The Chicken, The Mashed Potato, and The Stroll. That girl had the patience of a saint because I was anything but graceful. She was pretty, but kind of heavyset.

Two of the girls from the "prestigious" table - Kay Coffey, who I had been in Girl Scouts with, and Diane Kanuth, a friend from Junior High - came over to me and said, "Bev, we'd like for you to join us at our table."

I looked at them, smiled, thanked them, and started to stand up. I glanced over at Wanda, who had by this time lowered her head, and said, "Come on, Wanda, they have asked us to sit with them."

Diane quickly stated, "Oh no, Bev, not her, just you."

I sat back down and said, "No thanks."

Kay and Diane were astounded by my refusal to join them. They just rolled their eyes, huffed at me, and walked away. They couldn't believe I had turned them down.

Wanda informed me that I had just probably made the worst mistake of my life, and I would pay for that decision for the continuation of my High School days. I was feeling uneasy because I knew that she was probably right, but I just couldn't see my friend hurt like that. "Hey, so what, who's my best friend?" I asked her.

"I am," Wanda stated.

"Well, I'm where I should be then."

Whoa, was Wanda right! The whole table of girls treated me like a leper from that day on. They would plan parties in front of me, making sure I heard them, and then they would look at me and walk away. Ouch, that really hurt! Did I regret my decision? Honestly, at times, I did, especially when Wanda moved away.

I guess that the invitation was a "one time" offer, although I did get my revenge at my 30th High School reunion. Thank you Lord! That reunion and my revenge were two of the greatest experiences of my life. I'll share this unbelievable weekend with you in this book's sequel.

The American Airlines interview made all of those insecurities flood back into my mind and body. What in the world was I doing there? I gave Karen a dirty look, which she completely ignored, and then tried not to make eye contact with me the rest of the time we filled out the applications.

Mr. Kistler, a nice looking man in his thirties, called me into the room. I was "loaded for bear" — this was a mistake, and I wanted to get it over with just as quickly as I possibly could. I strutted over to the seat beside him. I was ready for the dress size question, and I was going to let him have it with both barrels.

"Why do you want to be a Stewardess?" he kindly asked me.

I was taken aback by the tenderness in his voice. It was almost like he actually knew what I was feeling inside. I put my guard down and answered that I really enjoyed being with people and that I had dreamed of traveling for a long time. We chatted for a while, and he seemed pleased with my comments and answers.

Mr. Kistler asked about my family, and then he made mention of the diamond on my left hand. He asked how my fiancé was going to feel about me flying off into the wild blue yonder. We both exchanged smiles at that terminology. I told him Alphie wanted me to be happy, and he knew I was miserable at the phone company. I said I felt like Alphie would be okay with me flying, which I knew was not true, but I didn't really expect to get the job anyway. I hadn't even discussed it with Alphie. One thing that had crossed my mind was that I wasn't sure I was ready to get married since I was only 20 years old.

Mr. Kistler asked me how soon I thought I could report to Stewardess School. I flippantly told him two weeks after giving my notice at Ohio Bell. He looked at me, smiled, and said I would be hearing from him soon.

I honestly never expected to hear from American Airlines, so I was completely surprised when I received a letter telling me that I had been accepted as a Stewardess trainee and to report for school in a few weeks.

Sadly, Karen didn't get accepted. I never understood why, although later one of the pilots told me that my friend obviously didn't pass the "Hula Hoop Test." When I asked him what he meant, he replied, "You take a Hula Hoop and drop it over the girl's head. If the hoop sticks around your bust, you fly for Delta. If it stops at your hips, you are TWA material. If it goes all the way down to your feet, you're destined to be an American Airlines Stewardess!" In some respects I think that was pretty factual. HA! HA!

Now I had to tell Alphie that I had been hired as a Stewardess. I think I would have rather faced a firing squad.

I was so excited when Alphie picked me up from work that evening because I could hardly wait to tell him about the letter I had received from American Airlines. Stupidly, I thought he might be happy for me, but when I told Alphie, he had to hold back the tears and not let his true emotions get the best of him. I knew he was hurt and angry with me when I told him that I really, really wanted to be a Stewardess. I told Alphie that it wouldn't affect the way that we felt about each other and that I would only do it for a little while, save some money, and then we would get married and have those three kids that he was always talking about. There were to be two boys and one girl, Damon, Donato and Deanna - his choice of names, not mine, but I didn't care. If it made Alphie happy, that was okay by me.

Alphie wasn't listening. "How do you know that you will even like doing this kind of job? Aren't you going to have to move away from Columbus?"

"You did too when you went into the Reserve." I tried to make a comparison to his leaving for training, but that wasn't making an impression either.

"That was just basic training; I only had to do it for six weeks, and then once a month; that whole Weekend Warrior thing. I didn't really move. You knew I was coming back home after it was all over." he said. "It's just not the same. You could be moving off to God-knows-where for God-knows-how-long."

Alphie was right, but I was grasping for straws to try to make him understand. I tried to sweet-talk him; I tried being stern with him. I tried everything I could to get him to understand that this was important to me, but he wasn't happy no matter what I said.

Neither were my parents. It was one thing to talk about being a Stewardess, but it was an altogether different thing to actually do it. When I told them I would have to go off to Dallas, Texas for training and that I really had no idea where they would send me to live and work, they were extremely nervous. They asked, "What about Alphie? I thought you two were getting married."

I had to smirk when I replied, "Oh, so now Alphie is good enough for me, huh?"

Mom said, "You know your Dad and I really do like Alphie, that he has come to mean a lot to us. We just took a while to actually get to know him. He is not the easiest guy in the world to talk to, but he is a good boy. It was just that he wasn't exactly the kind of guy we thought you would end up marrying." Dad just sat there, not adding to the conversation at all. He acted like his mind was a million miles away. Of course, this was so typical of Daddy – "mum's the word" with just about everything.

The worst part was telling Kaki and Mary. Needless to say, I got "the look," and Kaki was not happy! He did not want me to do this. He told Alphie right in front of me, "This is the end of you and Bev, Alf. You had better get used to it." I protested and tried foolishly to tell Kaki and Mary that I would only do this for a little while, and then I would come back home, marry Alphie, and we would live happily ever after. Kaki just left the room, then Mary did too. Alphie was devastated!

Here I was doing to Alphie what Jimmie had done to me. I remembered how much it had hurt when Jimmie went off to the Air Force. I had actually asked my parents if I could join the Air Force, and my Dad had roared and shocked the heck out of me by saying, "You aren't going off to become some officer's whore!" I was shocked to hear that come out of my father's mouth - my parents didn't talk like that. They had never even said a curse word around me. I was so hurt that my Daddy would talk to me like that, but he certainly made his point.

I truthfully didn't know what was going to happen when I left to become a Stewardess. I had been on an airplane only once in my life, when one of the girls from the phone company and I went to Ft. Lauderdale, Florida after seeing the movie *Where the Boys Are*. The flight was a satisfactory experience, but honestly I really didn't pay that much attention to what the Eastern Airlines Stewardesses did while working. Instead, I spent the whole trip talking to this attractive guy sitting beside me. I couldn't tell you what the Stewardesses were doing in the cabin.

I couldn't believe I had been accepted, and I was so proud! I thought about all of the girls in High School at "the table" and how shocked they would be to find out I was going to be a Stewardess. Me, a girl who would have loved to have tried out for cheerleading but knew in advance I had a snowball's chance in hell of ever being selected. I thought of Chris Graham and the TWA fellow on Career Day and how shocked he would be to see me getting a chance to do what he made sound like "mission impossible" to all except for a select few. Chris would probably faint, too.

I wanted to try this. To me, this was almost as exciting as being a movie star. American Airline's Mr. Kistler had told me that about one in 5,000 applicants were accepted for training, and not all of them even managed to graduate. Though that had scared the stuffing out of me, I just knew that when I got accepted, I would make it through to get my wings. I wanted the opportunity to prove myself right.

MY, MY, YOU'RE AWFULLY TALL

Jean Marie White, Beverly Golden, Bette Johnson, Nancy Lane, and Johnni Schumick

I'm really going to do it! I've quit the phone company. I'm committed now.

Mom, Dad, Karen's parents, Mr. and Mrs. Roth, and Alphie took me to the airport on February 12,1966. Alphie had a terrible time with my decision. I kept telling him it wouldn't change us, and, at the time, I meant it with all my heart.

At the airport, I met another gal going to school. Johnni Schumick, a cross between Shirley MacLaine and Cher, was tall and slender and had brown hair and eyes. She tried to act tough and, at times, seemed to act a little like the "Vamp" character from Cher's show, yet deep inside Johnni had a great heart. Her boyfriend, Stosh, was with her, and he reminded me of Robert Redford. Stosh had beautiful blonde hair, the kind most girls would kill for, and blue eyes. Johnni and I were both relieved to get on the airplane because the good-byes were getting tough!

We were so excited! We had little pamphlets to fill out on the way to Dallas. These had been sent to us with our acceptance letters and contained all sorts of information about the school, what to observe on our flight to Dallas, and questions to ask about the flight, the airplane, and, of course, the Stewardesses.

The very first page had "The Goal" with a drawing of Stewardess Wings. It read:

The Goal

If you who enter here have come sincerely
And know exactly where your interest lies
Have tried of office job, or school, or nursing----
Yet thrilled to the flash of silver in the skies;
If you have longed to see our nation's beauty

Not limited to east or western shore;
Can love all people, knowing each can teach you
And make you bigger than you were before;
If you have learned to sympathize with sorrow,
Open your heart to everyone you greet----
And if you honestly respect the culture
Of any creed or color you may meet;
If you have patience born of understanding
And pride not lessened though the task be small;
If you can gain the joy from helping others'
And have the will to give this job your all;
If you have loyalty unswayed by cynics,
But kindness far above your own demands,
Can realize all aviation's problems
But aid the vision of its future plans----
Then you will know this miracle of flying,
The comradeship, the progress, and what's more----
You'll feel the very pulse of our country!
Welcome to the Stewardess Corps (A.F., 1949).

The brochure from Miss Hazel Fitzgerald, Superintendent of Stewardess College, gave us the following instructions: "Introduce yourself to your stewardess shortly after take-off. Observe their procedures, as these will be the duties you will be performing within a few short weeks. When one of them has time, ask her to show you around on the airplane, because this will help you in answering the questionnaire. She will understand your feelings and enthusiasm, because she well recalls the day she, too, was on her way to the Stewardess College."

The Stewardesses on our flight may have understood, but our plane was completely full, and they were so busy they could barely spare a word or two for us. Although they tried to be cordial, Johnni and I kept asking questions because we couldn't show up our very first day without having those pamphlets filled out. (It all goes around, though; needless to say, I had my turn on the other side of that questionnaire.)

The pamphlet also mentioned that we would be kept busy studying. We had been sent a list of Airport Codes, three-letter abbreviations for cities where American Airlines flew, and we were required to have them memorized before we registered for training. My mom's brother, Billy

Bryant, sat at the kitchen table and helped me memorize all of the cities. He had made it easy for me to remember the codes by making up silly words for the call letters, such as Columbus, Ohio or CMH. He told me to remember to Call Mom at Home. SDF for Louisville, KY was So Damn Far. His way of learning was fun and easy and helped me get prepared for that part of my classroom work.

There was an explanation in our information packet by C. R. Smith, Chairman of the Board and Chief Executive Officer at American Airlines, that explained how he felt about the Stewardess' role in the overall picture of running an airline:

> "The future leadership of American, will depend, as it has in the past, on the faith and industry with which its high standards are maintained by the individuals in its organization.
>
> American has a responsibility to its passengers, who should be served well, with courtesy, and whose patronage should be appreciated. All of American's employees share this responsibility. Some have a greater responsibility than others, because they come in direct contact with passengers every day. Included in this group, vital to American's leadership in service, is the Stewardess Corps.
>
> American's Stewardesses are attractive, intelligent, courteous, solicitous and friendly young ladies. They are exceptional, because they must be able to carry out the responsibility of providing the best possible in-flight passenger service."

This sounded like a mighty tall order to me, but I was definitely up for the challenge. I was so excited about the opportunity to shine on my own and be one of those 5,000 applicants who made American proud they had hired me.

When we landed at Love Field in Dallas, I couldn't help but think this was the last airport President Kennedy ever saw. I think I was the only kid at North High School that wanted him to be President. My classmates had the same narrow-minded opinion as their parents. "He's a Catholic. He will populate the White House, Senate, and Congress with Kennedys.

He's going to try to start his own dynasty." Needless to say, I was so pleased when he won.

"Bev, we're here. Oh, do you believe this?" Johnni asked me.

"No Johnni, I don't. But please don't pinch me. I'm afraid I might wake up and find out this is all a dream."

We were all eyes as we rode in the limo to the Stewardess School in Arlington, Texas that would be our home for the next six weeks. The school was made of white brick and looked majestic nestled among the trees off Highway 360. There was a fence all around the property, and we wondered if that was to keep other people out or keep us in. We found out later it was for both.

The real shock occurred when I entered the door. The floors were like glass, and you could see your reflection in them. Out of the corner of my eye I saw a portrait. When I went to get a closer look, it was of a petite, pretty blonde with gorgeous light blue eyes in a pale blue Stewardess uniform. She was so attractive! (Little did I know that someday I would fly with that lovely lady, Mrs. Julie Redmond. I made her blush when I told her my feelings upon seeing her portrait for the first time.)

This portrait looked like what I imagined a Stewardess should look like, which puzzled me. What in the world was I doing there? I wondered how long it would take them to realize they had made a mistake and send me packing? Whew, did I feel insecure at that moment.

Johnni and I signed in and went up to our room on the second floor. The excitement in the air was intense. There were girls running all over the place, girls of all different shapes and sizes, from all walks of life. The other two girls in our room were Bette Johnson from New Bedford, Massachusetts and Nancy Langston from Winchester, Massachusetts.

Bette was real short, about 5'3", with light brown curly hair and blue eyes. She had an abundance of bubbly energy and was constantly in motion. Bette had the best attitude of any of us about this Stewardess thing. If she made it, great. If she didn't, so what? She was hysterical! You could usually count on "Bet" to perk you up when you got down.

Nancy was the oldest gal in our class and reminded me of Olive Oyl, Popeye's girlfriend. She was super thin with dark hair and deep blue eyes. She was a nervous wreck because she probably wanted to be a Stewardess more than anyone else in school did. Nancy had just ended a long romance she had expected would result in marriage. It was so important that she make good as a Stewardess. She felt terrible about the breakup and was really counting on the job to fill the void in her life.

We sat around and talked and read and discussed the information sheets they had given us when we registered. There were so many pages of rules and regulations to learn! We didn't care. We just wanted Monday to get there so we could get started.

Monday rolled around much too quickly. We shared a bathroom with four other girls in the next room. Getting eight girls in and out of one bathroom early in the morning would prove to be more chaotic than any of us had expected. There were naked girls running from shower to room. You could hear hair dryers blowing and see makeup strewn about. Clothes were pulled out of, and thrown back into, closets a million different times. We decided to try getting ready in shifts the next day.

At last, it was 9:00 AM - time to start class.

The instructors were unreal! There was never a hair out of place, their clothes were all so stylish, and their figures perfect. It was enough to keep me asking myself over and over for the next six weeks, "What am I doing here?" It was bad enough the instructors looked as if they had just stepped out of *Vogue* or *Bazaar*, but some of my fellow classmates were unbelievable too. We had former models, homecoming queens, cheerleaders, and teachers.

One girl that none of us could believe was Paula Kline. She had diamond rings, gold earrings, the most incredible wardrobe, and an unlimited bank account. While most of us were counting pennies, Paula was writing checks for her every whim. Her roommates reported that every piece of her underwear was color-coordinated. Every morning, all of us, including the instructors, looked forward to her appearance in the classroom. I guess she was the Paris Hilton of her day, but she had class. My classmates and I just couldn't get over her. One day her daddy sent her a trunk of clothes by helicopter - not a suitcase by bus, but a trunk by helicopter! What was THIS girl doing here?

We were quite a mixed group, fifty in all. Even though we were pretty different in appearance and backgrounds, we all had a similar look about us. I think we seemed pretty naïve, easily manipulated, polite, bubbly, and eager to start new lives.

There was one gal, Linda Ryner, who only lasted three days. She never spoke to her roommates or her instructor until they told her she would be sent home if she did not start communicating. Linda told her

Personal Instructor that was exactly what she wanted because she had met a fellow after her interview and wanted to continue the relationship. Her parents had recommended strongly that she pursue her career and forget this guy. To appease them, she came to school and had quickly decided it was not right for her. Linda said she would be happy to return to Chicago and tell her parents she gave it a try, so they gave her a ticket home.

On the first day, as our instructor, Miss Sandy Beane, was explaining our expectations, she was interrupted by a knock at the door. In walked C. R. Smith, the patriarch of American Airlines. He gave us a speech about being the backbone of the industry and how important our job was to the company. He then christened our class "C. R.'s Sweethearts" - after all, it was February 14. Mr. Smith was such a likeable person and a bigger man than he appeared in photographs. Because of his white hair and sparkling eyes, he reminded me of Santa Claus. In a way, he was Santa Claus. If he hadn't started American Airlines, we wouldn't be here about to embark on a whole new lifestyle.

Miss Beane introduced us to "Name Association." Before the class ended, she said we would all know each other's names, all 49 of them. The first girl stood up and said her name. The second girl introduced herself and repeated the first girl's name. This went on throughout the entire class. I was lucky I only had twenty-one names to remember! The poor gal in the last seat had 49 names to repeat. When she did it, we gave her a raucous round of applause.

I had an opportunity to use Name Association frequently as a Stewardess. On a flight from San Francisco to Oklahoma City, I was in the Coach cabin with only 46 passengers. Just for fun, I took all of their names. They looked at me rather strangely, since taking names is something usually done in the First Class cabin only. During the 2 1/2 hour flight, I used their names to ask for drink and dinner preferences or just to chat. By the time we landed, I had all 46 passengers in awe - they couldn't believe I had learned the name of every passenger on the flight. I even said good-bye to each one by name. The girl I was flying with couldn't believe me either. It was fun for me and a rewarding thing to do, since I made all of those people feel important; which in turn made me proud.

The next six weeks of class were jam-packed and intense. We had sixteen different courses we had to pass, not to mention the pressure put on us to look perfect for ten to twelve hours a day. After the makeup artists told us they were going to turn us drab-looking "Plain Janes" into future

"Miss Americas," I think we all felt like ugly ducklings. It was left up to each of us to follow their beauty advice to the letter.

By the way, I had dyed my frosted hair before I came to Stewardess School. I wasn't taking any chances. Another precaution I took was to be at least five pounds under my maximum weight. To be sure my hips weren't going to interfere with my chances, I exercised every single day after I received my acceptance letter. Later, my mom would laugh about my crazy exercise routine, saying she could still see me doing hip walks down the hall and hear me in the shower pounding my thighs against the wall. Thank goodness the foundation was strong at 2213 Case Road!

You may think I'm kidding about the pressure. Believe me, I am not! Classmates would just disappear, and no one ever knew why. They would just no longer be in the classroom when you returned from lunch or they'd he missing from class the next morning. New classes came in about every two weeks, and these girls were our "little sisters." We were supposed to give them the lay of the land and be there for them just like our "older sisters" were for us. Sadly, my little sister, Beth Ann Madsen, didn't finish training and went home about two weeks before graduation.

Of course, the "Newbies" (the new gals coming to train after us) were in awe of us as we had already been there for two weeks. We were starting to look more like what American Airlines wanted us to by the time we graduated. Every single day, you fretted about what to wear, you had to have your nails polished, your hair was to be in the latest updated style, and your makeup perfect. Even our eyebrows had to be perfectly groomed! Poor Bette's eyebrows were never right, at least not according to the grooming instructor. So one day Bette shaved them off and then had to pencil them in every day. What a hassle!

Some of the courses were easier for a few of the girls than most of us. For me, it was both terrifying and exciting. I had never been one to wear a lot of makeup. Growing up, I dressed as nice as we could afford, and my clothes were always clean and pressed. But this? This was like a runway for models, and you were constantly "ON." Not only did you have to look good, you had to watch how you replied to questions, your facial expressions, the way you walked; it was an unusual world for many of us.

I recall one class when an instructor shared the expected longevity of a Stewardess. "The majority of you will fly approximately two and a half years, and then you will get married. You are exceptional women. You are out there working in a man's world. You carry yourselves confidently, you have wonderful social skills, you can communicate on so many levels with people from all walks of life, and you are glamorous. Ladies, what more could a man ask for in a wife?"

Needless to say, you weren't allowed to be married and fly; you had to resign when you turned 32, you were expected to adhere to weight restrictions, and if you didn't make it through probation at your assigned base, you were history.

Know that pressure I was talking about? This was part of it too. I was determined to make it no matter how hard it was, both physically and emotionally. I just couldn't fail. I had to do this!

Another difficult task for me was learning all of the types of liquors, liqueurs, and wines, not to mention all the names of fancy foods I had never heard of before. Beer was the only drink I ever knew about in our household. Mom did mention two mixed drinks, a Tom Collins and a Whiskey Sour, but I had no idea what they were. Mom told me she and a few of the girls from work went out to a club one night after work, and those were the drinks that had been ordered. I just knew some poor passenger would ask me for a specific drink, and I would have no idea what he was talking about, so I paid particular attention in this class and the ones where we practiced serving meals.

Serving meals was tricky. We were expected to serve the meal graciously. You didn't dare plop that tray down in front of a passenger —you were supposed to "present" the meal to him or her. Filet and Mignon were totally Greek words to me (yes, I know they are French), but when you have never been exposed to that type of gourmet food, you feel insecure about how to explain and market it to your passenger. Even though I made it through this class, I still didn't feel confident in my ability to actually serve meals and drinks.

We were expected to make our passengers feel comfortable, at ease, welcome, and to try to meet and anticipate their needs. It was definitely a challenge, and all the while you were supposed to smile, smile, and never look flustered in any way. You had to act confident and reassuring in everything you did because, at times, all eyes would be on you. You couldn't ever act angry or negative. "Never discuss sex, religion, or politics with your passengers," we were told over and over again. We had classes on the different types of people that we might encounter on flights, unusual situations and circumstances outside the norm, and lessons how to handle them.

In High School, I had actually seen a movie with Doris Day called *Julia* where she played a Stewardess. She made being a Stewardess look so easy. Everything we were being taught seemed second-nature to her in this role. I found the job of a Stewardess fascinating, but because of my height I never dreamed I would ever get a chance to do something so spectacular.

My roommates and I all swore the rooms were bugged because somehow things said in your room always seemed to float into the classroom. At one point, Johnni climbed up on her desk in our dorm room to get a better look at a loose ceiling tile. She was convinced there was a bugging device installed in the ceiling that sent our every word back to the head of the school, or at least to the instructors. As Johnni tried to peek between the tile and the ceiling, she pulled a little too hard, and the tile came crashing down on top of the desk breaking into two pieces.

"Shit!" exclaimed Johnni, as we all burst out laughing. "Alright you hyenas, how do we get it back on now?" she asked.

Bette suggested we glue it back with nail polish. What a sight, Johnni on top of her desk holding the tile until the polish dried, Nancy standing guard at the door in case an instructor walked by, and Bet and me nervously laughing. What if someone saw us? How would we explain this? Much to our surprise, the nail polish held it in place. (If I could only recall the room number, I'd love to see if there's still nail polish behind that tile - twenty-seventh from the doorway and thirteenth from the middle window).

Perhaps some of our classmates were spies. Maybe they made deals to become Stewardesses by telling tales to the instructors. We racked our brains a few times to come up with names of the spies, but we could never all agree on the same people. One of us always stood up for someone the other three suspected. We finally agreed the walls must have had ears. I thought I was doing relatively well until one day, as I was standing in the lunch line, Miss Vi Luenburg, the Grooming Instructor, approached me. "Beverly, I'd like to see you after lunch." Gulp! I felt my heart sink, I couldn't swallow, I was weak in the knees. I knew the lunch I thought I was about to eat would never stay down, so I didn't eat a thing. "Bette, my God, what do you suppose she wants?"

"Damn if I know. They're so picky around here. She probably doesn't like the color of nail polish you have on."

"No, Bette, I just know it's more than that I just can't imagine. I've tried to do all the things they've suggested."

"Don't worry, Bev. After lunch you'll know what it is she wants, and it'll be all over. Now let's change the subject so you don't break out in that red rash again." Every time I get nervous my neck and chest get covered with bright red blotches.

"It is too late. I feel like I'm on fire."

"Did I tell you they sent Lucy Samuels home today?

"No, Bet, you didn't."

"Her roommate Elizabeth went back to the room before lunch to get a book, and all of Lucy's things were gone. No one knows why."

"Oh, that's great! Thanks a lot. That really does it. Now I feel just super! If you don't see me after lunch, it's been nice knowing ya."

"Bev, they're not going to send you home. You haven't done anything."

"Oh yeah, what did Lucy do? Tell me that."

"Well, you"ve got a point," Bette agreed.

"Good God, Bette, what are you trying to do to me? You are not helping. I'm going to go see what she wants. I can't stand this another second."

"You didn't eat lunch."

"It would have probably been my last supper. Say a prayer for me. I am really scared, Bet."

"You are going to be okay, I promise," Bette said as she tried to encourage me. I left the cafeteria to find Miss Luenburg.

My heart was pounding so hard when I caught up with Miss Luenburg. "You wanted to see me about something, Miss Luenburg?" I asked, as I tried to sound like I wasn't ready to suffer a coronary. She looked right at me and had to think for a second.

Miss Luenburg was a very attractive woman, tall with short blonde hair, and her clothes were always immaculate. She sort of waltzed or glided when she walked - a walk each of us tried endlessly to emulate in our rooms after grooming class. Johnni came closest but never quite perfected it.

"Ah yes, Beverly. I observed you standing in the lunch line with your arms folded beneath your bosom. That presents a very negative appearance. It's almost one of defiance and is extremely unattractive to our passengers. So that you'll be reminded next time you are so inclined to cross your arms in that fashion, I think it would be wise for you to ascend and descend the staircase ten times."

I thought my eyes would pop out of my head. At first I couldn't believe Miss Luenburg was reprimanding me for something so insignificant. That was bad enough, but then she was asking me to go up and down the stairs in front of her!

The first three times weren't so bad, but then I could feel my legs and knees getting weaker and weaker. They were turning to Jell-O. Fortunately, one of the other instructors came up to Miss Luenburg to ask a question, and she turned her back to me to answer. Thank God! I ran up and down those stairs like Mercury and was amazed I didn't faint and fall down them.

After what seemed like hours Miss Luenburg turned to me and asked, "How many trips is that?" I started to answer her, but she interrupted me to say, "Never mind, dear. I'm sure you got the message."

"Oh, yes, ma'am, Miss Luenburg, I certainly did." As she glided off into the grooming room, I sat down on the stairs to try and regain some strength in my legs. My hands were wringing wet. The red rash had spread from my chest to my neck up to cover every inch of my face.

I made my way back up to our room where Johnni, Bette, and Nancy were all waiting. Johnni was drumming her fingers on the desk, Nancy was pacing the floor, and Bette was plucking the new hairs that were growing into the place where her eyebrows used to be. She was always so cool.

I dropped to my bed as Nancy and Johnni rushed towards me. "What happened with you and Ole Vi?" Johnni asked.

"They aren't sending you home, are they?' Nancy blurted out.

Bette kept right on plucking.

"No, they aren't sending me home." I said.

"Oh, thank God," said Nancy.

I told them the story.

Johnni asked, "Are you shitting me? Because you stood in the lunch line with your arms crossed? Oh Lord, she'd die if I stood there and picked my nose or scratched my ass."

I cracked up. I really needed some stress release at that moment. I looked over at Bette, still plucking away.

"See, I told ya it was no big deal. You got your rash for nothing," she said.

"Nothing? I could barely breathe!" I exclaimed. "You try walking up and down those stairs seven times..."

Before I could finish, Bette cut me off. "I heard seven times? Did you say seven? I thought she told you ten. Where is ole Vi? Wait until she hears you only did seven."

With that she laid the tweezers down and made a mad dash for the door screaming, "Vi, oh Vi, where are you?" I took off in hot pursuit after her, laughing all the way back to the classroom.

That wasn't my only scare; the other was "Weigh-Ins." The food was just too good, unlike anything I ate growing up. Many times, I had to close my eyes and say "No" to lots of goodies I could have eaten if I didn't want to maintain being five pounds under my maximum weight. I also realized the height limit was indeed 5'9", and I was nearly 5'11" in my flat feet. On the day we were supposed to be measured, I panicked. Fortunately for me, my Personal Instructor was only 5'2", and the minimum was supposed to be 5'3", so when she measured me at 5'10 1/2", I literally looked down at her with the best "beagle sad eyes" I could muster.

"Don't worry," Miss Harrell said with a smile, "Your secret is safe with me." I wanted to pick her up off the floor and swing her around in utter joy. Of course, that would have probably drawn attention to both of us, and I don't think either one of us wanted that to happen.

Another time a doctor named Dr. Portland came to lecture us about how to stay healthy while being with the traveling public. He was so boring, I had a terrible time staying awake. It wasn't entirely his fault; we had just returned from lunch with full bellies and were trying to be alert. Plus, we had stayed up late studying for exams the night before, which didn't help either. At one point, I couldn't stand it any longer. I had visions of my head falling out of my hand, which was propping it up at this point, and hitting the desk. I nudged Johnni in the ribs, "Give me a cigarette, please."

Johnni's eyes got as big as golf balls. "A what? You don't smoke."

"I know, Johnni, but I can't keep my eyes open. Maybe it will help."

"Nothing's gonna help this guy sound any better, trust me. But here ya go. This ought to be good," she laughed.

I lit the cigarette, took a puff and could not believe the taste. "Yuck, this is awful! How do people smoke these things?" I asked her in amazement. "But if it'll keep me awake I'll give it a try."

The second puff went down the wrong way. I started to choke and cough. I thought Johnni would split a gut trying to keep from laughing. I tried to ask to be excused but I couldn't get the words out.

Dr. Portland finally asked me if I'd like to go get a drink of water. I nodded my head and zoomed out of the classroom. I heard Johnni telling the class, 'She hasn't been smoking long," as everyone burst out laughing. They all knew I didn't smoke.

It took all my intestinal fortitude to return to that room. When I sat down, Johnni leaned towards me and asked, "Care for a smoke?"

I thought I was bad about being nervous, but Nancy was the worst one in our whole class. Every night before a test, we'd quiz her until we were blue in the face. We kept trying to instill self confidence in her, but every test was sheer hell for Nancy. After we'd drill her, she'd go down the hall and get Jean Marie White, another Massachusetts gal, to quiz her some more.

Nancy always did well on the tests, never failed any, but when the test was completed, there was no need to ask, "Where's Nancy?" We always knew she was upstairs "blowing her cookies." No wonder she never gained any weight.

This brings me back to Jean Marie. She had an unusual sense of humor, a sort of dry wit, you might say. She was about 5'8" tall, dark brown hair, hazel eyes, and a chalk-white complexion you normally see only on Southern Belles who never go in the sun. Jeanie was constantly fighting the battle against the dreaded Weigh-In, where you had to get weighed in by the doctor practically every week. Jean's favorite saying was, "I may be fat, but I have a pretty face." We never thought of her as fat. She was a little heavier than most of the girls down there, but we were all really skinny.

Back to poor Nancy, we had sixteen tests at school in the six weeks we were there. She made sixteen trips up those stairs, once after every single test. She wasn't bulimic, she was just a nervous wreck. I guess you might say we all had our "Achilles Heel," so to speak. And taking tests was hers.

As I mentioned, there was a fence around the property. Well, not only was there a fence, but it was an electrified fence.

The school was nicknamed "The Nunnery" and "Stew Zoo." It probably could have qualified as a nunnery because there were no males anywhere on the grounds except the guard at the gate, our room parents, and the groundskeepers. If one of the maintenance men had to come upstairs for a repair, there was an announcement made of "man on second floor!" Every door was then expected to be closed with every female behind it. Honest! We had curfews. American Airlines was very serious about them - when they printed curfew times in our information sheet, they meant it.

We had strict curfews, but we did get to go out a couple of times to a club. I met a very good-looking student from Baylor University who was tall with dark brown hair and eyes. Bill Borland had broad shoulders, and his smile was definitely as big as J. F. K's.

I almost didn't meet Bill at all. I was missing Alphie, and sometimes after I talked to him, I wondered if I really was doing the right thing by being there in Texas instead of in Ohio with him. I really did love Alphie, but I knew once we got married, it would be kids and Columbus forever. Johnni told me she was leaving Stosh behind and making new acquaintances, and I was either going to go with her to this club willingly or she was going to drag me. I figured she meant what she said, so I went with her.

Bill and I hit it off at the club, and were enjoying talking and dancing. I didn't drink, so I noticed Bill had quite a few beers. He and his buddy Jeff offered to take Johnni, Bette, Bette's friend Tom, and me back to the school. Nancy wasn't with us because she was studying for the big Emergency Test. Although we all were really uptight about that one, we figured we had to have a break or we'd crack.

The six of us piled into Jeff's car; Bill and I got stuck in the back with another couple who were friends of Jeff. That made eight of us. I had to sit on Bill's lap, which I wasn't too crazy about. (I truly was a prude.) Only a few blocks down the road, Bill started to kiss me. Then he started to get fresh, so I grabbed his hand. He looked at me kind of funny, then kissed me again and made a grab for my chest.

I grabbed his hand again and said, "Look, fella, I am not that kind of a girl!" (How many times did I use that line in High School? Ask any fella I ever went out with. They would say, "You just don't get anywhere with Bev Golden. She's got the sharpest elbows at North High School.")

Bill got mad and pouted all the way back to the school and didn't even try to kiss me good-bye. I didn't blame him. Most guys would have tried the same thing. He just obviously had the wrong opinion of me. If only he knew how many guys had been shot down after I had dated them for a long time. What in the world would make him think he was going to get away with something like that after just meeting me? I sure never expected to ever see him again, and that was fine by me.

Some Stewardesses did have wild reputations. All of those girls locked behind the electric fence, far away from men. I'm sure the men in Dallas thought we were sex-starved "hot tickets," as Jean Marie used to say.

I was truly surprised when I was called to the phone the next Friday to find Bill on the other end. He wanted to know if Jeff had called Johnni and if Tom had called Bette.

I said, "Yes, why?"

"I was just wondering if you'd agree to go out to dinner with me and them on Saturday."

"I don't know, Bill. I should study. We only have one more test before graduation."

"Before you tell me no, I want to apologize for the incident on Saturday. I guess I just had too much beer. It's not like me to be so forward. It is really unusual to find such a nice girl, and I kind of like it. Come on, go out with me. I promise nothing like that will happen this time."

I said I would go, and Bill was true to his word. We enjoyed each other's company and got close, but we only had one more date before I got sent to New York. Although we wrote and talked on the phone, it was hard to keep a relationship going with that much distance between us. We probably would have been good friends if we had had the opportunity, but, more importantly, there was Alphie to think about.

Alphie and I wrote and called each other frequently. I guess he kept hoping I'd flunk out and get sent home. The situation was the same with Johnni and Stosh.

Johnni and I talked a lot about our future plans. We both figured we'd fly for a year or so then probably go back to Columbus, get married, have a house full of kids, and be friends forever. (Boy, were we wrong. Our futures didn't turn out that way at all.)

Thoughts of Alphie had to be put on the back burner because the next day was Emergency Procedure Day, and I was terrified. This was the scariest day at the school. For three different planes, we had to know where the emergency equipment was positioned, the locations of the door and window exits, and all of the commands to get the passengers out of the aircraft in a timely fashion. Three didn't sound like much, but this test was a "make it or break it" situation. If you screwed up here, you were not going to get those wings pinned on your chest. I had one goal in front of me and that was to pass this test with flying colors. Do or die. I was terrified because each evacuation procedure was timed by an instructor with a stop watch and each command had to be worded perfectly. (Fortunately the stop watch was dropped years later but everything else still had to be perfect.)

I did it, though, getting those doors and windows opened and making my way down the inflated slide with time to spare. Damn, I was proud! I had made it through this tremendous test of knowledge, skill and pure guts. We all made it, even Nancy.

School was tough! American wasn't kidding when they said, "You have to study?" We did. They also reminded us numerous times that out of 5,000 applicants a day, we had been chosen for the Stewardess Corps. Of the original fifty hopeful candidates I had started class with, only forty-two remained.

It was hard to believe at times that I had been chosen and not Karen and that I was still there after all of the challenging classes. As much as I wanted to make it, I would not have been surprised if they had sent me home for any number of reasons; especially the fact that I was too tall to be there in the first place. It was amazing to me that I had not only completed all of the tests, but I had done quite well on them, even the liquor and food services.

Now it was all over, and graduation was only two days away. I could finally breathe a sigh of relief and look forward to the reason we were all here: to graduate and join the American Airline Stewardess Corps.

We made up songs for our Graduation Ceremony and picked Jan Weirzba as our "Junior Birdman." This award voted by secret ballot, was for the girl who best personified what a Stewardess should he. She was to be a leader, cooperative, helpful, educated, and friendly. In other words, she was most likely to succeed as a Stewardess. Actually, it was more of a popularity contest since we were all expected to succeed.

American Airlines didn't spend all of that money just to have us fly few trips and then quit, although it did happen. Two of my classmates only flew a few flights and decided being a Stewardess was not for them. Guess who one of them was? Yep, it was the fancy Miss Paula Kline. She later made an appearance in *Bazaar* at her megabucks wedding. I think Paula felt serving people was beneath her. The other was a gal from Ireland who was way too shy for this outgoing job. She said she had gotten airsick on her trips (do you believe that?) and decided she wanted to go back to Ireland.

When my favorite instructor, Miss Azcapetion, entered the room to tell us what bases we had been assigned, she was wearing her Stewardess uniform. We all gasped. Of course we had all been fitted for ours, but somehow it just didn't look the same on us as it did on her. I think she was Greek, and I thought she was perfect. She had all the flair and finesse you'd expect of a Stewardess. Besides that, she was beautiful with dark brown eyes that flashed with excitement, particularly whenever you did a good job in one of her classes. Miss Azcapetion made you feel she was genuinely proud of what you had done and that you had lived up to her expectations for you.

At that time, American Airlines had eleven bases for Stewardess, and eight of them needed new ones. Everywhere except Boston, San Francisco, and Los Angeles opened up for class.

Jean Marie, Nancy, Bette, and I ended up at LGA (LaGuardia airport in New York). We were so upset that Johnni would not be going with us — she had been assigned to Chicago.

It broke my heart that my newfound best buddy was going off to a different base. Johnni spoke Spanish, and the silly girl had taken and passed the Spanish test. I wanted to choke her for having taken that test. She told me later that she wished she had failed it because all she could actually do was read the announcement in Spanish; that she really wasn't bilingual. Damn her!

We bought Johnni a little skunk to remind her of us. Although Johnni didn't like to show emotions, she actually cried when we gave it to her. The sight of Johnni crying got to us, so we had a major flood going on between the four of us.

Our image of Johnni was this crazy, wild, do-anything-for-a-laugh girl. Like the time we went to the shopping center near school to buy Stewardess shoes. Johnni made tracks to the lingerie department and bought a bra that you inserted a tube into so you could blow it up to almost any size. When she showed us, we laughed until our sides hurt. Only Johnni would do something like that. "All those passengers will think I have big boobs, but only a select few will know for sure." She laughed.

"Let's hope the pressurization doesn't go haywire while you are at 30,000 feet. You just might blow a boob," added Bette.

March 31, 1966. All my classmates were running into each other all morning. Every one of us couldn't believe Graduation was finally here. Our hair was combed and in regulation hair-dos and our nails were polished. Our makeup was as perfect as we could get it, except for Bette, who no longer had to worry that she couldn't get her eyebrows to suit Miss Luenburg. She figured no one would notice her eyebrows weren't picture-perfect. We just dared a piece of dust or lint to land on our crisp, navy-blue uniforms.

We were the crème de la crème, and in only a few hours, we would be Stewardesses. We knew all of our songs, and our Junior Birdman (aka Miss Congeniality) had her speech memorized. We were ready.

I was disappointed that Mom and Dad couldn't be there, but I knew there was no way they could afford it. They had sent flowers, beautiful red roses, which I really appreciated, and I know they would have been there if they could. Still it was one of the most important events in my life and no one from my family was there. I knew it was senseless to ask Alphie to come because I would not have been able to spend any time with him. Right after the ceremony we were going to be put on airplanes to go to our bases for indoctrination classes. I doubted seriously if he would have come anyway. None of my roommate's parents came either, so it wasn't all that bad.

Still, I would have loved to share this moment with Mom and Dad because I had never been so proud of accomplishing something in my whole life! I had done it! I was going to be a Stewardess!

There was one ceremony that I found particularly touching. It was the Kiwi Ceremony. (For those who don't know, a kiwi is a fruit, but it is also a bird from New Zealand that has wings but cannot fly) American Airlines Stewardesses who no longer fly join a club by the same name. They usually do good deeds in the community and host American Airlines functions.

Part of the ceremony was to put a penny in a statue of a kiwi bird and make a wish. My wish, one I meant with all of my heart, was to be able make at least one passenger on every flight sincerely happy and glad he or she had chosen American Airlines for their travel. Selfishly, I hoped I would learn something from one of my passengers on each flight that would help make me a better person. This seems like a mighty big wish, but I was young, naïve, full of promise, and I was about to graduate from American Airlines Stewardess School, so I figured I could handle it. I was very proud of myself and so thankful for this opportunity.

Getting My Wings

Each one of us went to Miss Hazel Fitzgerald to receive our wings. When my turn came, I confidently walked up to her. She was such a tiny lady. She looked up at me as she was pinning my wings on my jacket and said, "My, my, you are awfully tall."

My heart did flips. I envisioned the old "stage hook" coming out from behind the curtain to grab me by the neck and pull me to the side before she could actually pin those little silver wings on my chest. If you think for a minute I wasn't scared, you are wrong. I gulped so loudly that I know she must have heard it, then I managed a very meek, "Yes ma'am, I am tall and proud." Miss Hazel Fitzgerald smiled as I tried not to fall flat on my face getting back to my seat. Thank God I made it!

What I didn't realize then, in my youth and naïveté, is being a Stewardess/Flight Attendant is not just about looking pretty and making our passengers feel at home. It's about much more, and we have many different jobs onboard an airplane. To mention a few: Fire Fighter, Doctor, Peace Maker, Referee, Psychiatrist, Emergency Evacuator, Baby Sitter, and sadly, did we ever imagine that we would have to deal with Terrorists? So, the next time you fly, don't look at your Flight Attendant as just another pretty or handsome face; realize he or she is also the person responsible for and trained to save your life.

NEW YORK – NEW YORK

Summer Uniform in Chicago

Limos took us to the airport to catch our planes to our various bases across the USA. This was the last time we would all be together. There were some tearful good-byes as each group of girls boarded their airplanes. By a stroke of good fortune, Nancy, Bette, Jean Marie and I all ended up in New York, along with eight others. We were so excited!

As we waited for our plane to arrive, we watched other Stewardesses coming off flights. We were so critical and really picked them apart, I'm ashamed to say. One particularly tired-looking girl came off the plane we were about to board, followed by three others who also looked pretty beat. At the time, we didn't realize this was more like reality. We thought we were only there to be pretty, do our Phase 3 (communicate with our passengers), and serve an occasional meal with time to spare.

Silly, silly girls we were. Little did we know that one day, some of us would be getting off an airplane looking a whole lot worse than these ladies.

The flight to New York went so fast we could hardly believe it. The Captain said we would be landing at LaGuardia in twenty minutes. I was sitting beside Nancy, and she leaned over to share the incredible sight out of my window as we made our turn over the city. It was nearly 11:30 p.m. when we viewed the sights of downtown Manhattan; it was a spectacular sight at night! All of the buildings were lit up, and little did I know then that N. Y. never sleeps.

The view was something this girl from West Virginia and Ohio never, ever dreamed she would see in her lifetime. I was just a High School graduate with a little working experience, twenty-one years old, about to embark on a career I never imagined would be mine. I just couldn't believe it. I was terrified but giddy with excitement about my new future. I had called Mom and Dad to tell them where I was going to be based, and they acted excited for me. Later, Mom shared with me that Daddy was terrified, saying I was too naïve, that I would get hurt, and that he was scared for me to be in a place like New York. Of course, typical of Dad, he never told me.

From LaGuardia, the twelve of us were taken to the Travelers Hotel near the airport. We would be staying there during our indoctrination classes, which would last about a week. The hotel was not exactly the Ritz, so Nancy and Jeanie told me. It didn't make any difference to me one way or the other, since I didn't even know what "The Ritz" was anyway. We were told that the hotel was run by the Mafia, and there were all kinds of things going on there. Whether it was true or not, we never found out, but it sure was a fascinating place.

Our imaginations ran wild as we checked out every man who looked particularly "tough" in the lobby. There might not have been any Mafia men there, but there sure were some "ladies of the night." As we walked towards the desk to register, Jean Marie jabbed Nancy in the ribs. "Look, Nancy, there are some Hookers."

"Hookers? What are Hookers?" I asked them both.

"Sh-h-h, Bev, not so loud. You honestly don't know what a Hooker is?" questioned Nancy.

"Uh, no, I have never heard that expression before. What does it mean?" I looked sincerely puzzled.

"Well, look over there against the wall," instructed Jeanie.

As I turned, I expected to see longshoremen that worked on the docks or butchers; instead, I saw three women with tight, low-cut clothing and enough makeup for five of us. One was an attractive black girl in a flashy, red, satin-looking dress. The other two were white, and the taller one with the reddish-colored hair had on a skin-tight pair of black slacks and a sweater with a plunging neckline. I could not believe how busty she was. The shorter of the three had sort of yellow-gold hair and had on the shortest skirt I had ever seen in my life. They started to glare at me.

I turned back to Nancy and Jean. "I still don't understand."They burst out laughing.

By this time, Bette had returned from the ladies' room. "What's so funny?" she inquired.

Jean Marie regained her composure long enough to tell Bet that they really had a "live one" in me, that I didn't even know what a Hooker was.

Bette grinned as I turned bright red. "That's okay, Bev; I'll explain it to you when we get to our room."

Once we got into our room, she looked at me and asked, "What do they call prostitutes in Columbus, Ohio?"

"Prostitutes, I guess," I replied. I had just never heard the word hooker before.

"Well girl, get ready for a whole new education about the big ole world of life," she said. "One I am sure you were never exposed to back home."

"I am sure you are right, Bet," I said as I yawned and fell onto my bed.

The first day of indoctrination wasn't too bad, although it was a little scary for me. The instructors told us we had to fly out of three different airports, JFK, LaGuardia, and Newark. In order to get to some of these, you had to use the subway, which was a truly scary experience in itself until you get used to it, which I never did. I had a terrible case of claustrophobia. Yeah, I know, why was I not afraid of airplanes? I guess because they weren't underground and between two walls. We could also use the Carey Bus or New York Airways, a helicopter company.

I made up my mind right then and there that I only wanted to fly out of one airport, the one that ended up being closest to the apartment we found. Of course, Crew Schedule would have other ideas, and since they gave us our schedules when we were on Reserve, we had to go to whatever airport needed us. I must, admit I was very lucky that one of the Crew Schedulers took a shine to me for some reason and never gave me a trip out of Newark. Thank you, Lou Pappas.

After class let out, the instructor recommended that we set out to find a place to live since American was only footing our hotel bill until Friday. Bette and I decided to go for a walk over toward a restaurant we had spotted the night before. We had seen some apartments on 92nd Street.

As we walked into the office to inquire about vacancies, a man approached us from the lawn. He was short with sandy hair and kind of skinny. He looked at Bette, and we could both sense he was smitten. "Are you girls looking for an apartment?" he inquired.

"We sure are," answered Bette with a big ole flirtatious smile. "Do you live here?"

"Yeah, me and my roommate Nick; we are pilots for American Airlines. My name is Ron Baxter."

"How wonderful; we're new Stewardesses, just graduated. Say, do you know if there are any apartments available here?" asked Bette as she cocked her head to one side and flashed those big blue eyes his way.

"Yes, as a matter of fact, there is a two bedroom available down at the other end of the building. I doubt Mel will rent it to you, though."

"Why is that?" I asked.

"Because he said he is tired of renting to girls. He said they are far worse housekeepers than guys. That apartment had been rented to three Eastern gals, and they really did leave it a mess. Whew, was he ever pissed off. Oops, excuse me ladies."

"Oh, what a shame Ron; these apartments look like exactly the kind of place we'd love to live in. Do you have any influence on this Mel person?" Bette asked as she looked deep into his eyes. What a flirt she was. She really knew how to work it.

"I don't really know, but he is tight with Nick. They both enjoy working on little projects and things that get broken around here together."

"Gee, do you suppose you could talk to your roommate and see if there is anything he can do? We'd be so grateful." I looked at her out of the corner of my eye, as Bette leaned towards him. What a character!

"Sure. Nick gets in from his trip tonight. I'll see what I can do to help out. By the way, what are your names and where are you staying?"

We gave him the information and told him we'd walk over the next day after class to see what he found out. He waved to us as we walked down the sidewalk.

"Bette Johnson, you little flirt," I exclaimed. "I am amazed at how you can turn on the charm. Can you teach me?"

"No way, it is my charm! Besides we want the apartment, don't we? I mean look how close it is to LaGuardia. All we'd have to do is come over here to get a Carey Bus to JFK or Newark. It is a perfect location. We'd have it made."

"That sounds terrific to me. I don't relish the idea of taking one of those subway trains or a taxi, not knowing where I was going, and then ending up in Harlem."

Bette started laughing, "That is all you would need, Bev. Nancy, Jean Marie, and I could handle it, but you...no way! You would freak out. Of the four of us, though, I must admit I would probably handle it best."

"Know something, Bet? You're absolutely right," I told her with a giggle in my voice. "I bet you could handle just about anything. Because you are so awesome!"

She laughed. "I'd at least try almost anything once."

"I know you would, Bet, I know you would," as I smiled in her direction.

Jean Marie and Nancy were not too excited about our find. We were so pleased that we just naturally assumed they would be happy too. They had designs of living in Manhattan.

"What kind of men are you going to meet out here in Jackson Heights? Nancy and I want to get into the city to meet some real neat men, not pilots! We'll be working with them every day. I'm more interested in meeting stockbrokers or lawyers. All of the exciting people live in the city!" Jeanie stated.

Nancy just agreed with her.

"Nevertheless, Jean, Bev, and I are going to go back over to those apartments tomorrow just in case you don't find your penthouse in Manhattan," stated Bette with a load of sarcasm.

There was always a little tension between Jean Marie and Bette. It wasn't something we couldn't live with, but it was always there.

After class, we went over to the apartments to talk to Ron. He wasn't there because he had gotten called out on a trip. We were so discouraged because the manager was out too. "I guess we'd better wait and at least try to talk to Ron before we see the manager anyway. Don't you think so, Bet?" I asked.

"Yeah, I suppose you are right. I just hoped we'd find out something today."

Discouraged, we went back to the hotel.

Nancy and Jean Marie had gone into Manhattan apartment hunting and didn't return until late. I was surprised to see such long faces on them when they came to tell Bette and me about their adventures. "Well, how'd it go?" Bet inquired.

"Not too good," answered Jean. "Everything we found to be halfway decent was way too expensive for even the four of us. We would have to room with at least eight girls to afford some of those places."

"What? No penthouse?" Bette chimed in.

"Knock it off, Bet," I said. I didn't think Jean was in any mood to take Bette's comments right then.

Nancy and Jean Marie told us in detail about the tiny studio apartments that were renting for $500 and $600 a month. (Of course those same tiny apartments probably rent for $3,000 a month now, if you can even find one.) They asked what we found out about the apartment on 92nd Street. We told them that Ron had been called out on a trip and that we would try to see him tomorrow after class.

Jean Marie said, "Maybe we'll just go over with you to see it, if that's okay."

"Sure, Jeanie, that's fine. We'll all go right after class," I told her.

Once again, the instructor reminded us that we had better get really serious about finding places to live if we hadn't already found them because as soon as indoctrination was over, our rooms would no longer be paid for by American Airlines, so we wouldn't have a place to stay.

Thank heavens Ron was there when we went to the apartments after class. He had just returned from his trip and was still in his uniform when he opened the door. There is some truth to the statement that pilots really do look better in their uniforms, and Bette seemed impressed.

Ron told us he had spoken to Mel, the manager, and he wanted to meet us. Mel was a little apprehensive about renting to four girls, no matter what Ron said, but at least he was willing to meet us. Ron changed and took the four of us down to meet Mel.

Mel looked as if he was part Italian or Greek, with very dark, black hair, dark eyes, and an olive complexion. Actually he was kind of handsome. He was too short and old for us, of course, or so we chuckled about many times later. Mel talked to us and asked a bunch of questions. He was very frank about how disappointed he had been with the mess left by the previous tenants. We promised we would take good care of the apartment if only he'd give us a chance. Mel told us he would have to think it over and let us know the next day. We agreed to return after class to find out what he had decided.

We must have said something right because the next day Mel told us he would give us a chance, although he warned us that he would be doing periodic and unannounced checks on the apartment. That was the only way he would agree to let us live there. We would be on a three-month trial basis, and if at any time he didn't like the way we were taking care of the place, out we would go.

We were so happy to have found a place that we probably would have agreed to almost anything. After all, it was Thursday, and the next day was our last day at the hotel, which we were all glad to be leaving.

Ron took us back upstairs to his apartment to have a drink to celebrate our new home. Mel was still painting our place, so we didn't get a tour of the apartment, but he did say it was set up the same as Ron and Nick's.

"Speaking of your elusive roommate, Ron, when do we get to meet him?" asked Jean. This seemed like a funny question coming from the gal who only wanted to meet lawyers and stockbrokers.

It was a rather perfectly-timed question because Ron had been standing at the window and glanced down just as Nick was walking up the sidewalk. "In about three minutes, I would venture to guess."

"What!?" we all exclaimed at once as we ran to the window to look out. By this time it was too late to see Nick's face; all we saw was the top of a pilot's hat and a uniform walking in the front door.

Nick Zawaki was really nice looking. Jean looked over at me and mouthed, "He's mine," when he walked in the door.

I shook my head and mouthed back to her, "Why, Jean Marie, he's just a pilot."

"Funny, very funny" she said.

"What's funny?" Nick asked as he entered the room.

"Oh, nothing really, we are all just glad we got the apartment. Now we'll have an opportunity to get to know you and Ron better. To learn about the airline industry from a pilot's point of view," stated Jeanie.

"Better raise your feet, Bev, it's getting pretty deep in here," said Bette with a big smirk on her face. We all burst out laughing, and poor Nick and Ron had no idea what was so funny to us.

Nick and Ron helped us carry our suitcases and clothes from the hotel over to the apartment. Even though the apartment was furnished in a way I would not have done it, we were just so happy to have a roof over our heads we didn't care about the furniture.

There was one small problem. One of the bedrooms had twin beds but the other had just a double. Jean refused to share a double bed with anyone. She said she had a hard enough time sleeping at night, much less trying to sleep with someone.

So I looked at Bet, "I had to sleep with my little sister at home. It doesn't bother me if it doesn't bother you."

"Shit, I don't care. I can sleep anywhere with anyone. Just don't go having any romantic dreams about Alphie and reaching over and trying to hug me. I may be little, but I'll kill ya." We cracked up. The sleeping arrangements were set.

I was the first one to be sent out on a trip. I nearly died when Crew Schedule called that Monday. We had just gotten the phone installed 30 minutes before it rang. I was going to San Diego on a non-stop flight with a 30-hour layover.

I couldn't believe it. I was beside myself with joy because I had always wanted to go to California. Given a choice, I would have chosen Los

Angeles because I had hopes of seeing a real live movie star. San Diego was fine with me, though, until I realized that we would be serving one of those elaborate meal services. Thank God it wasn't First Class!

I ran into my room, grabbed my manual, and began going over the whole service, step-by-step. I even made myself a "cheat sheet" in case I forgot something. I checked and rechecked my emergency equipment and my uniform. I must have packed and repacked my suitcase at least four times. Poor Bet, I don't think I even slept a wink that night. I finally got up and went in the front room and just sat.

It was unreal to believe I was going to be flying my first trip as a Stewardess in about six hours. In school, we had observation flights where we watched the other Stewardesses work, but we didn't have an actual "work trip" like the students did in later years. The work trip was a much better idea, actually working instead of just sitting there craning your neck to watch some other girls try to do their jobs with a bunch of rookies watching their every move.

I had to go out of Kennedy Airport, and, fortunately for me, so did Nick. He offered to let me ride over with him. Although his sign-in was later than mine, he said he had some paperwork he could do before his trip left. I was so thankful that I didn't have to take the Carey Bus.

I was sitting in Operations reading my manual again when the rest of my crew signed in. I was so nervous!!! I walked over to them and asked if they were going out on trip #343 to San Diego. Melanie West, our first Stewardess, answered me, "Yes, we're your crew, and I'll just bet you are new."

Oh my, how could she know, I wondered. Did I look different? "Er, uh, yes I am, this is my first trip."

"Okay, you'll want to make sure to meet the Captain. He's a real bear about meeting all of the crew before we leave Operations. I'll point him out to you when he comes in. In the meantime, this is Darlene Tracy. She is working the First Class cabin with me. You'll be in the back with Missy, who stopped for some coffee. Don't worry, we'll take real good care of you."

I must have sighed out loud because she smiled at me when I said, "Thanks so much! I really appreciate it. I'm so nervous!"

Missy showed up with her coffee in hand. "That's Missy," Melanie told me.

I walked over to this little, tiny girl with dark auburn hair, millions of freckles on her face and God forbid...GOLD wings! If you had flown five years, you were really, really senior, turning in your silver wings for gold ones, becoming what we affectionately called "Gold Wing Mamas." Some of these Mamas were nice, and some were downright scary.

I turned back to look at Melanie and Darlene - they all had gold wings. Oh my Lord! I felt a lump the size of a baseball in my throat. Oh well, maybe these Gold Wing Mamas would turn out to be nice.

"Hi Missy, I'm Bev Golden. I'm going to San Diego with you, and this is my first trip."

She spun around like some kind of startled beast. "Oh, shit! You have got to be kidding me! Your first trip? Damn my luck anyway. This is all I need, a fancy service, with a full load of people, and I get stuck with a new hire. Shit again."

I wanted to die on the spot. I was terrified. Oh my gosh! I thought I was going to be sick. I looked at her like a scolded puppy and said, "I'm sorry Missy, but we are all new in the beginning."

"Oh, really? I just don't need this today. My boyfriend and I had a hell of a fight last night, I haven't slept, this flight is always full, and now you tell me this is your first trip. I just don't need to babysit today." Missy walked off.

I walked back over to the other girls, "I don't know what to say. I can't help it that I'm new. She was new once too." I felt the tears burning in my eyes. No, I will not cry! I won't!

Melanie took hold of my arm. "It is going to be okay Bev; I'll go talk to Missy." Melanie assured me that things would get better once the flight got underway.

In the meantime, she wanted to take me over to meet the cockpit crew. The Captain was really short and old-looking, with white hair and so many wrinkles. I guess I never really expected him to be old, but this was a very senior trip I was about to fly. His name was Bud Anderson, and he was pleasant but corny. He tried to tell jokes but always seemed to mess up the punch lines.

The First Officer (F/O) was Will Tanner who wasn't much younger than the Captain. He was nice but very businesslike and cool.

The big shocker was the Flight Engineer. Usually if there is one, he is the youngest member of the crew. Not in this case. This guy, George Lindsey, was ancient!! He was what American called a Professional Engineer and not qualified to fly the airplane. As a former mechanic, George was now an engineer for the duration of his career, which judging by the looks of him, wasn't all that much longer. I don't mean to sound shallow, but remember I was only twenty-one years old and fresh from the "Charm Farm." I must admit that George was a real sweetie though. He wished me a good first flight and told me he knew I would do great. I wished I felt the same way.

I didn't see Missy Branson again until we boarded the plane. She was checking out the catering, which was my job, but she felt better doing it herself. That way she would be sure everything was there, she said, "It's not like there is a place to stop for missing supplies once we are airborne."

I put away all my personal gear and took some papers out of my manual.

"What are those?" Missy blurted.

"They're my notes. I wrote down a few things I wanted to be sure to remember about the service."

"Well, let me tell you, girlie, you won't have time to check any damn notes. I looked at the PRR (Passenger Revenue Report), and we are full. So you'd better forget about any notes."

"Okay then, Missy, you just tell me how you want to work this service and exactly what you want me to do. How's that?" I asked.

"I hope this doesn't come as a real big shock to you, but that is precisely what I intended to do." Whew, she sure didn't waste any time putting me in my place.

So for the next four and a half hours, Missy played Sergeant, and I played Private. We finished the service - not the way I had been taught but the way Missy wanted it done. If there was a shortcut, she took it. If she could eliminate anything, she did. Every time I tried to Phase 3, talking to my passengers like we were supposed to for good public relations, Missy would call me into the galley. "We don't have time for that shit right now. If we have time after the service is completed, you can talk to your little heart's content."

At one point, one of the male passengers approached me and asked if I had a sewing kit. I did, of course. "Great! Now do you by any chance have a small white button?"

"No sir, I am sorry, I sure don't. Why? Did you lose a button off your shirt?"

"Yes, I did, and I have an important meeting with the president of my company when we land."

"Let me see if perhaps I can pull a button off my extra Stewardess blouse." He smiled so gratefully. I went to my suitcase to take out my blouse and had it laying on the jump seat when Missy returned from the cockpit.

"What in the hell are you doing?" she asked as she observed me trying to remove a button off my blouse.

"This passenger needs a button. He has an important meeting he has to attend and no time to get one. He doesn't have time to change his shirt."

"What!?!? I'm sure if this meeting is that damned important he can find the time to get a button or buy a new damn shirt. Now put your blouse back in your suitcase." I was so embarrassed and so was the man. He turned around and returned to his seat.

Missy continued, "Bev that is above and beyond the call of duty. Besides he wouldn't have been grateful anyway. You have to draw the line somewhere. It was nice of you to offer, but let me tell you here and now, there are some passengers who will take advantage of you every chance they get. The majority of them don't even bother to say please or thank you. This is the real world out here, girl, not the "candy-coated" one at the Stewardess School. Get used to it."

I didn't know what to say to her, so I put my blouse back in the suitcase and put it away. Then I went out into the cabin to talk to my passengers. I just knew "my" passengers would say please and thank you to me. (I must admit this wasn't always the case, though. I remember a gal once saying to me on a New York trip, "If these people ever said please or thank you to me, the shock just might kill me.")

When we got to San Diego, I assumed everyone would go out, but I was wrong. The three girls I was flying with all wanted to go to their rooms and take naps. I was too excited to sleep. Besides, we shared rooms, and I wasn't sure that Missy might not choke me in my sleep. Instead, I put on my swimsuit and went out to lie in the sun. Although it was a little chilly, I enjoyed myself.

I could not believe I was in San Diego, California. Our hotel was downtown, so after the pool, I walked around a little to see some of the shops. The weather was picture perfect. I was probably beaming to myself as I walked the streets in awe because everyone who passed me seemed to smile especially wide when I'd look in their direction.

This was it! This was what I had worked for. To see places I had never dreamed I would ever see in my lifetime. I was so happy, even in spite of Missy.

Later that night, the Stewardesses invited me to go out to eat with them at a Mexican restaurant. It was my first time to ever see, much less eat, Mexican food. It was okay, but I wasn't crazy about it.

Missy was almost nice at dinner, although she did embarrass me by telling the other girls about me trying to pull a button off my blouse for that passenger. Melanie told me Missy was right, some passengers will take advantage of Stewardesses, especially new Stewardesses.

On the flight back home, Missy was much better. Apparently, she and her boyfriend had worked things out over the telephone while I was at the pool. She was still bossy, but she wasn't quite so curt.

I couldn't wait to get back to the apartment to tell the others about my trip. I had to ride the Carey Bus this time, but it wasn't nearly as bad as I had imagined. The only one home was Bette. She said Nancy had been called out for a trip and panicked. She was hyperventilating and throwing up. It was a horrible sight, Bette reported.

Jean Marie called Crew Schedule to see if there were any other positions open on Nancy's flight. Luckily there was one position open, and Jean asked if she could have it. Of course, Crew Schedule was delighted because that was one more reserve they didn't have to call out for the trip. Jean Marie and Nancy were off on a three-day trip with multi-stops across the country. I told Bet all about my trip and Missy.

"It's a good thing that bitch got you on the trip instead of me. There would have been a small-scale war going on in the Coach Cabin," Bette responded, and I was sure what she was saying was true.

I was just so glad my first trip was behind me. I made a vow to myself that when my turn came to fly with a new girl, I would go out of my way to make her feel at ease and help her anyway I could. I kept that vow time and time again, never forgetting how I felt on my first trip and never wanting anyone I flew with to feel that way.

I called Alphie and told him all about my trip, bubbling over with excitement at being sent to California for my very first flight. He listened and tried to seem interested, but I knew him too well. Alphie was already sad that I had graduated, and now I had flown my first trip and instead of hating it, I loved it! He was not happy. I ended the conversation quickly so I didn't have to feel guilty. I told him I missed him and that I loved him, and I would be home just as soon as it was allowed. Unfortunatley, I had absolutely no idea when that would be.

I called home and shared my trip news with Mom and Dad, who were so happy for me. Of course, they wanted to know when I would be able to come home, since it had been two months since I had seen them. It felt like forever, and I assured them I would be there just as soon as I could.

The month of mandatory Reserve was over, so we were no longer being called to fill in for sick Stewardesses. We were able to request our own trips, so Bet and I "Buddy Bid." This meant we would select a schedule we would like to have, and we would be awarded that schedule based on the lowest seniority of the two of us, but at least we would be together.

What a pair we made. She was the height minimum, and I was over the height maximum. The mini-skirt was in its peak of fashion at this time, so as a joke, most of the agents at LaGuardia airport nicknamed us "Mini" and "Maxi." I hated it, but Bet loved it; cute little Bette, who acquired another nickname as well, 'Bette Bird.'

Bette boarded more flights from the overhead rack than I care to remember. That was a big joke with some of the flight crews. On planes in those days, the overhead rack was like an open shelf, not an enclosed compartment as it is today. They would hoist Bette up into the overhead rack just as the agent said the passengers were on their way. She'd scream and yell until they'd get her down just before the passengers entered the airplane. Once in a while they wouldn't get her down and Bette would have to board the airplane by greeting the passengers from her perch. The passengers loved it. They all cracked up at the sight of her up there in the overhead rack, and then they all stared as I held a blanket in front of her so she could get down. Remember, we didn't have uniforms with pants in the early days of our careers.

Once, Bet and I ended up on a trip with Ron. He had some delusion that he and Bette were an item because he felt we owed him for talking Mel into letting us live in the apartment. In all fairness to Ron though, Bette was quite often guilty of leading him on. When she wasn't dating anyone else, they were as cozy as two peas in a pod. Then Bette would see greener pastures, and off she'd go.

The night before this trip, they'd had a big spat. So to get her even more upset, Ron put her in the overhead rack. Bet was not in the mood for this. Ron ran to the cockpit and closed the door, which left Gayle and me to get her down after the passengers were boarded. What a sight: Bette trying to hold her skirt down, Gayle holding the blanket and me pulling Bette onto the seatback and then the seat cushion. She was furious and cussing a blue streak! Once her feet hit the floor, Bette ran to the cockpit. Ron must have suspected she'd do that because he was holding the door shut on the other side. Bette was about to yell some four-letter words at him when I reminded her that we had already boarded.

Gayle and I had to practically physically restrain Bette from going to the cockpit the whole trip. She wanted to baptize Ron with a full pot of coffee. We kept telling her she'd endanger all of us if she maimed the Flight Engineer in flight. We convinced her to wait until the layover and then let him have it, or not, whichever she preferred. "Funny, you two are really funny; he'll never get IT, not as long as he lives; at least not from me!" she sputtered.

I really liked Bette a lot. She was hysterical, with never a dull moment when she was around. She was always buzzing around in ten different directions.

The next morning, Bette absolutely broke Gayle and me up. We were on the airplane checking out catering when Ron rang for a cup of coffee. Apparently, Bette and Ron had made up because she was so sweet to him on the phone. As she was preparing to take the coffee to him, I looked toward the cockpit to see Ron leaning against the back of his chair trying his best to look cool. It was sort of dark in the cockpit, and Ron was standing directly under a small overhead light with his hat pulled far down on his forehead. He had dark circles under his eyes naturally, but with his hat so far down and the lighting above his head, those circles were even more obvious than normal.

Bet looked at me, glanced at Ron, smirked, and broke into a little cheer, "R-a-c-c-o-o-n, Raccoon-Raccoon, he's my man." Gayle and I went nuts. We were laughing so hard tears were running down our perfectly made-up faces. There went our mascara!

Ron couldn't hear what Bette was saying as he just stood there trying to look suave, but I don't think he would have appreciated that cheer at all.

Of all the flights and incidents that happened with Bet and me, there are three that really stand out. We were very poor when we first started flying and just never seemed to have enough money left for food. On this one particular flight, we had several people not make their connections to New York, resulting in quite a few meals left over after the dinner service. It was fried chicken.

"Go get me a couple of those barf bags, Bev."

"Yuck, Bet, are you sick?"

"No, just go get me a few, and bring them into the galley." As I picked them up out of the seats, a few of the passengers noticed and looked very disturbed. I smiled and said, "New Stewardess" and they laughed.

I brought the bags to the galley. Bet pulled the curtain closed and started stuffing pieces of chicken in those bags like a professional packer. Then she crammed about six bags into her tote bag, which was an extra piece of luggage we carried with us on flights to hold our manual, makeup, and things we had to get our hands on quickly during a flight.

"What are you doing?" I asked, even though it was perfectly obvious to me what she was doing.

"Supper," she replied, with that ornery little grin of hers. "We won't starve tonight. All of this food is left over, and it is just going to get thrown out, except for what the caterers eat, that is. So why not take it with us? We are about to land, and there's no time to eat; therefore we are taking it with us."

We would be taking the food home with us, and we could sit at a real table and have a leisurely meal instead of standing in the galley scarfing it down like street people in a dumpster. "I don't see any of this, in case you get caught, Miss Bird. I believe I need this job more than you."

"Okay, okay, just go out in the cabin and make sure Patsy (the other gal we were flying with) doesn't come into the galley until I am done."

We made it off the airplane with our loot and boarded the local public bus to the apartment. We were just too tired and didn't feel like walking home tonight, even though our place was close enough. Bette plopped down beside me and scanned the people getting on the bus after we had boarded.

"Oh God," Bette said under her breath as she grabbed my arm.

"What? What is it, Bet?" There was Bette's supervisor, Miss Carsen, who sat right across the bus in front of both of us. She talked to Bette, idle chitchat about how things were going, did she enjoy her new career, just chatting. I chatted with her too, anything to try and hide what I'm sure were very guilty-looking faces.

When we reached our stop, Bette and I grabbed our belongings and practically fell over each other trying to get off the bus. Just as we were about to hit the front door we heard Miss Carsen, "Oh Bette, you and Bev have a real nice dinner."

"Huh? Er...uh, yes, yes, we will, thanks," replied Bette.

We jumped down the stairs to get to the ground as the bus pulled away. She knew, Bette," I declared. "I tell ya, she knew about the chicken."

"Yeah, I think so too, but if she were going to do something, she would have already jerked us off the bus and taken us back to the airport. She must have smelled it."

"No kidding. I think everyone on the bus caught a whiff of it." We did reek like a Colonel Sanders store. "I am going to have a little trouble eating this chicken tonight. I am afraid every bite is going to get stuck in my throat for fear she will call us both in on Monday," I said with remorse.

"Bev, when was the last time we had a chance to eat a good meal? We've been on duty since 6 a.m. today, and it is now nearly 8:00 p.m. Trust me, girl, you won't have any trouble. Besides, if you do, there is that much more for me."

I punched her on the arm and said, "Try getting my chicken leg out of my hand, I'll bury you." We both burst out laughing as we ran up the stairs to our place.

I guess I'm still talking about food for this next one. Bette and I were working a trip to Cleveland, with me setting up trays and Bet serving them to the passengers. It was one of those days when we hadn't eaten for hours, and I was starving. On the trays, I spotted these little vanilla puddings with a maraschino cherry in the middle. I picked off one cherry and plopped it into my mouth. Whoa, that tasted so good! I did it a couple more times, but in my haste to get the trays ready for Bette, I didn't notice the red ring the cherry had left in the middle of the pudding.

Bette had served about three full rows when she came into the galley and informed me that the man in seat 12B wanted to see me. "Me?! What in the world would he want to see me about? He hasn't even seen me, to my knowledge. I was in the cabin for the boarding process, but I haven't been out there since we started serving. What does he want?"

"I don't know, Bev, but you had better get out there and find out what it is so that we can finish the service," said Bette.

"Oh my gosh, I just don't have any idea what this is all about. I don't have time for this," I muttered to myself as I left the galley to go into the cabin.

I approached the man in 12B. "Was there something that you wanted to see me about, sir?" I asked. He was a really big man, tall and broad-shouldered, and he didn't look particularly happy. He had his arms folded across his chest (maybe Miss Luenburg was right about the negative response that position suggested after all.)

"Yes, I did, young lady," he said as unfolded his arms, reached for the napkin that he had spread across his meal tray, lifted it up, and pointed at his pudding, "You forgot one," he stated. There sat a maraschino cherry on top of his pudding!

I turned scarlet red, not quite knowing what to do. He was smiling, so he must have had a good sense of humor, so I leaned over the man in 12C, grabbed the cherry off 12B's desert and popped it into my mouth. All three of the men seated in row 12 burst out laughing.

When I got back to the galley, I looked at Bet who had been watching the whole ordeal and was doubled over laughing. "One of these days I'm gonna kill you, Bette Johnson!" I stated.

It seems all these stories revolving around Bette included a food issue, but it just happened that way. One time, Bette and I were on a layover and went out to eat. The place Bette chose was more expensive than either of us imagined. After we ate and were sitting there counting our money and continuously coming up short, Bette looked at me and said, "This calls for some serious action."

"What are you talking about?" I was dumbfounded.

Bette reached into her purse and pulled out a tissue wrapped around something. In the tissue was a small piece of glass. She put it on her plate and mixed it up with what was left of her gravy; which was very little since she had nearly licked the plate.

"Oh, Bet, you're not going to do what I think you're going to do, are you?"

"Hush!" she said to me as she motioned for the waiter to come to our table.

I put my head down and stared at the floor as Bette told him how she had found this piece of glass in her food. He was so upset and apologetic; he immediately summoned the manager. The manager looked at me and asked if I had found anything in mine. Fortunately, we hadn't eaten the same thing, and I assured him that my entrée was just fine, thanks. He kept apologizing to Bette, and then he picked up the check and insisted on taking care of our meal.

I was so embarrassed that I couldn't get out of there fast enough. Not Bette! She kept talking to the manager, assuring him that yes, she would come back in spite of what had happened.

She started towards the door where I was impatiently standing and made a quick turn to return to the table. "I forgot to leave a tip for the waiter," she said. She returned with the piece of glass nestled in her right hand, "You just never know when this may come in handy again."

I just shook my head and tried not to be too obvious by running out the door. "Bet, what am I going to do with you? I am so embarrassed."

"More embarrassed than you would have been not to be able to pay your bill and having to do the dishes?"

"You know something? You've got a point there, but let's not do that again, okay?"

When we got back to the prestigious Palmer House Hotel in Chicago, Bet pushed the elevator button for the fourth level, which was our room floor. Before she got off the elevator, however, she pushed every button on the top floors. "Have a nice trip." she muttered to the gentleman getting on the elevator. He smiled when his eyes caught sight of all of the illuminated buttons, then burst out laughing.

The most incredible story I have to share about Bette and me was our one and only trip on the Electra. It was being phased out, and even though we had to train on it at school, we never dreamed we would ever actually have to fly on one. As we went down the jetbridge, there it sat, this ancient chariot ready to take us on a multi-stop flight from LGA (New York) to DCA (Washington DC) then on to CSW (Charlestown, West Virginia).

We snickered to ourselves as we got on the plane. We had been flying jets - was this propeller plane beneath us or what? Oh well, it would be another experience. We felt like this was our first trip all over again, and we were just glad we were together.

We flew from LGA to DCA (Washington, DC) where Walter Cronkite boarded our plane. At least, I thought he was Walter Cronkite, but I wasn't sure. Since he was sitting in First Class, I decided to take names just to confirm that he was indeed who I thought he was. I approached him and said, "May I please have your name, Mr. Cronkite?" Oh brother, there was no hope for me!

He looked at me, smiled, and then replied, "Cronkite, Walter." When I told Bette, she just laughed. What a dummy I was!

We made it to Washington, D.C., but then we were supposed to serve a meal on the way to Charleston, West Virginia. We had just hand-delivered all the trays and were preparing to start the beverage service when I heard what I thought was a call button. I looked up to see the "No Smoking" sign illuminated. This couldn't be; we had just gotten the trays out, so we couldn't be landing! Perhaps there was going to be some clear air turbulence?

I called the cockpit - no such luck - we were indeed landing. I nearly screamed into the headset I had just been speaking to the cockpit on, "Bette, we are landing in five minutes!!!!!"

"Bev, that is not funny," she stated, thinking I was joking around with her. "We haven't even given out the first cup of coffee. This can't be happening."

"Bette, we are landing in five minutes, I promise!!!" I screamed at her. We panicked, grabbed a soldier out of his seat, and put him in the galley to help. A priest caught sight of our dilemma and offered to assist in our plight. We told the soldier we were going to be bringing him some trays and to open the meal tray containers and stuff, shove, push with his feet or whatever he had available to put those meal trays in there until we had brought all of them to him. The priest started picking up trays and heading towards the galley. The passengers hadn't had a thing to drink, and very few of them had even had the opportunity to take a few bites of their meal.

Suddenly the passengers put two and two together and realized what was happening. No wonder they could see the runway coming up towards the plane, we were about to touchdown. The soldier and priest managed to get back to their seats, but there was no way Bette and I could make it to our jump seats, so we sat down in the galley on the floor among all the crumbs, pieces of bread, salad, and spilled food. We both pushed our outstretched arms against the containers of trays that were bulging like never before. Even though the retainer bar was down, the trays were pressing against it with such force, we weren't sure the containers would hold. If they broke open, we would have been unable to use the emergency exit, God forbid!

As we touched down on the runway, a carton of milk fell down on top of Bette's head, spilling all over her hair and running down the side of her face. I burst out laughing and couldn't control myself. About that time, a soda hit the floor and sprayed all its contents in my face. This time, Bette went into hysterics. We were clobbered by all of the items left sitting on top of the galley surface. We were an absolute mess by the time the aircraft pulled to the jetbridge.

Cookie crumbs were stuck to our uniforms, soda and milk was on our faces, and who knows what was spilled all over our shoes. As we came out of the galley, our passengers gave us a rousing round of applause. Bette looked at me and said in a voice loud enough for the passengers to hear,

"And they told me this would be a glamorous job." The passengers went wild with laughter.

As I opened the door to let the passengers deplane, the agent nearly fainted. "My God, what happened to you, girl? Did you hit some awful turbulence?"

I looked at him from under my crooked hat and said, "Whatever do you mean?" as if nothing was wrong with my appearance.

Every passenger on that trip said it was one of the best trips they had ever been on, that they had never laughed so hard before. They patted our shoulders and shook our hands, and the soldier even gave us a hug.

Bette and I looked at each other, "If this is one of the best flights they have ever been on, I'd sure hate to have been on their worst one," I said to Bette.

When we finally ended our day in Charleston, we were absolutely exhausted. Still, we wanted to get something to eat. Bet sort of had a crush on F/O Roger Anderson, but when she mentioned something to him about the whole crew getting together for dinner, he said he was meeting a "friend."

"It's wonderful how this flying job of ours enables us to visit 'friends' and 'old war buddies' all over the country, isn't it, Roger?" Bette asked in her most pissy voice.

"Uh, yeah, sure is, Bette," he answered, knowing full well we knew he wasn't really meeting an "old friend."

For the first time we noticed he must have previously had on a wedding ring because there was an indentation on his ring finger on his left hand. So Roger was married, huh?

"It must be lust 'cause love can't keep you that warm, not in Rochester with its subzero temperatures," stated Bette.

"Now Bette, you must be jealous. You didn't notice the ring either, and we have been flying with this crew all month." I said to her.

At the hotel, Roger's "friend" was there waiting for him in the lobby. Although they made eye contact, she didn't approach him until after he had checked in and the Captain had left for his room.

Bette and I made our way to the elevator, and Bette peeked around the elevator door, "She's not that good looking."

"You are such a sore loser, girl. Besides you don't want to get hooked up with some married pilot. There are plenty of single ones out there." I said and she just rolled her eyes at me.

When I first started this job, I admit I was pretty naive. So much so that when a certain F/O, who is now a retired Captain in Dallas, asked just me to join him for dinner three trips in a row, I never dreamed he would turn out to be married and the father of three boys. I thought it was strange that he never asked for my phone number when we got back to N. Y. because he seemed so interested in me when we had dinner together in Cleveland.

This F/O introduced me to the old, "Let's go to my room and watch a little TV" line. After all, we gals had to share rooms at that time, and I didn't want to wake my roommate now, did I? We never turned on the television; we sat and talked for a long time. He was on the bed, and I was in a chair beside the bed in my prim and proper little position. He asked me to sit on the bed with him so that he could give me a nice back rub. Silly me, I believed him. He really was nice looking, favoring James Garner a lot, but he scared me a little. This was my third time to have dinner with him, and he had always been a perfect gentleman, but this was also the first time I had ever gone back to his room with him.

He started kissing me and trying to unbutton my blouse. I bolted straight up next to him, "Duke, what are you doing? I am not that kind of girl!" I told him in my most authoritative voice.

He looked at me so strangely and asked what I was saving it for. I told him I was waiting until I got married.

I don't think he could believe I was real because he stared at me for what seemed like forever. Then he suddenly became aware of the time and told me I had better get some rest because we had a long day ahead of us tomorrow. I think he had known deep down he wasn't going to get into any heavy stuff with me, yet I also believe he had hoped he was wrong. He wasn't. That was our last trip together that month — the next day he was cordial but very chilly.

I had the feeling he had told the Captain, who, by the way, just happened to look like Robert Stack. It was very rare for this to happen, to have two really exceptionally good-looking pilots on the same flight. If you join the airline thinking that you are going to open the cockpit and look eyeball to eyeball with Tom Selleck, Orlando Bloom, and Channing Tatum, you are in for a big disappointment.

Anyway, Captain Hal Benson was even nicer to me than he had been the previous trips, almost like he knew I hadn't turned out to be a "layover quickie" I think he may have been proud of me.

Captain Benson had been so funny in Cleveland when the entire crew had gone to dinner at a seafood restaurant. I supposed Hal zeroed in on the fact that I wasn't exactly "worldly," to say the least, because he told the waiter we wanted to sit near the kitchen so that when they threw the lobsters in the pot, Bev could hear them scream. My eyes became twice their size and everyone burst out laughing;

I honestly didn't know he was joking, since I had never even eaten steak, much less lobster. Daddy had always told us that chopped sirloin was steak, and I had no idea what filet mignon tasted like or even how to pronounce it. As I mentioned earlier, the food and beverage classes were a whole new world to me.

I leaned over and asked the gal I was flying with if that really happened, the lobsters screaming. She just shook her head and assured me that it wasn't true.

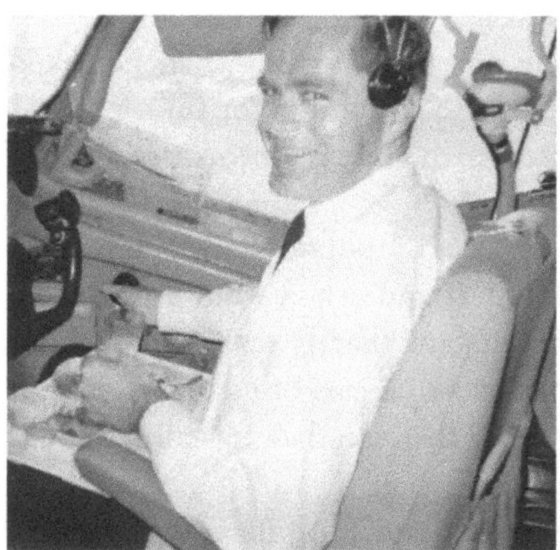

First Officer Donald B. Johnson

A particularly embarrassing moment comes to mind. I was on a flight with this oh-so-handsome Flight Engineer named Don Johnson (honest, that was his name). I had been up quite late the night before, and after the first portion, or 'leg,' of our trip, we had an hour holding time before we had to board the next load of passengers and continue on our trip. I grabbed a pillow, wadded it up, put my head down on top of it, and placed it on the divider table in First Class to take a little snooze.

I must have dozed off immediately into a deep sleep because the next thing I remembered was a gush of air going into my left ear. I jumped up, terrified and angry, and saw this massive-looking guy standing in front me. I couldn't focus immediately, but then I did, I saw Don standing there smiling. Instead of shaking my shoulder to wake me, he had twisted the air vent so it would blow right into my ear. I was so startled but had to admit it was an ingenious way to wake a sleeping Stewardess. I smiled back at him.

"I'm sorry, did I startle you?" he asked.

"Gosh no, you nearly scared me half to death. I must have been in a really deep sleep," I answered.

"That's what you get for partying late last night," he said.

"I only wish I had that as an excuse. The truth of the matter is that I just couldn't sleep. We live right near LaGuardia, and I'm still not used to all of the takeoffs and landings going on over there. Plus, we are so close I think we can honestly hear the caterers loading the aircraft."

Don laughed. "Well, I guess I'll have to make it up to you for waking you up like that. How does dinner sound after we get back from our trip?"

"Maybe I'll just take you up on that," I replied with a big smile.

After our trip was over, he asked for my phone number in N.Y. and wanted to know if I would have dinner with him the next night. I was definitely up for that. He was about 6'2" or taller, with dark hair, and John Travolta blue eyes. Yes, I was excited about our date because I kind of liked him already. He seemed so kind and sincere.

Don took me to this really, really nice restaurant. When he asked me what I'd like to eat, I told him to surprise me and order for me. I was terrified to order something I didn't recognize and be embarrassed out of my mind.

He ordered prime rib, broccoli, and baked potato after our salad. I leaned towards him after the waiter had left and asked what a prime rib was. He told me it was steak. I informed him that I wasn't crazy about steak, remembering that tough chopped steak we used to eat as kids, and I always seemed to get a piece with gristle. Because that was all we could afford, we had to eat it any way.

Don looked at me rather strangely and said, "I think you just might like this particular cut."

When the meal came, I looked at my plate and then at Don. I said, "This isn't steak."

He grinned and asked that I just try it. Perhaps it was a different cut than I had been used to. "If you don't like it, I will get you something else, okay?" he said with a gentle smile on his face. He knew I wasn't kidding, that this was a real experience for me.

"Okay, I'll try it," I told him. It was awesome!

Except for Don, I didn't date any crewmembers, even though there was practically a dating epidemic. There were new Stewardesses graduating weekly and new pilots leaving their military careers to be commercial pilots, so it was like a dating extravaganza.

There were a couple of pilots at the apartment I was close to. One of them was named Jerry "the Bear" Zeagler because he was so cuddly. All of the Stewardesses loved Jerry; every time they flew with him, the gals would run up and hug him in Operations. I know there were a lot of crewmembers very jealous of Jerry, but he was just that kind of a guy.

Besides Jerry, two others pilots were "Cousin Brucie" Denton and his roommate, Rick Brown, who lived right under our apartment. They were loud and had a constant string of girls in and out of their place, but to us they were just like brothers. You could always count on these guys if you needed something or if something broke in your apartment.

Of course, Bette could call on good ole smitten Ron.

Don and I had fun together. We dated off and on for several months when we weren't flying, but I felt so guilty dating him because I still hadn't figured out what I was going to do about Alphie. I was pretty darn sure I didn't want to leave this job and get married.

Still I didn't feel very good about myself for deceiving Don. I knew he was the kind of guy who would have taken off like a rocket if I told him about Alphie. He just had those kinds of scruples! I loved that about him, and I also didn't want him to think any less of me.

One time, I was on a date with Don, and his Dad called his place. Don was in a silly mood and told his Dad that he wanted him to talk to his future wife. I nearly died. Don told him my name and handed me the phone. His Dad said he was looking forward to meeting me and asked a few questions about how long Don and I had known each other and when we planned on getting married. I wanted to kill Don, but it was fun at the same time. I played along and told him that we just fell in love and decided we wanted to get hitched.

Fortunately, Don's mom wasn't home - I would have felt a lot guiltier if I had had to talk to his mom. Don played the same joke on his brother after we hung up from talking to his father.

I told Don we probably carried our joke a little too far, that we shouldn't have done that. He looked at me and asked, "Who was joking?" I just hit him on the shoulder and told him to call his Dad and brother after I left and tell them the truth. He half smiled and said he would.

It had been nearly four months when I finally got a chance to go home to Columbus, and I was excited and worried all at once. I couldn't wait to see Mom, Dad, Mike, and Charmaine, but I also knew I would have to face Alphie and decide how I was going to tell him about not quitting right now.

I loved, loved, loved my job! It was more than everything I had hoped it would be. I felt so glamorous and so proud of myself. I wanted to shout from the top of the Empire State Building to all of the guys and girls that made me feel insecure throughout High School, "Hey, look what I have done! In spite of my height, I am a Stewardess. I get to travel all over the United States. I fly with celebrities, politicians, people from all walks of life, and they depend on me to meet their needs in flight and to be able to save their lives through medical emergencies and, God forbid, in an evacuation. I am not just some tall, ex-Hillbilly from West Virginia without a college degree. I am going places!" That may sound a little conceited, but by damn, I earned it. Those six weeks at the "Charm Farm" were hard, and I did it!

Before I had left the apartment, I was talking to Don on the phone. He made me laugh when he said, "Tell Mom and Dad I said 'Hi.'" He was just such a great guy. We made plans to get together when I got back and he returned from his flight.

When I hung up, Jeanie came into the kitchen. I looked at her and stated, "I'm going to meet the man I'm going to marry today. He is going to be real tall with blonde hair and blue eyes."

She sort of huffed, "Yeah, right. Number one, you are already engaged to someone that you can't decide if you want to marry or not. Secondly, you don't like men with blonde hair and blue eyes. They have to have dark hair and eyes for you to even give them the time of day."

"Well, yes, normally that is true. But for some strange reason, that is what I feel, and it is going to come true."

"Don't forget to invite me to the wedding!" she laughed as she sat down to eat some breakfast.

After what I had just said to Jeanie, I nearly had a heart attack when I went up to the ticket area to turn in my pass, and standing there was an incredibly handsome, tall, at least 6'5", blonde-haired, blue-eyed agent with the longest eyelashes in the world. I must have gulped out loud. He looked up from his paperwork and smiled the most gorgeous smile I have ever seen. What beautiful teeth!

"Can I help you, Miss?" he asked.

I finally found my voice and answered with a question, "How do you pronounce your name?" I had seen his name plate in front of him on the desk and remembered how the instructors stressed the importance of people's names.

"How do you think you pronounce it?"

"Sko-n-man?" I asked. It was spelled S-C-H-O-E-N-E-M-A-N-N.

"Not quite. It is pronounced 'Sure-in-man.' It is German."

"Oh, that is a very unusual, but attractive, name," I stated with a big smile.

He asked if I was a Stewardess, and I told him yes, that I hadn't been flying very long but that I loved it. I asked him how long he had been an agent, and he corrected me by saying that he was not just an agent, but a Management Understudy. He would work as an agent and gain knowledge about different positions at the airport to eventually use when he became a supervisor.

He said that he had come here from California. Of course, with his "surfer boy" look, where else would he have come from but the beach?

We visited just a few more minutes because a line was forming behind me. I went over to a seat where I could see him clearly and pulled my already short skirt up above my knee a little higher. Daddy had always told me that I had great legs, and even Jean Marie said my legs were shaped perfectly. She told me that your legs should touch at the knee, the calf, and the ankle but nowhere else. She checked my "knee stance" and declared mine were perfect. I was glad I had nice legs because I sure didn't have a bosom, and I didn't think to buy one of Johnni's inflatable bras.

Management Understudy Schoenmann looked over, and I saw him scan the length of my legs with his eyes. Aha, he must have liked what he saw because he raised his eyes back towards my face and smiled. We both knew he had checked me out, and I was loving it.

He went onboard the aircraft and returned to announce we were boarding. He called my name, and as I went to get my boarding pass, he asked, "When are you coming back from Columbus?"

I told him it was a very short visit, and I would be back in about five days. He asked if he could have my phone number, so I gave it to him. "Maybe we could go out for a sandwich or something when you return."

"Sure, I would love that."

When I got on the plane, the Stewardesses were rushing all around like chickens. They offered magazines, pillows, blankets, and made chitchat with passengers all the while giving me frequent glances as I sat there in First Class. After the service, one of them finally got up the nerve to ask me a question that shocked me, "How long have you been a supervisor?"

I must have looked like she had just thrown ice water in my face. "A supervisor? ME? You have got to be kidding." I said.

"That darn agent, he came on and told us that we were getting a Check Ride and that you were a supervisor." A Check Ride was when a supervisor of In-flight Service came on and watched you doing your job and made sure you were doing everything that you were taught to do in school. They graded you on your communication skills, appearance, how you served, and just about every single function that you were supposed to have mastered at school. They could be really helpful and so unbelievably picky at the same time. It was something we all had to go through. Sometimes the agents would warn you, and sometimes they wouldn't if they didn't like you or just felt like being mean. You never knew the check riders were there unless you recognized them or until they handed you the paperwork and told you to come see them after your trip was finished.

"You just wait until I get back to LaGuardia; I am going to give that agent a good talking to," she said, and then we both started laughing. "He was pretty darn cute though, I must admit."

"I thought so too. We have a date when I come back from Columbus."

"Well, hopefully we'll get to fly together, and you can tell me how it works out because if it doesn't, I want to go for him."

I laughed and said, "He's open game, I guess."

"Nah, you two 'go at it,' and then I'll make my move."

Go at it? What a weird way to put it. Oh well, we would see what happens. What was Jean Marie going to say when Schoenmann picked me up? That was going to be a sight to see. I laughed to myself as I looked out the window and saw the Ohio State University Campus.

Mom and Dad picked me up. It felt so good and strange to be in my old home and to sleep in my old bed with my sister. I told them all about Stewardess training, finding an apartment, and about some of my trips. It was wonderful being able to tell them in person.

Alphie came over, and I was genuinely glad to see him because I had forgotten how cute he was and how shy. I grabbed him and kissed him in front of my folks, something he was never, ever comfortable with, but he smiled and seemed pleased at my reaction to seeing him again.

After we ate with the folks, we went over to see Kaki and Mary who were so happy to see me. Before I could even say a word or be prepared for his question, Kaki asked, "Are you ready to come home now?"

I was so flustered and didn't know how to answer or address that subject, but I guessed now I would have to. I told him that I was really enjoying being a Stewardess and that it beat the heck out of being a long-distance telephone operator. They all knew how much I hated that job because it was so confining. I told them about going to San Diego and how beautiful it was there, how I had three roommates, two reserved and one crazy. They laughed at some of Bette's antics. We visited for a while, and then Kaki and Mary went out.

Alphie looked at me and asked, "So I guess this means that you aren't ready to come home and get married yet, huh?"

I looked into those soft, dark brown eyes and said, "Please try to understand, I am just not ready yet. I worked so hard for this job, and I just want to do it for a year. Then I will be twenty-two, and I'll come home."

He put his head down and softly said, "Yeah, I'll bet."

"Alphie, please give me a chance. I have never been anywhere in my life except West Virginia and Ohio. Now I've been to Texas, New York, California, and places I never even dreamed I could possibly see. Just think about all of the things I will be able to share with our kids one day."

That still didn't encourage him the least bit. I might as well have been talking to the wall. This wasn't going to work; no matter what I said, he wasn't buying it. Alphie wanted me home with him, and that was the only thing that was going to make him happy.

We spent the rest of the evening just kissing and holding each other. He still made me feel so loved when he kissed me. At times when I closed my eyes, it seemed like just yesterday when we had been together for those two years. It was like this Stewardess thing didn't really exist, but in reality, it did and I just had to be a Stewardess for a little while.

I honestly believed that maybe we would settle down one day and get married, but I had no idea what my future would hold. I knew I loved Alphie with all of my heart, and if I hadn't become a Stewardess, we would probably have gotten married and lived happily ever after. But it had happened, and now I was all torn up inside about what to do.

I spent the next few days visiting my friends and a couple of special moms during the day. I saw Gussie, Karen's mom, who was like a second mom to me. When I couldn't talk to my Mom about something, which was very seldom, I could talk to Gussie, and she seemed to understand. The main thing Mom had no understanding of was how I had felt about Terry Kneisley most of my life, but Gussie understood I had a tremendous puppy love for him. Karen had married Nate Hanna and moved to North Carolina while he was in the service. It nearly broke Gussie and Chuck's heart, but what were they going to do?

Then I went to visit with Virginia and Jim, Jimmie Dale's mom and Dad. I caught up on Jimmie Dale and his German bride; that still stung a little, but oh well, that was my past, and this was my life now. It was great seeing all their kids that still lived with them. It was a wonderful visit, and they all said they were proud of me.

"Between you and me Bev, I think Jimmie Dale is proud too but he doesn't want to admit it," said Virginia. I thanked her and told her to tell him I said hello the next time they talked.

Alphie was helping Kaki, so he said he would call and come over later when they finished moving some stuff for one of Kaki's friends.

I called Terry Kneisley's house, and his mom said he was attending some night classes. I found out all of the information as to where and when, then made up my mind to go to his classroom and surprise him. I went to the building where Terry was taking classes and waited until he was finished. He came out, all tall and gorgeous as ever, walking with some other guy from class, and I called his name. He stopped and turned, and was so surprised to see me. Of course, I had taken extra time to dress beautifully, make sure my makeup was perfect, and get every hair in place. I really wanted to knock his socks off.

"Bev? Is that you?" he asked.

"Yes, Terry, it is me. I need a favor. My Dad was supposed to pick me up after I finished shopping, and there is something wrong with the car. Do you suppose you could give me a ride home? I would really appreciate it."

The fellow he had been walking with looked at Terry and said, "Kneisley, you have got to be the luckiest bastard alive."

Terry smiled and told me he had to wait a few minutes for Richie Irion to finish his class, and then he would drop off Richie and take me home.

It would be good to see Richie too. Richie was like one of the girls regarding his love of spreading gossip. He used to aggravate me so much in school, telling me about Terry's dates with Jan. He told me far more information than I ever wanted to hear. It would definitely be good to see Richie again, since I looked so good, and it would be all over the class of '63 in no time, just how different I was than in High School. Oh, yeah, I would gladly wait for Richie.

Richie came out of class to find Terry and me sitting in chairs right outside the front door to his room. He stopped dead in his tracks and blurted out, "Bev Golden, dear Lord, is that you?"

I slowly raised my eyes to meet his, smiled a sweet little smile, and answered "Why yes, Richie, it is me."

The three of us loaded up in Terry's car, with Richie blabbing like a girl, asking all sorts of questions about Stewardess School, where I had been, and who I had met so far. He just wouldn't stop asking questions, and I was loving it!

Terry was taking it all in as Richie asked all of the things Terry might have wanted to know. Richie didn't want to go home. He wanted to go out and grab a bite to eat or something. Terry said, "Irion, you are going home." Richie wasn't happy, but I was delighted to see Terry acting so forcefully.

After we dropped off Richie, we stopped for some pie and visited longer. I could tell Terry was impressed. He commented on how different I looked from our days at North High. I held my head up high and sort of cocked it to one side, smiled, and flirted with him. Yes, I was mocking Bette.

It was wonderful! I just don't understand what it is about your first puppy love. Yes, Jimmie Dale was my first real love, but there was just this chemistry I had with Terry that I still can't explain to this day.

Terry made me feel all weak in the knees every time I was around him. He finally drove me home and we sat in the driveway and talked a little longer. I asked him what he planned to do with his life and if he had a girlfriend. When he leaned over and kissed me, I was so happy, but he didn't ask me how long I was going to be there or if we could get together or anything. (Mercy, I guess some things never change, and this situation with Terry was one of them.)

To make myself feel better, I thanked Terry for the ride and told him that perhaps we could get together the next time I was home. He said he would like that, walked me to the door, kissed me again, went towards his car, turned around, smiled, waved, and drove off. I would NEVER understand that man!

Mike was going to his Senior Prom while I was there; he looked so grownup in his tux. I couldn't believe that he was old enough to drive and have a girlfriend. He had had the same one for several years, Carol Kellner, and they made a really cute couple.

Charmaine was still a little kid, only 12 years old. I loved her a lot, but sadly we were almost a lifetime apart. Ten years is a big difference, and we didn't have much in common. I wish there hadn't been such a big gap between us, but there was nothing I could do to change that. I tried to visit with her and play whatever she liked, but it was difficult. I was all grown up, and she hadn't even started growing up yet.

Alphie and I spent every moment together that we could cram into my three remaining days. We had so much fun. He was so affectionate and sweet and made me feel so good when we were together, but I just didn't want to quit flying yet. I had to do it for a while longer.

Our last night was so tearful. We would catch a look at each other out of the corner of our eyes, and both of us held back tears. When I had to say good-bye to his Grandma Jean and his parents the night before I left, it was so difficult that I wondered yet again if I had made the right decision. I was hurting physically about leaving again, but at the same time I talked myself into going because I had worked so hard for this job, and I just had to see if it was for me. I had to!

My visit went fast. Alphie drove me to the airport; I had said good-bye to Mom, Dad, Mike, and Charmaine at home. Saying good-bye to Alphie by myself was going to be hard enough without having to say it to the whole family at the same time.

I only wished I knew what I was going to do about Alphie. We didn't discuss us dating other people, but I guess I had done that. I wasn't really proud of the fact that I had an engagement ring with a promise to marry this wonderful man, but I was confused as to what I really wanted out of life.

I knew I wanted to fly for at least a year, and I thought Alphie probably wouldn't sit at home week after week with me flying all over the USA, meeting new people, seeing things I had never seen before, and doing things that were all new to me, but neither of us mentioned dating other people. Maybe we just didn't want to talk about it. Maybe if we didn't know about it and still came back to each other, it would all be okay.

Alphie kissed me, then turned and walked away even before I got a chance to tell him I loved him. I know it must have been difficult for him to take me to the airport not knowing if or when I would be back. He just wanted me to come home and get married and have those three kids we always talked about having.

My poor head was spinning as I got on the airplane. I thought I would do the marriage and kids someday, but for now I wanted to see what the world was like. I felt guilty and excited all at once. What was I going to do?

SCHOENBERG? IS HE JEWISH?

When I went into the apartment, all three roommates were there. This was unusual because it seemed at least two or three of us were always out on a trip, so it was seldom that the four of us were there all at once.

"So, Bev-a-lee, how was Ohio?" asked Nancy. I loved the way my roomies said my name. I had always hated my full name, Beverly, but the way they said it with their Massachusetts accents was so neat!

Before I could answer, naughty Bette asked, "Did you and Alphie finally get it on?"

"Oh my God, Bet! What is wrong with you?" I asked.

"Lord Bev, how long have you two been going together, two or three years? I just can't believe that you two haven't done it yet. Are you for real, girl?"

I must have turned red as a beet because Jeanie started laughing and chimed in, "Come on Beverly, don't tell me you really are a virgin?"

Nancy became uncomfortable with this conversation and tried to change the subject, "So how are your folks?"

I told them about my trip, having to tell Alphie I wasn't coming home for at least a year, seeing Terry. Talk of Terry drew oohs and ahhs because of what I had told them about him.

Then it dawned on me about Derek Schoenmann.

"Jeanie, remember when I left on this trip, I told you I was going to meet the man I was going to marry? I even told you he would have blonde hair and blue eyes, and you laughed? Well guess, what? I met a guy just like that. An agent; oops, I mean a Management Understudy, working my flight to Columbus. He was gorgeous!!" I tried to mock the way Jeanie said that word, it was hysterical. No matter how awesome the word 'gorgeous' sounded, it sounded even better in a Massachusetts accent.

"Seriously?" asked Nancy.

"Yep, his name is Derek Schoenmann."

"Schoenberg, is he Jewish?" inquired Bette with that silly grin on her face.

"I didn't say Schoenberg, I said Schoenmann. It's German, and he asked me for my phone number. We are supposed to go out tonight, but he hasn't called yet, has he?"

"No, not that I know of," answered Jeanie. "A blonde? Come on Bev-a-lee, you and a blonde? I just can't see that happening."

About that time, the phone rang. I ran to the kitchen to answer it, waiting for the third ring so I wouldn't seem too anxious if it was Derek. It was! I pointed to the phone and mouthed to my roomies, "It's him." They all giggled.

Derek asked me to go out for a bite to eat after work, to Long Island where he lived. I agreed on a time and hung up the phone. "Well, I guess you guys will get to see my 'blonde beauty' real soon. He'll be here in about an hour, after he gets off work."

"Alright," said Bet.

"This I gotta see - Beverly with a blonde," chimed in Jeanie.

"I bet he's really nice, Bev," smiled Nancy.

I fussed with my hair and outfit for several minutes. Nothing seemed to look or feel right. I finally settled on a sleeveless jumpsuit, since it was summer in New York and very hot.

When Derek showed up, I introduced him to my roomies. He looked even better than I remembered. Jeanie just stood there with her mouth wide open, until I looked over at her and motioned for her to shut her mouth. She just couldn't get over seeing me with a blonde-haired man. Mercy, Derek was indeed tall. He told me he was 6'5", and I smiled like never before. "This is awesome!" I said to myself.

We drove out to Long Island and stopped at a sandwich shop. Although I was much hungrier than a sandwich could satisfy, he was serious about getting a sandwich, and that was okay because he was so handsome, and I loved being with him and getting to know him better. We talked about our families. Derek had two younger sisters who lived in Pennsylvania, his Dad worked for the Insurance Company of Western America, as a Vice President or something, and his mom was a stay-at-home wife and mother.

Derek told me that he had only one roommate, Neil Casey, who also was in the Management Understudy Program. Even though they lived pretty far from LaGuardia, the beach was worth the drive even in New York traffic.

Beach? I was intrigued. I guess I never really gave that much thought to a beach in reference to New York, but that's where we ended up - walking on a beach. There were couples all over the place, kissing and enjoying being together. As we walked past one couple, a "Theme from Summer Place" was playing on their radio.

I looked over at Derek and my heart skipped a beat. Had I prophesied my own life? Was this really the man I was going to marry? I got chill bumps all up and down my arms. He saw me rubbing my arms and put his arm around me. I smiled, and he leaned down (oh happy days, he had to lean down!), and kissed me gently. It was wonderful!

Derek drove me back to Jackson Heights where my three roommates were all standing in front of and staring out the windows as we came up the sidewalk. I laughed and pointed at them, and Derek thought it was pretty funny too. He put his arm around me, and rushed me toward the door of the apartment so their view was ruined. We both laughed as we envisioned Nancy, Jean, and Bet craning their necks to try and see us kiss goodnight.

Bette and I had a trip together the next day, and we saw Derek at the airport working another flight opposite our gate. "Hey, Bev, there's lover boy over there. Want to run over and kiss him good-bye?"

"Bette, you know we are not supposed to show affection in uniform."

"So take off your jacket, run over for a little peck and run back."

"No way, I do not want to appear to be that crazy about him already," I replied.

"But you are, aren't you? I saw the look on your face when you came home last night. Even Jean and Nancy said they thought we had a problem. I told them it wasn't we girls who had a problem. It was Alphie. Isn't that true?"

"Come on, Bet, it is far too early to be jumping to conclusions. It was only one date."

Bette and I had a terrible flight because the weather was awful, causing delays everywhere. Finally we got back to LaGuardia and had only one turnaround to Rochester left. I went out to talk to the agent about how many folks we would have on our trip. His name was Joe Mascotti, and he was really cute and funny - oh no, not another nice Italian boy!

Joe just kept picking at me about the number of people and wouldn't hand over the Passenger Revenue Report. I finally reached around his arm to snatch the paperwork when I noticed what a handsome gold ring he had on. I mentioned how nice looking it was, and he handed it to me to get a closer look.

Next thing I know, a crowd of late arrivals showed up, and I had to get back on the plane. I tried to hand Joe his ring, but he motioned that he was too busy right that moment to take it. I went back to the galley and showed the ring to Bet.

Of course, Bette had to say something smart about it. "Lordy, it's always the quiet ones! You go off the aircraft to get the paperwork and come back going steady with this agent, you are engaged to your Italian Teddy Bear, and now you've met the new love of your life - all in the last few days. I knew I would have to watch you."

I burst out laughing, "Right Bet, I'm a real mover."

We got busy with boarding, and I still had Joe's ring on. The other agent working the trip apparently brought the final paperwork when I was helping a passenger with their coat, so I didn't have a chance to send the ring back to Joe. I felt terrible because he was going to think I was stealing his ring.

We flew to Rochester and back. When the door to the airplane was opened, there stood Joe, not looking happy. He practically yelled at me, "Give me back my ring!" The passengers had already gotten out of their seats and were standing behind me when he yelled.

I decided to play a little trick on Joe so I put my head down and softly said, "Joey, couldn't we talk about this after I get off the airplane? I mean this really isn't the time or place to break up with me, now is it?"

Joe was dumbfounded.

The man behind me commented to Joe as he deplaned, "You're a real jerk, buddy!"

The next guy gave him a glare and said, "You are pitiful. You could have at least waited for the poor girl to get off the airplane before you broke up with her, you ass!"

I could barely keep from bursting out laughing right on the spot. Joe just looked at me in disbelief. Was this really happening to him? I am sure he was wondering what kind of a nut I really was.

After all of the passengers had left I started up the jetbridge. Joe was waiting in the middle with his arms folded and shaking his head. "You are so crazy that I think I am going to have to take you out," he said.

"Before or after we break up?" I asked him. He chased me the full length of the bridge until right before we entered the terminal. I turned around and handed him his ring. "Thanks Joe, it was short but sweet."

"Hey girl, I am serious. You owe me a date for the chewing out I got from those passengers. They didn't let up, you know, and then the ones behind them started in on me."

I cracked up. "I am so sorry; I guess I do owe you a date," so we made plans for the following day.

Joe was from New York - what an accent he had - so he knew a bunch of restaurants that were family-type, not the touristy ones. We had a lot of fun together, doing really nutty stuff and laughing a lot! We were out with another agent, Noah Riley and his girlfriend Tracy Spencer, when, in the middle of the night, we decided to drive to Pennsylvania for coffee. I didn't even drink coffee, but it sounded like a great adventure. We didn't get back to my apartment until about an hour before my alarm would have gone off.

I could not believe I did something so crazy with a whole day of flying ahead of me, but I did. I jumped in the shower and went to work.

I don't know how I managed to stay awake, and I nearly fell asleep on the jump seat when we landed in Nashville for our layover. The crew wanted to get together for dinner, but I told them I was hitting the rack -and hard!! I took a bath, jumped into bed about 7:00 p.m., and didn't even hear Bette when she came back from dinner.

I was enjoying dating Don, Joe, and Derek because there were things I liked about each of them. I still hadn't faced the fact that I had Alphie's engagement ring hidden in a box in my drawer. Sometimes, when I had talked to him or missed him a bunch, I would wear it, but I'm sad to say that wasn't very often.

I really was ashamed of myself. I wasn't acting like an engaged woman because I wasn't sure I really wanted to be one. I honestly didn't know if I wanted to get married any time soon to anyone. I didn't want to give up flying, go home to get married, and then end up regretting it.

Yet Alphie was such a wonderful guy. He was so attentive, and he acted like no one and nothing in the world was more important to him than me or being with me. That made me feel so wonderful and loved, and I know I would have been content to just stay with him if I hadn't gotten the opportunity to become a Stewardess. We had our whole lives planned out, which was fine until I found out there was an entirely different world out there, beyond what existed within the borders of Columbus, Ohio.

I was just so proud of myself for accomplishing something that so few women would ever get the chance to try in their whole lives. This was the best of both worlds, getting paid to fly places I had only dreamed about and being on an airplane with movie stars, politicians, pilots, and company presidents. When I started working for American, it was such a glamorous job. Our passengers dressed up so nicely. We were taught to look our best at all times under any condition. When we walked tall and proud through the airport, we could feel eyes following us. Being a Stewardess was special!

(Later I read an interview with Robert Sean Leonard, an actor who played on the television program "House." The interviewer asked him what he thought about the young actresses of today. He replied something like this, "Give me a Stewardess from the 70s. They really had class." My flying partners and I would like to thank Mr. Leonard for his good taste in women.)

I had never known anyone who had tried to be a Stewardess. I wanted the whole world to know I was one, and I didn't want to settle for going home and becoming a wife and mother, not just yet. But I didn't want to lose Alphie either.

As I mentioned, neither one of us had brought up the subject of us dating other people. It would have killed Alphie if I had said something about it, and I didn't want to hurt him any more than I had already. Besides, he was thousands of miles away, and he wasn't going to find out. Alphie seldom ever called. I don't know if he didn't want to or if he was afraid to, but he always waited for me to call him. I felt down deep in my heart it might be better for us to break up, but what if we did, and then I decided I didn't want to do this job any longer? What a dilemma!

It was a terrible situation, and I felt so guilty dating other people. I justified in my own mind that it would be better if I dated around and realized I really did want to go home, instead of going home and regretting it later. I tried so hard to validate what I was doing, yet in my heart, I knew it was wrong. I guess I really was trying to figure out what I wanted, and I was having a hell of a time deciding.

I had fun dates with Joey. He always made me laugh, and we did such interesting things in New York since he was familiar with the city.

I know rumors got around the airport that I was dating both Joe and Derek. I don't think either one of them was too happy about occasionally meeting my flights together. I was always embarrassed, yet it was kind of funny when I came off a flight to see both of them there. I smiled, said "Hi," and then took off as fast as I possibly could to get home. Pretty soon one or both of them would call me to see how my trip was. I wasn't playing games; I was just trying to figure out what I wanted to do with my life and with whom.

Don was wonderful! He was so handsome and sweet. There was nothing in the world I could have asked of him that he wouldn't have done, but Don had that look in his eyes that said he was looking to settle down, and I knew I sure wasn't ready for that. We always had such a wonderful time together, and I truly enjoyed his company. We didn't fly together often, but when we did, it made my trips extra special. I was happy to be dating a pilot, my very own pilot, and we would have so much fun on layovers.

There was something about Derek. I can't tell you what it was exactly, but he seemed to be trying to steal my heart. Of course, I loved the fact he was 6' 5" and incredibly good looking! His blonde hair and blue eyes, with those foot long eyelashes, just captivated me. I would sometimes come into LaGuardia and see some other Stewardesses making eyes and flirting with him, and I couldn't resist the temptation to go over and interfere. Perhaps it was my height or the way Derek responded to me when I walked over that made them suddenly flee, but I loved doing it.

I enjoyed being seen with Derek because we made a striking couple. He was so smart and ambitious. I really admired that he had his life planned and was going after it. Derek wanted to be a young executive on the corporate ladder at American, and there was every reason to believe he would accomplish that goal, and I thought I wanted to be on his arm when he did.

We started spending more and more time together. We would often meet at Parker's, a local pub where airline personnel hung out after work, or Derek would come by the apartment for dinner, and then we would go out.

On occasion, Derek would spend the night on the sofa if he had worked a late shift and had to be back at LaGuardia early the next morning. Jeanie and Nancy weren't too pleased with that arrangement, and began telling me that I was a convenience to Derek, that he was only using me. I would often wash his shirt and iron it before he went back to work.

They just weren't too crazy about him, and it started to affect the way they were treating me. Bette told me to tell them to kiss my ass because it was my business, but since I never wanted to cause a confrontation, I tried to ignore the way they acted.

I made up my mind that I wanted to date Derek and no one else, so I stopped seeing Joey and seldom saw Don. Joe acted like it was no big deal. We had had a lot of fun together, but I don't think he expected any big romance to happen between us.

I knew Don had found out I was dating Derek because he made a surprising comment one day. I told Don I couldn't go out one Friday because I already had plans. He said, "Tell that long-legged agent he had better be good to you." That confirmed for me he did indeed know about Derek.

Don acted hurt, and I felt really bad about that. He knew I was dating other people, but I guess he had hoped that might end so he and I could have a future together. Perhaps I was all wrong about Don's intentions, but that was the feeling I got whenever we were together.

Although Don was wonderful, I just couldn't get Derek off my mind. He was the one I wanted to spend time with most often.

One summer evening in July, Derek drove up in his little red Chevy Corvair, and we went out. I could not take my eyes off him all evening, and I was hanging on his every word. I felt like maybe he really was the one I wanted. This meant actually breaking up with Alphie, but I felt like I was ready to make a commitment to this man and to a future for us together.

When Derek drove me home after what I thought had been a perfect evening, he leaned over to kiss me good night. When we parted lips, I looked him straight in his eyes and told him I loved him. He looked like someone had just thrown ice water in his face. He seemed to be upset, almost angry actually, and said, "Oh shit, I was afraid this was going to happen."

I must have had the same expression on my face. I could not believe my ears! I had never been the first to tell anyone I loved him, ever, in any relationship, and here I was saying it to someone who then reacted like that. Oh my God!

I turned around, opened the door to the car, ran up the sidewalk and up the stairs to my apartment. "Oh please, don't let Jean or Nancy be there," I remember saying to myself. I just couldn't face their wrath right now.

I was bawling! On the second floor landing, I paused, sobbing, and tried to catch my breath, when the door to the apartment beneath ours opened. There stood Cousin Brucie, one of my favorite pilots and friends. He looked at me in shock, "What in the world is wrong, Bev? Are you okay?"

I raised my hand and gently placed it on his face, "Not now, Brucie, please. I'll talk to you later, ok?"

"Girl, I'm here if you need me," Brucie called after me.

I could not get up the stairs and into the apartment fast enough. Thank God no one was there. I ran into my room, threw myself on my bed and cried myself to sleep. I cried for three solid days.

The phone would ring, but I refused to pick it up. It wasn't going to be Crew Schedule calling because I had trip schedule set for the month, and I didn't have to fly until the fourth day after my date with Derek. I just sat there wondering what in the world would make him say a thing like that. I honestly thought he cared for me.

Bette came home, and I told her what had happened and begged her not to tell Jean or Nancy. She said, "What an asshole! Even if he did feel that way, he should never have verbalized it. How inconsiderate! Maybe you are better off without him after all. Why don't you just wait and see what happens in the next few days?"

When she asked me if I had talked to him at all since the incident happened, I told her, "No, the phone has been ringing off the hook, but I never picked it up. I have no idea what I would say to him anyway. How do you respond to something like that?"

Bette again suggested that I tell him to "Fuck off!" jokingly, then seriously suggested I give it some time.

I went to the airport to fly my trip with Bette. I had her on the lookout for Derek so I didn't have to see him. She told me when she spotted him working a flight, and I hurried past him behind a bunch of passengers walking through the terminal. My heart broke when I caught a glimpse of Derek working at the gate, but I had a three-day trip to work and couldn't think about him now or for the next few days.

I was going to be a fabulous Stewardess and do the best job ever. He wasn't going to ruin that for me.

Bette and I had a good trip. Thank God for Bette. She always knew when to make me laugh. On this trip, I was running trays instead of setting up. We had pretty much perfected who did what best, and it worked out great for the two of us. Bette was good at catering and setting up drinks and trays, while I loved running them. At the time, we did not have carts, so instead, I ran every single tray on that airplane by hand. Because I had bigger hands, I could easily carry three trays at a time, which really helped get things done a lot faster. Plus, I loved to chitchat with the passengers, and Bette didn't particularly care to do that unless they were male and cute. Hey, she knew what she liked.

On this flight, I was running meals like a crazy woman in the back of a full 727-100. When I came out of the galley, the passenger in the middle seat on the left side of the front row had on a clown mask. When I went back up the aisle to return to the galley, he had removed it so when I looked over at him, he seemed perfectly normal. I thought I was seeing things. He started doing it just about every two or three times I left the galley.

I asked Bette to stick her head out of the galley next time I left with some trays and see if she saw what I thought I was seeing. When I returned to the galley, she said she hadn't seen a thing, and she had looked three times.

I knew for sure I was losing it. This time when I turned the corner I stopped right in front of him, and he had the mask on. "Caught ya!" I said to him.

He snapped his fingers, removed the mask, and replied, "Well Blondie, it took you long enough." The guys with him burst out laughing, as did some of the other passengers in the surrounding rows of seats. I found out later Bette had seen him in his mask on her third peek!

Bette made me go out after the flight to eat and mingle with the crew even though that was the last thing in the world I wanted to do. I kept thinking about Derek and wondering what in the world I would ever be able to say to him if and when I had to. If he worked one of my flights or I accidentally bumped into him at the airport, what in the world could I say to him after his comment? I had no idea and was dreading the time when it would happen, so I did what I could to avoid Derek at the airport.

I finally had to tell Nancy and Jean we weren't dating any longer, but I couldn't bring myself to tell them what he had said. They seemed so relieved that I wasn't seeing Derek anymore. They just didn't seem to like him for their own reasons, but I guess I never knew just how much they didn't like him. I never knew what those reasons were, except they thought I was a convenience to him, which I never wanted to believe.

Anytime Derek called the house, I instructed my roommates to tell him I wasn't there, and they were delighted to do so.

Of course, "dramatic Jeanie" always made up some outrageous story when he would call. Once, I had accepted a date with a Passenger Service Manager from LaGuardia named Sal Tatone, who had a reputation of being the Mafia contact for business at LaGuardia (I never knew if that was true or not). Sal was definitely slick and knew his way around. I don't know why I went out with Sal, but it just seemed like a good idea at the time.

Sal picked me up in a limousine in front of my apartment just as Derek drove by.

Derek called the apartment, and Jeanie really laid it on. She said I had left in a limo for my date with the president of IBM or some big corporation, and that this (imaginary) guy was "crazy for me." She had such a way with words. I laughed so hard when she told me Derek had called and what she had told him. Jeanie could be truly funny when she wanted to be.

A couple of nights my roomies came home to find me crying. They lectured me and tried to tell me this was for the best.

One weekend, Jeanie and Nancy were planning to go to Boston for some fun and so Jeanie could possibly decide again which man she loved. She was dating two fellows at the same time and couldn't make up her mind which one she wanted. Jerry Palazzo was a hunk and fairly wealthy. Richard Merullo, cute but older, had been her hairdresser she had known forever and had encouraged her to become a Stewardess in the first place. Jeanie couldn't seem to decide which one to give her heart to, so she went home to Massachusetts quite a few times to try and decide. Of course, Nancy always went with her because the two of them were inseparable.

The girls knew I was off that weekend and they wanted me to go with them to "Beantown." Bette had gone to New Bedford for a few days and wouldn't be back until Sunday, and they didn't want me sitting in the apartment alone crying over Derek. They told me I was going, like it or not, and Jeanie was going to fix me up with Richard's best friend, Bobby Bernhardt.

I loved to hear people from Massachusetts talk! Their accents were so thick, and they used strange words for things. Like a "frap" was a milkshake. "Soda" was any kind of beverage, like Coke or Pepsi. "Hookers" were prostitutes, as I had found out. I don't recall all the different words, but there were many others.

I packed my bag, and off we went in Nancy's little Volkswagen Beetle. Guess who ended up in the back? Me, of course! I was the odd man out, but I was glad to be leaving the apartment and going to do something fun.

We stayed at Jeanie's house, and she was giving me the "scoop" on Bobby when the phone rang. It was Bobby, and he wanted her to tell me not to bother even getting dressed because he didn't feel like messing with all of those clothes tonight. I nearly fell off the end of her bed when she relayed his message. I freaked! What kind of a guy is this? Jeanie had told me Bobby was tall and lanky with brown eyes and curly hair, a ski instructor, who owned his own TV repair business and was a thirty-two-year-old bachelor! She further informed me that all the women were after him, and he was considered a prime catch there in Watertown.

My mind went racing. I was petrified of this man, and I hadn't even met him yet. I was shaking so badly when Richard and Bobby came to the door that I could barely speak Nancy was with Tony, a friend she often dated when she was home, and she told me that she and Jeanie were going in Richard's car, and I was to ride in Bob's Caddy alone with him. My eyes must have bugged out of my head because they all burst out laughing. It turns out, they were joking about us riding alone, but they just couldn't resist telling me that. I wanted to choke all of them.

We went to the Playboy Club in Boston. Since those guys were regular visitors, they got the best tables in the place. We sat right in front of the stage where a gorgeous woman was singing. Everyone started to order cocktails, and I panicked. I didn't want to feel left out, but I had no idea what to drink. Then I remembered overhearing Mom saying she had ordered a Tom Collins once, so I ordered that. Our bunny served our drinks. We were all talking and laughing, then quieted down when the girl started to sing.

I glanced around to make sure no one was watching me as I leaned forward to taste my Tom Collins. As soon as I put my lips on the straw, Bob made a tremendous slurping sound. I practically jumped out of my seat, and the singer gave me a funny look. I sat back and rolled my eyes. "What an idiot!" I thought to myself as the singer tried again to concentrate on her performance. What in the world would possess a grown man to do something so juvenile?

I was getting pretty thirsty, and I figured Bobby had had his fun, so I leaned forward, and I'll be damned if he didn't do it again, only louder! The singer stopped in mid-song, looked at Bob, and asked "Blind date?"

Bobby grinned at the singer and said, "Yeah, some floozy Stewardess." Everyone went crazy! The whole area erupted in laughter. I knew I did not like this person, and the faster we could leave, the better.

After we had eaten, Tony and Nancy were dropped off at Nancy's parents' house. Jeanie told me that she and Richard wanted to be alone for a while, so they were dropping Bob and me off at Bob's TV repair shop to get his car so he could take me back to her house.

I thought I would die. "NO WAY, Jeanie!" I told her. She insisted Bobby was harmless and that he would take me straight to Jeanie's house. I was absolutely terrified of this man, and now she was asking me to ride in a car alone with him. I felt like I was indebted to her for taking me out of my depression in New York, although this was above and beyond the call of friendship, so I reluctantly agreed.

They dropped us off at Bob's shop. I followed him in to get a key, then he asked me to wait while he pulled the car around. The car was a big ole black Caddy. I took one look at that car and figured even as big as it was, I would still be too close to him.

Bobby opened the door, and I slid in and held onto the door handle. He got behind the wheel and burst out laughing. "Bev-a-lee (saying my name with the same accent that all of my roommates did), Hon, I am not going to bite you. I already ate."

I told him I knew that but that I felt much safer…er…better sitting where I was, thanks.

Bobby could not get me to Jeanie's house fast enough. I jumped out the door and headed down her sidewalk, as he yelled after me to slow down so he could at least walk me to the door. I slowed down for a moment and then walked quickly to her door. I thanked Bobby with my back to him and repeatedly rang the doorbell.

Jeanie's sister let me in. Bob yelled, "Goodnight, Bev-a-lee!" as I almost ran poor Peggy down getting in the door.

"Isn't he gorgeous?" Peggy asked, sounding just like Jeanie when she talked.

I didn't want to offend anyone so I said, "Gorgeous? Oh, yeah, he was gorgeous!"

"Are you gonna see him again?" she asked all excited.

"Peggy, I can honestly say I don't think that man will ever want to see me again as long as he lives." I went up to Jeanie's room to put on my pajamas.

On the way back to New York, Jeanie and Nancy kept telling me how funny Bobby thought I was. He could not get over the fact that a twenty-one-year-old woman acted like she was still in Junior High School. I was so embarrassed.

Actually, I was sort of mad at the two of them. I tried to defend myself, but they had both known Bob their whole lives and found him to be perfectly harmless. He was a real Romeo and wanted relationships on his own terms. I told them I really didn't think he would ever have to worry about being stuck with me again. They both laughed.

When I got into our bedroom where Nancy and Jean couldn't hear me, I told Bette about my disaster in Massachusetts. I could sense something was on Bette's mind because she was so quiet, then she told me she had heard Derek was dating some Stewardess named Phyllis and another woman who was a ticket agent. Bette felt like I should hear it from her instead of from somebody else, and I was grateful she had told me in our own room instead of me finding out at the airport in front of co-workers. I just quietly laid my head on the pillow and pulled the comforter up around my shoulders. Bette had a date, and I was glad she was leaving because I knew I would be crying myself to sleep that night for sure.

I finally saw Derek at the airport when he was working my flight. I gulped really hard because I was flying number one Stewardess, and I had to pick up the paperwork. When I approached him, he had his head down. "Mr. Schoenmann, may I please have the paperwork for my flight?" I asked in a very professional tone. His head jerked upward at the sound of my voice, and he smiled from ear to ear. "You bastard!" I thought to myself.

"Why, of course you may, Miss Golden. I'll have it for you in one second. I am just getting the final count now." I stood there smelling his cologne, looking at his eyelashes and hair and trying to be cool. It was very difficult to do, but I pulled it off even though my heart was breaking in a trillion pieces. Derek handed me the paperwork and started to say "I've tried calling you quite a few ti..."

Before he could finish, I looked into his eyes, said "thanks," and walked away as quickly as I could. He seemed surprised I had cut him off like that.

Derek ended up bringing the final paperwork to the plane right before departure, but I made sure I was in the galley so he couldn't get to me. He had to hand the papers off to the boarding Stewardess, which was supposed to be me, but there was no way I could be close to him and talk with him, then head out on this trip calm, cool, and collected. No way possible, and I wasn't about to put myself in that position.

I went out with Don a few more times, but my heart wasn't in it. He was so great and deserved better than me.

Derek called the apartment on occasion, but I always had Nancy, Jean, or Bette tell him I was flying or in Ohio or just anything. I wasn't going to put myself in a situation to be hurt like that again.

One late night I ran up to Parker's to grab a bite to eat and happened to see Derek in the bar. He motioned for me to come in, but I acted like I didn't see him. I was about to leave - without my food. I had not expected to see him there - he came over and asked me to come in for a drink. I told Derek I had to get back to the apartment, and then I spotted Joe Moscati who motioned for me to come in.

I left Derek standing there, went over to Joe, hugged him, and started talking. Derek was flabbergasted. He followed me and said to Joe, "She's going to be sitting with me, Joe. You are welcome to join us." Joe looked at me and could tell that had not been my intention, but I didn't want to cause a fuss, so I told Joey I would talk to him later and went to sit with Derek.

Derek ordered a drink, and I had a coke. I could tell by his breath that he had already had a few drinks. "So, why don't you ever return my calls?" he asked me.

"I hear you are dating quite a few Stewardesses and agents. Why would you need for me to return your calls?'

He was surprised I had heard what he had been up to. "I am just dating, no one special." I just ignored his comment. "Are you seeing someone now?"

"I'm dating, Derek. There are few people that I am seeing."

He lowered his eyes to stare at his drink and replied with a very faint, "Oh, that's nice. Are you seeing someone special?"

I was so uncomfortable talking about this; I excused myself to go to the bathroom and ran right into Joe coming out of the men's' room. He put his hands on my shoulders and said, "If Derek doesn't treat you right, I wish you'd give me another chance."

"Joey, I am not dating him. He just happened to see me come into Parker's. We haven't been out in months."

"Girl, I know where your heart is, but if you ever change your mind, call me." Joe squeezed me with a big hug just as Derek walked to the men's' room. He stopped dead in his tracks and glared at Joe and me.

I went into the ladies' room and snickered at the look I had just seen on Derek's face when he saw Joey hugging me. "You deserve to be hurt, you ass," I thought to myself. "Now you know how much I hurt that night." I came out and went to the table to finish my coke, thanked Derek, and left. He just sat there, and I could feel his eyes on my back. I felt pretty good about myself just then. I may have still been licking my wounds, but I didn't want him to know it.

Derek called one day, and I happened to answer the phone. I had such a terrible case of laryngitis that I could barely whisper and was so glad I wasn't scheduled to fly for a few days. It was the end of one month and the beginning of another, and I had about four days off.

Derek expressed concern over my illness and told me that he hoped I felt better. I hung up the phone and kind of stared at it. Why had he called? He didn't ask me out. He didn't ask to come over. He didn't talk but a few minutes. Why did he bother? Oh well, I grabbed a cup of tea and sat in the front room.

In came Jeanie and Nancy. "Bev-a-lee, I know you haven't felt good for a few days, but you need to get out of the apartment and go to Mass with us for a few days," Jeanie said.

I looked at them suspiciously and asked, "This doesn't have anything to do with Bobby Bernhardt, does it?"

"Why, Bev-a-lee, what makes you ask a thing like that?"

"Jeanie, I am not going out with that man again, and I am more than sure he doesn't want to go out with me either. Why would he? I am sure he thinks I am just about the most immature woman he has ever been with in his whole life. Isn't that what he said?"

"Actually, he really does want to go out with you again. He finds you to be a challenge, and he loves challenges."

"Are you nuts?" I asked her, as she burst out laughing. "Am I just the biggest source of laughter for you and Nancy to make fun of, or what?"

"No, seriously, Richard and I are going up to New Hampshire for the weekend, and Bobby asked me if I would ask you to come along."

"No, I will not!" I exclaimed with what was left of my voice.

"Come on, Bev-a-lee, he wants a chance to redeem himself with you. Poor guy has really been pining over you since you left him standing on the doorstep in front of my little sister. He was sure you were an Olympic track star the way you flew past him after you got out of the car."

"Damn, Jean, did he tell you everything?"

"Yes, even the fact that you held on to the door handle all the way back to my house."

"Okay, so he must be nuts! Why would he want to spend a weekend with me?" My throat was really hurting, and I wanted to end this conversation.

"I don't know, but he really, really does. Can I tell him that you will come with me?" she tried one more time.

I said "No," but Jeanie didn't give up all evening. She really wanted to see Richard, and the only way her Mom would let her go was if another girl went along. Nancy had a family get-together she absolutely couldn't miss – that's why I had to go. Jeanie was almost in tears when I finally agreed. After she jumped up and called Richard, Jeanie hugged me and asked if there was anything she could do to help me pack.

I just shook my head and whispered that I would take care of it tomorrow before we left. Jeanie was so happy, and I thought I must have really lost it. Why in the world would I have agreed to go off on a trip with a man that scared the beegeezus out of me? Too late now, I guess, so I would go.

When I got up the next morning, I tried everything in my power to get out of going. All night, I had thought about the whole weekend date, and I didn't want to do it. When Jeanie got down on her knees and starting begging, all in fun of course, I felt obligated to keep my word, so off we went.

I stopped and bought cough drops before the flight left for Boston, while Jeanie and Nancy proceeded to our gate. On the way, they saw Derek working a flight at another gate. They purposely got within earshot of him and started talking about me going with them to Boston. They mentioned Bob and how crazy he was about me and that we were all going to New Hampshire together.

Derek walked over to them asking, "Bev is going to Massachusetts with you two? I just called her yesterday, and she could barely speak. Why isn't she staying here in New York to get better?"

"I don't know for sure, Derek," said Jeanie. "I just don't think she wanted to disappoint Bob because he was so looking forward to this trip." Derek acted upset and turned around and walked back to the gate.

When Jeanie and Nancy spotted me walking down the terminal, they both rushed over and grabbed me, then shoved me past the gate where Derek was working, giggling like two hyenas. After they told me what was so funny, I grabbed both of them and hugged them tight. He so deserved to hear that. Yeah!!

Bob and Richard showed up at Jeanie's house about an hour after we had arrived. I still didn't have much of a voice. Bob was much nicer looking than I remembered, but he still scared me, although I tried not to show it. He ruined it when Jeanie informed him that I wouldn't be talking too much because I had laryngitis and was trying to save my voice. Bob smirked and asked, "She can't talk?"

Jeanie answered by saying I could but not very much or very loudly. He looked right at me and grinned, "I guess that means you can't scream either, huh?"

I flashed my panic-stricken eyes in Jeanie's direction, and she slapped Bob on the arm. "Oh, Bev-a-lee, he is such a kidder."

Oh Lord, what have I done? I asked myself.

The four of us took off for New Hampshire. Richard and Jean were all snuggled up in the front seat. I sat in the back a little closer to Bob than I had on our first date but not much. He had to know I was scared of him, but I honestly think he thought it was kind of cute. We talked a little, but not too much. I kept looking out the window trying to figure out why in the world this man would want to take a trip with me.

The scenery was absolutely beautiful. We ate in a really quaint restaurant along the way, with fishing gear and ship equipment on the walls. The food was delicious, and Bob wasn't making stupid noises to embarrass me.

Bob and I were getting along pretty well. When we got to the motel, we got two adjoining rooms, and the four of us all went into one room to hang out.

We were all visiting, laughing, and having fun when Richard got up and walked across the room, picked up his suitcase, unlocked the adjoining door, and went into the other room. I didn't think much about it - I told you I really was naïve - until Jeanie got up, grabbed her bag and followed. She closed the door behind her and locked it.

I bet my eyes got as big as saucers. Here I was in a bedroom with a man ten years older than me, and I had a feeling he would have a difficult time with rejection. I was furious with myself for doing this. I honestly thought Jeanie and I would share a room with Bob and Richard in the other. Scouts Honor, I did think that. Oh brother, now what was I going to do?

Bobby started to get undressed, and I stopped him in his tracks. "Look, I did a favor for Jeanie so that she could be here with Richard. I know I am stupid, but I never dreamed that she would not be sharing a room with me. I am not going to sleep with you, Mr. Bernhardt, so you might as well get that out of your mind if you think that is going to happen." My throat was killing me, and I was talking way too much.

He looked at me, put his clothes back on, and slept on the couch. I don't think I slept a wink because I kept thinking he would sneak over and attack me in the middle of the night. I pretended to be asleep when Richard tiptoed into our room, looked at Bob, and asked "So how'd it go?"

Bob sat up on the couch and said, "If you ever fix me up with the Blessed Virgin Mary again, so help me, I'll kill you, Richie." I had to push my face into the pillow because hearing Bob say that with his accent was absolutely hysterical.

We had fun sightseeing and goofing off the next day, and we were tired when we returned to our room. Again, I got into bed with all of my clothes on, only this time I told Bob he could share the bed as long as he knew it was only to sleep. He reluctantly got in and turned his back to me, and we both fell asleep.

On the way back to Boston, I began to trust Bob, and I respected him for not getting ugly with me. Maybe I was a little refreshing for him too, even though I know he was probably frustrated with me. When I kissed him when we got back to Jeanie's, Bob looked at me and said in a funny way, "Now the little whore wants to get romantic?" We all burst out laughing. (Bob and I have remained friends for years and still keep in touch. We adore each other and would do anything in the world for one another.)

When I got back to New York, the phone was ringing off the hook. It was Derek, and he acted all "huffy." He asked what was wrong with me going off to Boston feeling and sounding the way I did. I told him it was none of his business, and I didn't go to Boston, I went to New Hampshire. Derek got really quiet and said he hoped I felt better and hung up.

When I came in from a flight a few days later in the middle of the afternoon, I was exhausted and ready to get home. The agent meeting my flight, Bill Garner, came onto the plane and told me that Derek Schoenmann wanted to see me in the ACC room, which was where the ticket agents did all of their paperwork from the flights. I told Bill I didn't think so.

The ACC room was right beside the gate I had just deplaned from, and Bill grabbed me by the hand, threw open the door to the room, and more or less pushed me in. I was so embarrassed as I half-stumbled, half-fell into the room. All of the agents looked up, including Derek.

I felt my face go beet-red and my rash start to spread all over my chest and face. I looked at Derek and blurted out, "Did you want to see me for something?" Before he could even answer, I answered my own question by saying, "I didn't think so," and started out the door. Derek yelled at me to wait, caught up with me, then asked if he could come over to my apartment to talk.

I was dumbfounded; whatever could Derek want to talk to me about? I couldn't imagine, but I told him okay and asked what time he would be getting off work. He told me around 6 or 6:30 p.m., so I said I would see him then.

The whole time I was talking to Derek, I could feel my heart pounding. I just didn't understand why he made me feel this way.

I had to go through one of the hangers so I could walk home, and I swung my suitcase in the air, dancing and singing a song from *South Pacific* titled "Wonderful Guy." I can't sing, but I just felt like I wanted to. I heard some laughter coming from a catering truck that had just driven into the hangar. One of the guys leaned out the window and said, "I wish I were that guy." I laughed and took off running, in my heels no less, to the front of the terminal and half way home.

Thank goodness no one was home. I got cleaned up, searching my mind over and over for what could possibly be so important that Derek would ask to talk to me in person.

At 6:15, I heard Derek walking up the stairs and slowly went to the door when he knocked. When he came in, Derek went over to the couch, patted the seat beside him, and asked me to sit down. I really was curious.

Derek looked into my eyes and told me he had really missed dating me, and he wanted us to see each other again. I was so surprised, you could have knocked me over with a feather! I just sat there staring at him, fighting the urge to ask him if he was back with me because his dates with Phyllis and Ellen, the ticket agent, had fallen through.

He seemed so sincere and honest that I decided not to be a smart-ass. Derek told me he had really missed me, cared about me, and didn't realize how much until I went to Boston with Jean and Nancy. I did not expect this at all! I wanted to tell him I missed him too, and, while the guys I had been dating were really great, they weren't him. I wanted to tell him I would rather be with him than anyone else in the world. I didn't, though, because I was not going to set myself up for him to drop another bomb on me.

I remained calm even though I wanted to grab Derek around the neck and plant a big kiss on him. I told him we could try to see each other and see what happened. When he smiled and leaned over and kissed me, I thought I was going to faint right there.

For the next several months, Derek and I dated pretty steadily, and I fell right back in love with him.

Only this time, I knew I had to go back to Columbus and tell Alphie. I thought this was the real thing with Derek, and I couldn't go on living a lie.

I set out to go home and tell Alphie that I couldn't get married now or ever. Derek walked me to the airplane and stepped in the cockpit for an instant, pulling me along with him; he kissed me tenderly and told me he would miss me and to hurry back. I was surprised because Derek had always made a point of not showing any affection toward me while I was in my uniform. Of course, he was the only one in uniform, but still it was so unlike Derek to act this way. I was starting to believe he really did care.

Mom and Dad met my flight because Alphie was at work. When I. told them I was going to give Alphie back his ring, Mom begged me to let her keep it just in case I changed my mind. She reminded me I had actually paid for it because after Alphie had initially purchased the ring, he lost his job, and I had to pay it off. Alphie told me he would repay the money to me when he got a new job, but that just seemed silly to me. We thought of each other's money as "our money," so I didn't really care who paid for it.

I still felt like giving the ring back to Alphie was the thing to do, maybe as a gesture of closure.

When Alphie knocked on the door, my heart sank! I knew this was going to kill him. We had talked less and less on the phone, and I never seemed to be able to get home when he wanted me to, so I believed Alphie knew our breakup was about to happen.

As Alphie and I got in the car together, all the of memories of us came rushing into my mind: our first date at the drive-in, how he loved to put hickeys on my neck to embarrass me, our silly pretend fights. Alphie was so different inside than the exterior he tried to convey to outsiders. He was gentle, kind, fun, romantic, and would make a wonderful husband and father. He had always seemed to adore me. What was I thinking?

Still, I knew in my heart I didn't love Alphie the way I should for us to be together and have a future. If I did, how could I feel the way I did about Derek? Although I didn't want to end it with Alphie, I just had to. I thought I wanted a life with another man, and I had to be honest, which was something I hadn't been for over a year.

As I started to talk to Alphie, he just sat there staring out the front window. We were supposed to go out for dinner, but we never left the driveway. I honestly believed he knew this was coming, and I think he had prepared himself.

Alphie listened as I told him I wasn't ready to get married, and I didn't know if or when I would be. This wasn't fair to him, and we ought to end our engagement. If he found someone else to spend the rest of his life with, I certainly would understand. I told Alphie I still loved him and that I always would, that he would forever have a place in my heart.

His eyes teared up, and he wouldn't look at me. I finally reached over and put my hands on his face and made him look at me. A tear went running down his cheek, as he just stared at me. "I guess I always knew this day would come," he said. "The minute I saw you get on that airplane, I knew we would not be spending our future together."

Now it was my turn to cry. I felt awful, and the tears poured down my face. I felt like I was choking. When I tried to kiss him, Alphie pulled away from me as I thought he might. I had so many mixed emotions. I would always love him, and, Lord, what if I was making a mistake? I knew his heart was breaking as badly as mine.

We sat there, both of us crying and not looking at each other. He finally raised his head and said, "You have to tell Kaki."

I looked at him with great dread on my face. "Alf, there is no way I can go to your house and tell your folks. I just can't."

"They have been expecting it for quite a while any way," Alphie said. "So it probably wouldn't be as hard as you think."

Still I knew there was no way I could look at Mary and Kaki and tell them I was not going to marry their son. When Gary married Cheryl, Kaki put his arm around me and said, "I just can't wait for your and Alf's wedding day." I could still see that big ole grin on his face.

No way could I go tell them it was not going to happen, even if they suspected it. "I can't do it, Alf, I just can't," I repeated.

I felt awful inside. I couldn't stop crying and neither could Alphie. "I guess there is nothing more to say, is there?" he asked me.

"Oh, my God, Alphie; I wish I had never gone for that interview. We wouldn't be going through this right now."

"But you did, and we are. You seem to have made up your mind."

"What if I'm making a gigantic mistake?" I asked him.

He looked at me and told me I was.

I was so mixed up. "Well if I am, maybe somehow we will still end up together. We don't know what the future holds for us, now do we?"

"Bev, you know I am a betting man, and I'm thinking the odds aren't in our favor right now." Lordy, he was being so stern.

"Alf, we don't know that for sure, now do we?"

"I have to go," he blurted out. I looked over at Alphie and realized he was having a heck of a time trying not to bawl, and I knew I couldn't take looking at him, or feeling the way I felt, for another second.

"Alright," I said, quietly. "I'll always love you, Alf." He just shook his head and put the car in reverse.

I got out and went into the house, where Mom was sitting on the couch. I said, "Oh God, Mom, I hope I haven't just made the biggest mistake of my life."

She smiled and said, "Time will tell, Hon, time will tell."

I was only able to stay home one more day. I had planned to stay for two but just couldn't stand it. There were too many memories of Alphie in my house. I smiled to myself as I remembered all the pictures of us that he ruined by giving Dad "the finger." Alphie was always so uncomfortable having his picture taken that he constantly flipped Daddy off. It was just a joke between the two of them because Daddy knew Alphie pretty well by then, and he wasn't offended. I remembered getting engaged that Christmas and all of our wrestling matches and pretend fights on the couch. I just had to get out of there fast.

I called Derek and told him I was coming home sooner than expected. I felt guilty for never telling Derek about Alphie, but I just never thought it was the right time or even necessary, since I didn't know what I planned to do with my future. Why complicate it even more by telling Derek I had an engagement ring in my jewelry box? That I had been untrue to my fiancé and dated a bunch of guys trying to figure out what to do with my life? I just didn't want to discuss it with Derek. He seemed happy to learn I was coming back early.

Derek met me at Kennedy airport, and we drove out to his apartment. I was so glad to see him, but I couldn't get Alphie's face out of my mind. I felt so bad! I forced myself to concentrate on Derek and prayed I had made the right choice.

From then on, Derek and I spent more and more time together. It was late October and starting to get cold in New York. When I had first arrived in New York, it was March, and spring was right around the corner, so I had no idea what severe weather there could be in Jackson Heights.

We had so many snow days. It was beautiful and reminded me of Columbus and all of the winters I spent growing up there. I loved the snow, especially since I didn't have to drive in it. It was great just to sit and look out the window of our apartment and watch the big flurries fall inch after snowy white inch on the front yard - the same yard where we had spent many days getting sun, having cookouts, and getting to know our neighbors.

We really had some fun people in our complex, and you could always count on one of them to be having a get-together. Now the yard was barren and covered in beautiful white snow.

A blizzard hit New York in '67 that closed all of the airports. Thousands of people were stranded both in and out of the three airports. Hotels were filled to capacity, but some of their employees couldn't get to work because they lived too far away and were unable to drive, so Nancy, Jeanie, Bette, and I went to help out at the Travelers Hotel, the hotel where we had stayed when we first arrived in New York. Because flights were getting cancelled, we wouldn't be getting paid, so we had to make some money, and the hotel was delighted to see us. Stewardesses stranded in downtown New York were doing the same thing. It was a strange but fun experience.

One night Derek and I went for a long walk in the middle of the street in front of our apartment, slipping, sliding, and laughing as we nearly fell several times. It was a magical night I enjoyed so much.

A few days later, I was scheduled to fly a trip on a BAC 1-11, a British airplane American Airlines had purchased to do short multi-hops from ROC (Rochester), SYR (Syracuse), LGA, and BUF (Buffalo). I hated the plane with a passion because I was so tall, and it was so small. I felt like an Amazon, and when the passengers boarded, they sort of snickered. I could look directly into the overhead racks, and it seemed that every time I had to lean over to give something to a passenger, I would hit my head on the overhead compartment that held the air vents, call buttons, and oxygen masks. It was a nightmare for a tall girl like me.

That trip was going to be even more unusual because the girl I was flying with, Nancy Selken, was a redhead who was as tall as me. We were going to be quite a shock to the passengers when they boarded and saw the two of us. Surely, they would think they were boarding "Amazon Air."

It was Nancy's first trip, and, unlike my first trip, I wanted it to be a pleasant experience for her. We liked each other right away when we met in Operations. I could tell she was a nervous wreck, and I kept telling her everything was going to be fine.

Our trip consisted of several multi-stops, about fifteen all together over our three-day trip, with short layovers in Rochester and Buffalo. I warned her that the flights were pretty much always going to be full. This meant we really had to hustle to serve that Danish sweet roll and beverage to sixty-nine people in what seemed like a few seconds; it was actually only about twenty to twenty-five minutes after takeoff, if that long.

Nancy was terrified, and I tried my best to encourage her.

When we boarded the plane, I made an effort to have as much ready as possible before we took off. I set up the galley with various supplies, putting most of the items in storage compartments so we would have them close at hand and could get them in a hurry. I stashed a lot of the items in the ovens since they wouldn't be used for this service. Once we were in flight, there was a folding table at the forward entry door you could pull out of the closet and fasten to the opposite side above our Stewardess jump seat. On this table, we stored as much as we possibly could: creams, sugars, sodas, an ice container, trays for the cups, and sweet rolls.

Under the folding serving table, I pulled out the Service Kit that had all sorts of "just in case" supplies such as aspirin, matches, band aids, burn ointment, playing cards, seat-occupied cards, airline schedules, etc. I would generally place the Service Kit directly under the serving table so if I needed any of those items, I wouldn't have to go looking for them.

I briefed Nancy on how we were going to do the service once the smoking public announcement had been made. We were off and running.

"Miss, I need an aspirin," one of my passengers asked me in the middle of the service. I physically ran to the forward entry door to get under the table and retrieve the aspirin in the Service Kit.

The next thing I heard was a loud noise, and then I felt tremendous pain as the tray table hit me in the back of my head, followed by all the items on top falling on me.

When I woke up, the F/O was pushing the cockpit door against my body. Poor Nancy was crying, and a male passenger was pulling my arm trying to get me out of the way of the door. The passenger leaned over me and asked if I could hear him. I felt terrible; I was dizzy and my head was throbbing. I felt like I had been in a collision with a semi-truck.

The F/O got past me, and then he and Nancy picked up all the items that were around and on top of me. After that, the two of them and a few passengers picked up the trays. Half of the cabin didn't even get served. I wasn't sure exactly what we had accomplished.

I just sat on the floor feeling woozy. The F/O had to return to the cockpit as we were getting close to landing. Everything got picked up, and I managed to get into my jump seat and get my harness strapped. We were on descent in what seemed to be a matter of seconds.

As the passengers deplaned, I kept telling them I was alright, that I was more embarrassed than anything. But my head really hurt.

Before he went to Operations, the Captain, Tom Bender, asked me what I wanted to do. Did I want to be taken off the flight? I told him, "Oh no, I'm fine really. I am just a little unsteady."

Since we weren't at a crew base, it would have delayed the whole trip. Crew Schedule would have to get a Reserve Stewardess from LaGuardia to the airport and then to Rochester on the next flight. That could have meant several hours delay. My head was splitting, but I didn't want to be taken off my trip. Was I being a martyr or just stupid?

The Captain and F/O kept telling me if I didn't want to take the trip, they'd tell Crew Schedule and get me replaced for tomorrow. I insisted I was fine and that I only had a headache.

I filled out my accident report. I didn't have sense enough to go to medical there in Rochester, and with the rest of the crew as junior as I was, they didn't really think about it either. Everyone just wanted to continue their trip. Of course, Nancy never thought of me going to medical. She was too busy being even more terrified and didn't recall anything like this ever being discussed in training. Although Nancy would have a unique story to share with her roommates, she just wanted to get her first trip behind her like we all had wanted to.

The four of us ate together that evening, although I didn't have much of an appetite. I just wanted to get to the room, take some more aspirin, and go to sleep.

Captain Bender said, "Bev, I think we've made a big mistake. When we get back to LaGuardia, I want you to go see Dr. Shocken, and I'll get you replaced for the remainder of the trip. We should have done this earlier." I knew he was right, but I really didn't want to make any waves. I just wanted to fly my trip.

Before the flight the next day, F/O Jason Smith rang for me to come to the cockpit. He informed me we had the very same aircraft we'd had the day before and that the table had been written up in the log book for months. The fact that it had collapsed several times before had been noted, but sadly, it was "Checked and Deferred" by maintenance. He showed me the log book, which was a big metal folding-type book that stayed with the airplane to record any and all repairs done to it, from a screw missing in the galley to work done on an engine. Apparently, the holes in the wall that held the extended pieces of metal on the table had worn down and were no longer a tight fit.

"Don't use that table today, Bev." F/O Smith said. "Be sure to tell the company that this table had been written up numerous times and had not been fixed for almost two months." This was the case sometimes; an item would not get fixed until the aircraft went to Tulsa, Oklahoma for an overhaul. This was one of those items that didn't seem to be that important.

I made it to LaGuardia. And I was glad to see the Reserve Stewardess waiting for my flight. My headache was worse, and my vision was getting blurry. I went to see Dr. Shocken at medical.

I didn't have a lot of faith in Dr. Shocken. All the gals said the only thing he was good for was to give out birth control pills or diet pills. The company was so strict about our weight that when I first started, a supervisor might see you in Operations signing in for your trip and actually tap you on the shoulder, bring you into her office, and have you get on a scale. If you were overweight, you could be suspended until you lost the three or five pounds. It was really scary especially until you got off initial probation. During that six month period, the company could fire you for almost anything, and you had no recourse to get your job back.

Many girls went to Dr. Shocken to keep their weight down. Jean Marie was one of his frequent visitors. Although she never looked overweight to me, she was constantly being asked to come for a weigh-in. The thought of one of his girls getting pregnant was more than poor Dr. Shocken could bear, so he handed out birth control pills like M&M's.

Dr. Shocken examined me, wrote up a report, gave me some pain medicine, and sent me home. No one was in the apartment when I got there. Great! I climbed into bed as fast as I could peel off my uniform. I took the pills the doctor had given me and went to sleep hoping I would feel 100% better when I awoke.

Instead, I woke up to the sound of Bette's voice yelling, "Shit, Bev. What are you doing home? I nearly had a heart attack when I opened the door and saw a body lying in the bed. I thought you were supposed to be in Rochester tonight."

Before I could answer, she continued, "You should have at least left the light on in the front room to let someone know there'd be somebody in the apartment."

I sat up. Lordy, it was dark. I must have slept longer than I thought. My head was really killing me now "Bet, I had an accident."

"Oh shit, you didn't have an emergency landing did you? Oh, fuck, I'd die!"

"No Bet, not that. I was working this trip..."

Before I could finish, Bette interrupted, "Damn, I forgot all about Jack. He is still in the front room."

I looked at her inquisitively. "Jack Pearson, the Flight Engineer from my trip. He commutes from Nashville and I told him that he could stay here tonight. The weather was so bad that his flight home got cancelled."

"You had better be careful, Bet, if Ron sees you, he'll get jealous."

"Ron's on a three-day trip. He left yesterday morning. Besides, I'm free, white, and over twenty-one. I will date whomever I please."

"Ok, Bet, ok, when will Jean and Nancy be in?" I asked.

"Sometime tomorrow I think. Are you hurt or anything? Do you need me to do something?" she inquired.

"No, well yes, I guess I am hurt. I got hit in the back of the head with that serving table that comes out of the closet on the BAC 1-11. It collapsed while I was under it getting something out of the Service Kit. I was knocked out for a little while."

"What did 'Dr. Quacks-a lot' have to say? Did he give ya birth control pills?"

I had to snicker, "No, Bet, he didn't. He gave me some pain meds that don't seem to be working too well. I am going to take another one and try to go back to sleep. So get in there with Jack what's his name."

"I can at least get you some water," She did.

"Thanks, Bet, I'll see ya tomorrow."

"Oh, ma'am; if you need anything, please don't hesitate to call," she smartly stated. I threw one of the pillows in her direction as she slammed the door.

"Thanks a lot, Bet; that really helped my headache."

"Sorry!" she yelled from the other side of the door.

"Bette, keep it down will ya?"

"Sorry again," she whispered. I dozed off.

I never heard Bette come into sleep, so she must have slept in Jean and Nancy's room. I didn't get up until 11:00 a.m. — whew, those pills must have been stronger than I thought since I slept so long. It was just a shame they didn't take the headache away. I stumbled into the kitchen thinking I was hungry, and that if I ate some toast, I might feel better.

There was a note from Bette: "Damn airline can't live without me. Screw Schedule (as she called Crew Schedule) called at about 6:15 a.m. for a 7:05 sign in; didn't help that I got to bed at 2:00 a.m. I won't be back until tomorrow. If Buddy calls, tell him I'll call him when I get back. Take care, Love Bets." I really liked Bette even though she was nuts.

The phone rang. It wasn't Buddy but my supervisor, Pam Danaher. "Bev, what happened? I just got Dr. Shocken's report."

I told her about the table and how I progressively got worse as the trip continued. She took down my information, asked me to write her a report and one for the Union. I told her I would.

Then she shocked me by asking, "When do you expect to be back to work?'

I felt like saying, if I had a medical degree, I wouldn't be working as a Stewardess, but I controlled my desire to be a smart-ass. I told her I would let her know just as soon as I felt better "Right now my head hurts quite a bit. I will go see the doctor again if I am not better by tomorrow." She told me that was a good idea. Duh!!!!

I ate my toast and took some more Darvon. Feeling sorry for myself, I called Mom and Dad who began to worry. I probably shouldn't have called them, but that's what kids do sometimes no matter what age: call their parents. Mom offered to come to New York to help me, but I told her I thought I'd be fine in a day or so.

Mom suggested I see another doctor, not just a company doctor. I was beginning to think so too, but didn't know any and hated to get out and around in New York, especially in the winter.

I was afraid of getting lost. I wished I could have been more like Jeanie and Nancy, who were always on the go. I wanted to ask them to show me their secrets for finding their way to so many places, but our schedules were always conflicting. Plus, they took the subway a lot, and with my claustrophobia, there was no way I was going to go underground and ride on a train between two walls to get somewhere.

I told Mom and Dad I would find someone who knew a doctor if I didn't feel any better in a day or two.

As I put the phone back on the hook, it rang again. It was the calm, quiet, soft voice of Don. He asked me about my trip, and I told him the story. He said I should have gotten off the plane when I first got hurt, regardless of if it was a crew base or not, and gone to see a doctor. I told him he was probably right, but I just wanted to fly my trip, and I honestly thought I would be alright. He told me if I didn't feel better by tomorrow, he could take me to a doctor he knew in Manhasset.

I told Don I'd go with him to his doctor, but according to my supervisor, I first had to go see Dr. Shocken at AA Medical again. Don told me the same thing about Dr. Shocken I already knew, but I told him I would go to appease American Airlines.

Don said he was going to let me off the phone but that he would give me a call the next morning. In the meantime, if I needed him, I was to be sure and call any time night or day. I thanked Don and told him I would call if I needed him. He really was a thoughtful guy.

As soon as Derek heard what happened, he stopped over to check on me and bring me some food. I told him I was just going to try and sleep and that a friend of mine had offered to take me to a doctor they knew if I didn't feel like I was getting any better. There was really no need to mention that it was a pilot I had dated. Derek was glad someone knew a doctor other than the company doctor. He was sorry he didn't know any, but he hadn't been in New York much longer than I had.

Derek kissed me and told me he would call me the next day, but if I needed anything, to let him know right away. I appreciated it, but I really didn't feel like having company of any kind at that moment. I just wanted to go back to sleep.

The next day, I didn't feel any better, so I called Don. He took me to his doctor who checked me out and told me to go to the hospital. Don took me to the hospital, and after a bunch of tests and x-rays, the hospital doctor concluded I had a concussion and needed to stay in the hospital. It was bad enough for me to stay in the hospital for three days, far away from my apartment, but I also had to be watched over by a bunch of nurses and doctors. In addition to not being too crazy about hospitals, I was even more anxious because the headaches were getting more intense and frequent.

I was surprised when Joey showed up at the hospital. He had called the apartment, and Bette had told him I was in the hospital. He even brought flowers. Joe was actually a really nice guy, and I just loved to tease him. We basically started dating that way, and our relationship stayed in that mode. He made me laugh a lot, which I needed in my life right then. Even though it hurt when I laughed, it still seemed worth it and took my mind off being in the hospital.

Don came and visited too, with his wonderful, reassuring self. He even snuck me in a pizza. Don told me he was there for me no matter when or whatever I needed, and I knew he meant it. What a great guy.

The funny thing was when Derek showed up, all of the nurses called him "Mr. Golden." I guess they thought he was my husband, but if that were so, who in the world did they think Joe and Don were? I found that to be so odd - of the three male visitors, the nurses all thought Derek was my husband. Maybe it was because he came to take me home.

I called Mom and asked her to come to New York to be with me. She came the very next day using one of my passes. I felt bad she had to miss work, but then again, that's what you do for your kids.

Joe picked her up at LaGuardia and brought her over to the apartment. I had shown him a picture of her so he would recognize her when she arrived.

I was so glad to see my Mom. I grabbed her and cried like a little girl. It seemed every time I had ever needed her for anything in my life, she was always there. No matter how small or how devastating, she would be at my side. I knew I could always count on her to make it all better. I wished Dad could have come also, but someone had to be there with Charmaine.

Mom stayed with me for a week. She seemed a little confused at all of the attention her daughter was getting from three different men. Joe met her at the airport and took us out to some of his favorite spots, including Coney Island. Don took us to the doctor and out to eat several times. Derek came over and did whatever he could do to help, and he also took us out for dinner.

One day Mom asked me, "Hon, which one of these men are you interested in?" I just sat on the bed and shook my head. I told her I really liked Joey because he was so much fun. Don was wonderful, so kind, and caring, but I felt sure that my heart belonged to Derek.

When I was in Columbus, I hadn't shared with Mom that Derek was one of the reasons I had broken my engagement to Alphie. I just didn't want to have to explain myself to her at that moment, especially since I wasn't sure I had done the right thing and wasn't in the mood to hear "I told you so."

I didn't want Mom to think I had jumped from being engaged to a man I had known for two years to having a serious relationship with a guy I had only known a few months. I sure didn't want to tell her about what Derek had said that night when I told him I loved him. Mom would probably have told me to drop him like a hot rock.

I told Mom I wasn't really serious with any of them, but I did care a lot for Derek.

However, I would not be willing to give up my job for any of them. I absolutely loved my job, all the places I got to visit, and the different types of people. I had even seen a real movie star in Los Angeles! James Garner was every bit as good looking in person as I ever imagined he was in his TV series, *Maverick*. I giggled when I told Mom that Mr. Garner was on the opposite moving walkway going towards the gate area when I was on the other moving walkway headed out to the front of the airport. I caught his eye, and we both turned around at the same time for a second look, then grinned at each other. I was so proud I made James Garner give me a second look!

Mom and I had grown up on movie magazines together. We read *Photoplay* and *Modern Screen*, and I knew who Elizabeth Taylor was before I was a teenager. One of my greatest treats as a young girl was being allowed to watch the Academy Awards show with Mom. We would sit there together and "ooh and ahh" over the dresses and hairstyles of the actresses. Mom would give me all the scoop on who was dating whom and who was having affairs, even though when Mom said "affair," I didn't tell her I really didn't know what she meant. In those days, that was not the kind of thing to discuss with your Mom.

If I remember correctly, the magazines were twenty-five cents back then, but it was still a challenge to save the money to go to the Rexall drugstore to buy one, or on occasion, two of them to share. I tore out pictures of my favorite stars and pinned them all over the walls at our old home on Hudson Street. There was wallpaper in my room, but you couldn't see it for all of the star photos. My third fantasy choice for a career would have been to be a movie star, after singing (which I could not do) and writing. Writing was something that always came easily to me, and while it's debatable whether I am any good at it or not, I sure have enjoyed it over the years.

Growing up, Mom and I were really close! Daddy worked at night, and there was just too much of an age difference to share with Charmaine. Mike could have cared less about his big sister's boyfriend or friend problems. He just liked to be annoying and make some spending money by selling pages of my diaries to the fellows I was dating. The little shit!!!

Mom, Dad, and I visited about Mike and Navy boot camp. In September 1967, Mike had made it through boot camp in the unbelievable cold of the Great Lakes Area and was then stationed on an aircraft carrier, the USS Forestall. It was hard for me to believe this was my little brother.

Around the time I got hurt and couldn't fly, Mike had finally gotten to come home, although not for long because he had to get back to the ship. Mom was so relieved to spend that time with him, and I was just sorry I hadn't been able to make it home to see him.

Although Mom loved Bette, she wasn't quite as accepting of Jean Marie and Nancy. She didn't like it that Nancy wouldn't look you directly in the eye when she talked to you, and she said Jeanie was kind of a snob. Of course, I defended my roommates, telling her she hadn't really had a chance to get to know them.

I was sad to tell her my precious "Bette Bird" was transferring to BOS (Boston) to be near Buddy with whom she had finally actually fallen in love.

Shortly thereafter, Jean Marie and Nancy informed me they were putting their transfers in to Boston too. It would be about two months before they would leave, so I had better be looking for some roommates. I was hurt that none of them asked me if I wanted to go to Boston with them, but I guess they all knew I wouldn't go because I was getting really close to Derek.

Mom went home after that very short week. I cried pretty hard because it had been so great having her there with me. I didn't want to be alone, and although I knew she had to get back, that didn't make it any easier. Even though I was the oldest child, I liked feeling like the baby again. Mom did promise that she and Dad would both come to see me soon.

Since I still hadn't been cleared to return to flying, I was feeling pretty cooped up in the apartment.

Derek and I were seeing a lot of each other. When he spent the night, he had started sleeping in my bed with me. Derek would sleep in his boxers and t-shirt, and I always had on my pajamas, but he was in my bed, which really didn't sit well with Nancy and Jean.

They were so weird, making fun of me for being a virgin and then acting all pissy when Derek slept in my bed with me. Nancy and Jean had no right to judge me, but it seemed they did anyway. We were starting to have some real issues, and I was glad they had both gone to Massachusetts for the holidays.

Mom and Dad came up after Christmas to spend part of the holiday with me. With Nancy and Jean gone, I had the apartment to myself with Mom, Dad, and of course, Derek. Derek didn't sleep in my bed when they were there, however. He slept on the couch the few nights he worked late at LaGuardia and had to be back at the crack of dawn the next morning. Dad and Mom didn't seem to mind.

I think my parents liked Derek, but were a little leery of him because he came from a completely different background than I had. His parents were pretty well-to-do and belonged to a country club. Derek"s sister Pam had gone to Bryn Mar, and his other sister, Janet, would be going to a fancy school when she was old enough. Both of his parents were college grads, I believe. Neither of my folks graduated from High School, but to my amazement, Mom and Dad held their own when talking with Derek.

At the same time, I was dealing with a very traumatic issue involving Derek. One evening, November 12, to be exact, Derek and I were involved in some really serious necking. No one was home nor expected that night. We were making out on the couch when Derek suddenly stood up and offered me his hand. I looked at him rather strangely but put my hand in his and stood up too. I don't know why Derek laid on the floor, but I followed him. The next thing I knew he was taking off my sweater, and I didn't stop him. I was embarrassed that I was so flat-chested, but there was nothing I could do to change that.

My emotions were all out of sorts. I never ever considered having full blown sex with anyone, not until we got married. In High School, if a guy I was parked with tried to touch me anywhere that I thought was too personal, I elbowed him really hard. I guess word got around that I had the sharpest elbows at North High School, so not too many guys even tried. There were "fast" girls for that sort of thing.

One thing led to another, and the next thing I knew, Derek had slipped my slacks down and was on top of me. I panicked! I had never found myself in this position in my life. I was breathing heavy — not because I was excited but because I was terrified! Derek suddenly stopped and looked at me and asked if I had ever done this before. When I told him I hadn't, he pushed himself off me and laid down beside me. He started running his hand over my stomach and speaking gently to me, but I tensed up like a taut wire. Derek asked me to trust him and just let him touch my stomach. I breathed a deep breath, closed my eyes, clinched my hands into a fist and said he could. Derek ran his hand over my chest and stomach.

Then he leaned down, hugged me, and said we ought to get up and get our clothes pulled back up.

I was so grateful! I wasn't ready for this, but I didn't want to lose Derek either. I felt so guilty the rest of the evening. You've got to take into account here, folks, that I was raised in the 1950s and '60s and "good girls" just didn't have sex until they were married. I had many "battles royal" with Jimmie over sex. Alphie was never like that; he never pushed me. Now here I was getting almost naked in front of a man I was in love with, but I was filled with so much guilt that it made the whole experience unpleasant in some ways. I was just so scared!

One evening after Mom and Dad had gone home, Derek and I found ourselves again in a position devastating to me, only this time it was in the bedroom. Before I knew what happened, I was naked, and he was too. He got on top of me and I could feel him between my legs. I started to cry, and he immediately stopped and stared at me. I don't think Derek himself knew if he was angry, hesitant, or frustrated beyond belief. He sighed a deep sigh and pushed himself off me and laid beside me. I was bawling. Derek put his arm around me, and I laid my head on his chest. He held me and we fell asleep in each other's arms.

Whenever he wasn't with me, I relived that moment over and over in my head. I had such intense emotions that were all attacking me at once. Did I really love him? Yes, very much. Did I want to have sex with him? I thought I did, but I had never had sex before, so I wasn't sure what it would be like or if I would even know what to do. I didn't know any books to buy, and because I had never done "it" back in High School, I had no one to talk to about it.

Damn it, Bette, I wished you were there. I think she must have seen the look in my eyes when I was with Derek because she warned me before she left to be careful. Yet, I guess she and Jeanie figured that I had made it that long without sex, why would I do it now? Sex was never brought up around Nancy.

I thought I was ready one night, and I wasn't too embarrassed like I had been before when we got naked in the bed together. I started kissing Derek, and he responded by getting very aroused. The next thing I knew we found ourselves back in that position with him on top of me. This time he actually entered me, and I thought I would die. I had never experienced anything like that in my life and thought I was going to shatter into a million pieces because I was so tense and upset. Derek almost immediately pulled himself back.

This was more than I could handle; I froze and felt like I had gone into shock. Oh my God, what had I done? I was going to go straight to hell. I had just had sex with a man. How could I look myself in the mirror tomorrow? Would everyone know? How will I face my parents now that I had done "it"?

Derek fell off to sleep. I laid there as tears poured down my face trying to hide the sound of my crying in the pillow. I wasn't a bad girl. What if I just ruined any chance of marrying this man? Why would he want to marry me now? Why would any man? I wasn't a virgin anymore. Oh, my God!

I couldn't wait for Derek to leave the next day. I acted like I was asleep as he quietly tiptoed out of the bedroom to take a shower and go to work. I just laid there looking out the window with tears streaming down my face. What in the world had I done? I thought my life was ruined forever, and I didn't have anyone to talk to. I didn't even want to see my own face in the mirror. I never should have become a Stewardess and gone off into the big bad world and allowed this to happen to myself I should have stayed in Ohio, married Alphie, and then had sex. That was what you were supposed to do. I'd gotten it all wrong. What had I done?

I was so glad to get released from my head injury by the American Airlines medical department and return to flying on January 20. Although I was still having headaches, I needed to get back out there in the sky, and get back to doing the job I loved so much.

I was a different person then, but I hoped no one would know. I needed to be away from Derek for a while to think things over. Although I was tormented, I just couldn't confide in anyone. I felt like Derek really did care for me, but he never told me he loved me. I sure wasn't going to tell Derek how I felt again and take the chance of him reacting like he had before. That truly would have killed me.

I didn't know how I would handle our relationship now that we had crossed the line, now that I wasn't a virgin any longer. Worse yet, I wasn't sure I even liked this sex stuff. It had been painful, and I didn't understand why he pulled away from me after he had entered me. I didn't think I was ready for this aspect of our relationship to continue.

But it did. We found ourselves getting naked and "fooling around" often. Derek told me he wanted me to get some birth control pills. I felt so ashamed, but then I knew it would be twice as difficult to deal with if I suddenly found myself pregnant. Derek and I had not discussed having children or getting married.

I was one confused woman. Yes, I guess I was thinking of myself as a woman now, not a girl. Even though I was twenty-one, I had never felt like a woman.

Now it was different. I still wished I had someone to talk to. I went to Dr. Shocken and got some pills. I just hated the look he gave me over his glasses as he handed me the prescription. I felt so dirty. I knew he knew I was no longer a virgin. What he didn't know was that I had waited twenty-one years to do this. I hadn't jumped into bed when I was sixteen even though I certainly had the chance to. What did it matter anyway, really?

I took the pills for a few days, and they made me really sick. I didn't like the way they made me feel, so I took them fairly sporadically. Stupid me, I didn't know what I was doing. My periods were never regular, so I would have no way of knowing if I got pregnant until it was too late. I didn't want to get pregnant because I didn't know what would happen to me and Derek if I did, but I didn't want to take these pills either. So I didn't.

I awoke on a trip in St. Louis in a bed soaked with blood, feeling weak and in a panic. I thought I had started my period, but I had never seen so much blood. When I got up, I felt light-headed and faint. Fortunately, I had been flying number one Stewardess, so I hadn't had to share a room with anyone. I managed to get myself up, showered, and dressed for pick-up. I called housekeeping and told them that I had gotten my period, and I was putting the sheets in the tub. I don't know why I did that, but I did.

I had a feeling I might have been pregnant and lost it because I had never seen that much blood, and after that incident, I didn't get my period for a very long time.

I went back to Dr. Shocken, and he lectured me, telling me I might have been pregnant, and if I was going to continue this intercourse, I needed to become a responsible adult and either take the pills or get married. Yuck, no one had ever said the word "intercourse" to me, ever. It was the first time I had ever heard it spoken. It sounded awful.

I put my head down and walked out of his office with a new pack of pills. I suffered through the upset stomach, horrible headaches - just what I needed to be doing, taking a pill that made my headaches even worse - the bloating and all of the other side effects, but I was NOT going to get pregnant and have to quit flying either.

Don had transferred to Los Angeles sometime in early 1967. I missed his gentle ways and how kindly he spoke to me. I bet he would have been so ashamed of me for what I was doing with Derek. Don never once tried to get me to have a physical relationship with him. My first trip of 1967 was to Los Angeles, so I called him. He and I went out to dinner every time I was there. It was so much fun to see him, to talk and to pretend to be something I no longer was: a virgin. I knew it was silly, but I felt better about myself.

Don told me this girl he had been dating back in New York had transferred to Los Angeles, and he was feeling a lot of pressure from her about their relationship. Her name was Sally Grant, and she was a really pretty girl.

I flew with her one time, and she totally shocked me with what she said to one of our passengers. Apparently, they had gotten into a heated discussion over something he was angry about, and he kept saying something to Sally frequently throughout the flight. I could tell she was getting really upset. We took an awful lot from passengers as Stewardesses, but I think our submissive personalities was one reason the majority of us were hired. Anyway, Sally had had just about enough of Mr. Bad Manners, and she was about to lose it. I went and talked to him, and for some reason he didn't react to me the same way he did to Sally. Maybe it was because I was so much bigger and taller than she was. Who knows? He finally calmed down for the rest of the trip.

As he got off the plane, he was saying good-bye to Sally and me. When he got right in front of her, he said, "Good-bye, Sally dear." Sally looked him right in the eye and said, "I hope you break your ass." I nearly fainted. He obviously didn't hear what she said because he proceeded down the martin stand (a staircase on wheels that had to be used when there was no jetbridge). I looked at her, and she just shrugged her shoulders. I was kind of proud of Sally; she had stood up for herself in a way that most of us would never have thought of.

Don said they were dating, and he was pretty fond of her. I was glad for them but sort of sad too. Don and I were now just friends. I supposed it was for the best any way, considering my situation with Derek.

The next month I flew to Dallas, Texas. I hadn't been back there since I had graduated in March of '66. I called Bill Borland on a whim, and he asked if we could get together next time I was in Dallas. I told him sure. He was still a student at Baylor, and he actually hitchhiked from Waco to come to Dallas to see me. We had a lot of fun together, walking over to the Kennedy Plaza, and sitting and talking.

Bill asked me if flying had turned out to be everything I had hoped. I told him it definitely had and that I loved my job. He asked if I had met anybody special. I told him I had, and he said he was glad for me. I probably dropped my head a bit at the thought of what a gigantic prude I had been with poor Bill, but I really didn't regret it.

Bill had a girlfriend, and he was having a time of it juggling college and a relationship. I told him that I was happy for him. We went out two more times when I was there but just as friends.

Jean Marie and Nancy told me they were leaving on February 24 for Boston, so I had better find a roommate. Our landlord, Mel, agreed to help me find some other Stewardesses to share the apartment.

One day, Mel called to tell me that an Eastern Stewardess named Joyce Carter had stopped by the office looking for a place to rent, and he told her about me. She was really cute, beautiful blue eyes, a tremendous smile, and curly, curly light brown hair. She had a similar background to mine, from Cape Girardeau, Missouri, so we had that Midwestern thing going on for us.

Joyce and I seemed to get along right from the start. It was fun learning how things were done at Eastern vs. American. I failed to mention in the beginning that I had interviewed with Eastern in Miami, Florida before getting hired by American. I had received a letter of acceptance about the same time the one showed up from American, but I decided I wanted to fly for American because they flew to California. When I was a little girl, I was watching the *Wonderful World of Disney*, and they were showing film of Disneyland. When Jiminy Cricket sang "When You Wish Upon a Star," I would wish with all of my heart that I would get a chance to take my family there. I made up my mind that someday, somehow we would go there, and we did with my first non-revenue pass.

Joyce and I had both been flying since 1966 and loved our jobs. She used to crack me up with stories about the "San Juan Roach Coach" (the non-stop flights from New York to San Juan). I guess that plane was full to capacity and then some. She told me she loved working it though because it was so funny to hand out fruit to those folks and say "El Fruita" to them as they boarded. Joyce said it was her little way of "sticking it to them" for some of the crazy things they tried to sneak on the airplane within their suitcases and hanging bags. She shared with me that passengers had smuggled chickens and all sorts of things. I don't know if that was true or not, but she sure made me laugh every time she had a new tale to tell after one of those trips.

Joyce was in love with a Captain named Hank Cameron. They had one of those on-again, off-again relationships like Derek and I had originally. She would be so happy one day, and then her chin would be dragging the floor the next. They dated for quite a long time.

Joyce and I tried to find other roommates. We had one from American Airlines named Margaret Campbell who was a slob that neither one of us could stand. Margaret would make tomato soup and put kernel corn in it. It wasn't bad if she ate it all, but then she would go off on her trips and leave it sitting in the pan until one of us returned and saw it all crusted over on the stove. It was pretty gross! Plus, I don't think she ever cleaned the tub one time after she bathed. She didn't last long with us.

Then there was a girl named Candy Greenlee who slept with just about every pilot at our end of the complex. That didn't work out either.

We ultimately decided we didn't want any other roommates. Although it would be a financial struggle for both of us, we just didn't want to have anyone else there.

One day, Joyce seemed really down. As we sat talking, she shared with me that at the age of 12, she had found her Dad, who had committed suicide. Needless to say, it was a devastating thing to happen to a 12-year-old girl. I listened and tried to comfort her as best I could, but I had never known anyone who had experienced something so traumatic in her life. Joyce wasn't always open about her life, and I was pleased she had felt good about telling me this. Sometimes I think she was so fond of Hank because he was much older and that she had missed out on having time with her Dad.

To say that Joyce and Derek didn't get along was probably an understatement. They would get into arguments over things that happened at American Airlines or EAL day in and day out, about how a passenger should have been handled in a situation, how to deal with your finances, what time of day it was, etc. You name it, they were just like water and oil. I got so tired of the two of them getting into it, but I honestly didn't know which one to be the angriest with. They just rubbed each other the wrong way.

In March, Derek and I were both on vacation, and he wanted me to join him in Acapulco, Mexico for a few days. I was so excited! He went down before me because I didn't have my birth certificate. I flew into CMH (Columbus, Ohio) so Mom and Dad could bring me the birth certificate and I could continue my trip to Mexico. They kept teasing me that I was going to Mexico to get married and, Derek and I were meeting somewhere secretly to do it. I assured them we weren't getting married and that they would be the first to know if it was going to happen.

After Derek met my flight, we had a wonderful dinner, then went on a cruise. It was so much fun. On the boat, the guy playing a pirate decided he liked me and ran over to Derek with a knife like he was going to stab him. I think Derek was a little startled and I wasn't really comfortable with the drama, but I played along as he tried to get me to leave Derek and go with him. The other cruise passengers laughed.

When we went back to the hotel, Derek and I made love. I still wasn't really sure about sex because it wasn't what I thought it would be. Then again, I didn't honestly know what to expect. I loved the cuddling and holding part after Derek had finished, but I just didn't find the physical part to be something I had missed out on. Sadly, though, I was not experienced at all, and I don't think Derek had much previous exposure to the art of making love either.

Still, I loved him. After all, I gave Derek my virginity, and to me, that was the most precious gift I could ever give someone I hoped to marry. Of course, I had thought I would be married before I did "it."

I don't know what possessed me, but I asked Derek if he loved me and he said, "No." I nearly died!

Derek went on to tell me that I was a convenience to him. He said if he had to leave New York, he would get over me and it wouldn't bother him for long. This was the second time he had said something so devastating to me that I didn't think I'd live through it. I felt like he had just kicked me in the teeth AGAIN!!!! How could he be saying this to me after we had just finished making love?

I got so pissed I told Derek that when we got back to New York, this relationship was going to be terminated, and we were going our separate ways. I said I would be transferring to Los Angeles just as soon as I could get there.

I didn't sleep at all that night. I tossed and turned and cried until I thought I was going to throw up. Derek slept right through the night. I wanted to haul off and kick him right out of the bed. How in the world could he treat me like that? Was he nuts, or was I?

When Derek woke up, he rolled over toward me and tapped me on the shoulder. I asked what he wanted. If it was sex, he was definitely out of luck. Derek asked me if I meant what I had said the night before about us not seeing each other anymore when we got back to New York and about the transfer to Los Angeles. I turned over and looked him in the eye, with my swollen-frog eyes, and told him yes, that was absolutely what I planned to do.

Derek put his hand on my cheek and told me he really did love me. He told me three times, saying he just had a difficult time expressing himself and that he was afraid to let go of his feelings.

I knew Derek hadn't had many girlfriends in the past, but I would have thought he knew how to treat them better than he was treating me. My head was spinning. I wanted to slap him, hit him, kick him, but instead I reached over and held him. Derek cried on my shoulder and told me that he was so sorry for the pain he had put me through the previous night. Oh my Lord, there I went again, forgiving him when I should be running out of his life forever.

We left Acapulco and decided to go to Los Angeles for dinner. It was a wild and crazy thing to do, but we were young and we were airline folk, so why not? It wasn't going to cost that much, and it would be fun to be that spontaneous. We ended up having a great time.

When we got back to my apartment, Derek told me he would be going to Phoenix, Arizona with his sisters and parents the next morning for the remainder of his vacation. I wished so much that he would ask me to go with them, but he didn't. I accepted it pretty well because I knew he deserved some alone time with his family since he hadn't seen them in a while. Derek told me to remember that he really did love me, and he was so, so sorry for all of the horrible things he had said to me in Acapulco. He was just afraid of commitment. I hugged him, and he left for his apartment to repack for Arizona.

I spent the weekend alone, feeling sorry for myself. Joyce was gone for the weekend with Hank, and it was just me and my record player playing sad songs. I rehashed some of the hurtful things Derek had said to me and tried to convince myself he did mean it when he had apologized the next day and told me how he really felt.

I just wasn't sure I believed him, so I decided to go to Phoenix and see if I could find out if he loved me enough for me to spend some time with his family.

I went to Kennedy Airport and ran into Derek's seldom-seen roommate, Neil Casey. I had met Neil a few times, but we really never spent much time together because he was always gone whenever I was at Derek's place. The three of us might have gone out to eat a few times, but he and I didn't exactly have a friendship. Like Derek, Neil was in the Management Understudy Program. He started out as a ticket agent too, but he worked out of Kennedy while Derek got assigned to LaGuardia.

Neil just happened to be working my trip to Phoenix, and asked me if Derek knew I was coming. I told him no, that I just wanted to go somewhere to get some sun and relax and that I had always enjoyed my layovers in Arizona. This was so much B.S. I did enjoy Arizona, but I wanted to go there to see Derek and meet his parents.

By the time I got to the hotel in Phoenix, I was having second thoughts about seeing Derek. I called Neil at home and asked if he would call Derek and tell him I was in Phoenix, but to act like it was his idea to call and not mine. I didn't want Derek to think I couldn't live without him for a few days and that I was chasing after him.

Neil said he would call Derek and asked me the name of the hotel where I was staying. I went out to the pool and got some sun. When I returned to the room, I checked for messages, but there weren't any. I took a shower and turned on the television. Since it was too early to eat supper, I thought I would just take a little nap.

Derek called about 4:00 p.m., and I tried my best to act surprised. He sounded so pleased with himself that he and Neil had pulled one over on me. Ha, if only he knew.

Derek and I went out to a disco called the Red Dog, then went back to the hotel and had sex. After he had laid there a while, he brushed my bangs over on my forehead and asked, "How would you like to meet my parents tomorrow?" Of course I wanted to since that was the whole purpose of my trip in the first place. I was happy and terrified all at the same time.

Derek picked me up the next day, and we went to the Camel Back Inn where his family was staying. First I met his father, Derek, who was a really nice man and easy to talk to. Finally Derek's mom Claire showed up. She was so beautiful! She was tan and wearing tennis shorts. I could not believe how attractive she was. She smiled at me, and I just knew we were going to like each other. Derek's parents invited me for dinner the next night, and I was so happy when I got back to the hotel.

The next day, I bought a few dresses so I could decide which one to wear for our dinner date with the family. Looking back, I hate the dress I wore to that dinner. It was a light-blue dress but not appropriate for the desert. It almost made me look pregnant because it was very full.

We had a delightful dinner together, and I hoped his family liked me. I kept asking Derek when he took me back to the hotel if he thought they had liked me, and he felt certain they did.

I went back to New York and left Derek in Phoenix. I flew my regular trip, and when I got back to the apartment, I was missing Derek so much that I called Crew Schedule and asked them if they had any trips they needed covered to PHX (Phoenix.)

Bless his heart, I got Lou Pappas, and he gave me a trip to Phoenix. He knew about Derek and me, and I guess Lou was a romantic at heart, plus he had always been so good to me when I was on reserve. He would try to give me the best trips with the most time so I could get my flying done and be home with Derek. Lou was a sweetheart.

When I called Derek to tell him I would be back in Phoenix the next day, he seemed happy.

Sadly, that evening with Derek and his sister Pam was not very pleasant. We had dinner at the Camelback Inn and she was with some of her snooty college friends who decided they would speak to each other in French in front of me. Pam told Derek to go dance with one of her girlfriends, which left me there at the table with her and another little bitch. They didn't say two words to me as they just conversed in French and giggled.

Mrs. Schoenmann came over to the table and asked how everything was going. She must have seen the look on my face because she asked me to come sit with her and Derek's dad. I was overjoyed to be leaving that table. When Derek returned from his dance, he seemed surprised I wasn't there, but he came over and sat by me. Mrs. Schoenmann told him it would be real nice if he danced with me, so Derek got up and extended his hand as I turned to smile at his mom with a great big smile of gratitude. The night ended well, and I was so happy to have been able to spend some more time with Derek's family, except for Pam.

I do not know what ever possessed me to nickname Derek "Poopsie," but for some strange reason I did. I guess it was just so ridiculous to call this 6'5" manly man such a goofy name, but it made me laugh. At first, Derek acted like he didn't like being called Poopsie very much, but then he sort of shrugged it off and just pretended he didn't hear it half the time.

I was careful to never said it in front of anyone, but Joyce overheard it one day. Cousin Brucie, his roommate Casey, and a former fellow Marine named Wesley were in the apartment visiting with Joyce when Derek and I walked in. All of the guys turned around and said, "Hi POOPSIE!" I thought Derek was going to kill me, he was so angry. I gave Joyce the look of death as she burst out laughing.

Derek finally got over it, so much so that when he sent me flowers for my birthday he signed it "All my love, Derek 'P.'" I was so surprised he did that.

On occasion, Bruce would call him Poopsie if they ran into each other or just whenever he felt like embarrassing Derek. Bruce hadn't forgotten what happened between Derek and me that fateful night after I had confided in him about Derek's reaction when I had told him I loved him. Bruce had told me the bastard didn't deserve me, that any guy he knew, including himself, would be proud to have me be in love with him. Brucie was like the big brother I never had.

It was nice knowing most of the pilots looked out for me and Joyce.

Derek and I became pretty much inseparable, always together when one of us wasn't working. Derek was promoted to Supervisor of Ticket Agents.

Joey had gotten fired. I was so sad for him but never knew exactly what happened, except there was a rumor that he had given a couple of tickets to people. I found that hard to believe, but all I knew for sure was Joey wasn't at LaGuardia anymore.

My headaches kept flaring up, and on one trip, they were so bad I had to be taken off the trip. I caught all sorts of static from my supervisor, Pam Danaher, when I got back to my base. Dr. Shocken jumped all over me too when I went over to medical to be cleared to fly my next trip.

An attorney had called me one day begging to represent me in a lawsuit against American Airlines for negligence, but I told him I wasn't interested. I wanted to be a Stewardess, and if I sued them, they would probably fire me. The attorney said, "Yes, that may be true, but at least you'll be rich." I told him I wasn't interested.

I used to fly through Columbus a lot on the way to Dallas or some other layover city, so I always called Mom and Dad to get the latest. During one call, Mom told me she heard that Terry Kneisely had gotten drafted.

Silly me, my heart dropped. I called Terry's mom, and she told me Terry had been reclassified 1-A, whatever that meant, and she fully expected him to have to go to Vietnam. I told her I would pray for him, that he would be alright, and he would come back safe and sound. She seemed so appreciative. After all, Terry was her only child, and I could only imagine how it must have felt to know what was going on over there and think that you had to let your son go into harm's way in a country nobody thought was worth fighting for. His mom sounded a little teary but thanked me for calling and said she would tell Terry I had called. I always felt like she thought I wasn't good enough for Terry, but this day it seemed she saw me in a whole different light.

When I was young, I thought Jimmie had me going in circles, but Derek was the master at keeping me confused. He would act like he absolutely adored me, and then he would say something that would rip my heart out and shatter it into a million pieces.

We made each other crazy at times. Derek would take some Stewardesses home after work, then come over to my apartment, tell me all about it, and not understand why I was so upset. I trusted Derek; it was other women I didn't trust. I saw the way some of the gals looked at him at the airport when they didn't know he was taken. How dare they? It made me so mad. I was just so insecure that I'm sure I drove him nuts too.

Derek and I had a lot of fun together exploring in New York. Angela Lansbury had been on one of my flights, and she invited me to bring a friend and be her guests at the Broadway production of *Mame*. I was so excited because it was my first Broadway play. I just never dreamed I would be seeing something so awesome.

Derek's favorite time was when Bette was dating a New York Mets baseball player named Dave Eilers who gave all of us tickets to a baseball game. We visited many different restaurants and drove to a few tourist attractions. We occasionally went into the city, but I didn't like riding the subway. We often double-dated with Derek's friend, Ernie Jacobson, and his wife Linda, who were a great couple.

At times, Derek could not have been more attentive. When I had one of my headache days or the cramps that I was forever getting, he would actually fix me breakfast or lunch and pamper me, and I felt so loved.

Yet we still kept doing and saying things to each other that made no sense. We would get into stupid fights over nothing. Derek would leave and then be back apologizing either a few hours later or the next day. We couldn't be apart, but we also couldn't seem to keep from hurting each other whenever we were together.

VIETNAM, A DIFFERENT TYPE OF WAR

Our Favorite Uniforms

My brother seemed to be enjoying the Navy. We were glad he had joined the Navy instead of getting drafted because he would most likely have been sent to Vietnam. On May 19, Mike called me to say his ship was being sent to Vietnam anyway. I couldn't believe my ears. He told me he loved me and thanked me for all of the silly cards and letters I had sent him.

When Mike was a kid, I had given him a nickname that stuck with him for years. There was a show on television that we used to watch together called *The Addams Family*, and for some strange reason, I decided to call Mike "Pugsley." It stuck, and whenever I would send him a letter, I would write "Dear Pugsley." Rudy, one of Mike's friends, thought it was hysterical, so he decided to change it to "Pugsley Fucker." I don't know why. Why do servicemen do such nutty stuff? Perhaps it was to entertain themselves, to get their minds off their situation, or just for a laugh? The new part of Mike's nickname stuck as well, and his shipmates called him that the whole time he was in the service.

I couldn't believe Mike was actually going to Vietnam. Even though he wouldn't have to get off the ship and go on the ground to fight, I was still scared but believed he would be safe way out in the ocean. Little did I know how wrong I would be.

On July 30, 1967, I remember my mom calling me hysterically to tell me that she had seen on the news that Mike's ship, the U.S.S. Forestall, had been reported as having caught on fire on July 29. Several of the sailors had been injured and some had even died. Mom was hysterical, and I became pretty upset myself.

Not my baby brother! We had seen each other when he was home on leave after boot camp and had had a great reunion with Mom, Dad, and Sis at the house. I was only able to stay home for two days because I couldn't get a trip trade, which was when I would trade flights with another Stewardess, and she and I would fly each other's schedule giving us both the days off we wanted.

Although it was only for a short time, it was fun to see Mike in his sailor suit, looking so cute with all of that beautiful dark, curly hair sticking out from under his sailor hat. His hair had finally grown back from boot camp, and he looked absolutely adorable! I have a picture of Mike in his uniform and me in mine, and we both looked so cute. I know Mom and Dad were so proud of both of us. Mike was still seeing his old girlfriend Carol at the time, and although I think they wanted to get married, somehow that didn't happen.

I asked Mom if she knew how bad the fire was or how to find out if Mike was okay, but she was just mumbling and not making any sense at all. I felt so bad for her. She burst out crying and asked me to come home. I couldn't because I had to fly. Later I learned I probably could have gotten a leave, but I was too green to know that at the time. I promised to come home as soon as I could and told Mom to call me if she heard anything at all.

I shared with Derek what was going on with Mike, and he could tell how upset I was. He offered to take me to his apartment where we could walk on the beach and just be together, which sounded wonderful to me.

During the night, I woke up and felt like I was freezing. I sat up in the bed and leaned towards the bottom of the bed to pull the covers up over myself.

When I looked at the foot of the bed, there was a vision. It was of the flight deck on the aircraft carrier Mike was on. There was smoke and twisted metal in various places along the edge of the flight deck, and standing in the middle of my vision was Mike.

I opened my eyes wider trying to focus. I rubbed my eyes and leaned forward as if to reach out and try to touch him. He backed up and said to me, "Sis, tell Mom I am alright." I shook my head and could not believe I was hearing his voice. I said, "Michael, are you okay? Are you hurt?"

He told me again to call Mom and assure her he was not hurt and that he would be calling her soon. Then the vision faded right in front of me. I felt a complete sense of peace come over me regarding Mike's safety.

The next morning I called Mom when I got up and told her about my vision or dream, whatever it was, and assured her that I felt like Mike was going to be fine. She cried and cried.

Later that morning, a ham radio operator called Mom and told her he had a message from Mike. He said Mike was okay and that he would be coming home soon. Mom called me to let me know what the radio operator had told her and that my vision was correct; Mike was indeed alright. We were all so relieved! One item of interest that freaked me out was when pictures of the Forestall were printed in *Life* magazine, the deck was exactly as I had seen it in my vision.

Mike had gotten burned on his chest, shoulders and back because he was a firefighter and had tried to rescue some of the other sailors that were trapped. He had a terrible time with the whole incident and lived with flashbacks for years. Every July, we all knew Mike wouldn't be getting much sleep because he would be hearing the sounds of those poor sailors screaming. Although it was a difficult time for him, Mike finally did get over it, but it took years and years before he could put it behind him.

In June of the following year, Mom, Dad, Charmaine, and I went on a family cruise on the U.S.S. Forestall. I had traded two trips and flew them back to back so I could go with them to Norfolk, Virginia on this cruise.

I was exhausted. Although it was good to see Mike, I was having one heck of a time keeping my eyes open. He had just seen the Clint Eastwood movie, T*he Good, The Bad and the Ugly*, and wanted me to go see it with him again. After the movie and dinner, Mom, Dad, and Sis showed up, and we all went to our rooms. I remember falling asleep long before we had much of a chance to visit because we had to be up really early the next morning to leave.

Being on that ship was unbelievable. It was huge! We strolled all around the deck. Mike, Mom, Sis, and Dad went down into the ship; Mike knew I was claustrophobic, so he didn't expect me to go with them.

When they finished the tour, Mike got upset with me because I had sat down on a pile of duffle bags to wait for them and fell sound asleep. The next thing I heard was Mike's voice saying, "Damn, Sis, getup. I can't believe you did this. I told all of the guys about my sister, the Stewardess, coming on this cruise and how cool you were. Then I find you sleeping on bags of dirty skivvies." I was so sorry I had embarrassed Mike, but I was just so tired from all of that flying.

We watched the planes do "touch and go" flights off the deck. It was amazing how quickly they could stop. The hooks had a lot to do with it, but it was really interesting to watch. We also saw some helicopters. It was a great day for all of us, being together as a family like we used to be.

Thank God Mike came back home safe from Vietnam. I don't know what would have happened to Mom and Dad if they had lost him. I guessed they would have had to endure what so many other families had to go through who lost their sons or daughters.

It was such a difficult war, with so many people against it. The sad part was the lack of support for all of the men and women who served. They would arrive back home and some of the "tree-hugging hippies" would antagonize them at the airports calling them "baby killers" and spitting on them. That made me crazy! Those ignorant "draft dodgers" had no respect for these men and women who were fighting for their freedom.

I shared with Mom about this military charter Bette and I had flown together. We were called out to take a whole 707 full of soldiers to some stop-off point where they would board flights to Europe and then on to Vietnam. These boys were all so cute and young and were so excited to get the least bit of attention from a woman, much less a Stewardess. Bette and I must have given out 200 decks of AA playing cards before they got off the plane via a martin stand.

The soldiers all lined up at the bottom of the stairs. One of them made a funny-sounding noise, and they all raised their right hands, saluted the four Stewardesses, and yelled in unison, "You're what we are fighting for!" Bette and I turned from the top of the stairs and ran into the airplane in tears as did the other two gals. It was a very quiet trip back to base as we worried about just how many of these young men would never come back to the U.S.

One of the gals had a poem a soldier on one of her Military Airlift Command (MAC) trips had written to her. MAC flights were charters from 1969 to 1973 that actually took the guys to bases close to, or even in, Vietnam. The girls that flew these charters were very senior. While a lot of the gals loved to fly MAC trips, I don't think I could have even if I had been senior enough to do it, because I would just be too emotional to handle it.

I'd like to share that poem with you. The soldier's name was Kenneth W. Johnson, and I did not get permission from his family to publish this because I have no idea what branch of the service he was in or whether or not he even came back.

To Kenneth's family, I say "Thank you for letting me share his poem with some people today who may have no idea what it was like back then." I feel sure he would be proud to know his poem is being published here.

The poem was written on flight C2C3 from Washington to Japan to Vietnam on December 22-24, 1968:

"REMEMBER US"

Airline Stewardess, queen of the sky
Whatever possessed you to live so high?
Was it the promise of adventure, travel, romance?
Was it money, excitement, or merely chance?

To live by no timetable or rhythmic clock
To rise, to rest, to sleep where you dock.
Does it ever get tiresome this endless change?
Or do you grow with your travels and expanding range?

To walk the long aisles meal after meal,
And fend off fingers that seek to feel
To breathe the dry air and pull a balancing act
Each time you must walk from the front to the back.

Yes, oft I wonder what holds you here
But I'm glad you stay and look after us Dear.
Your beauty delights me with its simple grace
And it helps me go to what I soon must face.

For there's a danger on ground perhaps more than above
Men can be cruel when they forget to love
And to face whistling bullets and hot hardened steel
We need a reason to fight and our safety repeal.

Toward this you're great, though perhaps you don't know
You represent what we live for and why we must go
Because only if you're free can you fly in the sky
And our job is to ensure that freedom won't die.

So as you fly us soldiers across the globe
And travel the world on your special road,
Please understand that we love you quite well
And remember us, won't you, while we're stationed in Hell.

Those were really tough times for the guys my age. Several of my classmates were drafted and sent to Vietnam. It was not a popular war with the protests of the servicemen and all the hippies leaving for Canada. It was definitely not like the wars of the past when people appreciated our servicemen and honored them for the sacrifices they were making for our country. When Mom told me Mike was thinking of joining the Navy, I nearly died. He was my baby brother; there was no way he could be old enough to do something like that. I hoped he would reconsider, but she told me he was seriously considering joining the Navy before he ended up getting drafted into the Army.

I wasn't sure I understood why we had to send troops over there, but I supported the actual service people no matter what I felt about the war. We had so many guys and girls on our flights either coming back from, or going over to Vietnam. The flights bringing the soldiers back were wonderful when they weren't trips for the troops to do "R and R" (rest and relaxation). R and R meant the soldiers had to go back.

The soldiers all seemed so young and hopeful going over, but the ones coming back had a faraway look about them. It was like they had experienced things they couldn't grasp or comprehend people doing to each other. I don't know how anyone can go through a war and ever be the same again.

Everyone just wanted the war to be over and for our servicemen and women to come home. I don't know how many of my graduating class died in Vietnam, but I believe it was three. It was such a senseless war, yet the people doing the fighting believed they were doing what was right, and they put their lives on the line for what they believed in. God bless them.

FLYING, FLYING, AND MORE FLYING

A man was flying from Seattle to San Francisco. Unexpectedly, the plane was diverted to Sacramento along the way. The flight attendant explained there would be a delay and if the passengers wanted to get off the aircraft, the plane would re-board in fifty minutes.

Everybody got off the plane except one lady who was blind. The man had noticed her as he walked by and could tell the lady was blind because her seeing-eye dog lay quietly underneath the seats in front of her throughout the entire flight.

He could also tell she had flown this very flight before because the pilot approached her, and calling her by name, said, "Kathy, we are in Sacramento for almost an hour. Would you like to get off and stretch your legs?"

The blind lady replied, "No thanks, but maybe my dog Scout would like to stretch his legs."

PICTURE THIS! All the people in the gate area came to a complete standstill when they looked up and saw the pilot walk off the plane with a Seeing Eye dog! To make matters worse, the pilot was even wearing sunglasses. People scattered. They not only tried to change planes, but they were trying to change airlines as well.

I certainly can't confirm this, but supposedly this is a true story. If not, it's a pretty funny joke, don't you agree?

THINGS AREN'T ALWAYS AS THEY SEEM.

I had a funny thing happen to me once during a delay. It was the early seventies and Clint Eastwood as *Dirty Harry* was the movie to see. We had a mechanical delay in San Fran, so we asked the passengers if they wanted to get off the plane since it would be one and a half to two hours before we departed while we waited for a part. This one gentleman from First Class had been complaining about everything: we didn't have the magazine he wanted, he didn't like our choice of entrees, we dared to inconvenience him by having a mechanical delay. Yup, it was always us Stewardesses who planned to delay our passengers. It never messed up our own flying schedules, our already-short layover times, or our lives. We did it on purpose! We were the scourge of the earth.

This man was out on the jetbridge yelling at anyone who would listen - the pilots, the agents, a passenger service manager, just anyone whose attention he could get. He finally started in on me. After he vented for what seemed like forever, I turned my back to him, spun around, put my hands together in an attempt to appear to be holding a gun and said, "Go ahead, PUNK, make my day!"

He burst out laughing and asked, "Have I been that much of an ass?"

"You betcha!" I replied. (See, I had this 'catch phrase' long before Sarah Palin made it famous.)

He asked if I wanted anything from inside the terminal then went to get the magazine he had originally wanted at the beginning of the trip. After we took off, he was great.

I am so lucky that I can only recall one or two incidents where passengers confronted me about something. I don't know if it was my size or what, but seldom did anyone get upset with me about anything.

Once, when the agent started boarding before the cabin had been cleaned up completely, I had placed a large stack of magazines in a seat since I hadn't been able to get to the magazine rack. The man who was to sit in that seat bluntly told me, "Get those magazines out of my seat!" Since I was hanging another passenger's coat at that moment, I assured him I would move them in just a minute. Apparently, that was too long, because he picked up the magazines, and when I came towards him to retrieve them, he shoved them into my stomach as hard as he could. Two of the other passengers seated across the aisle from him were shocked and sat there waiting to see how I would react. I just looked at him and said, "Thanks so much for picking those up for me. I really appreciate it." He turned red as a beet but didn't say a word. I walked up to the magazine rack and put them in their slots before going into the galley and doubling up in pain. It hurt badly when he shoved the magazines into my stomach, but I wasn't about to let him know he had hurt me.

In Philadelphia, one of the passenger service managers sought my crew out in the cafeteria where we were relaxing before boarding our flight. He asked for the number one Flight Attendant (me), and then told me we had twelve travel agents on the trip back to Dallas, and he wanted me to, "Lay it on thick. Give them anything and everything they want. Treat them like royalty," were his exact words.

I looked at him and told him that all of my passengers got treated that way.

He informed me, "No I mean bend over backwards to be sure they have a great trip. They send lots of business our way." I thanked him for the information and again told him I would treat them just as well as I did the family that had saved up for years to take that one vacation on our airline. He seemed pretty miffed, but I assured him that the travel agents would have a great trip.

It just made me angry. Yes, of course I understood we wanted to have these folks send us their business, but I wanted him to know that all of my passengers meant a lot to me. And they did.

One of the girls I was flying with told me she hated old people and babies on her trips. She said both of them demanded too much attention. Old people always wanted to tell you about their aches and pains, and babies just threw up or squalled the whole trip. I said to her, "How sad for you because that is where you came from and where you are going." I didn't have a whole lot of patience with my co-workers who didn't appreciate their jobs. I was so grateful to be doing this job and felt there was almost always something good about all of my passengers.

On one trip with a tour group of elderly folks, mostly women and a few men, I had a ball teasing the men about how outnumbered they were. I said they must have felt like roosters in the hen house. I made a point of saying I hoped they had brought more than one pair of dancing shoes because they were going to use up that first pair in no time. They loved it! They were so cute and fun. The ladies all giggled, and the two men I had been talking to just winked at each other and grinned. What was not to like?

I had always loved babies. Nothing smelled better to me than a little baby who had just had a bath and been powdered. I loved the way they nuzzled under your neck when getting sleepy. More than once one of my flying partners made the comment, "If you've got any babies on board that you're having problems with, hand them over to Bev." I was so flattered.

I was flying so much and loving it. I went to many places and learned many things about different cities that I had only heard of before. This was the best job ever! Never in my life did I think I would be flying all over the country and meeting so many folks from all walks of life. It was the best education ever for a gal from Ohio.

We Stewardesses were getting new uniforms, and I wasn't sure if I liked them as well as the one I wore when I graduated. I was proud of that graduation uniform because it was a classic. There were so many dressing rules that it was like the military in some ways. We were not allowed to have our hair touch our collar, we had to spit shine our shoes, we had heels for wearing in the airport and "alternates," or flat heel shoes, for wearing on the plane during the service. The emblem on our hat had to sit directly over our left eye. We wore white gloves and didn't dare get a spot on that beautiful navy blue suit that was buttoned at the waist and made us look like Scarlet O'Hara in her corset. I had never felt so attractive.

Now we would be getting light blue uniforms with a pillbox-type hat. The uniform was supposed to be summer weight, but it always seemed warm to me, and it just didn't hold its shape as well as our old ones. But I wore whatever they gave me and was proud to do it.

Throughout my flying career, I think I had ten different uniforms. My favorite was the one we got in 1968 with the "go-go" boots. For those of you unfamiliar with that term, there used to be dancers in cages at the discos where people went to dance, and they were called "go-go dancers." I'm pretty sure it was the precedent to today's pole dancers, only they kept their clothes on.

You could wear white heels or you could wear these go-go boots that were white plastic and went to mid-calf. They looked awesome, but after you wore them for a while, your legs were so wet with sweat you literally had to peel them off your feet. I had to put some powder in the boots to prevent them from smelling bad because my feet sweat so badly anyway, but we looked good!!!

Some of the gals got a little crazy with the length, or lack thereof, on their uniforms. A few had to wear some sort of shorts under their dresses because when they leaned into the overhead rack, you could see way up their dress. I do believe a couple of gals didn't care; they just wore pretty underwear or shorts with smiley faces.

At one time, we had coonskin caps, fake not real, like Fess Parker used to wear as Davy Crockett. Of course, when this uniform was introduced, there were publicity pictures with Fess Parker and some of our gals showed up in various newspapers all across the USA. I don't know who thought that one up, but please. I never wore that hat!

My last uniform was the blue-black one we had in the late '90s. Those of us on International flights also got to wear different styles of muumuus on our trips to Hawaii. The first one wasn't all that pretty, but the royal blue with red flowers and white hibiscus was really nice.

It was always fun to have celebrities on board. One of my favorite stories was about Sidney Poitier, who was on my flight from New York to Cleveland, Ohio for a meeting. We were on the runway when we found out there was going to be at least an hour delay waiting for a position in line to take off. After an hour, Mr. Poitier motioned for me to come over to his seat and asked me to inquire of the Captain if he could be taken off the plane because he had already missed his meeting. I aimed to please, so I went to the Captain to ask if this was possible.

Boy, did I pick the wrong guy. This Captain, "Cotton" Bransley, was infamous for being a racist. I asked him the question about Mr. Poitier being able to deplane. He spun around in his seat and asked me "Isn't he that nigger [Sorry!] actor that made that movie with a white woman?" I answered him affirmatively. He practically yelled in my face his reply, "Not just NO, but HELL NO! Even if I could let him off on an active runway, I wouldn't. Not even if he was dying. And he ain't dying, is he?"

"No, Captain Bransley, he's not dying. I told him I would ask" I turned around and looked in the direction of the F/O who was busy looking out of his cockpit window so he didn't have to get involved. The Flight Engineer was reading his manual. I had to laugh; yeah, right, he's reading his flying manual. There was no way he was actually reading it, but he had to pretend to be doing something so he could avoid the conflict.

When I returned to Mr. Poitier's seat, he was gone. I checked the restroom to see if it was occupied, then went into the galley to find Mr. Poitier pretending to beat his fists against the door of the airplane yelling "Let me out! Let me out!" While it wasn't loud enough for the passengers to actually hear him, I could, and I was so shocked to see him doing this. Just as I was about to step back out of the galley, Mr. Poitier turned and grinned at me, then winked and returned to his seat. He was having some fun at my expense.

I gave Mr. Poitier a gentler version of Captain "Cotton's" reply stating that we were on an active runway, and the only way we could remove anyone was for a medical emergency. He looked at me a little suspiciously, because I am not a good liar, then smiled and thanked me for inquiring. He was a great passenger and a charming man.

Several other celebrity passengers were on my flights. I kept a list of who, and whether they were nice or not, but somewhere in my travels that list got lost. I wish I had it to recall how many and who they were.

I was lucky because I seemed to get along with just about anyone, both passengers and crew members. I did run into a lady based out of New York named Louise Godell. She was very, very senior, and she didn't let you forget it for a second. She was in command, she was the boss, and you would do as she said or else. Louise would get on the plane with her can of Lysol and spray the telephones (the ones we used to talk with the cockpit and with each other), the galley trash cans, the serving tops in the galley, and the lavatories. It was funny to watch her do this, but no one dared to say a word or ask her why she did it. We just let her do her thing.

Oh, and God forbid if you ever were brave enough to take anything from Louise's galley supplies. She didn't care if you ran out of soda, condiments, napkins, stirrers or any other supplies; what was on her galley serving area was for First Class and First Class only! Forget the coach passengers if they ran out of things. On occasion, I would snatch something if I needed it, but I was careful to check she was out in the cabin before I did it.

One time, on a flight to Cleveland, we had this television personality from a local talk show and a newspaper reporter who was doing a story on him. The agent came on the plane and wanted me to give a cake to this man while the photographer took a picture. He had no more than handed me the cake when Louise asked him if the passenger was going to be seated in Coach or First Class. When the agent told her the television personality would be seated in First Class, Louise came up to me and jerked the cake right out of my hands and informed me that since he would be sitting in her cabin, she would be presenting him with the cake for the photograph. I could have cared less, but the photographer and reporter weren't too happy.

I guess for some reason Louise liked me. Maybe it was because I never gave her any grief, and I never called her "Sergeant Godell" like some of the other girls did. We got along fine.

Derek thought it was a real credit to me that I could get along with just about everyone; everyone except for my roommate, Joyce. We usually got along, but we had our major differences. And she sure didn't like Derek as I mentioned earlier, not one bit.

Once I had been sick all night and decided that instead of puking my way across the country, especially with fifteen stops in three days, I would call in sick. Joyce was upset when she got home from her trip and found me at the apartment. She woke me and asked if I would please go to the Travelers Hotel for the night since I wasn't supposed to be home anyway because Hank was coming over after he got in from his trip.

I was so upset with Joyce for even asking me. I didn't understand why my being in the other bedroom with the door closed was going to upset Hank. She got so mad at me and again asked me to go to the hotel, stating that she would pay for it. I didn't want to go, but I didn't want to fight even more, so I packed up my bag and walked to the hotel after I made Joyce give me the money for the room. She was mad, and I was pissed.

When Derek came over the next night, I told him I had spent the night in the hotel feeling the way I did, and he hit the roof. He wanted to confront Joyce, but I told him to just let it go. He told me in no uncertain terms this would not happen again, ever! I felt grateful that Derek was so protective of me because the Travelers Hotel wasn't a very safe place to be.

When Joyce returned from her flight, she left a little stuffed bear with a bag of candy on my nightstand. When I asked her what it was for, she told me it was a "happy day" gift. Although she was a sweetheart, I sure hadn't been happy with her asking me to leave when I had felt so bad.

I had my first medical emergency on the trip from LGA (LaGuardia) to ORD (Chicago.) This beautiful pregnant lady was traveling with her three- or four-year old son. Shortly after takeoff, she rang her call button, and I rushed to her seat because we had a meal service to do and a full load of people. She was sitting in the aisle seat with her hands folded in her lap. When I got there, she leaned towards me and opened her hands to reveal she was covered in blood. I got her up out of her seat and helped her to the bathroom, asking the lady sitting by the window to please visit with her little boy until I could find out what was going on. As the pregnant woman proceeded down the aisle, the blood was running down her legs. She went into the bathroom while I stood outside. She told me she couldn't seem to stop the bleeding, that she was soaked through and through. I took off my serving topper and gave it to her, and offered to rinse out her dress and hang it somewhere to dry. She said she wanted to return to her seat, but as I helped her up from the toilet seat, she fainted. I held onto her as she fell and placed her on the floor.

I ran and got a stack of pillows and blankets and put them under and around her. She came to and told me she didn't want to return to New York, that she wanted to go on to Chicago. I called the cockpit and let them know what was going on, and they decided to make an emergency landing in Cleveland. She didn't want to do that, but we were all afraid she was hemorrhaging and that she was going to lose the baby right there. She was eight months pregnant and flying against her doctor's wishes but wanted to go to her sister's wedding.

Her little boy came back and asked, "Momma, what are you doing on the floor?" I told him his Mommy was tired and had to rest for a few minutes. I told her I was taking him back to his seat, and I would be right back. I was supposed to be on the forward jump seat, but I opted to stay on the back one of the 727 between the two lavatories to be able to hold onto her until we landed. She was getting scared and thanked me over and over again for staying with her. Of course, I wouldn't have left her for the world. It was a burden on my flying partners to deal with the passengers that weren't getting fed, but all in all, they were pretty understanding.

The emergency squad came with a stretcher and wheeled her and her little boy off the airplane to the hospital. She had asked for my address so she could return my serving topper. I had placed her wet dress in a plastic bag and put it on her lap before they wheeled her off.

I heard from the woman about two weeks later. Sadly, she had lost the baby, but it had died from respiratory problems and not because of what had happened on the airplane. She thanked me for all of my kindness in staying with her and taking care of her and her little boy.

One of my other inflight emergencies started when a First Class passenger, dressed like a rock star with jeans and a wild looking shirt, made an immediate entry into the lavatory when he boarded the plane and stayed in there for quite a while. Later, when I passed by his seat, he asked for a glass of water. When I handed it to him, his hand reached out and went to the side of the glass. I moved the glass, and again, he wasn't able to grasp the glass, so I sat it down on the small serving table beside his seat. I asked him if he was okay, and he assured me he was.

After we took off, I walked past his seat and noticed the large vein in his neck was pulsating rather obviously, seeming larger and much more active than I felt it should be. The man appeared to be asleep, so I decided to just check on him periodically as I served. He slept through the service.

When I tried to wake the man to see if he wanted anything, he didn't respond. I asked the passenger beside him to please get out of his seat. I stood to the side, out of the man's reach, and tried again, unsuccessfully, to wake him. Although he was breathing, he would not open his eyes or respond to me.

I reported to the Captain. Since we were almost ten minutes away from landing, the Captain would wait until we landed to see if he could wake the man up. Once everyone had deplaned, the Captain tried to wake him, but still the man just sat there with his head against the window.

The paramedics were called and showed up with a wheelchair. They tried to wake the man, but ended up lifting him and placing him in the chair to take him off the plane. Before they left, they asked me if he had communicated with me at all on the trip. I told them about his long visit to the forward lav and his request for a glass of water, so they had me check for anything suspicious in the lavatory's trash bin. I wasn't too crazy about this idea, but I did as I was told.

Rummaging through the trash, I found a syringe and picked it up with several tissues wrapped around it. When I took it to the paramedics, they searched the guy's shirt pocket and found a substance wrapped in foil. It was "Mississippi Mud," a drug the guy had apparently injected when he was in the lav and, perhaps, had taken too much. I walked off the airplane to see two policemen sitting with what appeared to be the guy's wife and son as they placed handcuffs on the man and wheeled him out into the terminal. My heart ached for the little boy, who got so upset when he saw the police officer had placed those cuffs on his Dad. The wife looked sad too. We found out later he had almost overdosed to the point of no return, but fortunately, he was helped at the hospital before being sent to jail.

I had met the Captain for my flight, Brian Reynolds, in Operations and he was known for being a real nut. He loved his job and loved his flight attendants. Brian handed me a piece of paper and asked me to read it:

> An airline Captain was breaking in a new blonde stewardess. The route they were flying had a layover in another city. Upon their arrival, the Captain Showed the stewardess the best place for airline personnel to eat, shop, and stay overnight.
>
> The next morning, as the pilot was preparing the crew for the day's route, he noticed the new stewardess was missing. He knew which room she was in at the hotel and called her up wondering what happened. She answered the phone, crying, and said she couldn't get

> out of her room. "You can't get out of your room?" the Captain asked, "Why not?"
>
> The stewardess replied: "There are only three doors in here," she sobbed, "one is the bathroom, one is the closet, and one has a sign on it that says 'Do Not Disturb'!"

"That was cute, Brian, real cute. You gave me this joke because I have blonde hair, right?"

He laughed and asked, "Why, Bev, whatever gave you that idea?" Some of our pilots were so much fun to fly with.

On another trip, I was boarding the flight when the Captain and F/O came on board. The Captain, Rick West, was behind the F/O, and I was taken aback by his height - he could not have been over 5'5", if that. They introduced themselves and entered the cockpit.

When we got to Philadelphia, the whole crew decided to go out for Italian food. We had the best time eating and laughing. Everyone decided to go back to the hotel except Rick and me. I was so full I wanted to take a walk, so Rick offered to go with me because I might need some protection. I could barely keep from laughing in his face. He knew how silly it sounded because he looked up at me and winked. So off we went, 5'5" Rick and almost 5'11" me. As we were walking by a bus stop, several men were staring at us. Rick looked over at them and said, "You want to know how I do it? I do it with mirrors." They all burst out laughing! I turned nine shades of red.

I thought that was the end of Rick joking about our height difference. Not so. The next morning, I was at the front door when he and the F/O came on with the passengers not far behind them on the jetbridge. Rick looked at me and said, "I just want to play windshield wipers with you, Bev," as he moved his head back and forth in front of my bust line. I nearly died! He cracked up and jumped into the cockpit leaving me there to board the passengers with a crimson face.

Hopefully, you are laughing at these stories. I have to share with you one of my all-time favorite airplane jokes.

On a transatlantic flight, a plane passes through a severe storm; the turbulence is awful! Things go from bad to worse when one wing is struck by lightning. One woman in particular loses it. She stands up in the front of the plane screaming, "I'm too young to die!" and continues to wail.

Then, just as suddenly she yells, "Well, if I'm going to die, I want my last minutes on earth to be memorable! Is there anyone on this plane who can make me feel like a WOMAN?"

For a moment, there is silence. Everyone has forgotten their own peril. They all just stared, riveted, at the desperate woman standing in the front of the airplane.

Finally, a man from Texas (of course, where else?) stood up in the rear of the plane. He is handsome, tall, well built, with dark brown hair, and beautiful hazel eyes. He starts walking slowly up the aisle, unbuttoning his shirt.

One button at a time...

No one moves...

He removes his shirt...

Muscles ripple across his chest...

She gasps...

As he gets closer, she reaches out her hand...

He reaches out his hand...

And softly whispers...

"Iron this, and then get me a beer!"

I loved flying, and am pleased to say that in the years I flew, I never got a bad passenger letter. I honestly loved my passengers. I only had maybe two or three encounters that got heated. Thank the Lord, I was given the gift of a sense of humor and could pretty much deescalate any situation to a less volatile state.

I did, however, on occasion, get a little fiery with one or two of my crew members. The majority of them were pretty good guys, but one or two of them could really get under my skin. I recall a Captain, Les Rogers, who drove me nuts calling for coffee. He didn't care what we were doing, how busy we were, or how little time we had to do our service. He wanted his coffee when he wanted it. I finally had had just about enough of his constant calling, and I took an entire pot to the cockpit and instructed Les that he could not call any of us until every bit of it was gone. Fortunately, he took it well and didn't call the rest of the trip.

There was a F/O I flew with for a whole month who was the rudest, most negative person I think I had ever encountered. He complained about everything and seemed to delight in making comments about how bad his crew meal was. It was either not what he wanted, not cooked enough, cooked too much, or he just didn't like it. I had my fill of him and did something so out of character, but I thought it was justified because I was so fed up with him and his antics. I had been in a goofy card shop and saw some beautifully embossed five by seven cards that said some pretty horrible things on them. One of the cards said, "You are cordially invited to go fuck yourself." It was decorated beautifully and written in calligraphy.

After this F/O called for his meal, during our last trip as a crew that month, I placed the card on his tray. I no more got back into the galley when the call phone dinged, and he demanded I return to the cockpit. He wanted to know the meaning of the card he had found on his meal tray. When I told him he had been a total ass all month, and his actions had caused me to feel the way the card expressed, he was shocked, to say the least. He told me he was sorry and asked me to forgive him for his actions. I was floored, then felt bad and accepted his apology. I suggested maybe next time a Flight Attendant served him his meal, he might try to find something positive about it, and he said he would. The Captain and Flight Engineer looked in opposite directions as I left the cockpit.

Speaking of the cockpit, here is a joke that made the rounds. "As the airliner pushed back from the gate, the Flight Attendant gave the passengers the usual information regarding seat belts, etc. Finally, she said, "Now sit back and enjoy your trip while your Captain, Judith Campbell, and crew take you safely to your destination."

Ed sitting in the eighth row thought to himself, "Did I hear her correctly? Did she say the Captain was a woman?"

When the attendants came by with the drink cart, he said, "Did I understand you right? Is the Captain a woman?"

"Yes," said the attendant "In fact, this entire crew is female."

"My God," said Ed. "I'd better have two scotches and sodas. I don't know what to think of all those women up there in the cockpit."

"That's another thing, sir," said the attendant, "We no longer call it the cockpit. It's now referred to as the 'Box Office.'"

One of my biggest pet peeves was that generally the cockpit crew had meals provided for them if the flying time was during a meal service. Sad to say, we gals and guys on the other side of the cockpit door only got something if someone refused a meal. I had pilots eat their meals and then call back to see if there were any meals left from the cabin. How thoughtless! Some of them could not have cared less if we had anything to eat; they were just thinking about themselves.

There were a few pilots who were so tight they squeaked or squawked like chickens, "CHEEP, CHEEP, and CHEEP!" We didn't expect the pilots to buy our meals, but this one guy went too far. On an evening layover in Tucson, Arizona, the three cockpit guys and the three Stewardesses went out to eat together. After this poor gal had run her legs off serving us, we were figuring out the check. The Captain divided it up among the other five of us and we all threw in our tip. As we were leaving, I went back to get my lipstick I had left on the table. I could not believe my eyes as I saw the Captain pick up the girl's tip and put it in his pocket. The F/O was standing right beside him.

I looked at the F/O as the Captain walked toward the hotel limo that had come to pick us up and asked rather loudly, "He did not just do what I think he did. Did he?"

The F/O put his head down and replied, "I'm pretty sure he did, but please don't say anything to him. We still have two days on this trip, and you don't have to sit in the cockpit with him."

"You have got to be kidding me if you think I won't say anything to him." I spun around and when we ended up in the elevator together, I boldly asked the Captain, "You didn't actually pick up the waitress's tip from the table back there, did you?"

"What are you talking about?" he blurted out.

"I saw you pick up the tip money back at the restaurant and didn't see you do it to make change." He got all upset and assured me he had done just that, he had a large bill and made change and definitely left her a tip.

I knew in my heart he was lying because I never saw him put down a penny. It is no wonder some airline personnel get horrible reputations of being cheap. I was so embarrassed. The F/O wasn't too happy with me, but at least I let the Captain know the jig was up, and I could hope maybe he wouldn't do it again. None of us went out to eat with the Captain the next night. The Flight Engineer told us the Captain was building a runway by his new home, so he had to figure out a way to get some extra money. That was pitiful!

A few pilots were funny about getting extra things from us. We might have gotten a little aggravated, but they did it in such a way that giving them extra things was worth doing because they were so funny. One pilot came on the plane to introduce himself to us with a linen napkin sticking out of his uniform in the front of his jacket and informed us he was the "designated eater" for our trip. Now that was cute and clever!

We had a nickname for one of the notorious offenders. F/O Pete Jenkins looked so much like Ted Kennedy that we used to make jokes about never getting into a car with him. He was known as "The Driver." Pete would always come back to the galley right before landing and get several soft drinks or Bloody Mary mixes to take to his room along with any bread he could find. Then he would have the nerve to ask us to pick him up a few newspapers for the layovers. We pretty much instructed him to fend for himself. Oh brother, like he couldn't afford a newspaper.

In all of my years of flying, I was only afraid on an airplane twice. This one Captain had a well-deserved reputation for being an alcoholic. Occasionally, the entire crew would meet after a flight on a layover and have what was called a "debriefing." This just meant we got together to talk and maybe have a glass of wine or a drink in one of the crewmember's rooms. However, this Captain brought two or three bottles of J&B out of his flight bag, and by the time we all headed to our rooms, the bottles were empty. He never had an accident, but I was always scared when I saw his name on the crew list.

My scariest incident involving a drinking crew member was on the BAC 1-11. (Why did everything bad seem to happen to me on that airplane?) I answered a call from the cockpit, and the Captain told me to come up front. When I opened the door, he was standing behind his seat and instructed me to sit in his chair. I looked at the F/O, and he turned his head. I could smell the liquor on the Captain's breath and told him I didn't have time because I had a service to do in the cabin. The Captain said, and not in a very nice way, "I said sit down."

To avoid any further confrontation, I sat in the Captain's seat. He leaned over me, stinking like a bar, and told me he was going to give me a flying lesson. My eyes must have bugged out of my head, but I was so new I didn't dare say a word. At Stewardess School, we were told the Captain was the boss and not to question him or his actions.

The Captain showed me this dial that had an orange-looking set of wings in the center of it. He told me to use the steering wheel to keep the orange-looking wings horizontal and level in that dial. I got to thinking this was probably a joke he and the F/O made up and that the F/O was actually flying the plane, so I turned the wheel a little too far to the left to try and call their bluff. The entire plane leaned sharply to the left. I burst out crying, and the Captain started yelling at me, telling me to get out of the seat and back to the cabin. The F/O didn't say a word! He just returned the orange wings in the dial to the proper level while the Captain climbed back in his seat. I ran out of the cockpit with tears pouring down my cheeks.

After we landed, I looked at the F/O and asked him how he could let the Captain do that to me. He just shrugged his shoulders and said, "He's the Captain." I wanted to report the Captain, but the F/O said he would not back me up.

The majority of our pilots are fantastic flying men and women, who would be appalled if they ever knew what had happened to me. I don't recall ever sharing this story with anyone other than Derek, whom I told long after it had happened. Derek wasn't pleased either, but I was new and didn't have the courage to say anything about what had happened.

Later on in my flying career, I had a wonderful Captain stand up for me against a supervisor in Los Angeles. I had let my hair grow really long, but we weren't allowed to let it hang down our backs while on the airplane, in the terminal, or, heaven forbid, while in uniform. In the Operations, area where the crews sign in for trips, I was in the crew lounge where we would take a break, nap, or grab a snack. We had been up since "zero dark thirty" as we called early morning sign-ins, and I had a headache so I let my hair down while we were sitting there.

A supervisor went by the room, stopped, came back, then asked me to step into her office. I didn't know why she was doing this, but I went any way. With her manual opened to the part about grooming, she told me my hair had to be confined while in uniform. I tried to explain to her I had a headache, and I was not out in front of our flying public, and I would definitely have it "confined" when I went to my aircraft and during my trip. She wasn't taking that for an answer and insisted I pull my hair back. I did as she requested but didn't like it one bit.

Once I was on the plane, I was checking catering when the gal who was going to be boarding came back and told me the supervisor was on board and wanted to see me. Our Captain had heard about what happened in Operations but hadn't said a word to me. As I came up to the boarding door, the cockpit door opened. Captain Don Holson, a huge man with white hair, sparkling blue eyes, and usually the most mischievous grin, stepped between me and the supervisor. He was a very intimidating figure! "You aren't here to check Bev's hair, are you?" he asked in his big burly voice

"What?" she nervously replied.

"I asked if you were here to check if Bev's hair was regulation or not?"

"Er, uh, no, I am here to make sure you all got everything from cabin service and catering."

"Good, then if you are finished with that, I suggest you get the hell off my airplane and leave my girls alone." To say she was shocked was an understatement! She backed up and nearly fell out the door onto the jetbridge and left.

I grabbed Don around the neck, hugged him, and thanked him for standing up for me. "Nobody messes with my girls!" he stated as he went back into the cockpit. What a sweetie! Our crews generally stuck together no matter what, and it was a really good feeling to know most of the guys behind that cockpit door had your back.

I did a terrible thing to a wonderful pilot once. I wish I could name all of my favorites, but sadly I can't recall all of them. He was one of the nicest, most polite and gentle pilots I ever flew with. He was truly one of the good guys. I was feeling goofy one day when this passenger asked me if I knew Jerry Garland, that he was his brother-in-law. Instead of telling the truth and raving about what a great guy he was, I told the most preposterous lies about Jerry, all in jest. I rolled my eyes and stated that all of us girls had to double-lock our doors when we flew with Jerry because he would bang on your door trying to get in. When you went into the cockpit, it was at your own risk because given half a chance, Jerry was all over you. This was the absolute furthest thing from the truth!!!!

I guess Jerry's brother-in-law believed me. Jerry told me later on a flight about his brother-in-law confronting him for being such a Romeo. I wanted to die right there on the spot! My apologies were nowhere strong enough to convince Jerry how sorry I was for having done that. I offered to write his brother-in-law a letter and tell him I was only joking, but Jerry was afraid that would only make things worse.

No one deserved this, much less Jerry. I felt terrible! I just figured his brother-in-law should have known Jerry well enough to know that it was a big lie, but maybe he was living vicariously through the lies I told about Jerry. To this day, however, every time Jerry and I see each other, he laughs about it. Fast forward to 2010 or so, my husband and I met with Jerry and his wife Trisha, and I had an opportunity to apologize to her in person and set the story straight. They are wonderful people I am proud to call my friends.

AN UNEXPECTED SURPRISE IN OKLAHOMA

Derek and I went to Devon, Pennsylvania where his parents lived. Although we only planned on being there for the weekend, because Derek had to go to work, Janet asked me to stay longer with them since I had more time off. Pam had been pretty chilly towards me when I first arrived, but we managed to talk our way through things. She just wasn't used to having to share her big brother with anyone, and she wasn't sure if she liked me all that much at first, but I finally won her over.

We girls had a great time. Claire showed me Derek's yearbooks and his baby pictures. What a cutie he was. I could only imagine how tall our children would be if Derek and I ever got married. Mercy, they would all be at least 6' feet tall, both boys and girls. I hated to say good-bye after my time alone with Derek's family, but I was pleased I had been able to get along with them without Derek there. I was especially happy Pam and I were getting closer.

I had many opportunities at that time to date other people, but I just didn't want to. I was on a flight to Dallas one day and met this adorable soldier named John Piccione (another Italian boy; what was with me and those dark haired men?). John was on his way home after boot camp, then he was being sent to Vietnam. We made plans to go out for dinner in Dallas. John had a girlfriend, and I had Derek, but we enjoyed each other's company.

After dinner, John asked if he could come back to my room to continue our talk. I looked at him rather suspiciously, but I trusted him. When we got to the room, he kissed me, and it felt so weird to kiss someone other than Derek; I felt guilty but I didn't expect to ever see or hear from this fellow again, so I let him. Suddenly, John asked me if I would marry him, so I laughed, but he said he was serious. When I asked what his girlfriend would say, he told me she would just have to get used to it. I told him I was flattered, but I was in love with Derek and didn't think it would work out for us to marry.

John asked me if I would write to him when he went to Vietnam, so I did for several months. He sent me a beautiful turquoise, oriental robe and a gold bracelet with some sort of Vietnamese symbols on it. Both gifts were really pretty and so unexpected. After several months, I never heard from him again. I don't know what happened, but maybe I don't want to know. Although I felt guilty writing to John because I knew I wouldn't be happy if Derek were writing to a girl in the service, I made up excuses to myself to justify writing to this young man, like I was just trying to help a poor soldier get through this terrible war. After all, it was just letters, and I figured it really wouldn't hurt if Derek didn't know. Still I was a little relieved when we weren't writing any longer.

A few pilots asked me out, but I always said no because I was afraid it would get back to Derek I didn't really want to go out with them anyway, but I was pleased that other men found me attractive.

I started getting frustrated with Derek and our relationship, so I more or less gave him an ultimatum. That went over really well...NOT! He didn't seem to like being pushed into a corner, so I decided I would never again mention marriage to him. It was just that several of the guys and gals from the airport and a couple of Stewardesses who knew me were all asking if and when Derek and I were going to get married. It was getting to me.

One day Derek was at the house after I had been figuring out my bills. I had put them on top of the fridge thinking he couldn't see them up there, but I was wrong. Derek started giving me all kinds of grief over my charge cards and other expenses. Joyce walked in about the middle of this conversation, and she flew into Derek that my bills were none of his business and for him to stop snooping around in our apartment. She was right, but I felt she was as out of line, as was he. I just hated confrontations with anybody about anything. I ran into my bedroom and Derek followed. He looked at me and said, "Bev, I can't marry you with all of this debt. You are going to have to do something about getting these cards paid off before we get married." I was dumbfounded. What kind of an announcement about our future was that?

We took a trip to San Francisco together in September, and I kept hoping he would propose there, if he was ever going to. How romantic that would have been! He didn't propose but did ask if I wanted to wear his crest ring backward on my ring finger to make it look like we were married before we registered at the hotel. I don't know why I bothered to do this, since we didn't know anyone in San Fran any way.

Derek bought me a beautiful pair of earrings and some flowers. We ate at Fisherman's Wharf and in Chinatown. We walked everywhere or rode the cable cars. It was so much fun! This was probably our best trip together ever, and we never fought.

I don't know what I would have done about my frustration with Derek if I hadn't been able to fly. Whenever I left New York on one of my three-day trips, I would just enjoy being a single girl. I flirted with a few of my passengers and enjoyed the company of some of our crew members but never on a dating basis. Still, I felt like I had to keep my options open since I had no idea if Derek was ever going to ask me to be his wife.

I felt I had ruined my chances of going back to Alphie, since I didn't think he would be able to forgive me for what I had allowed to happen to me and take me back. He might have taken me back, considering how much we loved each other at one time, but I didn't want to ever go through leaving him again if I did decide I had made a mistake. I did know I was not ready to go home to Columbus.

I had pretty much given up on Derek asking me to marry him. I just kept flying and spending time with him.

On November 8, 1967, I had a trip through Oklahoma City, Flight 209, that ended up in Dallas. I was getting ready to leave LaGuardia and it was past departure time. The agent came to the plane with the final paperwork and I asked him what the holdup was. He said there was a late passenger that we were waiting for.

I was about to leave the forward entry door when I saw Derek come running down the jetbridge with a carry-on suitcase in his hand. I smiled from ear to ear. He sat down in First Class, and we pushed back. I was so surprised to see him, and it was great to have him on board watching me perform in my element. I was a damn good stewardess, and it made me happy to see him watching me interact with my passengers. I didn't want to bring any undue attention to him during the service, so I treated him just like any other person onboard.

After we had landed in Oklahoma City, I sat and talked with Derek for a few minutes before the agent boarded our next load of passengers on the way to Dallas. Derek asked me what I would be doing this time next year, which I thought was an odd question. I told him I wasn't exactly sure, why? He said, "Why don't you spend all of your next years with me? Bev, will you marry me?"

I nearly fainted right there on the floor of the First Class cabin as he handed me this beautiful platinum ring with a one carat center stone surrounded by 52 other diamonds. It was gorgeous! It had been his grandmother's ring, and now Derek was offering it to me. (His grandmother was nicknamed "Guagy." I never knew her real name or how to spell her nickname either but that is what it sounded like.) Sadly, it was too small but, I took it anyway and put it on the little finger on my left hand.

I reached over and hugged and kissed Derek even though the passengers were boarding already. One of the men looked at us rather oddly and said, "My, this certainly is a friendly airline." I ran up to the cockpit to tell the crew and the other Stewardesses.

Derek had finally made it official. We were actually going to get married. Thank God!!!!

We left the ring at Neiman Marcus in Dallas to have it sized, and I would pick it up on my next flight.

I was so happy! I just couldn't wait to call Mom and Dad. Derek told me his parents already knew he was going to ask me, and they were delighted. I felt like we were going to be alright. Even though it had been a long struggle to get our lives together, it seemed we were finally on the right track. Everyone was happy for me. Even Joyce said she hoped everything worked out for us. She still didn't care for Derek, but if marrying him is what I wanted, she just wanted me to be happy.

JUST PLAIN ELVIS

If someone had asked me, "Okay, Bev, what celebrity would you most like to have on one of your flights?" I would have answered without a moment's hesitation: Elvis Presley.

In the beginning of the Elvis Era, I was not a fan. I was madly in love with Frankie Avalon, all 5' 6" of him. Boy, ole Karen had a field day teasing me about the difference in our heights. ""Gee, Bev, when he walks you home, he'll have to stand on his tiptoes or use a ladder to kiss you good night." It didn't matter to me because I thought Frankie was so-o-o-o cute with all that wavy hair and those mushy brown eyes. I just knew he was singing directly to me when he sang "I'll Wait for You."

I'll never forget the time I saw Frankie in concert. It was January 24, 1960, and the concert was *The Biggest Show of Stars for 1960.* There was Freddy Cannon, Bobby Rydell, and several other groups but the most important star was Frankie, who of course, was the last to come on stage. I had saved all of my money to purchase a loudly-striped sweater, one I was sure would stand out in a crowd. I just knew Frankie would spot me in the masses, and it would be love at first sight.

No such luck! Frankie would've had to have hawk eyes to have even gotten a glimpse of that fuzzy sweater. If he had seen me, he probably would have thought, "Yuk, what an awful sweater." I just knew he did see me though, because he was facing my direction even if there were twenty rows of screaming girls in front of me. I got the last laugh on Karen when I read that Frankie married a gal 5' 8", and they had eight kids together. What ole Frankie lacked in height...well.

Anyway, back to Elvis. I had always thought of him as a good-looking, greasy-haired "hood" or "rebel." When I was growing up, that's what we called those outcasts who wore black leather jackets and smoked cigarettes. Seriously, I lived the *Grease* generation, so I knew a Thunderbird when I saw one!

The biggest hood in my school was a guy named "Toobie" Farley. He used to terrorize all the jocks, and they lived in constant fear that Toobie might be waiting for them after school to pick a fight, just for kicks. "Toobie" may have been small, but he was someone to be reckoned with.

He was the "Fonzie" of my High School years, but their appearance was where the similarity ended. "Toobie" was not a nice guy, while The "Fonz" appeared to be a genuinely kind, sincere guy who was always helping someone. After reading articles about Henry Winkler later, I think that was the true heart of "Fonzie."

My cousin, Sandy, was madly in love with Elvis. She had all the paraphernalia associated with him, such as combs, bracelets, purses, lipstick, and records galore. She told me if I would just watch him on *The Ed Sullivan Show*, she was sure I would understand then why he was so cool! So I watched Elvis and thought he was absolutely disgusting, with all of that yucky, greasy, slicked-back black hair. Could you ever imagine touching it? Oh, how gross! That was pretty much how I felt about "Elvis the Pelvis" for a very long time. I bet he was crude, just as crude as his nickname.

At least that's what I thought until I let Karen con me into going to see Elvis in *G. I. Blues* when I was 16. That was the beginning of my long, one-sided love affair with Elvis Presley. When I saw that beautiful face without all the greasy hair hanging in his eyes and those gorgeous blue-green eyes with long eyelashes, I mean to tell you, folks, I was hooked!

In the theater, I sat there spellbound by the man who was accused of leading the youth of America astray. (He could have led me anywhere at that moment.) As Elvis leaned over in the ski lift to plant that French kiss on Juliet Prouse, I thought I would faint. People weren't supposed to kiss like that; that was supposed to be bad, but I sure was intrigued. I asked myself how something supposedly so bad could look so good.

I leaned over to Karen, who sat there with her mouth wide open in either shock or disgust, I wasn't sure. She had been in the process of cramming a handful of popcorn in her mouth when Elvis kissed Juliet and then stopped mid-cram as I said to her, "Someday I am going to meet Elvis Presley and he is going to kiss me just like that." I must have startled her because she dropped half her popcorn in her lap and the rest onto the floor as she burst out laughing.

"Shh, quiet!" warned some folks sitting near her.

"How someone could be laughing at a time like this is beyond me!" stated the girl sitting on the other side of Karen.

"Sure, Bev, sure, and I'm going to be Mrs. Ricky Nelson too." Karen replied to me.

"Karen, I am serious. It's just a feeling I have," I said.

"Bev, you really are a dreamer. Do you know that half of the Hollywood starlets can't even get him to notice them, much less ask them for a date? How in the world do you expect to even get close to him, much less kiss him? Elvis can have any woman in the world he wants!"

I just shrugged my shoulders, looked back at the screen and knew; I didn't know how, when, or where, but I knew it was going to happen.

Fast forward to February 24, 1968, I'd been flying flight #299 and #90 for two months in a row. It was a killer trip to work — we would leave LaGuardia at 5:00 p.m., serve dinner on the way to Nashville, serve drinks to Memphis, then fly nonstop to Los Angeles with drinks and snacks. It had gotten to be a big joke between the gate agents at the Memphis airport and me every time I'd hand them the papers from the trip. I'd ask, "Well, is he out there waiting tonight?" and they all knew I meant Elvis. I had heard American Airlines was his favorite airline, and I was determined to be his favorite Stewardess. So what if I was engaged to be married in less than two weeks? I mean, Elvis Presley isn't just any ole passenger.

One agent in particular, Jess Jones, smiled and said, "Not tonight, Hon. We forgot to tell him that it was you that was gonna be on here tonight." He was so silly to tease me like that.

This time it was different. Jess said, "Bev, I'll need to talk to you prior to boarding the outgoing passengers." He seemed so business-like I guessed he wasn't in the mood for our usual Elvis banter.

"Sure," I replied, deciding not to chide him about Elvis tonight.

All of our inbound passengers had deplaned, and I had gone into the galley to make sure we were getting all the supplies needed for the service to Los Angeles. Jess came into the galley and told me to put three "Occupied" signs in an inconspicuous row towards the back of the First Class cabin. I couldn't help myself, "Oh, is that for Elvis and his buddies?"

"Yes, as a matter of fact it is for Elvis and two body guards. He's really on your flight tonight, because he has to go to Los Angeles to make another movie." This was just a little too coincidental. Since this was my last trip through Memphis before the schedule changed for March, I had a difficult time believing Jess.

Still, I decided to play along with him just in case he wasn't teasing. I went into the cabin and placed three "Occupied" cards in the seats furthest back on the right side of the plane at seats 4E and 4F and the left side at 4B. If Elvis really did show up, I wanted him as far away from the other passengers and as close to my galley as he could be.

All the passengers had boarded the flight when Jess came down the jetbridge with the paperwork in his hand. "You really had me fooled, Jess. I even put the "Occupied" cards in three seats. Did you agents gang up on me, or was this all your idea?"

"Bev, he'll be here. I'm serious. Elvis just wanted to wait until everyone else was on the plane, then he, Joe, and Alan are going to board." It was departure time, and I was convinced I had been the butt of his joke.

I started towards the galley to get the Captain some coffee when one of the passengers stopped me. "Why are those men walking under the airplane?" he inquired. "What men are you talking about, sir?" I asked and he pointed out his window. I assumed they were mechanics or cabin service personnel. As I leaned over him to look out the window, I saw the legs of a man in civilian clothing climbing up the stairs leading to the side entrance of our plane's jetbridge. Honestly, it never dawned on me Jess could be telling the truth.

I was still bent over straining to see who the men were and what they were doing out there when I heard a man's voice say, "Nice view." As I realized my derriere was sticking out into the aisle, I quickly stood up, barely missing the overhead bin to look eyeball to eyeball with Elvis Aaron Presley. I was utterly flabbergasted and didn't even notice poor Joe Esposito in front of Elvis or Alan Fortas behind him. I only saw that sensuously smiling little curl on the lips of Elvis Presley!!

I must have looked foolish standing there with the reddest face I had ever had and my mouth wide open like a bass mounted on the wall. Nice way to greet the King of Rock and Roll, one of the sexiest men in the whole world! Somehow, I gathered my composure long enough to direct them to their seats.

Once we were then in the process of pushing away from the gate, I went into the galley to share with the other girls that Elvis Presley was indeed on our flight. Diane Totino, a darling little gal who was working in Coach, could not have cared less. She said she thought he was a greaser and I could have him all to myself as far as she was concerned. "YEAH!" I could hear myself say inside. After all, Diane was darling, and I wasn't sure if Elvis would prefer one of those petite types to me or not.

Linda Kirkland was as excited as I was, but she didn't want to show it, so she nonchalantly walked up to the forward magazine rack to get a particular issue for one of the Coach passengers (yeah, right). She snuck a quick glimpse as she passed by my galley. "Seniority, it sucks," Linda said, laughing as she went back to Coach.

I could barely stay on my jump seat long enough to take off. I couldn't believe Elvis was really here, right there in 4F in my cabin, on my flight, as my passenger. WOW!!!!! Could life get any better than this?

After the "No Smoking" sign turned off, the cockpit rang for coffee. Ed Montgomery said poor Captain Pat Matthews was about to pass out from lack of caffeine. Then I heard Skip Cline in the background ordering another one of his special pain-in-the-ass drinks. Skip always had to have something different like a squeeze of lime in his 7UP or half a sugar and a quarter of cream in his coffee. Then he would ask if we had any condiments for his meal or any leftover snacks. He was driving me nutso! I was so glad this was my last trip with him for the month; maybe even forever because he was transferring to ORD (Chicago) in March. Thank heavens, some other poor number one Stewardess would have to put up with him in Chicago.

I made a beeline for the galley to get their beverages and peek at Elvis one more time before I started my service. Linda was already in the galley, and she was as excited as I was. We were acting so goofy! We were ridiculous, giggling and stifling our oohs and ahhs as if we were sixteen. Diane came into the galley and told us we were absolutely "goosey." "He's just a man, for crying out loud. He puts his pants on the same way every other man does. What is so special about him?" she asked with such disgust in her voice.

"Only a man!" gasped Linda. "He's only a man? Dare we tell her that ain't no ordinary man sitting up there in First Class or shall we just let her wander around in utter stupidity?"

"Let's leave her be. She's entitled to her opinion, even if it is wrong. She must be crazy. An ordinary man indeed!" I stated, and we both burst out laughing. Diane shook her head and headed to the Coach cabin.

We were enjoying our laugh when the cockpit call button chimed again. "Damn," I said under my breath. I had forgotten Pat's coffee and Skip's 7UP. I picked up the phone and said, "I'm on my way, honest."

As I entered the cockpit, Pat, one of my favorite Captains, turned around and said, "Well, Bev, I guess we won't be seeing much of you this leg of the trip, will we?"

I giggled, "Why, Pat, what in the world gives you that idea?" I knew they had overheard me teasing with the agents all month and were aware of my desire to meet Elvis. They would have known Elvis would be on board before I did since they got the paperwork first. I handed them their drinks so quickly I nearly spilled Skip's 7UP.

As I turned to leave, Skip called out, "Oh, Bev, you forgot the squeeze."

I wanted to scream, "You'd better just squeeze yourself!" but I thought better of it.

Pat said, "We've seen the last of our Miss Bev." I went back and got Skip a few pieces of lime and a full can of 7UP. When I thrust it at poor Ed, the Flight Engineer, he said, "Don't be upset with me, Bev. I didn't order the squeeze," as he looked right at me and crossed his eyes. Skip's requests were getting to him too.

I smiled and said, "Perhaps if you had, it would have been a different kind of squeeze I delivered to the cockpit, Ed." He grinned from ear to ear and handed Skip his drink. Skip gave me a dirty look, and I just smirked in his direction. I saluted them and said, "See ya in Los Angeles, guys." They all just looked at me as I closed the door behind me.

Oh my, in all of the excitement I forgot to get Elvis' and his buddy's drink orders. I stood beside Joe and asked what he wanted to drink, then looked over in Elvis's direction. "May I get something for you, Mr. Presley?" I asked, all calm and cool.

"Mr. Presley, uh, did you say Mr. Presley?"

"Yes, that is your name, isn' it?"

"No, hon, it's just plain Elvis," he replied with a big, beautiful smile.

"Ok, Just Plain Elvis, would you like something to drink?" Joe started laughing, Elvis did too. He ordered Mr. and Mrs. T's Bloody Mary Mix with no liquor, calling it by the term "Virgin Mary." I had always hated it when people ordered the mix that way. I don't mean to sound even more like a prude, but it embarrassed me, and it was especially uncomfortable coming out of the mouth of Elvis Presley. "Okay, thank you, sir, er uh, I mean Just Plain Elvis."

Elvis looked at me and said to Joe, "We're going to have our hands full with this one." Then Elvis looked up at me and told me he was sure I would get the hang of calling him just Elvis eventually, and I assured him I would try my best.

I served everyone their drinks and sandwiches. Gradually many of the passengers started to doze off. Bless their little hearts, I was so grateful to them. It took a lot of sleeping pills and some very stiff drinks to get them to do that. Of course I' m only teasing, but I sure felt like I wanted to do something to make them all go to sleep. That would have been a pretty drastic way to get to spend time with Elvis Presley, but I doubt if anyone would have blamed me.

Elvis was staring out the window and didn't appear to be the least bit tired. (Little did I know at that time he was nocturnal.) He really was good-looking. As a matter of fact, he was almost pretty. His nose was just perfect, and his forehead and chin looked as if they had been carved by some master sculptor. He was wearing a light-blue turtleneck sweater under a royal-blue suit jacket. If you have seen the movie *This is Elvis*, the outfit he had on that night was the same one he wore in the movie when he was bringing Pricilla and Lisa Marie home from the hospital. He had longer hair than I was used to seeing him wear in his movies, but it wasn't greasy-looking at all.

"Could you take this?" Joe asked me as he handed me his tray. He startled me, and I almost dropped it right into his lap.

The sound of Joe's voice brought Elvis's eyes in my direction. They were so striking, a combination of blue and green! Elvis looked up at me and asked, "When are you going to quit all of this running around and come sit and talk to me?"

Whoa, was I thrilled! "Uh, I, er, uh should be finished in just a few minutes." I told him.

"Good," he replied, "I'll be waiting."

OH MY GOD! I thought to myself. Elvis Presley will be waiting for ME!!!!!

Linda had been standing right outside of the galley in front of me, and she grabbed me, "I heard that! You are the luckiest woman on the face of the earth!" She went on to mock Elvis, "When are you going to come and talk to me? I hate you, Beverly Golden, I hate you! I heard that flirtatious tone in his voice. He wants you."

"Oh, my God, girl you have lost it. He could have any woman in the world. What in heaven's name makes you think he wants me? He is probably just bored and wanting to have some fun."

"Yeah, some fun with you, Bev."

"Alright, that is enough. I need to get the galley picked up."

"I know you want some help because you don't want to keep Elvis waiting now, do you?"

I gave up. "No, Linda, I don't. Now get your junior ass in here and help me so that I can go visit with the King." We both burst out laughing.

Diane walked by shaking her head, "There's no hope for you two; none whatsoever."

I walked through the cabin to see if any of my passengers had the nerve to ask me for anything. Not really, but I did want to check on them so that once I sat down, I could stay for a while. Oh, thank you Lord, they were all asleep. How did I get so lucky?

I returned to the row in front of Elvis's seat and sat down on the divider table facing backwards towards him and Joe. "Now what was it you wanted to talk to me about?" Boy, was I cool or what? I thought to myself.

Elvis leaned toward me and looked directly into my eyes; I could feel the cool evaporating out of me. "Tell me about yourself," he demanded in the most alluring way.

I lost all my false feeling of calmness as I gazed into those blue-green eyes. He was staring at me and grinning that famous grin. Dear Lord, it must feel incredible to know you can just look at someone and watch them turn into silly putty right before your very eyes. I took a deep breath; my heart was pounding so hard I found it difficult to breathe normally. I thought to myself, "Just where is the nearest oxygen bottle located? I may need it before this night is over."

I started jabbering. I told him about how long I had been flying, about my family and my hometown. I even let it slip I was getting married in about two weeks, but I didn't really want to elaborate on that. Elvis reached up and grabbed my left hand and looked at my engagement ring, which was quite awesome, "So who are you marrying, some millionaire?" Oh, how cute, look who's talking, I thought to myself. I told him Derek worked for American Airlines too, and the ring had belonged to his grandmother.

I heard the cockpit call light. I excused myself. "Damn it, guys!" I wanted to yell into the phone, but I didn't. It was my ole buddy Skip wanting to know if there were any extra sandwiches left because his meal hadn't filled him up. If it had been anyone but Skip I wouldn't have cared, but him of all people. Still I didn't yell, I just took the whole tray of leftover sandwiches and some beverages, then reminded them I would be busy for the rest of the flight. "Yes, Mrs. Presley, we hear you," said Ed with a snicker. I just smirked at him and left again.

As I walked slowly through the cabin, I checked on each passenger to see if anyone needed anything, but they were all still sleeping. Oh happy days, I can go back and talk to Elvis some more. As I approached his row, I noticed Joe Esposito had moved over to sit with Alan Fortas. I was delighted and terrified all at once, especially when I caught Elvis's eye and he patted the seat beside him for me to sit in. GULP!!!!!

Linda was standing behind Elvis's row and motioned for me to come to her. I smiled at Elvis and told him I would be right back. When I got to her, she informed me she was giving me until the count of three to get my ass in that seat because if I took longer, I would be sitting in her lap. I laughed and turned and plopped right down, then turned around to look at her, stuck out my tongue as she flipped me off and again mouthed that she hated me.

Before Elvis and I could begin a conversation, Linda squatted down in the aisle beside me and asked Elvis if he had any pictures and if she could get one with his autograph. I know she just couldn't help herself, and I honestly couldn't blame her. Elvis leaned over me to ask Joe if they had any pictures. I inhaled deeply when he was leaning across me. He smelled so good, and I hoped I could remember that smell forever.

Joe pulled out a briefcase from under the seat in front of him, sifted through some papers, and handed Elvis a couple of pictures. They were of Elvis and Priscilla looking longingly into each other's eyes on their wedding day. God, did Priscilla look happy. Who wouldn't in her place?

"Who do I make this out to, Honey?' (I loved to hear Elvis say "Honey." It was so-o-o-o sweet, and with his southern accent, the word just rolled off his lips.)

She told him "Linda" would be just fine. Elvis leaned against me as he chatted with her for a few minutes. Oh, be still my heart! I felt like I did back in High School next to Terry Kneisley at the party when he kissed me the first time. This was so foolish, but I could not help myself I only hoped that what I was feeling on the inside didn't show on the outside. Elvis smelled so yummy — he wasn't even wearing cologne or aftershave — it was just the smell of him, and that smell was really getting to me.

Diane came by to ask Linda to cover for her in Coach while she went to the cockpit for a break. Elvis looked at Diane and said, "Hi." She just uttered a "Hi" back and honestly could not have seemed to care less. "She reminds me of Nancy Sinatra," Elvis said, and I got the impression that Diane's aloof attitude had hurt his feelings a little. Linda stood up, thanked Elvis for the pictures, and told us she had better get herself back to the Coach cabin before the "animals" got too restless.

"Animals? Is that what you girls call us?" Elvis asked me, and I was a tiny bit uncomfortable with his question. That was one of the nicer things

I'd heard used to refer to our passengers. Of course, the girls were usually joking but once in a while, well, the description fit.

"She was just joking around," I told him.

Then Elvis grinned rather sheepishly and asked me, "Don't you want a picture too? I can cut Priscilla off this photo if you want." Now why would he want to do a thing like that? (I must explain something here. I wanted to include the picture Elvis gave me but I wasn't permitted to because it had Priscilla in it. And I didn't know how to go about getting her permission to use her likeness.) Of course I wanted a picture, but I didn't want to appear too excited about receiving one.

"Yes, as a matter of fact I would like one for my little sister. It was her birthday three days ago, and I can't think of anything she'd rather have than an autographed picture of you." Elvis autographed the picture with a note for Charmaine and handed it to me.

"Now what about you, don't you want one?" I was surprised at how Elvis was reacting to me not getting all excited about wanting a picture, but I also remembered how he had seemed almost sad when Diane had been so cool to him.

"Yes, of course I would love one too."

Elvis turned his back to me so I could not see what he was writing on the picture. When he gave me the picture, he said, "Read it," which I did right away.

The autograph read, "To Bev, Well uh, kid, I don't know." I turned towards Elvis, sort of cocked my head to one side and looked puzzled. That was exactly what I think he had wanted me to do.

"What in the world does this mean?" I asked him.

Elvis smiled and answered, "It means this: If I wasn't married already and you weren't getting married, well..." his voice sort of trailed off into silence. Like that was supposed to make his meaning clear to me. I looked at him even more puzzled than before. "You really don't know what I mean do you?" he asked.

"No, I honestly don't."

He smiled a sweet, sensitive smile, as if to say he could not believe I could be so naïve. Then a twinkle came into his eyes, and he said, "Think about it, Hon."

We sat there and talked for what seemed like a long time. Elvis told me about the problems he had when he tried to go places, saying he really would enjoy being able to go to a nice restaurant just once like a normal person. Then he laughed and said, "If you want to call some of the kooks walking around the streets normal."

Elvis said he probably wouldn't feel comfortable in one of those fancy restaurants anyway because he wouldn't know which fork to use first. I told him how I nearly had a heart attack the first time I ate dinner at my future in-law's house. All the forks and spoons sitting beside my plate made me panic, but I managed to survive, and I was sure he would too. He laughed. (Oh my God, he had the most beautiful teeth!)

Then suddenly, like a plague, it hit. There was a deadly silence between us, and I felt so uncomfortable. We had been sharing and talking almost nonstop, and now I was panicking as I tried to think of something to say to him, something other than the stupid questions he was constantly being asked.

I had to say something. "Do you enjoy making movies?" I blurted out, almost too loudly. I was embarrassed. Elvis glanced at me with relief on his face because I had said something, even if it was something he had been asked numerous times before.

"Well, let me tell you, I have a good time. Unfortunately, I probably ruin more film than most of the other actors in Hollywood because I usually end up breaking up right in the middle of a scene. As a matter of fact, the scenes I ruin most are the so-called "love scenes." It is so silly to pretend that you and this girl are alone in this room about to start kissing when there are people all over the place. There are light technicians, script people, cameramen, directors, you name it. The place is crawling with people trying to do their jobs, and you've got to attempt to fool the audience into believing it's just the two of you. I am famous for bursting out laughing at the most inopportune times. It's a real problem for me."

"Have you ever had to kiss someone that you just hated to kiss?" I asked. "I know I have. It is so terrible to be attracted to this person and then they kiss you, and it's a total zero. That is so bad, don't you agree?"

"Yeah, that has happened to me a couple of times," Elvis replied, "but there is nothing you can do but fake it."

Elvis had turned and was looking out the window, and there was that awful silence again. I was about to get up and go check the cabin when he turned to me and said, "You are going to think I am absolutely nuts, but I feel like a guy on his first date with you. I want so much to say so many things, but everything I think of sounds so silly. Just like saying there is a beautiful view of the moon out of my window. It just seems odd to mention it to a Stewardess at 30,000 feet in the air."

I sighed a big sigh of relief. "There must be a million things I want to say and ask of you, yet every one of them sounds, as you said, so silly."

"Well, I'm sure glad that we got that out in the open," Elvis exclaimed.

Yet another silence was to follow.

I had just looked down at my hands, which were folded in my lap when I heard him move in his seat. I raised my eyes to see a hand coming in the direction of my cheek. I nearly jumped out of my skin; it caught me completely off guard. But it happened so quickly I don't believe Elvis was aware of the fact he had perhaps just robbed me of at least ten years of my young life.

Elvis placed his right hand on my left cheek, pulled my face towards his, leaned forward, and kissed me right on the mouth. If he had opened his eyes, the poor man would have surely screamed because my eyes were wide open staring at him in disbelief. I looked into that incredibly handsome face with those beautiful eyelashes resting on his cheeks. Oh my goodness, I couldn't believe this was happening to me! I imagined this had to be the worst kiss Elvis had ever received in his life because I was so totally unprepared.

It must not have been the worse kiss ever though, because when he finished kissing me, Elvis pulled his face a little away from mine, looked into my eyes, leaned forward, and kissed me again. But this time I was ready for him, and really laid one on him. My heart was about to explode, to think of all the women in the whole wide world who would have given anything to trade places with me at that moment.

All kinds of things were racing through my head, including a flashback to when Karen and I had gone to see *G. I. Blues*. It would be worth a million dollars to have Karen Hedwig Roth see me now. Then the thought rushed through my head about one of my passengers getting up and seeing me. Oh, Lordy, I'd be fired for sure. I could just imagine the gossip in Operations as it was reported I had lost my job over kissing Elvis Presley inflight. What Stewardess in her right mind would have blamed me? I couldn't think of any, and probably even the supervisors would have understood and wished they had been me.

(Now for all of you ladies sitting out there clutching this book or your Kindle, or whatever and wondering just what it was like to kiss Elvis Presley, let me tell you this: it was FABULOUS!!!! Unlike the movie, he didn't try to French kiss me. I was so grateful because I had very little experience in that type of kissing, except with Alphie. His lips were so tender, yet there was passion in the way he pushed his mouth against mine. You could tell Elvis really enjoyed kissing as much as I did, and believe me, I enjoyed kissing Elvis!!!!!!!)

I sat there staring at Elvis after he had finished kissing me the second time. Then, for some reason, I felt sad. I imagined Elvis sitting in the limo with Joe and Alan boasting about the great big thrill he had given to the Stewardess on his flight. Then he'd laugh at me because this kiss didn't mean a thing to him; it was just something to do to kill time on an airplane trip. I felt my face turn deep red as I got angry. I stood and walked to the cockpit without saying a word. I heard Elvis call my name, but I just kept walking. I was really upset because I just didn't want to be laughed at.

As I entered the cockpit, Ed looked up at me. He seemed to know there was something wrong, but he didn't say a word. Instead of sitting on the jump seat directly in back of the Captain like I usually did, I sat on the jump seat back in the corner. Skip turned around and inquired with his horse's ass attitude, "What"s up, Bev, did you and Elvis have a fight?"

Apparently, Pat hadn't heard me come into the cockpit. When he saw me, he sensed this was not the time for Skip to be an ass. Glaring at Skip, Pat turned to me and asked if I was alright. I nodded my head that I was. I just didn't feel like talking right then and knew Pat would understand. I sat there for what seemed like an eternity, probably more ten minutes tops, when I realized I really didn't want to be there either, so I decided to go back to the galley. As Skip turned around and started to ask me for something, Pat cut him off, "Not now Skip," he said with such kindness toward my situation.

As I passed Elvis's seat, he spoke my name. I turned and looked at him. He looked so pitiful, like he truly didn't understand why I had jumped up and left him like that. Frankly, I couldn't explain it to myself either. Elvis leaned toward me and handed me a little piece of paper. I looked at him rather strangely and took it into the galley to read, thankful he didn't attempt to follow me. (You may think I was acting very peculiar, and I admit I was, but I am very sensitive and just didn't want to feel like he was making fun of me.)

I opened up the paper, it was a beverage list; written on it was this message, "Don't think we were bad; I loved it. A passenger."

Tears burned in my eyes. Damn! If I were Elvis Presley, I would go around giving poor little Stewardesses thrills to talk about too. Is that so bad? Why was I acting like such an ass? Everything doesn't have to be so serious. I thought about my vision of Elvis laughing at me and making fun, and I just knew he wouldn't act that way because he just wasn't that kind of person. He seemed to be sensitive too, based on how he reacted to Diane and the fact he didn't think I wanted a picture of him.

I took a deep breath, blinked my eyes to erase any trace of the tears that had just been there and went back into the cabin to sit beside Elvis. As I sat down, he put his hand on mine and patted it. "Everything okay?" he asked, looking like a little boy who had just considered doing something wrong and had changed his mind at the last moment hoping to be forgiven. He was waiting for me to tell him everything was okay, and that I was okay. I assured him I was just fine.

Elvis sighed, a big sigh, and grinned at me as he sank back in his seat. It was such a cute gesture, I had to giggle. He looked over and seemed so relieved that everything was fine between us. I can't believe how silly this sounds, but I felt privileged that Elvis had worried he might have offended me in some way and wanted to be sure I was okay and not upset with him. This all made him that much more endearing to me.

An announcement came on, "Ladies and gentlemen, we have just been informed by the tower in Los Angeles that our landing conditions are below minimums, and we may have to proceed to Oakland for landing. We will keep you further advised." I couldn't believe Pat hadn't called me up to the cockpit to tell me about this before he made the announcement, perhaps he thought I was still upset.

"I'll be right back," I told Elvis.

"Hurry," he responded.

"I will, just as fast as I can." I took all of the cockpit crew some coffee, even Skip with his half sugar and a fourth cream.

"To what do we owe the honor of this unexpected treat? You and Elvis make up?" Skip snidely inquired as I handed out the coffee.

"Don't push it, Skip. There may be arsenic in yours," I replied. "Pat, are we really going to have to land at Oakland?"

"There's a real good chance of it, Bev. If the fog doesn't clear in the next twenty-five minutes, we have to. We don't have enough fuel to spend any more time than that up here circling. I'll let you know just as soon as we have made a decision. Thanks for the coffee."

A few of the passengers were awake by now, so I served them coffee and juice. The others I just let sleep because there was no reason to wake them until we had some definite news.

When I sat down beside Elvis, he seemed very excited. "Bev, if we have to go to Oakland, will you ride over to Los Angeles with Joe, Alan, and me?" He seemed so pleased to have come up with this idea.

"I really don't know if I can, Elvis. Generally, the whole crew has to stay together. You can bet that I'll check though." He had a happy look of anticipation in his eyes, which I found to be so strange. Why would he be so excited about me riding in the limo with them? I was definitely pleased he seemed to be looking forward to the possibility of this happening. Oh, how I wished.

Unfortunately, my wish didn't come true. The fog cleared and Pat announced we'd be able to land in Los Angeles after all. Elvis looked at me with such disappointment in his eyes. "Sorry," I said, and really meant it.

"Yeah, me too," he replied.

We prepared for landing, and when I sat on the jump seat, Elvis waved at me like a little kid. I was a little embarrassed, but the gesture was so darling. Although I tried to keep staring at the floor, I just couldn't. I just wanted to look at Elvis and soak in as much "Elvis time" as I possibly could before he was gone forever.

As I looked at him, Elvis started blowing me kisses. I couldn't believe this! I giggled to myself. What in the world had gotten into him? How could he be acting like this? Was he really acting so silly because of ME? WOW, this was just amazing!!!!

Some mechanics were on the jetbridge as Elvis was leaving. He stood right in front of me, smiled and said, "See you, kid."

"Get off my plane, mister," I said to him jokingly. I wished so much this trip had never ended. I could not have dreamed a better outcome and was so happy Elvis turned out to be a wonderful man.

The two mechanics stood there with their mouths open, hanging on every word. Elvis took a few steps, turned around and winked at me, then said "Good night."

"Yeah, it was a good night, Elvis, a very good night!" I exclaimed with a hint of mischief in my voice as he grinned and walked away.

I wonder what those mechanics were thinking; perhaps they thought Elvis and I had joined the "mile high club" during our flight or something. I blushed at the very thought of it but also felt a bit impressed with myself they might have been thinking that. For shame! (For those of you who aren't familiar with the term "mile high club," it means you had sex on an airplane inflight, be it in your seat or in the lavatory. I experienced a few people getting very familiar with each other under blankets on night flights, but I never stuck around long enough to see how far they actually went. And yes, I did see a few couples emerge from a lavatory together, but fortunately, never heard anything from inside. Thank goodness!)

I walked about ten feet off the ground to the area where the crew limo was to pick us up. As I sat there on the bench reliving the events of the flight, a soldier approached me and asked for directions to Western Airlines. As I leaned forward to direct him, a big black limo pulled up in front of us. The rear window rolled down, and I stared at Elvis sticking his head out the window. "Hey, Bev." I grinned at the sound of his voice. "Good night again," he said.

"Good night to you too," I said, sounding a little sad that my wonderful evening had ended.

The soldier stood there with his mouth in the same drooped position as the mechanics had on the jetbridge earlier. "Oh, my God," he yelled, "that was Elvis Presley! Wasn't that Elvis Presley?"

"Yes, it was Elvis Presley. He's a friend of mine," I told the soldier with a big grin on my face.

"Wait until the guys back at the base hear about who I saw. They are not going to believe it," he stated in disbelief.

"Yes, I know that feeling. I'm having trouble believing it myself," I replied. The soldier walked towards Western Airlines muttering to himself that he had just seen Elvis Presley and how no one would believe him.

I was smiling when the rest of the crew came out. As we headed towards Santa Monica, Linda said to me, "Bev, I've just got to ask you something. I was walking through the First Class cabin and I could have sworn I saw you sitting there making out with Elvis. Did I?"

"Don't be ridiculous, Linda. You must have been seeing things" I looked over at her and winked. I was grinning from ear to ear at her question but didn't see any reason to tell anyone. It was between me and Elvis. Of course, I would be calling Karen the first chance I got!

Needless to say, Karen was completely blown away when I told her. I asked if she remembered what I had said to her when we saw *G. I. Blues*. She said she did but she never ever, in a million years, dreamed it would come true. "Come on, Bev, there are women all over the world who would give everything they own to have been in your place on that airplane. Me included."

"Now, Karen, just what do you think Ricky Nelson would do if he heard you say that?"

She giggled, "Hey, how about Frankie Avalon?"

"Well, I guess he has finally been replaced," I told her. We both laughed and accepted the fact I must have really had a vision of my future after all, that day back in 1963.

Fortunately, this was not the only time fate brought Elvis and me together, but hey, that's another story. As they used to say on the radio, "Stay tuned." Or in this case, keep reading.

WE'RE GETTING MARRIED

Derek got a kick out of my story about Elvis, but of course I didn't elaborate on the kissing part. As a matter of fact, I don't think I mentioned it at all. When I showed Derek the picture with the autograph, he asked what it meant, and chuckling to myself, I told him he would have to ask Elvis.

Joyce wasn't too pleased about me marrying Derek. She thought he was too controlling and really didn't like the way he wanted to dominate me and our lives. I guess I was too in love to listen to anyone - Jean Marie, Nancy, Joyce - and had no idea how my future would turn out.

I knew Derek could be loving and tender when he wanted to be. He just was so big and tall and domineering in his presence that I guess he felt like he always had to be the person in control of everything. I would never really know why he was the way he was. He was just Derek, and I saw things in him that he didn't allow others to see.

We were trying to plan a wedding in Ohio while living in New York, which wasn't easy. Plus, my parents had no money for a wedding. I didn't think there would be too many people at the wedding anyway since I hadn't lived in Columbus for over two years and had lost contact with many people. I never saw Godee or Laura. I did keep in touch with Karen after she had married Nate and moved to North Carolina while he was in the Army.

I couldn't afford to buy a wedding dress, so Karen's mom, Gussie, told me Karen would be proud for me to get married in her dress. There was only one problem, Karen had boobs and I didn't I didn't have a whole lot of choice, though because I knew Mom and Dad couldn't afford a dress and neither could I, and I had too much pride to ask Derek to buy it. So I would be wearing Karen's dress even if it was too big and short (In the wedding pictures later, it didn't look too bad because I wore a heavily-padded bra.) Derek wasn't too happy when I told him we would have to pay for the reception, so it probably wouldn't be anything like what his parents were expecting.

When Mrs. Schoenmann, Pam, and Janet came to our little dinky house on Case Road, I was so embarrassed. Their home was huge and ours was like a matchbox in comparison. Claire was sitting beside me on the couch and asked, "Bev, dear. I would love to see your room." (For some reason I hated being called "Bev, dear." I don't know why, but it almost felt like Claire was talking to a servant or something. Of course, I never told her that, but I hated it!) I tried my best to discourage Claire but nothing would do except for her to see my incredibly small room. So I took her down the hall and opened the door to the room I used to share with, Charmaine. Claire peeked in, looked at me, and stated, "How quaint."

I was embarrassed, but there was nothing I could do about it. It was what it was and that was all there was to it. My folks were middle-class, ex-hillbillies who had made it out of the hills of West Virginia and were doing really well by some of our family's standards, just not in comparison to the Schoenmann clan who had ambassadors and all sorts of upper crust folks hanging from their family tree. I knew Derek's grandmother, Aida Schoenmann, was an ambassador's wife, but I tried not to let their situation of affluence affect me. (I found out later, Claire thought that by Derek marrying me, he would become financially responsible for not just me but my whole family. This never was the case, but I resented the fact she even thought that.)

March 2, 1968 was our wedding day.

Mike had told me he couldn't get leave to come to the wedding, but then he suddenly let me know he was coming. I was excited when he and another sailor showed up so Mike was able to be in the wedding. Little did I know that Mike and his friend had gone AWOL to come to my wedding and had to sit in the brig when they returned to the base. Even though we had always been close, I never would have asked Mike to do that, but it meant the world to have him at my wedding.

Derek had asked his Dad to be his best man, which I thought was so touching. I had Pam, Janet, and Charmaine as my bridesmaids in light turquoise dresses. Mom looked so pretty in her pink outfit. Sadly, all of the men's tuxes were too short except Daddy's. I don't know how that happened, but it was too late to make any changes before walking down the aisle.

It was a really small wedding. My uncle Buck was there with his family, my Granny Dickson, Aunt Kat and Uncle Bill, Karen's folks, Derek's grandmother, and one gal I had worked with at the phone company. I felt bad that so few people were there, though I really hadn't expected many, but a few more than that handful would have been nice. Since Mom and Dad had lived in Columbus for so long, I thought more people would have come.

I found myself hoping I would not find Alphie waiting outside the church for us. Fortunately, if he was, and I do think he mentioned to me later that he did come by the church that day, I didn't see him. But I felt his presence. I knew I loved Derek, but he didn't always treat me the way I thought a fiancée should treat his future wife. Little did I know what troubles were ahead of us in this marriage.

We went to Honolulu, Hawaii for our honeymoon. Derek had arranged for us to go First Class on Pan American, which offered such a lovely service. I loved that we were served bananas foster, a dessert the Stewardess lit on fire. I would have thought that was too dangerous, but these gals had been flying a while, and I doubt seriously if there was anything they couldn't handle. Pan Am put on quite a show for their First Class travelers. I think we were both impressed by our competitor's service.

In Hawaii, everything seemed to smell of flowers, and there were tons of different types everywhere you looked. Leis were placed around the necks of visitors - Derek and I got one when we deplaned, and they were sold at just about every little shack along the way from the airport to the hotel district.

We stayed in a condominium in the Ilaki Resort, which was a beautiful place. With the time difference, we were so tired after we checked into the hotel that we actually fell asleep in each other's arms. There would be plenty of time, years I assumed, to make love to each other.

The next morning we woke up rested and did make love. Silly me, somehow I thought maybe married love would be different from engaged love. It wasn't. We had agreed to abstain from sex for two months before we got married, so I had thought it would be much more passionate after our wedding than it turned out to be. But then again, I had nothing to compare lovemaking to because I had never been with anyone other than Derek.

It seemed making love was always done the same way, and it was very frustrating for me. I had heard an expression when I walked into the cockpit one day, one of the pilots said his wife had accused him of always doing, "Slam, bam, thank you, ma'am." I wasn't exactly sure what that meant, but I was beginning to get the feeling that that described our lovemaking. As I mentioned, I don't think Derek had much previous experience, and I sure didn't have any. I just expected more feelings, I wanted fireworks and heavy breathing, but that wasn't the case. Then again, I never really sat down and talked to anyone about sex because I was too embarrassed to discuss it. Based on some of the conversations I accidentally overheard in High School, sex was supposed to be something fantastic, thrilling, and exciting. I knew I had experienced some pretty tremendous butterflies in my stomach when kissing Jimmie or making out with Alphie. I had felt that way about Derek too, but this just wasn't what I expected to feel after "going all the way."

We rented a jeep and drove all around the island. Derek got sun poisoning and had to go to the doctor. I guess he had no idea how intense the Hawaiian sun could be. We did go out to a luau, which was a lot of fun, although the poi (a famous Hawaiian dish) was gross! I really couldn't imagine anyone actually eating that stuff - it looked like grey wallpaper paste. I liked the rest of the goodies they served though. Derek and I even dressed alike - he in a beautiful dark blue shirt with flowers on it that matched the muumuu I had. (Why these were fashionable was beyond me. Everyone I saw in a muumuu looked either overweight or pregnant. Yes, I imagine it was a great cover up for heavyset gals, but why would skinny women want to wear one?)

We did the tourist thing and took a few tours. One morning when we had a slight rain, I suggested we stay in bed and cuddle and experiment with being together. For some strange reason, Derek got out of bed and told me he didn't intend to spend his whole day lying in bed. I was devastated! I thought that was what honeymoons were for, getting to know each other and pleasing one another. Derek wasn't having any part of that and informed me he was going downstairs to the coffee shop for some breakfast. I told him I wasn't hungry. When he left, I just laid there crying into my pillow. Is there something wrong with me? I knew I didn't have any experience, but how was I supposed to learn if we didn't spend any time together getting to know what made each other happy and feel good? I sat there looking out the window at the first of many beautiful Hawaiian rainbows I would see over the next twenty or so years. What I didn't know was that as I saw those future rainbows, I would recall how sad I had been during what was supposed to be the happiest time of my life.

Derek and I returned to work at LaGuardia. Right before we left to get married, we had found a really cute, one-bedroom apartment, not far from the airport. This was great because both of us could walk to work. Some days, Derek would drive me when I was going out on a three-day trip, and if it was late, he would pick me up or I would do the same for him.

We were Mr. and Mrs. Derek Schoenmann, Jr., but somehow things weren't as I thought they should be. I had made this commitment, and I was determined to have a marriage that would last as long as my parents' marriage had. I thought marriage was forever; you have a little house, two kids and life goes on. I didn't know you were supposed to be happy and content in your marriage. In spite of the fact that on our wedding day, Pastor Darnell said from that day forward we would be one, I never felt complete in that statement no matter how hard I tried. I always felt for some reason, Derek was the boss and I was his partner, but not an equal one. I'm not exactly sure why I felt this way, I just did. Although I wasn't sure how it was going to change now that we were married, I was going to do everything I could make the best of it.

We double-dated with our friends, Linda and Ernie Jacobson, and at times we had Neil Casey (Derek's old roommate) over for dinner. If I met a Stewardess I really enjoyed, I'd invite her and her husband over to join Derek and me for dinner or a movie.

My favorite couple was Helen and Jim Kirkman. She was a Stewardess, and he was an attorney. Jim and Derek had some great conversations, since their personalities were very similar, as were mine and Helen's. She and I would "Buddy Bid" like Bet and I used to and fly trips together so the four of us could do things on our days off. One time, Helen and I were flying to Los Angeles and staying at the Miramar Hotel in Santa Monica not far from the beach, so we talked Derek and Jim into coming with us for some sun time and dinner. It was always so much fun when the four of us got together. We loved cooking crazy meals or going out to new kinds of restaurants.

Derek was interviewing for jobs within the company so he could climb up that corporate ladder. He had been an understudy and then a supervisor of ticket agents and now he was looking for something much more advanced, to get more exposure to the company and see how it worked from another perspective. So started Derek's venture into the automated world of Sabre, American Airlines's automated reservation system, where he was hired as a systems analyst. What I didn't realize was this meant we had to leave New York and live in Tulsa, Oklahoma.

It was 1970, and American Airlines was flying to the South Pacific. I was barely senior enough to get on the International operation, and I was ecstatic! We flew 707s for seven-day trips from JFK nonstop to Honolulu, spent the night, then on to St. Louis, Missouri, stayed over, back to Hawaii, another layover, and then nonstop back to New York. It was so exciting! I just loved this new kind of flying with a fabulous service and good loads of passengers. The whole crew was together for the entire trip, and we all seemed to get along great. There was now an extra crew member, the Inflight Service Manager, who would zoom around the airplane doing public relations, finding out about new groups of folks that might want to book transportation to one of our new destinations. He was basically a member of management there to "schmooze" with potential future fliers.

Some of the guys were great and others were pompous jerks. Some wouldn't even pick up a glass if one of the passengers offered it to them, instead coming to get one of us to pick it up. Others were great and helped in any way they could, including on occasion taking a couple of kids and entertaining them while we were doing the meal service so Mom and Dad could actually enjoy themselves for a few minutes.

It was a whole new world flying to Honolulu, Australia, and New Zealand. I didn't get to go to the latter two destinations very often because they were so senior, but once in a while, on reserve, I would get called for one of those trips, and it was unbelievable! I struck up a friendship with our American Airlines representative Graeme Thompson, from Auckland, New Zealand on a trip from New York to Honolulu. He was staying in Hawaii for a couple of days and asked me to go to a luau the hotel was sponsoring to entice tourists from "Down Under" to stay at the Ala Moana Hotel. It was so elaborate! They had a huge spread of food, a Hawaiian floor show with dancers from several different locations in the islands. Some of the dancers, Maoris I think, were pretty scary looking with their makeup and tattoos on their faces and bodies.

I had a wonderful time. Graeme told me he would be delighted if Derek and I would come to Auckland, New Zealand some time and meet his wife Cheryl. I told him I would discuss it with Derek because we actually had our vacation coming up soon and that sounded just wonderful. He assured me I would never get better tasting lamb in my life. I had never eaten lamb before and sort of wrinkled up my nose since I couldn't get past the sight of a little, white, fuzzy critter being eaten. I told Graeme we would be happy to visit him, but I wasn't so sure about the lamb dinner.

When I got back to New York, I told Derek about Graeme. He looked at me suspiciously, but I assured him that Graeme was just a really nice married guy who had invited us to visit him and Cheryl on our vacation. Graeme and I corresponded for a few months before our vacation in the fall. Derek had given in and decided it might be a lot of fun to go someplace so far away, where not too many folks from the U.S. had ever been. Derek wanted his parents to go too, so we were disappointed they couldn't tear themselves away from Janet's parents' weekend at college. Since I hadn't gone to college, I asked Derek if there would be other parent weekends they could go instead, and he told me there were. But his parents had made their choice, not realizing how much it would have meant to their son for them to go with us. We had taken a trip with my parents to San Francisco in November of 1972 and had the most fun together sightseeing and eating out. It is one of my fondest memories of the four of us together.

We had to stay over in Honolulu for almost a day before going on to Auckland. It was so green and beautiful there. At the Duty Free Shop, Derek took me in and bought me a watch. I hadn't had a new watch since Daddy bought me one for Christmas when I was a teenager. I loved that watch so much, especially since it had been Derek's idea to buy it and not mine.

When we finally landed in Auckland, we rested at the hotel. The next day we called Graeme and Cheryl, who suggested we come to their home for dinner since we were tired from the trip, and then we would start our tourist travels the next day. It was fun being with them, and with their British-sounding accents, I could have listened to them talk forever.

We traveled over the island going to different tribal villages. I had no idea there were so many primitive people there. We visited this one area that was supposed to have springs that were medicinal and made you feel better. They smelled awful to me, like rotten eggs. I jokingly asked Graeme if the people got well in a hurry just to escape the smell. He and Cheryl got a good laugh from that; they were used to the smell.

One of the funniest things was getting Derek into Graeme and Cheryl's car. It was a purple Mini K, and Derek and I named it the Purple Grape. It was an Australian-made vehicle obviously made for very short people, close to the size of a Mini Cooper today. Derek had to practically curl up just to get in the car and then didn't have room to stretch out his 6' 5" body. Cheryl and I sat in the back seat, me behind Derek so he could push his seat as far back as I could stand it. While it was funny to all of us, I don't think Derek enjoyed it half as much as we did as we watched him get in and out and heard other people nearby snicker at him.

Our last night in Auckland, we went out to a really nice restaurant for dinner, and I finally gave in and ate lamb. I didn't know what it was supposed to taste like, but it was delicious! Derek had had lamb before; his family quite often had leg of lamb for Easter Dinner. I could not get over how wonderful it tasted. I felt guilty eating a fuzzy little lamb, but it was a unique and pleasing dining experience. (I still love eating lamb to this day, but I don't serve it very often. None could compare with that New Zealand lamb.)

When we got back from vacation, Derek found out he and I would have to go to Tulsa, Oklahoma for a visit to decide if he was going to take the job as a systems analyst or not. We said we would go after we got back from spending Christmas with his family.

The Schoenmanns had their Christmas tradition of having eggnog and decorating the Christmas tree the night before Christmas. I thought that was kind of sad because it meant the tree wasn't up very long to enjoy, and it seemed like a lot of work for such a short time, but I wasn't going to buck tradition. Another thing I had a problem getting used to was that Derek and I had our presents placed on a loveseat, his Mom and Dad each had a chair for theirs, Pam and her husband, Jeramie, had the couch, and Janet was the only one whose presents were around the tree. That was so odd to me. We had always put all of the presents under the tree, everybody's. It would have made a lot more sense if Janet had been a little girl, but she was in college. Again, who was going to say anything; definitely not me.

We filled them in about our awesome trip and how we wished so much that Derek and Claire could have been with us. Derek, Sr. actually acted like he was disappointed not to have gone along, but Claire was insistent they had made the right choice in joining Janet at college because it was such an important time in her life. She assured Derek and I we had plenty of years to travel to places together. Well, those plenty of years never happened, and I never got over seeing how sad Derek was they didn't go with us then.

When we returned to New York, we made plans to fly to Tulsa for a visit. It was a nice enough city, clean and growing with lots of potential. It would be nice living in Tulsa, but the thought of moving from New York to a city I didn't know, with absolutely no one I knew, was terrifying to me. I know I had done it as a Stewardess, but this seemed completely different to me. At least I had had three roommates who were in a similar situation for the last move, and we were all starting out together. But now it was just me and Derek. When we first started dating, I knew he planned to climb that corporate ladder. Now I was married and had agreed to spend my life with this man, so I was going to be by his side even if it meant moving. The worst part was I could not get a transfer to DFW (Dallas-Fort Worth) for several months, so that meant I had to fly back to New York before my scheduled trip, work my schedule, and then fly back to Tulsa. I was on reserve on International, and I was scared what would happen to me if they knew I was living in Oklahoma and couldn't get there when they needed me. I did not like this way of living.

DEPRESSION REARS ITS UGLY HEAD

Muskogee and Me

In 1970, we found a really cute apartment in Tulsa. After living there for about six months, we decided to build a house, and I was so excited about the prospect of us having our very first home together. I had never known anyone who built their own house before. Mom and Dad's first new home was a tract home, ready to move in, and they never picked out anything. Now Derek and I would be choosing the style of house, the layout of our floorplan, the wallpaper, carpet, and just about everything right down to the fixtures on the cabinets in the kitchen and bathrooms. It was going to be a three-bedroom house with a combined living-dining area and a big den or family room. It was more than I ever dreamed I would have in my life. It was beautiful, and we were so proud of it the first time Derek's folks came down to visit. We even got a golden retriever puppy we named Muskogee because we liked the way the name of the Oklahoma city sounded. Derek's parents had always had golden retrievers, so of course we had to have one too. When Claire met "Kogee" as we called her, she dubbed her "Grand-dog." Little did we know then that Kogee would be as close to getting grandkids from Derek and me as she would get.

Our life should have been perfect but...I was having difficulty dealing with a problem. I felt like I was living with one foot in the past and one foot in the present, and because of my commuting back to New York to fly, I felt like I was in the Twilight Zone. While Derek was concentrating on his new job, I was trying to keep my spirits up, but it wasn't working. I found myself getting in more and more "blue moods" with crying jags. I could almost feel myself falling deeper and deeper into a depression I felt I wasn't going to be able to handle. I was getting worried about how much time I spent crying both at home and, occasionally, on my layovers. I don't think I broke down on my trips but I sure shed a bucket of tears over the next few months. I could not keep myself busy - I mean, how many times can you clean a brand new house, do the wash and ironing, and still find something else to do? I was falling deeper and deeper into this emotional well that made me feel awful, and I couldn't explain how I got here or what caused this to happen to me, other than this move to Tulsa.

I was fortunate enough to have met Derek's aunt Dori and her husband Gary when we were traveling to Ohio for Christmas one year. They lived in St. Louis, Missouri, and it was great we had fallen in love with each other because several of my trips laid over in St. Louis (STL). Dori was the Mom of four, and she was so wonderful to me that it was like I had known her my whole life. It was hard to believe she and Claire were sisters because they were so different, but then again so were Charmaine and me.

When I had layovers in St. Louis, I would visit Dori and Gary's house. One trip in. particular, Gary came to the hotel to pick me up because Dori was cooking supper. I had purchased two beautiful leis for them in Hawaii. I came into the hotel lobby all tan, tall, and blonde, approached Gary from behind, and when he turned, I placed the lei around his neck and kissed him on the cheek, saying, "Aloha from Hawaii." The lobby was filled with mostly businessmen, and they all turned to see me kissing Gary. He puffed up like a blow fish, telling me later his status in life definitely took a soar in that lobby. I laughed so much when he would relate this story to anyone willing to listen. We left the lobby for their home arm-in-arm.

I always felt like I could talk to Dori about anything, so I shared with her about how sad I had become when we moved to Tulsa, that I really didn't like it there. I didn't want to stand in the way of Derek's advancement, but I wanted to be back in New York for flying instead of having to leave hours, and sometimes days, in advance to cover my schedule. I told her I felt bad about imposing on former roommates and friends for a place to stay or rides to and from the airport. I was worried about how depressed I had begun to feel. Dori understood all about depression because her daughter Claire (named after Derek's Mom) had some really trying times herself with depression. They had finally found some medication that helped her deal with her problems.

I shared with Dori that I didn't want to burden Derek with how I was feeling, but she recommended I talk to him because, as she reminded me, we had married in sickness and in health, and it probably wasn't fair for me not to tell Derek what I was dealing with. I knew she was right, but I just didn't understand what was going on inside me. I told her I might go see a doctor in Tulsa. (Dori and Gary Ferguson are two of the most wonderful people I have ever met. They both have remained my friends through all of life's events. She is the one woman that I admire more than any other. I am blessed to call her and Gary my friends, and I love them both with all my heart.)

I finally shared with Derek what I was feeling, but I don't think he understood. He just thought I was missing my friends and living in New York, but I knew it was much, much more. When I returned to Tulsa, I called and got an appointment with a psychiatrist named Dr. Lynwood Heaver. I went for an office visit and explained to him what I was going through. He recommended I start taking some antidepressants to see if it would help.

Dr. Heaver gave me medicine, but he also wanted to treat me through hypnosis. I wasn't sure how I felt about that, but I was pretty desperate. I probably would have consented to almost anything to get these bouts of tears to end, but I didn't like that Dr. Heaver kept bringing up my sex life. He was probably one of those Freudian-type doctors that thought all problems in your life were based on sex. I never discussed sex with anyone, ever, and I sure didn't feel right talking to this man about it, even if he was a doctor.

Dr. Heaver asked specific questions, some of which I had no idea what he was talking about, but I didn't want to ask him what he meant. I didn't feel comfortable with the questions he asked at all, so I always tried to change the subject or pretended I didn't hear what he had asked. He would want to hypnotize me, turn out the lights, and then sit there and talk to me in the dark. I don't think I was ever really hypnotized because I was aware of everything that was going on during our sessions, everything that he asked, and everything that happened in his office.

I shared with Dr. Heaver I sometimes felt like I couldn't do anything right when it came to Derek. He was constantly correcting my grammar and my manners. Derek didn't like the way I pronounced "aunt." I had always called my mother's sister "Ant Kat," but Derek informed me that ants crawled on the ground, and she was my "aunt" (like "haunt"). Mom, and therefore I, always referred to facecloths as washrags. Derek nearly had a fit the first time I said that. He told me you cleaned the house and worked on the car with rags and that cloths were for washing your body, not washrags! He was never happy that I didn't want to read a newspaper to stay abreast of the world situation so I could converse accurately with people at my job and in everyday conversations. Although I read *Time* and *Newsweek*, he was especially unhappy about my love for reading movie magazines.

Once we moved to Tulsa, Derek completely took over the paychecks, his and mine. I was given an allowance, usually twenty dollars to go on a flight, while he put the rest of my money in the bank. I was constantly reminded when I would buy something, "There are wants and there are needs. First you get the needs, and then if there is anything left over, you can get the wants." I found myself hoarding money from my trips to buy things I wanted when I returned to Tulsa. Or if there was something I bought on a trip, I would wait until he went to work to take it out of my suitcase and hang it in my closet. If Derek mentioned a piece of clothing looking new, I would always let on like it was something I had had for a long time.

Derek had no complaints with how I kept our house, his clothes, or how I tried to cook for him I loved learning to cook, and Derek loved to eat. I don't recall ever fixing anything he didn't seem to enjoy, and he was especially fond of the pumpkin bread I made around Thanksgiving. Derek did compliment me more times than not on my cooking.

Still, I could not help feeling like there was so much more Derek wanted me to do or be. That I was never good enough, or smart enough, or gracious enough for him or his family. I couldn't help but feel I wasn't the woman his family had expected their first-born and only son to marry. I was self-conscious around them when we were together, and I felt bad that I didn't have more than a High School diploma. Yes, I had become a Stewardess and had done it on my own, but it never seemed enough to match up to Derek, Pam, and Janet's college degrees. Maybe they weren't really thinking this, but I always felt like they were, so I was even harder on myself.

I didn't feel like Dr. Heaver was really helping me that much, but I was actually to the point of being scared about how I was feeling. I just couldn't stop crying. I had no self-worth, and I didn't know how it had gotten this bad. Dr. Heaver suggested to Derek I be hospitalized, not once but two times in 1971, once in June and again in December. Being hospitalized didn't seem to make much of a change in me either. Dr. Heaver finally admitted he felt like he was not successful in treating me, so he referred me to Dr. Thomas Turner, a neurosurgeon, for further treatment. Dr. Turner suggested electroshock therapy be considered.

After examining me, Dr. Turner told Derek I was severely agitated and depressed, with the inability to cope with even simple situations, and he felt like I had definite suicidal tendencies. I was admitted to St. John's Hospital on January 19, 1972 to be evaluated. I seemed to improve so much that Dr. Turner discharged me on January 29, telling Derek he was pleased at how much I had improved but not to be surprised if I suffered a recurring bout of depression. I don't know what triggered it, but I became so upset that I was readmitted to the hospital on January 31.

When Derek took me back to the hospital, Dr. Turner noted I was extremely distraught, crying, behaving in a somewhat infantile manner. He reported I had laid on the floor kicking and screaming and was extremely indecisive, quite agitated, illogical, depressed, and threatening suicide and all sorts of dire attempts to run away from myself and my feelings of frustration and inadequacy. I was a complete mess, and I had no idea why or how I got this way. I just knew it was something I couldn't fix.

I became angry with Dr. Turner and, unlike my true personality, became combative with him. I didn't like him, and I didn't want to do anything he said or be treated by him, so I fought with him at every turn. I know this whole experience was devastating to Derek. Bless his heart, I know he was going through absolute hell. Here he was in a new job, trying to learn something completely different than he had done in his career with American Airlines, moving to a new state, having to deal with a bawling wife who cried at the drop of a pin. A wife who couldn't seem to face every day living. I know he suffered terribly during this time, but I was miserable! (I am sincerely sorry he went through this difficult time, but there was absolutely nothing I could do to change how I felt at that time or I would have. I never meant to cause him or anyone else any pain.)

Dr. Turner suggested I start electroshock therapy to save me from myself and Derek finally gave in and agreed. I honestly never knew what that was, and I was too afraid to ask. My parents were so upset about what was happening to me that Mom even went to an attorney and asked if there was any way that she and my Dad could intervene and get me out of the hospital and back to Ohio. Of course, the attorney advised her that I was Derek's wife and as my husband, he could make any and all decisions involving my health and the type of treatment he and the doctor felt were necessary to help save my life.

I received twelve shock treatments from January through March, when I was finally released from the hospital. I have little or no recollection of my time in the hospital or of the treatment, with the exception of the severe headaches I always had after each procedure. I only have what I wrote in my diary during that time. "It was a hellish experience! I couldn't write or contact my family. I wasn't permitted to use the phone. The only outlet I had for joy was to do some baking at the hospital. I made all sorts of brownies, cookies, and fudge for the other patients, which gave me so much pleasure. I became close with one of the nurses, Linda Mortan, who would accompany me whenever I had to go for the treatments and hers was the first face I saw when I woke up. She was wonderful and so kind, with a real heart for giving. I hated having to have those treatments, but somehow it was made a little easier with Linda's help. Thank God for people like her; people that help folks like me through these terrible times in our lives. I am forever grateful to her for being there."

I was only twenty-six years old; I could not believe this was happening to me. I didn't know how it started and wasn't sure what triggered it, other than the move from New York to Tulsa and all of the commuting back and forth. I hated feeling like I was such a burden to my husband. I thought maybe I was losing my mind. The hospitalization, shock treatments, and therapy were the most difficult things I ever lived through, but I made it and wouldn't wish it on my worst enemy. However, those treatments may have saved my life.

After I finally got released from the hospital, I was terrified of everyone and didn't want Derek out of my sight. That must have been so difficult for him to handle. To his credit, he had come to the hospital almost every time Dr. Turner allowed it. Derek always tried not to upset me and tried to be supportive, but I am sure he had no real idea of how to cope with what I was going through any more than I did. I knew he had talked numerous times to Dori, who tried to encourage and support him by sharing some of the things she and her daughter had gone through.

I had often told Dr. Turner I wanted to go back to New York, and that I wanted Derek to quit his job and go with me. I was talking crazy, but to me it made all the sense in the world. I had felt like I was living in my past and my present, and I couldn't adjust, which was driving me nuts. After all the treatments, I felt better, but I still had no self-confidence and had forgotten so many things. I didn't even remember how to drive a car. I never really knew what was involved in those treatments until years later when I happened to see a documentary on EST. I could only watch it for a few minutes; I felt so unsettled knowing that had been done to me twelve times. I guess I owe my life to those treatments because my depression lessened, but things still weren't right in my life, and I didn't know why or how to fix them.

During my hospital stay, Dad and Mom came to see me. They were in the room when I woke up, and I was so glad to see them. Though I was pretty groggy, I managed to sit up in the bed, smile, and tell them both I loved them. Mom said, "I love you too, honey." Daddy said, "I love you, Bev, and I want you to concentrate on getting better." Tears poured down my face as I realized this was the first time I had ever heard those words come out of my Dad's mouth. It meant the world to me!

Dad was only able to stay for the weekend, but Mom stayed with me for a week after I got out of the hospital. It was nice to have them both with me my first weekend home and great to have Mom there when Derek was at work during the week. She and I worked on the yard, had cookouts, went out to eat, and just spent time together. I felt safe with my family around me.

Mom and Dad weren't too happy with Derek, but there wasn't anything they could do about it. I tried to tell them the decisions Derek had to make on his own weren't easy for him to do. I asked that they try and understand he had been through an awful lot himself, that he had been there with me throughout the whole hospitalization, and he had come to see me almost every single night. Still, I think they blamed him for being part of the reason I ended up in the hospital in the first place. It wouldn't make any difference how I tried to convince them, Mom and Dad had their minds made up. They just never said anything to Derek about the whole ordeal.

After I felt a little more confident, Derek and I went on a trip back to New York in early April, 1972. We had fun seeing a lot of our friends. We stayed with Derek's parents, who had moved to Morristown, NJ where Derek, Sr. had gotten a new job and had started a new life. I was envious since I had not been able to accept my new life and adjust to it like a normal person. His parents didn't treat me any differently than they had before my hospitalization, but I always felt embarrassed. It just wasn't discussed, at least not with me.

After we returned to Tulsa a few days later, we were sitting in the den of our house when I told Derek I honestly didn't want to go back to New York ever again. I told him our future was here in Tulsa and that we would get through it together. I thanked him for helping me during the most difficult experience of my life and told him I couldn't have done it without him. I cried, but not uncontrollably like I had in the past, just tears of relief and realization that we had made it through this thing together. I hoped it would make our marriage stronger and better equip us to handle anything after this horrible heartbreak.

I still had to see Dr. Turner occasionally for checkups. He finally released me to return to flying on April 21. I was so excited as I flew down to Dallas to talk with the American Airlines doctor to get his release to return to flying status. After I left there, I called crew schedule to tell them I was delighted to be able to return to work. Two days later, I got a call from my supervisor telling me I couldn't go back to work until I passed the Emergency Procedure Training (EPT) since I had been off work for about ten months. Although I was not happy about it, I understood because I didn't feel all that confident about my memory of some things I felt I should know, particularly regarding emergency situations. So going through EPT was, in reality, a very good idea because I needed to feel like an asset and not a liability in an emergency.

I had a difficult time passing the emergency evacuation drills. I knew the commands I needed to to say, but I was so nervous I kept getting them jumbled up in my head, and they would come out of my mouth wrong. Some of the instructors knew a little about what I had gone through, not the details, just that I had had some issues with depression, because they were very patient with me. They allowed me far more chances to pass the drills than they should have. I finally got through the EPT class and returned to Tulsa to tell Derek I had passed and would be returning to flying in May.

Derek said he was so glad I was returning to work because he really needed for me to get back to doing something constructive. I was so hurt! I am sure he didn't mean it the way I took it, but I was not pleased with the way he worded what I had hoped would be words of support and encouragement. Sadly, Derek had a way of saying things that made you feel really bad when I don't believe it was his intention to do so. It seemed I was always making excuses for or trying to defend something Derek said or did to my friends, co-workers, and family. I was sure they didn't understand him the way I did, or thought I did.

I finally met another Stewardess who was in the same situation as me. Cheri Depue was commuting from Tulsa to Dallas to work her schedule too (I had transferred to DFW from LGA in early 1970). She was absolutely adorable, tiny with a cute pixie hairdo, sparkling brown eyes, beautiful skin, and a megawatt smile. Her husband David was a pilot stationed in Tulsa, so they had moved there for him to build up flying hours to apply for a job with a commercial airline one day. The four of us started spending a lot of time together. Dave and Derek got along really well, and of course, Cheri and I had a lot in common with our job. She and I went to art classes together, went shopping, or we would just lay out in the sun and chat. She taught me how to do needlepoint, which came in handy while commuting and sitting around airports waiting for flights home or before signing in for a trip.

I was starting to feel better about our life in Tulsa. We made friends with an older couple named Paul and Josey Horn, whom we absolutely loved. They built their house a little further down the road in another new development. We would go out to eat or go to each other's homes for dinner or to play cards. I was beginning to adjust to what I thought would be our "happily ever after life." Sadly, I was wrong again.

Derek traveled a lot. I did better being by myself, but I was always sad when he had to go and delighted when he came home. I spent a lot of time with Muskogee, our golden retriever. Derek and I bought me a 1966 red and white Mustang, something I had wanted all of my life but could never afford. I had my first car now, one I could call my very own. I loved this car so much and was so proud of her. I washed and waxed her so much it is a wonder her paint didn't come off. My Mustang was one of a kind, different from any Mustang on the car lot, with running horses on the doors just like the ones on the back of the seats. (Later, my Mustang-loving older son, Josh would inform me that "Rosie" was one of 250 cars made for a special promotion of the Mustang, and she was probably worth a whole lot of money, especially now. Little did I know.)

The first time I drove my Mustang alone, I turned on the radio and Neil Diamond was singing "Cracklin' Rosie," so that became her name. Every time I went for a ride in Rosie, Muskogee was with me, seated in the right front bucket seat. If the dog saw me go after the keys, she would bounce around and stand on her hind legs, ready to go with me. We had so much fun in that car. Muskogee was essentially my child, and we did just about everything together. Everyone knew us at the grocery store, and every time we went, one of the cashiers would give me a little sack for Muskogee to carry into the house as I unloaded our groceries. We spent endless hours going to parks and running in the field outside Sabre where Derek worked. He told me he always enjoyed looking out the window watching Muskogee and me running through the grass when we would go to pick him up from work.

In April 1972, I was reading the newspaper and ran across an article written by Jan Fulsom, a former Eastern Airline Stewardess. It was entitled "Airline Stewardesses Send Glamour Job Image Crashing." It made me so angry. The article said a drunk passenger had ripped the Stewardess's skirt off inflight, and when she complained to the Captain, he laughed at her. She claimed to have been pinched, fondled, leered at, asked out on dates, and propositioned more times than she cared to count. She claimed the airlines promoted us as "sex objects," and they expected her to accept it and expect it. Mrs. Fulsom claimed to have lost her self-respect, become cynical, and had begun to hate people. She was particularly upset with National Airlines' new "Fly Me" campaign where Stewardesses named Beth Pam, Susie, or Becky would come on television and announce, "I'm Becky, fly me to Miami." I didn't care for it very much either, but it didn't really offend me.

She and some other Stewardesses were starting a group called Stewardesses for Women's Rights. One of the members had filed charges with the equal employment commission against Eastern Airlines, claiming sex discrimination. They stated they had weigh-ins and makeup checks, comparing this to being treated like jockeys. Mrs. Fulsom complained of having her hair cut, being made to wear a certain type of makeup, and being told what she was allowed to weigh. She downplayed her emergency training, saying she was taught emergency procedures, about delivering babies and helping sick passengers, but the whole emphasis was on how you looked. She bitched about her uniform being made to fit to accent her body for the pleasure of the male passengers. Their new organization wanted to get the airlines to concentrate on cleanliness and courtesy, and they wanted the position of Stewardess to be opened up to males.

I was upset because Mrs. Fulsom was badmouthing the job I loved with a passion, so I wrote a letter to the editor in defense of my job as a Stewardess:

> I hate to differ with one of my colleagues, but the pictures she painted of the airlines and the Stewardess profession are definitely not the same ones I have. I have been a Stewardess for nearly seven years, and I feel the advantages far outnumber the disadvantages.
>
> What profession involving women does not make reference to 'sex objects'? As long as there are men and women on this earth, there will be sex and sex

> objects. Why should I expect the job as a Stewardess onboard an airplane full of mostly men to be a sterile atmosphere? But in nearly seven years, I've never had a passenger try to 'paw' me or get out of line to the point I couldn't handle him. That's why I find it extremely difficult to believe a passenger, intoxicated or otherwise, could 'de-skirt' a Stewardess.
>
> I don't feel the airlines, at least the airline I work for, has tried to brainwash Stewardesses into believing they're sex objects. As far as losing my self-respect, I haven't lost that either. I love my job and feel you get out of it what you put into it. And if Mrs. Fulsom was cynical and began to hate people, I am sure it showed. That's probably why she found herself in those awkward situations. There are times when I lose my temper or get disgusted with a passenger, but that happens in every job that involves the public.
>
> I thank American Airlines for the opportunity to work for them. I've been places I would normally never in a lifetime be able to visit, and I've made friends everywhere.
>
> In conclusion, I don't feel I'm treated as a sex object by my employer or my passengers. I am a woman who is here to make the most of a job she's sincerely proud of. To grow and learn from it and the opportunities it provides me. If I'm ever lucky enough to have a daughter, I hope she'll have ambitions to be a Stewardess. I'll certainly encourage her in every way I can.

I received letters from George A. Warde, American Airlines Executive Vice President, from Lyman K. Randall, American Airlines Director of Flight Service, supervisor Kathy Schroeder, and from my father-in-law in reference to my letter. I was so proud they wrote to thank me for defending my job. I think Derek, Sr.'s letter meant the most to me. He wrote, "Your letter was one of the best things I've ever read. You had something to say and you said it very well. Congratulations."

I had hoped our lives had settled down and we would live happily ever after. Derek and I took wonderful vacations and trips. One of my very favorites was a wine and cheese tasting tour to Switzerland. It was fantastic!

Although we had so much fun together during the day, our intimate relationship was not going well. One night, we had gone back to our room with intentions of making love. When we got there, it was as if someone told us we weren't really compatible in our lovemaking. I mean, no one really said that, but at almost the same time Derek and I realized things weren't the way they should be between us, that something was very wrong. We discussed that fact that Derek had had to suppress his feelings of intimacy towards me when I was dealing with all of that depression because I wasn't taking the pill during my hospitalizations, and Dr. Turner said it would be a tragic mistake if I ended up pregnant.

I disagreed with Dr. Turner. I always felt it would have been better if I had gotten pregnant and had a child. Perhaps I would have had to grow up and stop being so self-centered and thinking about myself. We will never know, but if I had had a place to channel all the love I wanted to give, maybe, just maybe, things would have been different. Some of you may be thinking that could have been the most awful thing to do to a child, but I'll never know because it didn't happen.

Derek said he had difficulty thinking it was alright now to be physical with me again. We sort of just gave up on making love and lay in bed holding each other. We assumed that part of our lives would come around in due time.

We both went to see Dr. Turner for a few visits to see if we could work things out, and he suggested a marriage counselor. Sad to say, but the woman we chose had an immediate crush on my husband and made no bones about her attraction to him. She basically blamed all of our marital troubles on me, which really pissed me off! When she kept finding reasons to touch Derek in front of me, I got more than perturbed and decided I didn't need her or her crap. We stopped seeing her after four visits. We never went back, and we never got our issues resolved either. I knew I loved Derek, but there was a void in our lives neither one of us knew how to face or repair. Derek ended up seeing Dr. Turner for a while, but nothing pertaining to us changed, and we just went on living our lives as if there was nothing wrong.

To the outside world we were "Mr. and Mrs. American." We made the most beautiful couple, tall, blonde, blessed by our jobs and material possessions, and we had each other. Everyone we socialized with didn't have a clue there was trouble in paradise. Derek and I knew things weren't right, yet we didn't have any idea how we could make our lives and our marriage become the way we both wanted them to be. I used to tell Derek there was no such thing as a mistake as long as you learned from it. I didn't think our marriage was a mistake, but we didn't seem to be learning how to deal with the issues we needed to face to grow together. Both of us had had to put our emotions on hold to help me get over my depression, and now we couldn't seem to get our feelings back to where they had been when we first fell in love. We were both frustrated and felt helpless. Dr. Turner tried to work with us, but I always felt there were unresolved past issues we both had brought to our marriage that were hindering our lives from being the way we wanted. I had no idea what was going to happen to us, and I was scared.

WENDELL LARRY LADNER

Wendell

So many things had changed since I started with American. We no longer had to quit at age thirty-two. As of August 11, 1968, you no longer had to quit if you were married, thank God, but American Airlines did not hire ladies who were already married. Pregnancy was still a cause for termination.

American had hired some Stewards from Hawaii for our South Pacific trips in 1970. In March of 1971, when we bought Trans Caribbean Airways, we acquired several male members for our flying team. Suddenly, we were no longer called Stewardesses — we became Flight Attendants. It didn't sound nearly as glamorous as being a Stewardess, and I never understood why the guys couldn't be called Stewards.

Several of our passengers did not like having guys serve them. They pretty much assumed all the guys were gay. Some of the male Flight Attendants were gay, but others had families. I was so naive that I didn't always know when one of the guys was gay. It took some getting used to, but most of the guys were great and really funny.

A former Trans Caribbean Flight Attendant named Richard Leslie told me this joke, and I didn't really know how to react.

> *An airline's passenger cabin was being served by an obviously gay flight attendant, who seemed to put everyone in a good mood as he served them food and drinks. As the plane prepared to descend, he came swishing down the aisle and announced to the passengers, "Captain Marvey has asked me to announce that he'll be landing the big scary plane shortly, lovely people, so if you could just put up your trays, that would be super."*

> *On his trip back up the aisle, he noticed that a well-dressed, rather exotic-looking woman hadn't moved a muscle. "Perhaps you didn't hear me over those big brute engines. I asked you to raise your trazy-poo so the main man can putty-pat us on the ground."*
>
> *She calmly turned her head and said, "In my country, I am called a Princess. I take orders from no one." To which the flight attendant replied, without missing a beat, "Well, Sweet Cheeks, in my country, I'm called a Queen, so I outrank you. Now put your tray table up, bitch!"*

After Richard finished telling the joke, he burst out laughing. Since I thought it was rather funny, I laughed too, but I was still having difficulty knowing the boundaries for when it was okay to laugh at a gay-related joke and when it wasn't.

Another time I was flying a Hawaii trip with this crazy gay guy named Ray Nastasi. He and I were sitting on the jump seat chatting. It was a really hot day, so the doors to the plane were open to the Hawaiian heat, and Ray had his uniform shirt unbuttoned to his navel. (It looked like some furry animal had crawled up and sat on his chest. He always made jokes about how he wished he had that much hair on his head.) Ray was a riot! The Passenger Service Manager (PSM) came and told us we had a group of 150 John Deere tractor salesmen on board that night. Ray's eyes got as big as golf balls, and he started buttoning his shirt up as quickly as possible. Then he looked at me with fear in his eyes and stated, "Oh my God, Bev!!! They are not going to like me one bit. I'm sure they are a bunch of 'Red Necks'! You are going to have to work the cabin all by yourself!" I burst out laughing and so did the PSM. Ray would say anything to make you laugh. That's why I loved flying with him.

One change American made I did like a lot was dividing the cabins into smoking and non-smoking sections, although it was somewhat ridiculous since the air circulates all throughout the entire cabin anyway. If you were seated in the non-smoking section, you were going to get it in your face anyway. Finally there was a complete ban on smoking on flights lasting less than two hours.

There were two big aircraft changes with the introduction to our fleet of the Boeing 747 airplane and McDonnell Douglas DC-10. Both of these aircrafts held over 300 passengers; it felt like a flying city. The 747 held 366 passengers, sixty-six in First Class and 300 in Coach. It was an awesome airplane with a piano bar in it. The DC-10 was introduced on August 5, 1971 with its forty-four First Class and 264 Coach passengers. Both aircrafts had elaborate services on them, with galleys below the main cabin galley where the meals were prepared and sent upstairs in elevators.

All the Flight Attendants had to go to special classes for these new aircraft and their incredible new Flagship Food Services. It was almost like being back at school - exciting, fun, and challenging, and I was ready. We had new emergency equipment, new evacuation commands, and a different set of drills for the windows and doors. It would be more difficult to remember so much equipment, but I was up for it. We were all so proud of the newest members of our fleet and what our company had to offer.

In spite of everything, I was never so happy as I was to be able to return to flying. It had been such a battle to lose all of the weight I had gained in the hospital. I weighed 156 pounds when I was released. I think my maximum weight was around 140, so I had to lose 16 pounds before I was allowed to come back to work. I had fought so hard to maintain my weight and to look good in my uniform. I wanted to lose the weight also because I didn't feel good weighing that much, so I would starve if I had to. I would do whatever was necessary, no matter what I had to do to feel good about myself. I think Derek was prouder of me for losing the weight than he had been in a while. All in all, I thought our lives were humming along just great.

We had gone to Columbus to celebrate Dad's fifty-third birthday on New Year's Eve with Mike and his fiancée Bernadette. Although Derek and I couldn't stay very long, it was nice to be there to celebrate the dawning of 1973.

Derek was already dealing with a lot of frustration in his job. I always thought he should have stayed in Passenger Service because he was always so good at it. Some of those enraged passengers had a second thought about acting like bastards when this 6'5' man came up to them to settle whatever problem they had, or had imagined they had. His size definitely benefited him in some situations that would have probably destroyed someone of lesser stature. But if the only way for him to get back into Passenger Service meant returning to New York, I was not going to go there again. I suppose I would have gone wherever Derek's job called him to go, but emotionally I was just starting to get my feet back on the ground, and I didn't want to go through any major changes for now.

Derek proposed what he felt like were some good ideas for changes in Sabre, but they weren't as well received as he had hoped they would be, so he wasn't feeling very confident in his position. I felt like I was partially to blame for his stress and lack of confidence because of what we had been through during my bout of depression. I tried to encourage him and be supportive, but I think this was something inside Derek he felt he had to overcome by himself. I knew he was an awesome employee, and I hoped American Airlines would realize that too.

I was back flying and having a ball. I loved sharing "war stories" about flying with the other Flight Attendants. I got this crazy idea from one of the girls to submit my story about my night with Elvis to see if I could get it published. Why not? After all, I had experienced something that some women would give everything they owned to be able to do. So I submitted the story, never dreaming someone would buy it. But *Motion Picture Magazine* actually paid me $150 for my story! I was so proud, even though they changed a lot of it and made me sound like a real airhead. Only a few lines of the story were actually the words I had written, which made me sad because I thought it was better the way I told it than how they changed it. At least they didn't use my real name. I asked that they call me Heather Stiles.

Dad, Mom,Bernie and Mike

I wheeled and dealed with Crew Schedule to get time off for my brother's wedding, begging them to give me any trip I could fly back-to-back so I could be at my brother's wedding. After all, he had gone AWOL for my wedding and spent time in the brig; the least I could do was fly my butt off to get time to be with him on his important day. I had told Mike there was a chance I wouldn't be able to make it to the wedding. Even though he said he understood, I could hear in his voice how sad he was that I might not be there.

Crew Schedule gave me a charter flight to Las Vegas. It was my first time to go there, and I was so excited! I had never seen so many lights in my life. I saw a sign that Elvis would be there January 26 through February

23. It was only January 11, and I wondered if there was any way I could get back to see one of his shows. That would be so cool!

Derek and I made it to the wedding by the skin of our teeth because the flights were so full, and we were traveling on passes. (Passes allowed us to get on a flight if there were any seats left over after the paying customers were boarded. We only had to pay a service charge, and we could go anywhere in American Airlines' system unless there was an embargo.) As Mike came out of the groom's room on January 13, 1973, he made eye contact with me, and I could see the tears of happiness in his eyes. He smiled and winked at me. He and Bernadette, who was French, Chinese, and Hawaiian, had a beautiful ceremony with a Hawaiian theme; they wore Hawaiian leaves around their necks, and she had flowers in her hair. After the ceremony, she danced a traditional Hawaiian dance as a token of her love for Michael. Mom bawled. Daddy and Uncle Buck got drunk and were hysterical! Derek had too much to drink too, and he was acting so stupid. He kept asking me why I didn't like him. I just couldn't understand why he was asking that, and I wanted to get away from him because he was really getting on my nerves.

I had the best month flying with Carole Sanders, who was a riot! She had read my Elvis story and decided to introduce me by my pen name, Heather Stiles. No one knew why she was doing it, but Carole loved to make people laugh and embarrass them.

I was surprised that my in-laws had read the Elvis article and made mention of it. Even Granny Schoenmann told me when she went to get her hair done, she had picked up both a *National Geographic* and *Motion Picture Magazine* and had hidden the movie magazine inside the *National Geographic*. After all, what if someone saw her reading a gossip magazine? She told me she enjoyed the story and laughed when I told her they had edited it so much I barely recognized my own story. She may have been an ambassador's wife, but she was cool, and I liked her a lot. The word got around the Dallas base about the story, and a few Flight Attendants told me they were waiting for the more graphic sequel. Oh, how I wished! Little did I know what the future held for me and Mr. Presley.

I continued buying things at sales and sneaking them into the house so I didn't have to listen to Derek's "wants and needs" lectures. Only this time, I was not reacting the same way I had before. Before I had just listened meekly and felt guilty even if I bought a set of sheets without his permission. Now I was getting angry. I felt like since I was working and had a paycheck, I ought to be able to buy whatever I wanted as long as we covered any commitments we had for house payments, utilities, etc. I wanted to spend my money as I saw fit, and I was starting to feel like it was time to stand up for myself for once. We got into it over this, and Derek didn't quite know how to react. He just listened and then brushed the whole encounter off. I had made up my mind I was not going to sneak another thing into that house. If I wanted to buy something, he would just have to live with it.

I had a trip to Boston and Phoenix, and Derek kept calling me on my Boston layovers just to chat and tell me he missed me. What was that all about? I found it rather odd, until I remembered Bobby Bernhardt.

So just to be a bitch, I called Bobby, and we told each other what had been going on in our lives. Well, not all of it, because I never told him about my depression or the hospitalization and treatment. There was no reason. I just wanted our conversations to be light and crazy like they always used to be. He was the same ole Bob. I loved listening to his thick Massachusetts accent; nobody said "Bev-a-lee" with the vigor he did. I loved it! We laughed and talked about old times. It was nothing romantic, just two friends catching up.

Derek even called me on one trip in Phoenix to ask me if I had gone out in Boston because he had called and no one answered in my room. Since I hadn't gone out, he must have been given the wrong number, but it was nice to know he was concerned and maybe a little bit jealous.

Randy Ray and Charmaine

My little sister Charmaine had gotten herself pregnant at sixteen. She married the baby's father, and they were having a hell of a time. They were living with my parents and trying to raise a baby boy when they were just teenagers themselves. It caused so much stress when Derek and I went to visit that little bitty house with way too many people in it, that we couldn't wait to head home. I was embarrassed for my little sis, but I had left when she was only eleven. Although I wished we had been able to be closer, we were worlds apart. Before becoming a Stewardess, I did try to take her places and do things with her that I thought might be fun, but my visits home were almost always short, so we never had much of an opportunity to get close. I just couldn't believe my baby sister had to grow up and become a Mom long before she was ready.

Derek and I were still dealing with problems in our physical relationship. Derek didn't seem to crave or need all the affection and attention I found myself needing and wanting. If he could sit in his easy chair, all leaned back with a thick book in his hand and be left alone to read, he was as they say, "in hog heaven." I would ask him to hold me or hug me. He would get that look of aggravation on his face and put one arm around me, squeeze, and go off to do something that really interested him. One day, I got angry and insisted Derek put both arms around me and really hug me. He could not be less interested if he tried.

I just did not get it. What was wrong with me? Why didn't my own husband want to make love with me? I knew I was lacking in experience, but I was more than willing to try to learn. I bought the stupid book *The Total Woman* and tried to do some of the things from that book to perhaps cause a spark - no, I did not meet Derek naked at the door wrapped in Saran Wrap, but maybe I should have. I bought *Everything You Ever Wanted to Know About Sex* and read it. Some of the drawings knocked me for a loop but I thought if it worked, it would be worth it. One evening, when I tried being the aggressor, Derek seemed to respond, but then we ended up in the same old missionary position with Derek going off, rolling off me, and falling asleep. Damn it, that was not what I had in mind, and I was really mad at him.

I had to fly a trip the next day, and I was still angry. Before Derek went to work, I tried talking to him, asking if maybe we might try something different next time we made love. I guess I insulted him because he turned to face me and said, "If you need all of this constant love and affection, why don't you get yourself a lover?" and then he stormed out the door. I was so shocked! I was his wife, and Derek was supposed to be my lover, not some stranger.

I felt awful as I headed to the airport for my flight to Dallas. At times, I resented Derek for me having a long commute because I always had to leave myself a back-up trip just in case the one I had thought I could catch cancelled. I was constantly worn out from sitting in airports, on airplanes, and then doing the reverse just to get home, but I didn't want to quit flying, so I had to make the best of it. Another thing that set me off was the hope that Derek would be inside the terminal waiting at the gate for me when I would return to Tulsa, but he seldom was there waiting. In fact, I could probably count on one hand the number of times he was. Damn him! I had to commute because Derek took this job in Tulsa; the least he could do was spend a quarter in the parking meter to come inside and meet me. When I mentioned it to him, Derek didn't think it was that important and said it was a silly thing to bring up in the first place.

I was starting to harbor a lot of resentment towards Derek for many little things that were turning into mountains. Get a lover, indeed. He would regret the day he ever said that to me.

I was on the second leg of a trip, and I was tired. I normally liked to fly First Class and be my own boss, commanding the cabin as I saw fit. That way, the service went pretty much the way I liked, and I didn't have to worry about my co-worker's attitudes affecting my passengers. That month, however, I bid an "extra" position, which meant there was already a crew of at least four Flight Attendants, but if the passenger load went over a certain number, then an extra Attendant was added to make the service go smoother and for safety. I didn't like this position because there were so many different ways of doing things and so many different personalities. Even though I had never had a confrontation with any other crew member, other than the gal on my first flight, I preferred the continuity of flying with the same people every month, getting to know one another a little and knowing more or less what to expect when it came to the service. I headed back to the Coach cabin to introduce myself to the two gals in the back I would be working with. As I looked about the cabin, I found it rather odd that there appeared to be an unusually high number of very tall men on board. It never dawned on me that these men were part of a professional basketball team. I thought to myself, did I just die and go to heaven? I snickered. This is so cool!

After I introduced myself to the girls in the back, Jill, the galley girl said, 'I can see by your wedding band that you are married, but I am sure that you can appreciate a good-looking man when you see one." (During this time, there was an ad campaign involving Tom Selleck as "The Marlborough Man." with him on gigantic posters along the road and in magazines trying to sell cigarettes. I think just about every woman I talked to about the ads could not have told you what Tom was selling though; we couldn't get past how gorgeous he was). Jill told me the guy sitting in the window seat beside the window exit right behind me was better looking than The Marxlborough Man. This I had to see, but I didn't want him to realize we were talking about him. So I slowly turned around and found him staring at my behind.

OH, MY GOD!!! This man was absolutely the most handsome man that I had ever seen! He must have been at least 6'5" with dark, almost black hair, a thick mustache, and a grin that lit up the whole cabin. I gulped hard, then hoped and prayed he hadn't heard me. I spun back around to Jill, acted like I was biting my own wrist, and said, "Girl, he is everything you said and more." I remarked to her that he was probably so conceited that he was his own number one fan. She had told me all of these tall men on board were part of an American Basketball Association team called the Kentucky Colonels from Louisville, Kentucky.

Then the agent was starting to board our aircraft with the rest of our passengers to San Diego, so I had to get out in the aisle to help. I almost tripped coming out of the galley, and when I looked in his direction, he smiled at me. I temporarily forgot about this gorgeous hunk as we were nearly full, and without carts, we had to hand-run every single meal tray and offer beverages from a separate tray. Of course, you always lost your train of thought while serving because some passenger inevitably had to have another cocktail while you were still trying to get other passengers their first beverage to have with their meals.

For the first time in the seven years I had been flying, I was rushing out of the galley with an entire tray filled to capacity with about eighteen drinks when a passenger headed for the lavatory. I stopped abruptly to keep from running into the passenger, and all the glasses tumbled either towards the front of my serving topper, off the edge of the tray, or over the end of it. I wanted to crawl under the seats because of course, the gorgeous guy saw the whole thing. Thank goodness he didn't laugh. I overheard someone say, "It wasn't your fault," but I didn't stick around to see who it was. I made a beeline to the lavatory to wipe up some of the sodas dripping from my topper. I wished I could stay in that bathroom forever, but the girls were counting on me, and I had to get my butt back out there, grab some more drinks and serve those passengers. I darted out of the lav, went into the galley, grabbed some more drinks, and took off into the cabin without looking in his direction.

After the service was completed, I grabbed the Service Kit (a small suitcase-like box that held all sorts of things we might need during the flight such as Band-Aids, aspirin, flying schedules, etc.) and sat on the floor in front of the man in 25E. I introduced myself, and when I asked, he said he was Dan Issel. I looked at the man in 25D, who immediately told me his name was Jimmy. (Why am I doing this? I asked myself. I'm a married woman acting like a High School girl with her first crush. I felt myself blushing.) I turned to the man in 25F, "And what is your name?" I asked him. He looked directly into my eyes, grinned and said, "My name is W-e-n-d-e-1-1." I swear to you it took him nearly thirty seconds just to say his name. I've never heard such a Southern accent; I found out later he was from Mississippi, a place called Necaise Crossing, to be exact.

In the course of our conversation, Wendell asked me how long my hair was. Since Flight Attendants no longer had restrictions about our hair not touching our collars, I had let mine grow. We still had to have it confined while in uniform in a neat coiffure, but it could be as long as we wanted. I often pinned my hair on top of my head in a twist or pulled it back with a tie around it in what we used to refer to as a "George Washington," which was actually a ponytail tied at the nape of your neck instead of the middle of the back of your head. Tonight my hair was neatly tucked in a bun. (Yeah, I may have looked like an old maid school teacher, but it was neat and met with the hair restrictions, so I didn't really care.)

I was talking to Dan when I realized Wendell had leaned over and was pulling the big bobby pins out of my hair, so it cascaded down my neck onto my shoulders and down my back. He made a small gasp and seemed surprised it was so long. I was pleased because I've always felt my hair was one of the prettiest things about me, even though Derek always told me it was my eyes and legs. Derek, oh my, he was the furthest thing from my mind at that moment.

I needed to check on the passengers, so I pulled my hair back into a bun after retrieving the pins from Wendell's hand, then went to finish picking up and putting all of the trash in the galley. When I returned to the galley, I noticed Wendell had moved and was now sitting in 25D. I was feeling silly, almost giddy, but I was having fun flirting. I remembered a card I had in my tote bag and went to get it to give to Wendell. There was a teddy bear on the front with his paw in a honey jar, and written on the card were the words "I believe in love at first sight." On the inside it said, "It saves time."

What had gotten into me? I wasn't normally so forward. It just felt so good to have this oh-so-attractive man paying attention to me. I stood beside his seat, squatted down, and handed him the card. I watched his eyes as he read it and then delighted in his laughter as he looked at me and said, "So do I." I took the card from his hand and started to walk away. Wendell reached for my hand and asked me where we stayed and if I would go out to dinner with him. "Dinner? You just ate a full meal. How can you be hungry?" He told me he was a big man, and it took a lot of food to fill him up. I laughed but told him I was sorry I couldn't go because I was married. Lordy, that was so hard to say. I really didn't want to tell him and felt like putting my ring in my tote bag or in my jacket, but I knew that was just something I couldn't do. Wendell seemed disappointed.

I suddenly remembered I had some of my homemade pumpkin bread in my bag, so I gave it to the three men. They devoured it like it was the first food they had eaten in days. There had been nearly a whole loaf, and then it was all gone. Oh well, if I can't go out and eat with Wendell, at least I could give him something to hold him over.

I overheard Jimmy calling Wendell "Elvis" and got tickled. He might not have been Elvis, but he sure was appealing, and boy, did he ever have a boatload of charisma. I bet Wendell had so many women chasing after him that he stayed out of breath.

When we landed in San Diego, Wendell again asked me where we stayed. I told him it was the El Cortez Hotel. Normally we never told anyone where we stayed on layovers, but I felt like it was okay to tell Wendell. He told me where he would be staying just in case I changed my mind or got hungry. I watched Wendell deplane and felt such a weird feeling of emptiness. I had so enjoyed my short time with him. Not only was he magnificent to look at, but he made me feel attractive too.

I had turned to get my bag when I heard someone running up the martin stand. I looked around and saw Wendell running up the stairs towards me. I felt my heart flip. "Did you forget something, Mr. Wendell?" I asked.

He seemed a little taken aback by the mister part, but he grabbed me by the arm and grinned, (God what beautiful teeth!), "Yeah, you, Baby."" My heart skipped several beats. Truthfully, Wendell said he had "forgotten" his travel bag, on purpose perhaps? He pulled me down the aisle behind him to where he had left it, picked it up, looked at me, and said, "Call me." Then he left the airplane while I stood there with my mouth wide open. Dear Lord, that man was gorgeous!!!!

The cockpit crew and the other Flight Attendants had all been standing in front and witnessed the whole incident. I must have looked silly being pulled down the aisle by this tall man. They said, "Well, I guess Bev won't be joining us for dinner tonight."

I told them I probably would.

Two of the girls almost chimed in at the exact same time saying, "Oh sure, I bet."

Jill said, "If you've got a lick of sense, we won't see you until tomorrow, if then." Everyone burst out laughing as I turned nine shades of red.

I thought to myself there was no way that was going to happen. I said, "You guys are awful. I am a married woman."

The F/O chimed in, "So when does that make a difference? I always say what my wife doesn't know won't hurt her." I could not believe he was saying that, although maybe I really wasn't too surprised, but I wasn't that kind of a woman.

I got to my room at the hotel and fought with my conscience. I couldn't get Wendell off my mind. Yes, no, yes, no, no, no, yes, damn it! I was going to call him! I knew I had better hurry because I was losing my nerve by the second. I wanted to continue that wonderful feeling of another man wanting me, flirting with me, making me feel so special, especially a man who looked like that, so I called his hotel.

Oh, horrors! I realized I didn't know his last name, and I panicked. When the hotel operator answered, I told her I had been the Stewardess (old habits were hard to break - I never liked being called a Flight Attendant) on a flight the Kentucky Colonels were on, and one of the players had left his lighter onboard. LIGHTER?!?!?! You idiot, basketball players probably didn't smoke. I felt so stupid that I almost hung up. I could tell by her voice she did not believe my dim-witted story. After I told her his first name was Wendell but did not know his last name, I heard her calling his room. Oh, I should hang ...00ps...a man answered the phone. "I have a call for Wendell Ladner," she said.

Hang up, Bev, you can't be doing this!

Then I heard his voice in reply, "This is Wendell Ladner."

I blurted out, "I'm hungry. Let's go eat," in this shaky, little voice I could barely recognize as my own. I was amazed Wendell could even hear me, but I could feel his smile through the phone. He asked me for my room number and said he'd be right over.

I guess Wendell knew all along I'd call, even though he mentioned later he was really surprised when I did. I AM NUTS!!!!!! My hands were trembling so hard I could barely hang up the receiver. "Now look what you've done, Bev, how could you?" I asked myself.

In the five years since I had gotten married, I had been asked out several times, but I always said no. What had happened to our marriage? I had never loved anyone the way I loved Derek. I still loved him, but I was disappointed by so many aspects of our life together. I never dreamed I would have to ask someone, especially my own husband, to hug me or make love with me. I guess I wasn't accepting the reality of how our marriage was turning out. I knew this situation was not all Derek's fault or all mine either, in spite of what that damn marriage counselor tried to make me believe. Maybe we just weren't compatible.

I didn't have much time to figure it out right then. By the time I jumped in and out of the shower, put on fresh makeup, and brushed my hair, there was a knock at my door. Oh God, he was knocking at the door. What was I supposed to do then? I wouldn't answer it. Stop! Wait! Who was this person walking towards the door? Who was opening it? I couldn't believe I had really called him. I don't know how I made it to the door, but I did, and there he stood grinning from ear to ear. My heart was just about ready to jump right out of my body. "Hel-l-er, uh, Hi, Wendell, are you ready? I'm starved."

"Yes ma'am, let's go," he said as he grabbed me by the hand, and down the hall we went. My God, I hope he couldn't feel how much I was shaking.

Please don't let the crew see me. Lord, dear Lord, I had never seen a more handsome man in my whole life! I couldn't take my eyes off him. That shirt with green roses would look awful on somebody else, but on him it looked great. Wendell would probably look good in absolutely nothing. OH, BEVERLY, what were you thinking? I embarrassed myself with my own thoughts; I meant he would look good in anything, even green roses.

There weren't many places open, so we went across the street to the top of the El Cortez. Since it was so late, perhaps no one from my crew would be out and about and see us. Other than the staff, we were the only two people in the restaurant. Wendell ordered shrimp cocktail, salad, steak, and a baked potato. Where was he going to put all that food? I only ordered a salad. "I thought you were hungry," he inquired.

"I was...er, uh, I am. I just hate to eat a big meal so late." I should have realized it was odd to be only ordering a salad after I had told him I was hungry. I hoped Wendell didn't think I had an ulterior motive for getting him over there. But then, I wasn't exactly sure I didn't have another motive.

When his shrimp cocktail arrived, he insisted on feeding me a bite. I was feeling so awkward and fidgety, I just knew I'd drop it right in the middle of my lap, but somehow I managed to eat it.

Oh my, here came the manager and our waitress. It's Derek, he was here hiding behind the potted palms, and he sent them over to tell me I had better get the hell out of there; they were coming to warn me or capture me I wasn't sure which. Looking at both of us, the manager asked so sweetly, "How long have you two been married?"

MARRIED?!?!?! Us?!?!?!

Before I could fall out of my chair, Wendell had placed his huge hand on mine and answered, "We're on our honeymoon." I put my head down. He looked at me and grinned. Oh mercy, I can't believe he said that. They both "oohed and aahed" at us and wished us years of happiness. Wendell thanked them, and they walked away remarking about what a striking couple we were. Wendell said, "I just hated to ruin it for them. Hope you don't mind."

"Mind? Ah, no, of course not." I found myself wishing it was true. Just get your big, hot hand off mine before I end up with first degree burns. I could not believe the heat. It started in my hand and was working its way up my arm and all over my body.

Wendell finished his huge meal, and I played with my salad. I was actually afraid to eat for fear I would throw up. We left the restaurant and got into the elevator that went down the outside of one part of the hotel to the ground floor. In the elevator, he leaned toward me and confided he was afraid of heights. I burst out laughing. For the first time since he had gotten there, I didn't feel so nervous.

Well, at least not until we walked back to my hotel room. I was shaking so badly I couldn't get the key into the keyhole. He put his arm around in front of me, took the key from my hand, pushed it into the lock, and unlocked it. I was in the process of thanking him for dinner when he asked if I minded if he came in and watched the last half of the Conquistador's basketball game. He was sure his roommate would be fast asleep, what with the time change and all, and Wendell didn't want to wake him. Would I mind, just for a little while? I hesitated and then decided I didn't really want him to leave right then, so I agreed. He turned on the television, pulled off his boots, and sat down in the middle of my bed. Now, I was getting really nervous!

We had talked at dinner about me overhearing Jimmy or one of the other ballplayers call him Elvis. We both had a mutual love for Elvis, and

I had told him I met Elvis on a flight. I shared with him about the article I had written for the movie magazine. He asked me if I happened to have a copy with me, and I handed him the one from my suitcase. I felt like I should apologize for the article making me sound like some starry-eyed illiterate who did well to pour coffee successfully, much less try to write. I told him they changed a lot of the story from how I had originally written it, that it was almost like they wanted to make me sound like a dingbat. Wendell said he was sure my original was better, but when he finished reading the article, he told me it was fine. He understood they had changed it, but that the best part was the paragraph I showed him that was totally mine. Oh, he was a charmer! He knew instinctively exactly what to say. (I was sure he'd had a lot of practice.)

I was sitting in a chair beside the bed. We started talking about his home in Mississippi and about his family. I couldn't get over the unusual names his brothers and sisters had: Bernell, Janell, and Berlin. But there were also Shirley and Glenn. His Dad was Aaron and his mom Ollie Mae, which I thought sounded so sweet, warm and "down home." I just knew you would have to love a woman with a name like Ollie Mae. (Little did I know how true this would be.) We were still engaged in deep family conversation when I realized the basketball game had ended. "Who won?" I asked him.

Wendell looked over at the TV, then back at me and grinned and asked, "Who cares?" He got up and turned the television off and returned to the bed. My eyes got bigger by the second, and my heart was jumping up and down like crazy (I wondered if he could see it through my sweater). He asked me to sit by him, so I reluctantly got out of my chair and sat beside him on the bed. He leaned toward me and lightly kissed me on the cheek, his moustache tickling me. Then he put his hand on my face and turned my lips toward his and really kissed me. It felt so weird kissing someone besides Derek. My head was spinning. I could not believe I was doing this, kissing someone other than my husband. It felt so strange to kiss someone with a moustache too, because it really did tickle. I was tingling all over my entire body. Wendell kept kissing me, and then he pulled me closer and held on to me like he never wanted to let go. I felt wonderful!

Wendell and I kissed for what seemed like forever. I was having trouble breathing, and so many feelings were rushing through my head when he slipped his hand under my sweater. I must have gasped because he stopped and looked at me. I looked straight into his eyes and told him, "I can't do this," as I tried to breathe normally.

He softly asked me, "Why not?"

I felt my voice tremble in my throat, "Because I've never been with anyone, ever in my life, except my husband."

Wendell looked right back into my eyes and asked, "Don't you think it's time you did?" I couldn't even think, my whole body and mind were spinning. I felt as if I were falling backwards from a cloud, but the chemistry between us was like lightening. He must have undressed me because the next thing I knew, we were lying on the bed completely naked. I couldn't believe I had allowed myself to end up in this situation.

Wendell made love to me. He was gentle, but so passionate! He would touch me tenderly, and then it was as if he just couldn't get enough of me. We were sweating like crazy and rolling around the bed. He was inside me, and he appeared to have no intentions of letting our bodies be separated. He held me so close and so tightly, as if he was afraid I would suddenly leave. I felt like my skin was on fire. The kissing was so intense, and the excitement was overwhelming! He was on top of me, and then I was beside him, but he never withdrew himself from inside me. It seemed like we had been entwined for hours. I wasn't used to this, and I wasn't sure how to respond to him. I touched him by running my hand across his muscular, somewhat hairy chest which felt so incredible. When Wendell finally let go, the intensity was overwhelming, and I thought we were both going to pass out. I held on for dear life, having never experienced emotions on this level. My heart was beating so hard, I was soaking wet, I was exhausted, and I had never gone through anything like this ever!

He was so incredibly beautiful! I know men probably would prefer not to be described by that word, but he was. Wendell reminded me of some Greek God; he was perfect in my eyes. I stared at him as he lay there beside me with his eyes closed. I could not believe a man who looked like him was here with me, making love to me, holding me like he never wanted to let go. I thought I was dreaming but then felt sad as I imagined I would probably never see him again. I decided I wanted to feel all of those feelings again, so I raised my head from his chest and started kissing him. Wendell responded immediately. This time it was even more intense than it had been the first time. We were more passionate and more demanding, and it felt like sparks were jumping off our bodies. I never knew lovemaking could be like this. We couldn't get enough of each other. We exhausted ourselves, and finally he fell asleep after 3:00 a.m.

I got up a little later and put my nightgown on. Although I was burning hot, I wasn't used to lying in bed naked. As I was about to fall asleep, Wendell put his hand on my stomach and sleepily, but sort of demandingly, whispered, "Get that damn thing off. I want to touch you, not some piece of material." I pulled my nightgown over my head, twirled it in my fingers, smiling to myself as I threw it on the floor. I was thrilled he wanted to touch me! I cuddled up next to him, exhausted but never having felt so fabulous in my whole life! His body temperature felt like it must have been 110 degrees, and I could not believe how hot he was - in so many ways. Still, that heat didn't keep me from wanting to be close to him. I put my head back on his chest and wrapped my arm over him, he put his arm around me, and we both fell into a deep sleep.

I woke up once, and the outside light was seeping in through the window. I looked at Wendell still asleep and just enjoyed the view. He looked like a sculpture! I had never seen anyone so unbelievably handsome. His dark hair was matted to his forehead from all the sweating, yet it still looked nice. His eyelashes were dark and thick. Oh, and that neat-looking moustache. I had always loved moustaches, and touched my lips as I thought how his felt when he kissed me. I giggled quietly to myself as I imagined how red my face must be from his moustache and heavy whiskers. My sensitive skin must look like a beet, but it was worth it. His lips were shaped perfectly in front of those absolutely straight, white teeth. Just thinking about his mouth and lips gave me chill bumps. I sort of shivered and hoped he didn't realize it. Whew, I thought, I needed to catch my breath.

His hand was resting on his chest and I couldn't get over how large it was with such long slender fingers. (I learned later he wore a size thirteen ring on his ring finger and an eleven on his little finger.) His chest wasn't as hairy as I expected it to be; I somehow imagined he'd resemble a grizzly bear. Wendell had broad shoulders and long arms. "All the better to hold you with my dear," I thought to myself and smiled. I felt so silly but so amazingly happy.

Growing up, I hadn't been a particularly religious person. I knew about God and His commandments and about going to hell for breaking them, and I realized I had just broken one. I had just committed adultery. I fully expected a lightning bolt to come soaring through the ceiling of my room and strike me right between the eyes. I thought to myself, "Lord, I know what I have done is wrong, but I know deep in my heart you understand how it happened. Please forgive me for what I have just done, but somehow

I feel like you brought Wendell Ladner into my life for a reason. I'm not sure what that reason is, but I think you know." I fell back to sleep.

I woke up with a start to the ringing of the telephone, which I assumed was my wakeup call. Oh, God, it was Derek! I nearly died. Wendell had rolled over, sat up, and was about to lean forward to kiss me when I mouthed, "It's my husband." Wendell smiled, got up, and went into the bathroom. I asked Derek if everything was okay and why he had called. He said he just wanted to chat. I asked if there was something in particular he wanted to discuss, which just didn't sound like me at all. Derek became defensive, sarcastically saying he was sorry he woke me. I told him I hadn't slept well at all last night (understatement!), so I was tired and just surprised by his call. About that time, I heard Derek being paged at work, and I was never so glad to have that happen. He said he had to go, and I told him I'd see him soon. He hung up. Oh, why of all days did Derek have to call today? Wendell came out of the bathroom. He had showered and was already dressed, looking and smelling fabulous! He sat down by me on the bed. I had pulled the covers up around my chest, having never wished more that I looked like Raquel Welch.

Wendell asked me if there was any way he could call me. I couldn't believe he was asking because I had supposed this would be a "one night stand" to him. I never thought I would see him again. I heard myself telling him my phone number in Tulsa and that he should call between 8:00 a.m. and 5:00 p.m. Wendell wrote the number on a notepad on the nightstand and put it in his shirt pocket. (I figured, that way if I ever ran into him again and he hadn't called, he could say he accidentally washed it. I just didn't believe he would ever call, so I was being really hard on myself, trying to get prepared for the fact I would never see him again.) He leaned over and tenderly kissed me and said, "I'll call you, Baby," then turned and walked out the door. My heart sank!

I sat there for a moment feeling so empty, staring at the door Wendell had closed behind him. I couldn't have gotten up and walked him to the door, though, because I was naked. I went into the bathroom, got into the shower, and sobbed. I cried so hard I thought I was going to throw up. I was so ashamed of myself, but I had never imagined lovemaking could be like that.

I felt so confused as I met the crew for pickup. While I was glad about what had happened, I was also very sad, because I felt guilty for having broken my marriage vows. I had been with a man other than my husband, and I wasn't proud of myself. One of the girls from First Class, Jan, asked me if I had gone out with that basketball player. I told her of course not, I was married. Jill looked over at me and said, "You're a better woman than I am, that's all I've got to say. I would have followed that guy anywhere he wanted to take me." I felt my face turn crimson.

When I landed in Tulsa I hoped that just this once Derek would spend the quarter and be there to meet me when I got off the airplane. No such luck! As usual, he was out in front of the terminal waiting in the car with Muskogee, our beautiful golden retriever. I was hurt, and then I was angry. Dammit!!!! He deserves to have a wife that cheats on him. He can't even invest a damn quarter to be at the gate when I got off the plane. If he hadn't taken this job, I wouldn't have been commuting in the first place. There he was and there was Kogee. She jumped around in the bucket seat of the car, wagging her tail and trying her best to get out the window to greet me. I think she was more excited to see me than Derek was, but I still grabbed Derek and hugged him tightly when I got into the car. "What's the matter with you?" he asked.

I curtly replied, "Nothing, Derek, not a damn thing."

I tried and tried to put Wendell Ladner out of my mind, but I kept reliving that night in San Diego over and over. I couldn't get over how he made me feel. I remembered his cologne, his hands, his voice, those eyes, that moustache! I could not get him or that night out of my mind. While Derek sat in his chair reading, I would be sitting on the couch, getting butterflies as thoughts of Wendell ran through my head.

I found myself doubting whether or not I wanted to be married any longer. I wanted to go places, do things, and be free. Derek got a call from a co-worker who asked if he wanted to go to an ORU (Oral Roberts University) basketball game. When Derek mentioned it to me, I told him to go. After he got ready, I asked him if he thought it would be okay for Elaine Grayson and me to go see Elvis in Las Vegas later in the month. He blew his top and said no, we didn't have the money, and I didn't need to be running off to Las Vegas with a gal who wasn't married. I got angry, and after he left for the basketball game, I called Elaine to see if she could go see Elvis with me. She told me she would love to, but she had forgotten about our trip and didn't figure Derek would let me go anyway, so she had made plans to go on a trip with the fellow she was dating. I was disappointed but figured it was probably for the best because pushing the topic would mean another fight with Derek. So I just gave up.

When Derek and I first got married, we did so many different things, went on trips, and out with friends. It seemed we always had something to do in New York. Since we had moved to Tulsa and bought this house, we didn't do much of anything, and I was getting bored and frustrated. I got ready for my trip the next day and never mentioned the Elvis thing again.

It was weird being in San Diego again and reliving that night with Wendell. I was sad he hadn't called, but I really and truly didn't expect to hear from him. I flew my trip and returned to Tulsa feeling sorry for myself. I didn't blame Wendell for what we had done. Lord knows, I was a willing participant. But I hated that something so important to me had probably meant so very little to him.

On February 22, exactly ten days since I had met Wendell, he called. I nearly died! I could hardly contain myself; I honestly figured I was just an evening's entertainment to him and that I would never hear from him again. He said the team would be in Dallas on Saturday and wanted to know if there was any way I could possibly meet him there. I told him I really doubted that I could, and he really wanted to see me again. Oops, there went my heart doing flips again. Before I knew what I was saying, I told him I would try, then asked for his phone number so I could call him if I could figure out a way to be there. Wendell told me to call him collect. That southern accent was even more prominent on the telephone, and I absolutely loved hearing it! I couldn't help myself, I was so excited. We chatted for a few minutes longer, and he again told me he hoped I could be there Saturday because he couldn't stop thinking about me. ME!?!? I had difficulty imagining he was going through the same thing I had been since our first meeting, but it was nice to think about, whether it was true or not.

I found myself reading the sports section of the paper after Derek went to work to see if anything had been written about Wendell. I just wanted to see his name in print. I thought about what he had asked me and decided, God forgive me, I was going to see if there was a way I could meet him in Dallas on Saturday.

I called Crew Schedule and told them I wanted to pick up an extra trip, but it had to end in Dallas early in the morning. Crew Schedule was always short on Flight Attendants and loved to have one call and ask for a trip, even one with restrictions. It would be one less trip they would have to call a Reserve out to cover. They gladly gave me a trip to Boston.

I was a nervous wreck. Derek wasn't too happy I was taking a trip over the weekend, especially to where Bob Bernhardt lived, but he was delighted I would be making a bunch of overtime. I had told him Crew Schedule was really short on Flight Attendants and they were panicking since it was only the twenty-third of the month. Derek didn't seem too fazed that I was leaving because he had some chores he planned to get done in the yard. Mercy, our lives were so boring.

Before my trip, I ran into Don Johnson in Operations. He looked good and seemed happy to be living in Los Angeles. He was still dating Sally and appeared to be content.

But I only had one thing on my mind...Wendell Ladner.

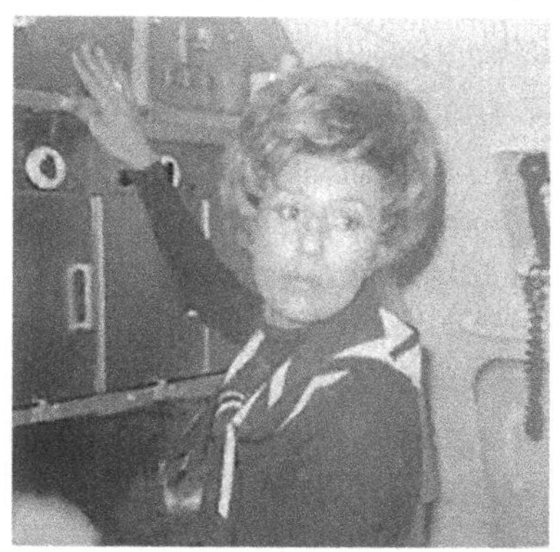

Carole Sanders

The next person I saw was Carole Sanders, who was getting ready to go out on a trip. The last time we flew together, I had told her I hadn't been exactly happy in my marriage lately, so she asked me how things were going. I told her it wasn't too great and then I asked if I could confide in her about something I needed desperately to talk to someone about. Carole looked at me and could see I was really upset. "Sure, shoot." she said.

I told her all about Wendell and what I was planning to do. Carole told me she knew this wasn't an easy thing for me to even consider, but she had a few ideas and I could do with them whatever I saw fit to do. She mentioned I probably really didn't want to spend the day with Wendell and then head home to Derek "all aglow." (Carole had a real way with words.) Carole suggested I call Derek and tell him she wanted me to come to a wedding shower for my Supervisor, who was getting married. I would spend Saturday night with Carole and then she would bring me back to the airport to catch a flight to Tulsa on Sunday morning.

What wicked webs we weave...I know. But this was such a brilliant idea, I just had to try. I called Derek and lied to him, and told him the whole story Carole had made up. He was angry and didn't see any reason why I had to stay all night. Couldn't I just go to the shower and then come home on a late flight Saturday evening? I told him I would be tired after my flight, that I had to go with Carole to get a gift, help her set up for the shower that started at 7 p.m., and I had no idea what time it would end. I just didn't want to have to run to the airport for a flight home at midnight.

Derek still didn't like it. As a matter of fact, he said, "Just do what you want because you are going to anyway."

Well, that pissed me off. I said, "Derek, I am staying. I'll see you Sunday," and I hung up. I grabbed Carole and swore I would be in her debt forever, then I called Wendell in a rush and told him I would meet him on Saturday. He sounded surprised and also very happy. Then I ran for my flight because I was almost late from spending so much time in Operations.

This was my first trip on the DC-10, and I was really nervous because it was such a big plane. I had studied the location of all my emergency equipment because I hadn't actually flown on the plane since I'd had my training class after returning to work. The Premium, or number one Flight Attendant as they were called on the 747 and DC10, wasn't overjoyed I wasn't familiar with the aircraft the way the rest of the crew was, but there really wasn't much she could do or say as long as I did my job, which I intended to do. The last thing in the world I wanted to do was be a burden to my flying partners. I had to be reminded a few times how to do the service because the way the instructors taught us in class almost always got revised on the line. We Flight Attendants were pretty ingenious in figuring out the best, most efficient, and sometimes quickest ways to do our jobs.

I was pretty tired when I got to Boston but went out with a couple of the gals for some famous clam chowder. Then I went to my room, fortunately, my own room, and called Bob to chat for a while. I jumped in a bubble bath and let my mind wander over what I had done. I felt bad about lying to Derek, but I was so wound up at the thought of seeing Wendell again. I was scared wondering if we would actually get along, since we really didn't know each other. I mean, we knew each other in the biblical sense, but we hadn't talked much after the kissing started. I wondered if we would have anything in common besides lust.

When I got to Dallas, I decided to get a room at the Ramada Inn near the airport. I used money I had saved from my "allowance" Derek gave me before my trips to pay for something special. This was very, very special!

I thought I would take a shower before it was time to see Wendell. I had told him to call me when he arrived, and it turned out we were staying at the same hotel. I took forever getting ready; I wanted everything to be perfect. I even brought a beautiful night gown that I thought was kind of sexy, but it never got used.

The phone rang. Wendell wanted to know when he could come to my room. I asked him for a little more time; I was getting cold feet and wasn't quite sure what to do about it. I was a nervous wreck!

The phone rang about ten minutes later. When I answered, Wendell said, "I'm on the way up," and hung up the phone.

Suddenly, there was a knock on the door. I had been sitting on the edge of the bed doing a needlepoint to work through my nerves. When I opened the door, there Wendell stood in a beautiful chocolate brown suede coat. He came through the door, slammed it behind him, pulled off his coat, flung it in the chair, gently pushed me onto the bed, then laid down on top of me. When Wendell landed on top of me, I could feel that he was already aroused. I don't know what came over me, but I asked, "Is that a pencil in your pocket, or are you glad to see me?" (A pencil, huh, it was more like a policeman's flashlight!) He burst out laughing. I loved that laugh!

We couldn't get our clothes off fast enough. When he kissed me, I felt like I was being touched by 120 volts of electricity. This was absolutely amazing! I felt like I was on fire. We made mad passionate love that lasted forever. Again, we couldn't get enough of each other. After our first round, we were laying in each other's arms when he suddenly sat up and started kissing my neck, my breasts, and my stomach. Then he kissed me below my belly button. I jerked straight up on the bed, with my eyes popping out, "What are you doing?" I asked. I had no idea what he was about to do.

Wendell took that big ole hand of his, put it on my shoulder, and gently pushed me back and told me, "Trust me, you are going to enjoy this." I just fell back on the pillow as I was told. He continued to kiss me in places I never dreamed anyone would ever be kissed. Suddenly, I felt my whole body explode! I could not breathe; I was engulfed in emotions I had never felt. I honestly thought I was going to die. (That I allowed this to happen to me was unbelievable in the first place because I had never let anyone touch me below the waist before. If anyone ever tried, I grabbed their hand and told them emphatically, "No!") So I really trusted Wendell.

I finally knew what it was like to have an orgasm. I had overheard two of the gals in the galley talking about it one day and got up my nerve to ask them what they were talking about. One of them looked at me and asked how long I had been married. When I told her, she had to control herself to keep from laughing. "You've been married five years, and you've never had an orgasm? I bet you've never even had oral sex." Dear Lord, what was she talking about? I had read about it in the *Joy of Sex*, but, no, I had never done that. I never even considered doing it or having it done to me. She put her arm around my shoulders and said, "Come here girl, we need to talk." Some of the things she shared with me nearly made me faint. People actually do things like that to each other? She enjoyed telling me and watching the shocked look on my face. I could not imagine what these things might feel like. But now I knew, and I wanted more.

We made love all afternoon, hugging, kissing, holding, touching, so into each other. It seemed we both wanted badly to please each other. Sadly, my knowledge was very limited in the lovemaking department, but what I did know, I did with much enthusiasm. We'd nap in between, and then one of us would wake up ready to start all over again. The man was insatiable! There was no end to his sex drive. Wendell loved for me to touch him as much as I loved for him to touch me. I experienced so many orgasms. Yahoo! It was a whole new feeling for me. I had never felt such intensity in my body in all of my life. It was incredible! How did this happen? How did I get it to happen again? Now I knew how awesome sex could be, and I loved making love with this man. I never wanted it to end.

At one point, after a particularly vigorous bout of lovemaking, Wendell looked at me and said, "I think I've died and gone to heaven."

I looked at him in a most mischievous way and asked, "So what does that make me; a fucking angel?" I could not believe I said that to him, but I did. Who was this person that had taken over my mind and body? Wendell laughed so hard I thought he was going to fall right out of bed. He laughed until tears came into his eyes. I think he was as shocked as I was at what I had just said, but he seemed to love my newfound wicked sense of humor. We just hugged each other and laughed some more.

"Wendell, I have to ask you something," I inquired of him.

"Sure, Baby, what is it?" he replied.

"Did you like the way I had my hair fixed before you demolished it?"

"Why yeah, it looked real pretty."

"I wasn't sure you'd like me in a ponytail," I said to him.

"You looked really cute," he told me.

I hit him on the shoulder, "Wendell Ladner, I didn't have my hair in a ponytail!"

"I'm sorry, Baby, but I really didn't take the time to notice."

"Oh really, what else did you have on your mind?" I teased.

"Ah, just this..."

"Oh boy, here we go again," I whispered in his ear.

Wendell looked at me, almost as if in amazement. Then at one point, he looked deeply into my eyes, all serious, and I stared back at him. I could not imagine what was going through his mind. Then he grabbed me and squeezed me so tightly I could hardly breathe. "I just can't believe you have been married five years and you've never done some of the things we're doing."

"I promise I'm telling you the absolute truth, especially that one particular thing that you did to me."

"What a waste of woman!" he stated. "You're so good at making love. You respond so passionately; how could any man not sense this in you?"

"I don't want to talk about that anymore, Wendell, I just want to learn. Teach me, please, teach me everything."

"Oh, I will, Baby, I promise I will. But if there is something you don't feel comfortable doing, just tell me and we'll stop," he told me.

I trusted him so much. We tried all sorts of positions; he even wanted me to agree to watch ourselves make love in a mirror. Before I knew it, he had taken the mirror off the wall and sat it on the bed. I couldn't believe this was happening to me. All of this sex, and I was loving it!!!!

The mirror, by the way, was too distracting to me. I told Wendell I didn't want anything to interfere with my concentration. My mind was on two things and two things only, how to do all of these things and how to please him. I must admit I had to ask some pretty silly questions. To his credit, Wendell didn't laugh at me once. I do think he was in his element. He was the teacher, and I was the more than inquisitive and willing student.

"Baby, I love being with you," he suddenly blurted out.

"I love being with you too, Wendell," I told him, "but I have a favor to ask of you."

"Sure, Baby, name it." he told me. Although I loved to hear him call me "Baby," I wondered how many other women he had called that very same name. "I'd like you to call me by my name whenever we are making love."

He looked at me with such question in his eyes. "Why?" he asked.

"Because, Wendell Ladner, I want you to know who you're making love with!"

Smiling that perfect smile of his, Wendell said, "If that's what you want, Bab...er, uh, Bev, you've got it."

This time I grabbed him around the neck and hugged him so hard I was afraid he'd lose his breath. "Wendell, I'm so happy!"

We fell backwards and made tender, sweet, love once more. Afterwards he said, "I do so enjoy making love to you, Bev. You're so soft, so responsive; any man would be a fool to pass up making love with you."

I felt tears burn in my eyes; I was embarrassed but so pleased he had said that about me. "Ah, shucks, Wendell, I bet you say that to all of your girls. But if you do, I don't want to hear about it." He laughed. There was one thing so vital and important to our relationship besides sex, and that was laughter. This may have been one reason why we lasted as long as we did. I laid my head on his chest, and we both fell asleep.

When we woke up we were both absolutely starved. "No room service," they told Wendell when he called downstairs. "Well, how about you fix it and I'll come after it?" he asked. They agreed, and he got dressed and went after it.

Kentucky Colonel's Uniform

When Wendell came back into the room, I snapped his picture. "Just wanted to see how you'd look serving trays."

"Cute, real cute," he said with a darling smile on his face. "Now get over here and eat. Then I've got to go get showered and dressed for the game. I've arranged for the bellman to drive you to Loos Stadium to watch the game. He'll have to bring you back too, Hon, if that's okay with you. The Coach has been on my ass about goofing off lately. Then I'll meet you back here." I told him that was fine with me.

I don't remember a thing about the bellman except he kept trying to make small talk. I didn't really feel like talking, but I tried to be nice. I felt a little uneasy with him, afraid he was thinking terrible thoughts about Wendell and me. I didn't want to be made to feel guilty about something so beautiful, even if it was wrong.

I sat in the stands and watched Wendell in utter amazement, not taking my eyes off him the entire game. I couldn't believe he was mine, at least for the evening, and that no one else mattered to him but me. If I had been a queen in another time, I would have gladly given up my throne for him. I knew I would have done anything for him!

As I watched him run down the court, I felt so proud. I had to chuckle to myself as I overheard some of the comments from the Chaparral fans sitting near me. "Ladner, you gorilla; go back to Kentucky where you came from." When Wendell played ball, he was like a steamroller. He played football on the basketball court. Some people criticized him for it, others admired his gusto. (If you'd like to learn more about Wendell's way of playing basketball and being "A Fan Favorite," type his name and "Fan Favorite" into a search engine.)

One of the kids sitting beside me noticed I wasn't cheering for the Chaparrals. He nudged his buddy, then turned to me and asked, "Excuse me, ma'am, but are you Dan Issel's wife?" I smiled at this adorable red-haired, freckle-faced little guy and answered, "No, Hon, I'm Wendell Ladner's girlfriend."

As I looked around at these six boys, two beside me and four in front of me, they all started to squirm in their seats. The red-headed fellow quickly apologized for their comments. I told him it was alright. We all had our favorites when it came to sports. He blushed, looked at me, and said, "You sure are pretty." His buddies cracked up and started teasing him. I was rather surprised myself, but I said, "Why thank you, kind sir, that was very nice of you to say," then leaned over and hugged him. His little face was nearly purple when I let go.

It was near the last few minutes of the game when a young boy approached me. He asked me if I was Bev Schoenmann, and when I said I was, he told me Wendell Ladner asked that I wait for him on the second floor after the game. Great! Oh super, I could hardly control my enthusiasm that I got to ride with Wendell instead of the bellman. Wendell had gotten hit in the mouth during the game, and I nearly died when I saw all of the blood on the towel he removed from his lip. I just wanted to run to him when it happened, but I couldn't. At least now I could comfort him on the way back to the hotel.

Wendell and three other men came out of the locker room. He walked towards me and asked if I would walk with Ron Franz to fool the Coach into believing I was with Ron. I agreed and walked over to Ron so Wendell could introduce me. Ron was a giant! Ron seemed a little annoyed at first, but he warmed up as we started talking. At one point, we were laughing so loudly that curiosity got the best of Wendell, who kept walking closer and closer to Ron and me. Wendell was dying to know what we were laughing about, and he got so close he walked on Ron's heel. "Christ, Ladner, why don't you just walk up the back of my leg; back off, man!" Ron roared at Wendell.

Wendell looked at me and said, "Screw the Coach, I'm walking with you Bev." Throwing that long arm of his around my shoulders, he said "Come on, Baby, you're walking with me." He sounded so funny because his mouth had a bunch of gauze in it because of the cut on the inside of his lip. I tried not to laugh, but it sounded so funny.

When we got to Ron's car, I burst out laughing. A Volkswagen!!! You have got to be kidding me; the four of us in a Volkswagen? Another player had asked Ron for a ride on our way out to the car. What a joke! Ron looked to be about 7', the other guy was at least 6'8", and there was Wendell at 6'5", and me almost 5'11".

"Anyone got a crowbar?" I asked. "We may get in there, but we're never gonna get out!" But we crammed into that little bitty bug, all four of us. Of course, Wendell's and my knees were under our chins as we sat in the back seat.

I looked at Wendell with his lip protruding out. How can one man look so many different ways at once? He was sexy as hell, wild yet innocent, boyish, manly, vulnerable (especially with his swollen lip), and downright gorgeous! Such contrasts, all in one twenty-four-year-old face. I was feeling silly and leaned over to Wendell and sort of sang (Lord knows I can't carry a tune in a bucket), "This time there'll be no good night kiss."

Wendell glanced in my direction, and I assumed that he had taken that as a challenge because he spit the gauze on the floor of the car and said, "Oh yeah, that's what you think, girl. Come here." I met his kiss with both eyes wide open because I had not expected him to do that; thank heavens, he had closed his.

Back in our room, we decided to change beds since we had pretty much demolished one of them. "Looks like someone staged an all-out war in that bed," Wendell laughed.

"It sure does, Wendell. Only the neat part about it is we both won."

He grinned and said, "I think you're right about that. Now let's see if we can't destroy this one the same way." Wendell jumped, like a little kid, right smack in the middle of the bed. "Get over here, woman!" he demanded. I leaped on top of him as his arms encircled my body. "Yahoo!!!" he yelled.]

"You're crazy, Ladner!" I told him.

"Yeah, you bet I am, I'm crazy, crazy about you!" he replied.

We exhausted ourselves in nonstop lovemaking again. "Wendell, how did you do it?" I asked him.

"Do what?"

"Make love to me all day and then turn around and play two hours of basketball? I wouldn't have been able to walk down that court much less run."

"Conditioning, girl, pure conditioning."

"In that case, let's just see what good condition you are in."

Wendell looked over at me all shy and inquired, "You don't mean... again, do you?"

"Yep, Superman…again!!!!" I said to him as I pulled him towards me.

It must have been nearly 4:00 a.m. when we both passed out. About 5:00 a.m., Wendell sat half up in bed and said, "Oh, Baby, I want to make love to you." I felt my eyes cross. I'll never be able to walk normally again, I thought to myself. Just as I was trying to figure out where I could get the energy, Wendell fell back on his pillow sound asleep. I stifled a giggle. I was exhausted too - there was the will but right now, no way.

I wanted to cry when the wakeup call came. Wendell rushed downstairs to get a shower and change, then came back to kiss me good-bye. I took his picture before he left. "You have a real thing about pictures, don't you?" he asked me.

"Yes, I'm afraid I do. I hope that you don't mind." He said he didn't. Quite honestly, I could tell the ham actually enjoyed having his picture taken. (One of my great regrets is we never had a picture taken together.)

Wendell grabbed me and kissed me, tenderly but passionately. Then he almost ran out the door to join the team in the lobby for the trip to Love Field.

I felt like my heart was broken in two. I could not believe how much I missed him already. I nearly jumped off the bed when the phone rang. I had been crying and couldn't imagine who would be calling me at the hotel. I tried to disguise my voice when I answered, "Hello?"

Wendell had gotten as far as the airport, which was less than ten minutes away from the hotel. "I miss you, Baby...er...uh Bev! I already miss you!"

"Not half as much as I miss you, Wendell," I told him. He hung up the phone, and I laid on the bed and cried. God, now I have to get up and go back to Tulsa. How am I ever going to be the same again? Little did I know I never would be.

For the next few days, I went up and down like a yo-yo. One minute I felt guilt, then the next I couldn't stop thinking about how much I cared about Wendell. He had really gotten under my skin (no pun intended). I would be enjoying just sitting out in the sun and suddenly my mind was on Wendell again.

I had tried to be sweet with Derek when I got home from that trip, but he was cold and stand-offish. I was almost glad he was because then we didn't have to talk to each other. Our fifth anniversary rolled around and Derek brought me some beautiful, coral roses. He also gave me a silly and a romantic card. But he never wrote anything in the cards other than "Love, Derek."

Maybe I was asking too much from Derek. All I knew was that I was frustrated with our marriage. I loved Derek, I really did, and I wasn't proud of what I had done with Wendell, but I somehow felt justified because of what he told me to do that morning before I left for my trip.

Wendell called a few days after I got back to Tulsa. He had told me he was married, but they hadn't lived together for a very long time. It was his second marriage, and he wasn't quite sure why he had even married her but intended to get a divorce soon. I don't know if that made me feel better or worse. Maybe I felt like we were partners in crime because we both were married and we both were unhappy.

Wendell told me the Colonels were playing in Memphis where Bessie lived and that he was going to see her and start the divorce proceedings. I believed him, but at the same time I was suspicious of whether he was actually going to get a divorce or not. I worried the whole weekend he was in Memphis, but just like clockwork, he called me on Monday and told me it wasn't going to work out with his "about-to-be ex-wife." Wendell really wanted a divorce. I didn't know if he was waiting for me to say I was going to get divorced also, but I had told him things were not going well with Derek and me. I didn't know what to do.

Wendell and I talked at least once or twice a week. He would tell me he really missed me and couldn't wait until we could be together again. I felt the same way, but with his basketball commitments and my flying schedule, we had to be satisfied with telephone calls until we could have an opportunity to meet somewhere.

I knew in my heart that someone who looked like Wendell could not be true to any one woman. He was constantly being chased after, and I was sure there were many times he allowed himself to be caught. I didn't want to think about him being with other women, but it was always in the back of my mind. No matter how much I tried to convince myself Wendell was not a one-woman kind of guy, I couldn't help feeling about him the way I felt.

One thing that surprised and touched my heart was how we would end our conversations. I would say, "Miss me!" and he would reply, "Always!" It felt so good to hear that.

I tried to concentrate on my flying. I flew with a neat gal named Bonnie Beckert. One day, she told me she had an appointment to see a fortune teller named Mr. Robert and asked if I wanted to go with her. I had always enjoyed going to fortune tellers with Mom because we never took them seriously but had fun doing it.

When I walked in and sat down at Mr. Robert's waiting room, I had a funny feeling. I couldn't put my finger on it, but I felt a connection or something, maybe a spirit in the room. It was odd, but I didn't give it too much thought until Mr. Robert walked out of the room to call Bonnie in for her appointment. He took one look at me and the necklace I was wearing that had moons and stars all over it, asked me to come in, and told Bonnie it would be a minute before he gave her a reading.

Mr. Robert asked me why I wasn't toning my spiritual gifts. I was surprised and asked what he meant. He told me I had so many ESP gifts I could use to help people if I would quit fighting them. I thought Mr. Robert was kind of nuts. Yes, I had had "gut feelings" in the past and whenever I ignored them, I always wished I hadn't, but he was a bit much.

Mr. Robert told me the man I was in love with, "WL," was married, that he wouldn't get a divorce, and that we would always have problems with his ego. He also told me that my marriage was pretty much over because I was miserable and so was my husband. He said I should attempt to do what I really had the heart for, which was to be an actress and that if I applied myself, it would happen. Mr. Robert mentioned my husband's and my mother-in-law's names, and was really starting to freak me out.

Wanting to prove I had abilities I wasn't using, Mr. Robert made a drawing on a piece of paper and handed it to me after he had folded it three times. He told me to tell him what was on that paper. I sat there thinking, "This guy IS nuts!" Then suddenly a picture came into my mind, and I described it to him. After I finished my description, he told me to open the paper, and the picture on it was just the way I had seen it in my mind. That was strange!

Lastly, Mr. Robert asked me to write down a frivolous wish and give it to him folded so he couldn't see it. I did, and after I handed it to him he said, "Bev, you will get that date with Elvis Presley. You just have to be patient." I looked at him oddly and got up and left his room. Outside, three people were waiting, and Bonnie wasn't happy. I apologized as she went into see him.

I didn"t realize how long I had been in with Mr. Robert, but it had to have been at least an hour or two. I tossed around all the things he had told me about Wendell and Derek and knew he was right. How did Mr. Robert know Derek's and Claire's names? I had never seen him before, and I had no prior plans to see him before Bonnie asked me to tag along. It was all very odd, and also a bit scary, so I never did anything about trying to develop any gifts.

Derek and I met his family for vacation in Phoenix again and pretended there was nothing wrong with our marriage. Pam commented on how long my hair was getting and said I reminded her of Cher, and I was flattered. When Derek and I went to dance, he asked me, "So are you going to divorce me the same way Cher divorced Sonny?" I didn't answer him because I didn't know. I just knew I didn't like feeling like I was leading a double life.

Derek and I took Muskogee to obedience school. Because she still had a lot of puppy left in her, Kogee was not the best student but did manage to get her diploma, probably because the teacher liked her so much.

We seemed to be getting along better, cooking out with other couples, and starting to do fun things like we used to in New York. I knew in my heart I still loved this man, but I wished I had the exciting sex life with him I had experienced with Wendell. I wasn't raised to be in a situation like this - I was supposed to be a loyal wife and not be doing what I was doing.

At times, Derek could be so sweet. If I couldn't go to sleep, he would read to me until I got drowsy and then would rub my temples until I dozed off. I adored him when he did things like that. I even found a couple of letters in an old diary he had written me when I was flying International. He would mail them to the Ala Moana Hotel, and they would be there for me when I arrived the second day of my trip. In the letters, Derek told me he missed me, loved me, and couldn't wait for me to come home and tell him all the "scoop" I heard about the airline. When I flew, it seemed I would hear things that were about to happen and then would tell Derek when I came home, along with what I had seen and what the crew did on the layover. I missed that side of Derek. After being with him for over five years, I knew Derek was not a romantic man, but he could be thoughtful when he wanted to be.

Derek was so good at putting up walls to keep people out, even me. He would just decide he didn't want to share what he was doing or feeling, and there was nothing I could do to make him.

I was still talking to Wendell every chance I got. He would call me on my layovers just to let me know what he was up to and tell me he missed me. I had such a problem believing him because I knew if there was one thing Wendell Ladner was never lacking, it was women! Even a few times when we were first out together, women would almost knock me over to get to him, which pissed me off big time. Of course, Wendell was always gracious and would sign an autograph or visit with them for a short period of time, and then he would turn his attention back to me and all was forgiven. He always made me feel like I was the most important person in the world when we were together.

About two months later, I was flying a three-day trip with the first night being in LAX (Los Angeles) and the second night in CVG (Cincinnati, Ohio). Wendell and I planned to meet in Cincinnati later in the month but just weren't sure which trip would work with our schedules. He asked me to call him as soon as I knew what days I was flying.

A cute, tiny, red-haired gal with tons of freckles, Kathy Winslow, and I hit it off and worked well together on our trip. We laughed at the same things and enjoyed talking to each other about our personal lives. I was sitting on the stairs outside the jetbridge in Los Angeles getting some sun on my face when she sat down beside me. "Okay, let's hear it," she prodded me. I looked at her rather oddly and asked her what she meant. She told me she had been watching me closely yesterday and today, and she knew there was something really bothering me. I trusted Kathy and wanted to tell her about Wendell, but I had already told Carole Sanders, and I was afraid, with Derek also working for American, that somehow it just might get back to him. Even though you fly together with the same crew members and rely on each other all month, you can't trust everyone.

But Kathy seemed so sincerely concerned for me, and I wanted to talk to someone. I told her about my marriage, how I wasn't very happy, and I didn't think Derek was either. I told her about our fight before the trip when I met Wendell and what Derek had said about finding myself a lover. "He was being rather prophetic, huh?" she asked.

"I guess so, but that doesn't make me feel any better about what happened between Wendell and me, and that it's still going on." I told her how much I cared for Wendell and how I knew in my heart we could never be together, that I was too insecure, plus he hadn't asked me for an exclusive relationship. I tried to make her laugh, but I could tell she was sensing my pain and didn't laugh at my attempt to be funny. Kathy asked me what I was going to do, but I hadn't the faintest idea. I was dealing with so much guilt eating me up inside that I had started to have some serious stomach problems. It was time to go, so we agreed to finish our chat later.

Later, when we got to Cincinnati, these two guys were standing in the hotel lobby watching us. One of them tried to strike up a conversation. "You two girls Stewardesses?" he asked.

"No, we're meter maids," Kathy replied in a snit. Duh, we were wearing our uniforms.

The talkative one invited us to a party at the Netherland Hilton where we were already staying, but we didn't want them to know that. We hoped they would leave so we could go to our rooms, but one of them just wouldn't give up. "Perhaps it would make a difference if you knew who the party was for. It is for Tommy Branch, the pitcher for the Cincinnati Blue Stars. He just got back from spring training and we're throwing a little get-together for him."

Kathy sort of rolled her eyes. "Well you're just gonna have to throw it without us!" she snapped at him. When the elevator came, we decided we had tried to stall them long enough and got in to go to our rooms.

The guys got on the elevator also. One of the guys was wearing a baseball cap pulled low over his forehead. He didn't say much of anything at first, but then he said, "Ah, come on ladies. He's serious about the party. Bobby Goldsboro will be there too." We came to our floor, and they remained on the elevator. The mouthy one said, "If you change your mind, ladies, the party is on the top floor. We'd love to have you there."

"You boys have fun at your party," Kathy told them.

We just looked at each other as we got off the elevator. I said, "Kathy Winslow, I can't believe you were so rude!"

Then she said, "Oh come on Bev, those two probably don't even know Tommy Branch."

I laughed at her, then said, "Kathy, the guy in the baseball cap was Tommy Branch!"

She stopped in the middle of the hall, spun around, and practically yelled in my face, "Are you kidding me?"

I told her no, that I was from Columbus, Ohio, and I sure knew Tommy Branch when I saw him. She screamed, "Go change and get ready! I'll be to your room in thirty minutes."

I was so tired and didn't want to go but Kathy insisted. She didn't want to go alone, and she promised me we would only stay a little while. I finally gave in. If it was that important to her, I would do it. We changed and went up to the top floor.

The talkative guy from the elevator opened the door, and you could tell we were the last two people he ever expected to see. Kathy said, "Okay, buddy, where's Tommy Branch?" He stepped back, opened the door wide for us to come in and pointed over towards a window. Tommy was over there talking to Bobby Goldsboro, the country singer.

Kathy barged into the room, only to stop dead in her tracks, and I almost ran right into her. The place was packed with women. All sizes, shapes, ages, and they were all lined up around the wall. Except for the guy who opened the door, Tommy, and Bobby, there were no other males present. I couldn't believe this. There must have been fifty or sixty women there all watching Tommy's every move and waiting their turn to talk to him. Some of these women were real beauties but some who looked as if they worked the local street corner (perhaps they did). I was pretty sure they all had one goal in mind though - meeting Tommy and becoming involved with him in one way or another.

I wanted no part of this ridiculous scene. I could feel several sets of eyes glaring at my back as we walked over to where Tommy and Bobby were sitting. Kathy grabbed me by the hand, pulled me right in front of Tommy, and then strategically planted her body right beside Tommy on the windowsill.

Tommy grinned because I don't think he expected us to be there either. He introduced us to Bobby. I was nervous and said, "Hi, Bev, I'm Bobby." They both burst out laughing as Bobby said, "No, Honey, I'm Bobby. You're Bev." Lordy, did I feel stupid. I just smiled and didn't say another word.

Bobby sang a few songs, and Tommy joined in on some of them. At one point, Bobby asked if there were any requests, and I stuck my foot in my mouth again by saying to him, "Yes, please don't sing 'Honey.' It is so sad and always makes me cry."

"How do you like that folks?" Bobby asked as he gazed around the room at all the other women. "A million-selling record, and her request is not to sing it." He sort of chuckled, and I'm not sure if he was upset or not, but he didn't sing it.

The party was starting to drag, and I was getting even more tired. Kathy and Tommy were really enjoying themselves. At one point they were acting like little kids, pouring their drinks out the window onto people coming into the hotel. I hated to tell her I was leaving, but I couldn't stay awake. I excused myself and went to the ladies room to splash some water on my face. On the way there a girl with dark, dyed-black hair grabbed my arm. "Look here, sweetie," she snapped in my face, "my friend and I are staying with Tommy. He flew us up here from Florida. Just where do you and your friend get off coming in here crashing our little party?"

I didn't like her or her attitude at all. "We were invited!" I hissed back at her. I didn't normally react in this manner, but she made me angry, and I was already in a bad mood because I was so tired. I could tell she wasn't expecting that answer.

Her mouth flew open, "Who asked you?" I jerked my arm out of her grasp, told her it had been Tommy, and went into the bathroom.

When I came out, she was still standing there. "I just want you to know that we're spending the night with Tommy."

"Congratulations, aren't you lucky?" I walked away from her.

I went to find Kathy who asked, "What's wrong?" I told her I didn't feel like playing high school games tonight and that I was leaving. Tommy asked me to stay for just a few minutes more because he was going to start sending folks out of the room. I really didn't want to stay, but Kathy caught my attention and mouthed, "Please just a few more minutes." I sat back down on the windowsill.

To this day, I still don't know how the kissing got started. Tommy kissed Kathy, and then he turned and kissed me. I was so flabbergasted I didn't quite know what to do. Then I spotted the witch with the dyed-black hair giving Kathy and me the dirtiest look imaginable. I grabbed Tommy, put my arms around his neck and really laid a big ole kiss on him. This time it was his turn to be surprised. I wondered what all those girls were thinking who had come here hoping to make a connection with Tommy while I couldn't have cared less. Somehow it didn't seem fair.

I looked at Tommy who was staring at me as if he was as unable to believe what I had just done. I was surprised at myself too. I thanked him for inviting me to his party. What party? This was an "opportunity," not a party, for him to check out a bunch of girls and decide who his next conquest was going to be. He looked at me rather peculiarly, and then in a cocky voice asked, "Oh, you're one of those nice girls, huh?"

"I guess you might say that, Tommy." I replied. Kathy told me she would see me in the morning at pickup.

I put the key into the door of my hotel room only to be startled by the persistent ringing of the telephone. Thinking it might be Kathy, I said, "Hello?"

"Hello, nothing. Where have you been?" I recognized that Southern accent. "I've been calling you all evening."

"God, Wendell, nice to hear from you."

He sounded pretty miffed. "You didn't answer me. Were you out with one of those pilots?" he almost shouted.

"Wendell, you know me better than that."

"Okay, so where were you?" Wendell asked again.

I said, "If I didn't know better, I'd swear you were jealous."

"Me, jealous? No way. Now where were you?"

I smiled from ear to ear. I wanted to laugh, but I thought better of it. "There was a party..."

"Where?" he abruptly asked.

"Here in the hotel. Some people were having a welcome back party for Tommy Branch. Oh, and Wendell, Bobby Goldsboro, the country singer, was there too."

He practically yelled into the phone, "Tommy Branch, Tommy Branch, big fucking deal, Tommy Branch!"

"Well, well what do you know? You are jealous!" I taunted him a little.

"Of him? You've gotta be kidding. Why would I be jealous of him?"

"Gee, Wendell, a lot of girls think he is kind of cute."

"I don't care what a lot of girls think. What about you?

"I'm afraid I'm hung up on a certain basketball player with this incredible southern accent."

"I'm sure glad to hear that. I'll be coming to Cincinnati next week when you get there."

I was so happy I could barely keep from screaming in his ear. "Let me check my date book," I smartly replied.

"You will be spending the evening with me, not running around with some baseball jock."

"If you say so, Wendell." I smugly replied.

"I say so!"

We visited for a little while, and I told him it was nearly 1:30 a.m., and I had a 6:00 a.m. wakeup call. "You might want to think about that next time you go running off to some party," Wendell declared.

"I will, sweetheart, I will." As usual, I said, "Miss me."

And as usual, he replied, "Always!" Our special way of saying goodbye was so sweet, and it meant so much to hear him say that.

We hung up, and I jumped into bed without washing my face, something I never, ever did. I was tickled he had sounded so jealous.

Kathy was smitten. She could not stop talking about "JB" as she called him. She ended up spending the night with him. I don't know what happened to the other two girls from Florida; I guessed he had sent them packing.

My weekend with Derek was like all the others. We worked in the yard, cooked out, went to see a movie. I felt as if I were living in two completely different worlds AGAIN! At home, I was the wife, and when I flew, I wanted to be single. I had gotten in a lot of trouble mentally the last time I found myself living in the past and the present. Honestly, I was scared I would end up getting sick again. I wasn't being honest with Derek or myself. I sat on the bed rubbing Derek's back until he fell asleep. I remembered doing that so many times in New York, hoping one day I would be able to do it forever and praying Derek would be mine. I felt sick at my stomach, went in the bathroom crying, and threw up. "Please don't let me screw up my life again, Lord, I'm really confused!"

Wendell called to tell me he was sorry, but he had to meet with his agent the night I would be in Cincinnati. He begged for me to forgive him and promised to be there the following trip. Actually, I was sort of relieved since I was having a really hard time with my life, so not seeing Wendell right then was probably a good thing.

I flew my trip, and while going through Memphis, I saw Jess, the Passenger Service Manager who had boarded Elvis on my flight that February. (I had gone off the plane to buy some watermelon sherbet - I had never had anything like it before, and the only place I knew that served it was an ice cream shop in the middle of the Memphis terminal).

Jess nearly ran me over as I was heading back to the airplane. He asked how I was doing and if I had enjoyed my trip with Elvis that night. When I told him I did, he smiled, opened a small book he had inside his jacket pocket, wrote something on a piece of paper, tore it out, and handed it to me. I just looked at him rather oddly and asked, "What's this?"

Jess smiled and replied, "Next time you're in Memphis, you might like to call this number. Elvis is divorced now." I got back to the airplane and opened the paper - on it was a phone number. I didn't really believe it was "THE" phone number for Elvis, but I put it in my tote bag anyway for future reference.

Kathy went out with Tommy on the Cincy layover, and I went to my room. While they had invited me to go, I knew she really didn't want me there. I knew I wouldn't want her there if I had been meeting Wendell. I read in the paper that Wendell had had an incredible game the night before, so I decided I would call him when I was sitting in Dallas tomorrow waiting for my trip back to Tulsa.

I tracked Wendell down in Greensboro, North Carolina. I found out from the Colonels' office where the team would be staying. I wanted to tell Wendell I had read the story in the paper and how proud of him I was. When I called the room, he sounded funny when he answered, acting like he didn't want to talk to me. Then it dawned on me, he wasn't alone. For some reason, even though I knew Wendell was with lots of other women, and I honestly didn't blame him, knowing it and experiencing it were two completely different things. He told me he would call me Monday.

I hung up the phone and lost it. I ran to the bathroom, crying so hard I thought I was going to be sick again. Then I got mad, really mad! I thought about Wendell telling her the same things he had told me. I didn't want to, but I envisioned him touching her, kissing her, and making love to her the way he had with me all of those times. I was so upset!

I dried my eyes and called Western Union. Billing the telegram to my Mom, I sent Wendell the following message: "Don't bother coming to Cincinnati on Tuesday, you probably won't have the energy to drive. I don't care to join your harem. Thanks for the memories." I told the lady at Western Union I wanted the telegram delivered tonight! She told me it could arrive as late as 2:00 or 3:00 a.m., and I told her that would be just perfect. She tried to discourage me by telling me it would cost more to deliver it that late. I said I didn't give a damn and to deliver the damn telegram when I wanted it delivered. I am sure she thought I was the bitch from hell, but she said it would be taken care of.

I cried all the way back to Tulsa. When I got there, Derek asked me what was wrong. I told him I had a terrible stomachache, which was the truth.

I had bought a mug in Mexico for Wendell and had it engraved with the words, "Always remember Flight 331, February 12, 1973. Love Bev." I went to the Post Office and sent it to him. He would probably throw it out the window after the telegram I had sent him.

Why did I send that telegram? I guess I had lost control of my emotions and my life.

When Derek went to work, I called Wendell, scared to death to have to face him. Jay Bauer, who used to hang around Wendell, answered the phone. After I asked for Wendell, Jay asked if it was Bev calling. I reluctantly told him it was. Jay said, "Whew, I'm glad I'm not you." I gulped so hard, then heard him put the phone down and call Wendell.

When Jay told Wendell it was me, I could hear Wendell almost stomping to the telephone. "What was with that 'fuck off' telegram that you sent me?" He was furious!

I half cried, half whimpered, "I am so sorry, Wendell. I don't know what to say. I just needed to hear your voice and to talk to you, and I was devastated when you seemed like you didn't want to talk to me. I knew you weren't alone, and that hurt me so much. Normally, I could handle that, but Thursday night I couldn't."

"I have never been as mad at anyone in my life as I was at you. My parents are old and to get a telegram at 3:30 a.m. scared the hell out of me. What were you thinking? Couldn't you have waited and talked to me in Cincinnati on Tuesday? What the hell, Bev?"

I started bawling and telling him how sorry I was and that I really wasn't thinking. I could barely speak to him. I knew he was furious with me, and I had to fix it. I was glad Wendell mentioned I could have talked to him in Cincinnati; I guess that meant he was still planning to come. Again, I told him how sorry I was, and he calmed down a little. He finally forgave me and told me he would see me on Tuesday. I hung up the phone and felt like the weight of the world had rolled off my shoulders.

I had to leave a day early for my trip because they were expecting really bad weather to come into Tulsa for a day or two. Kathy picked me up so I could spend the night with her. When I told her what I had done to Wendell, she couldn't believe it. "It is a wonder he didn't tear your head off, girl."

"I know, Kathy, it was a stupid, stupid thing to do, but I couldn' help myself. I am so damn insecure as it is, and my world is upside down right now I guess I did it to myself, but I just couldn't help what happened between Wendell and me, and I don't want to let go of him."

"Well then, you had better accept Wendell for the way he is and realize that those jocks lead a completely different lifestyle than normal males." I told her I knew that, but I was just having a difficult time living all of the lies and still not being able to walk away either.

On our trip through Memphis, I decided to call the number the PSM had given me just to see if he was pranking me or not. I nearly died when Elvis's Daddy, Vernon, answered the phone. He told me Elvis was performing at Lake Tahoe, and if I needed help locating him there, I could call back and he'd try to get a number for me. I ran on the plane to tell Kathy, who couldn't believe it either. It really was Elvis's phone number, and I had just talked to his Dad. That was so cool!

When I got to Cincinnati, I had hoped to see Wendell waiting for me in the lobby, but he wasn't there. I called his house, and the phone was busy for over an hour. I was getting really angry. When I finally got him, he told me he had to go see his lawyer and would come up right after he finished. I waited and worried for another few hours. I'd called his house and got no answer. I kept expecting him to show up any second. I sat on my bed and waited and waited.

Finally at 2:00 a.m. he called, drunk as a skunk. I was livid! Wendell told me he had met with his lawyer about getting a divorce, and they had gone out for a drink and ran into some Kentucky Colonel fans who kept buying them drinks, and the next thing he knew he was drunk. Wendell was afraid to drive from Louisville to Cincinnati feeling the way he did.

I was so angry I wanted to choke him. I had worried myself sick thinking maybe he had been in an accident. When I yelled at him, he acted sincerely sorry, and I remembered the telegram fiasco and that he had forgiven me. So I finally said, "Wendell, I was just so worried that something had happened to you. After you told me that you would only be with the lawyer for a short time, I guessed that you would be here in about two hours. When you didn't show up and no one was answering your phone, I got so worried."

"I know, Bab-...Bev, I am so sorry. I can't drive up there now, not in the condition I am in. I promise you that I will be there next week. Honest, Baby." I let that last "Baby" slide because it sounded so cute. I told him this wouldn't have bothered me so much if I didn't care about him the way I did.

Wendell told me he was really looking forward to seeing me and would make it up to me next week. I teased him about "making it up to me," telling him I expected a whole lot of "making it up." He laughed and promised he would do his best. I stated, "That's good enough for me." We made our usual exchange of words instead of actually saying "good-bye."

Terry and Me

After that trip, I went to Columbus to see my folks, and decided to call Terry Kneisley. I had written to him the whole time he was in Vietnam. (I had told Derek Terry was just a guy I had gone to junior and senior high with and that we had remained friends. I asked Derek if he minded if I wrote to Terry, and he said he didn't have a problem with it.) Terry came to the house to pick me up and looked so much older, more mature. He hugged me really hard when I came out onto the porch.

We grabbed a piece of pie at Max and Erma's and then went back to his apartment where he opened up and talked about Vietnam. Terry told me how much he appreciated those letters, how he looked forward to getting them, and how he and his buddies loved the pictures I sent. I had taken some bikini pictures when I was flying the Hawaii trip and some photos of me sitting on my brother's awesomely cool Mustang Mach 1. Terry laughed when he told me those pictures nearly caused a bunch of guys to go AWOL. Wow, hearing that made me feel good!

Terry had changed so much. He shared with me about how upsetting things were in Vietnam and how you never wanted to make friends with anyone because they could die in the next few minutes. With tears in his eyes, he shared a particularly disturbing experience about one of his friends getting blown up. My heart ached for him and all of the other men and women who had to be there. Terry informed me that a lot of the guys got into drugs to avoid reality. They felt that by taking drugs they had an "I don't give a shit" attitude. If you died, you died. You were braver, and you just didn't care what happened to you.

Terry also dealt with survivor's guilt. The guys who came back had trouble accepting they had made it through this hell, and they weren't sure why they hadn't been killed. Terry always struck me as being a sensitive guy. I could only imagine how difficult this part of his life had been to get through.

Terry asked me about flying and my marriage. I told him I loved flying, but I was dealing with some issues in my marriage, serious issues that were really getting me down. I didn't tell him about Wendell because I thought Terry would have been shocked since what I had done was so out of character for me. He said he hoped everything worked out and that he wanted me to be happy.

I hugged Terry so tightly when he walked me to the door, and then he kissed me. I always enjoyed kissing Terry. He thanked me again for keeping in touch with him and for being his friend. I wanted to tell him we could have been so much more than that if only he had given me a chance way back in High School, but I didn't want to ruin our evening together. I felt great that Terry had opened up to me about some things that I was sure were not easy for him to talk about. I told him I'd give him a call next time I was in Ohio because I'd like to take him out for dinner. Although he didn't think he would allow me to take him out to dinner, he would be glad to have dinner with me again. I hugged him really tight and told him to take care. We always had a bond without actually discussing it. Terry was my first crush and if only he had dated me, we might have ended up together one day. It just never seemed to work, though not for lack of wanting on my part, but maybe we were just destined to always be friends. Anyway, Terry was, and had always been, someone so very special to me.

On the way back to Dallas, J.D. Sumner and the Stamps Quartet (Elvis's backup singers) got on the plane in Nashville. I mustered up my courage and gave J.D. a note to give to Elvis for me. I asked him if he knew where to send Elvis a card in Tahoe, and he gave me the address. I sent several cards to Elvis, just silly ones saying "Hi" or encouraging him to have a great performance. A few months later, I was amused by an article in one of the movie magazines which reported that Elvis was dating up a storm and receiving a lot of mail, especially from a mysterious girl named "Bev." I had to laugh when I read that; I do believe some maid found all of my cards and notes and told some reporter about them.

The weirdest thing happened when Kathy picked me up for the next trip. She told me she wanted me to go out with Tommy on the layover, and I thought she had completely lost her mind. Apparently, Kathy and Tommy had gotten into a hassle over something, and she had agreed to go out with one of his friends on this trip and Tommy asked her if I would go out with him. I told her there was no way because I wouldn't feel right being there with someone she loved. Kathy begged me, telling me if I didn't go out with Tommy then she wouldn't be able to see him.

I told her I was going out with Wendell anyway. Then Kathy asked if I hadn't seen any newspapers of late. I had no idea what she was talking about, but apparently Wendell had been hurt at a game, in a head-on collision with a glass water cooler. I could not believe what she was telling me. Kathy said Wendell was in the hospital, but he had been fine when I talked to him earlier in the week. I called the Colonels' office and got the name of the hospital where Wendell was and called to find out he had just been released.

I called Wendell at home. "What in the world happened?" I asked. Wendell told me he was running after the basketball, turned to go back down the court, then misjudged how close the water cooler had been and collided with it. He had to have 48 stitches. I was upset because he sounded so pitiful. I asked Wendell if he wanted me to come to Louisville and take care of him. He said although he would like that (ever the diplomat), there was a nurse from the hospital watching over him. Hmm, I'll just bet she was. There goes that green-eyed monster again!

Kathy saw the look on my face and asked what Wendell had said. When I told her, she was all pissy and grabbed the phone, "So I guess this means you won't be coming to Cincinnati on Tuesday, huh?" Wendell must have said no because she told him, "Well that's probably for the best because Bev has a date with Tommy Branch anyway!" and hung up.

I could have killed her! When I grabbed the phone to call Wendell back, Kathy pulled it out of my hand, held it to her chest and said, "Now let him think about that when his pretty little nurse is tending to his boo-boo." I didn't know what to say since I didn't want to think about the nurse, so I decided not to call him back.

When I got to Cincinnati there was a note for me. I had hoped it was from Wendell, but it was from my in-laws. I nearly died right there on the spot because the note said, "We're here in Cincinnati with Granny S and want to take you out to dinner." Oh, my God, what if Wendell had been there? I was never so glad he wasn't there in my whole life.

I told Kathy I had to go out with my family, and she got upset because we were supposed to meet James and Tommy. I told her to call them and say I couldn't make it. Instead, she asked if we could just agree to go out for drinks with them when I got back from dinner. I told her I really didn't want to go, but she insisted that if I went, she would ditch James and then have a chance to fix things up between her and Tommy, so I finally agreed.

I had the best time with Derek, Sr, Claire, and Granny Schoenmann. They took me to a French restaurant, and Granny was speaking to the waiter in French. It was a nicer experience than my first encounter with a Schoenmann family member speaking French — Pam and I had since made our peace, and I thought the world of her and Jeramie.

We visited and caught up on everything going on in Tulsa. Derek, Sr. and Claire were hoping to come for a visit in the spring. I was very fond of my in-laws in spite of the fact I still thought I wasn't exactly the type of woman they hoped Derek would marry. I got this impression from Claire more than Derek, Sr., who was actually pretty easygoing. I thanked them for surprising me and taking me out to such a wonderful dinner and told them they could surprise me any time. Secretly, I was just so thankful I hadn't been surprised by them finding me with Wendell!

When I got back from dinner, Kathy was on pins and needles because Tommy wasn't too happy he'd had to wait for me to have dinner. Kathy didn't tell him it was with my in-laws because she didn't want him to know I was married. I just didn't feel comfortable doing this. I mean, there was no way I would have ever asked Kathy to go out with Wendell so that he and I could make up after a fight. This whole thing made no sense to me, but she was my friend and I would have done just about anything for her, even something as silly as this.

James picked us up and took us to Tommy's place, which was awesome. It was masculine, definitely a bachelor's place including his trophy room. Tommy had just opened a restaurant and told us he would take us there one day. Although he seemed really nice, I felt awkward. We went out bar-hopping, and since I didn't drink much, it was difficult for me when they were chug-a-lugging one beer after another. At one point, I was so uncomfortable I didn't know how to act. It seemed like every word I said, every move I made, every time Tommy looked at me, I could feel Kathy's eyes burning holes in me.

I decided to be a bitch, hoping maybe the evening would end sooner. We were standing at one of the bars when Tommy put his hand on my butt in front of God and everybody. I didn't like that one bit. I tried to move so as not to embarrass him, but he refused to move his hand. So I loudly said, "Get your hand off my ass."

He was taken by surprise and said, "What's the matter? You don't like being touched by me?"

I said, "I am not one of your girls, and I don' want to be treated like I am."

Tommy blurted back at me, "No you aren't, and I doubt if you would qualify to be one of them either."

I snapped back, "And I seriously doubt if you can chew gum and walk at the same time." The bartender's eyes nearly fell out of his head. The people standing within earshot of us gasped. They couldn't get over the way we were talking to each other. I went over to Kathy and James and told them I was tired and wanted to leave. Tommy followed me and told James we were going back to his place. I just rolled my eyes and let out a sigh. We left for Tommy's home.

After we had been at Tommy's house for a while, he went into the other room with James. I told Kathy I was miserable, and I was sure Tommy was too, so she had better tell him she needed to talk to him so I could get James to take me out of there. When they came back, James said, "Kathy, I have to get up early tomorrow morning so I'm going to need to take you to the hotel. Tommy's going to bring Bev."

I know my eyes must have bugged out of my head. Kathy must have thought James and Tommy had discussed this when they left the room and that she wasn't going to get a chance to talk to Tommy alone, so she jumped up, grabbed her purse and said, "Let's go, James."

I stood up and looked over at her and then at Tommy and said, "There's no need for you to have to take me to the hotel, Tommy, since they are going anyway. I'll just ride with them."

He looked right into my eyes and said, "No, I want to talk to you."

I was puzzled. Kathy said, "I'll see you later, Bev," and Tommy walked them to the door.

When he returned, he asked me, "So, why don't you like me?"

I was bowled over by his question. "It's not that I don't like you Tommy, but I am serious about someone else, and besides, Kathy is crazy about you. Can't you see that? This whole date was her idea; she wanted to see you and hoped that somehow you two would have a chance to talk and work out whatever happened between you."

Tommy said, "This date was my idea, not Kathy's."

"I don't understand. I thought you and Kathy were involved."

"I like Kathy, but I'm not interested in a long-term relationship right now."

"So you decided to move on to her friend? Is that your plan?"

Apparently, Tommy didn't like the tone in my voice. "Maybe you should leave."

I said, "Sure, I think that's the best idea you've had lately." He called me a cab and then went into his trophy room. I was grateful the cab got there quickly. I left without even saying good-bye to Tommy, which I'm sure didn't matter to him.

Kathy was furious, barely speaking to me at pick-up time. She wanted to know when I had gotten back to the hotel. When I told her that it was probably about thirty minutes after she got there, she didn't believe me. Then I told her what Tommy and I talked about, and she still didn't believe me. I told her bluntly, "Look, Kathy, my life is nuts right now. I am married to one man and think I'm in love with another. The last thing in this world I need is to have yet another man in my life. Besides, as cute as he is, Tommy is not my type. Wendell is my type." She seemed okay with that, but it wouldn't be the end of Kathy, Tommy Branch, and me.

I called Wendell to see how he was doing, When he asked me how my date with Tommy Branch went, I told him it was a disaster and tried to explain to him about Kathy's plan. Wendell told me he sure wasn't happy when Kathy told him I had that date, and I responded that I sure wasn't pleased to hear about his little "nursey poo" who was taking care of him either.

"And I would venture to bet she wasn't forty years old either," I said to him, which shut him up pretty quickly.

Wendell told me he was sorry he had missed me in Cincinnati because of the accident. He offered to come in May, but I told him I wasn't flying that schedule then, but I would let him know when I flew back to Cincinnati. He told me he missed being with me, and I told him that I missed him a bunch too.

Then I said, "Wendell, I am going to try really hard to make my marriage work. I feel like I just have to. I care deeply for you, but I think Derek and I deserve to try to make a go of it without you being in the middle." I couldn't believe I was saying this to Wendell. It just came rushing out of my mouth, and I wasn't exactly sure where it came from. Wendell told me he understood, and no matter what, he wanted me to be happy. He said he wouldn't call me, but I should call him if things didn't work out, but if I decided not to see him anymore, Wendell hoped I would still keep in touch. I promised him I would call one way or the other.

I ended our conversation the way we always did, "Miss me."

"Always," he quietly said.

I felt so sad when I hung up. Why did I do that? I felt like I needed to give my marriage one last try, and oh, I hoped I knew what I was doing.

Kathy and I decided we were going to go see Elvis at Lake Tahoe. I knew Derek would have a hissy fit, but I was determined to go anyway. Of course, when I brought it up, he didn't disappoint me, getting angry and saying he didn't see any reason why I should go to Tahoe with a girl to see Elvis Presley when he had taken me to see Elvis in Tulsa. Yes, and I had sat so far up in the "nosebleed" section that Elvis looked like an ant on stage. I appreciated that Derek had taken me, but I wanted to go to Lake Tahoe with Kathy for a girl's trip. He just didn't want me to go, period, but I stood my ground and was going, come hell or high water.

On my birthday, May 5, I was in Phoenix when Derek showed up to surprise me. I was so touched by his thoughtfulness. Maybe I had made the right decision in breaking things off with Wendell. Without thinking of Wendell every waking moment, maybe Derek and I stood a chance, and this surprise was especially wonderful. My only complaint was Derek drank too much at my birthday dinner. He was acting really weird - sweet one minute, then loud and obnoxious the next. He embarrassed me a couple of times by getting too loud in the restaurant.

Kathy and I went to Tahoe on May 7. It was an unbelievable day. We had to run through the San Francisco airport to board a helicopter in Reno, and then in Reno, Holiday Airlines actually held the airplane for us to catch. We didn't even have our tickets, but they let us on, and we paid for them when we got to Tahoe. We were absolutely giddy!

We didn't have tickets to see Elvis's show either, so we started down to the hotel lobby early to pick up a couple and nearly fainted when we saw the line wrapped all around the building. Oh, my gosh, we should have planned better. We were heading to the end of the line when Joe Esposito walked by. I don't know what came over me, but I grabbed him by the arm, told him that he, Elvis, and Alan Fortas had been on my flight once, and he had told me if I ever needed any tickets to any of Elvis's shows to let him know. Well, I was letting him know...we needed tickets.

I could tell Joe was startled. I had on a bright fuchsia knit dress that crisscrossed in front of my bosom, wrapped around my neck, and buttoned onto the back of my dress. Kathy and I had laid out in the sun so I was bronzed, and with my freshly highlighted, very blonde hair, I was a striking sight, if I do say so myself. Plus, I had on very high heels, so Joe was looking eyeball-to-bosom with me. Kathy said he didn't take his eyes off my bosom the whole time I was talking to him. I chuckled to myself, thinking, poor man, what a waste of his time.

Joe took Kathy and me by the arm and showed us into the room where Elvis would be performing. We could not believe our luck when he sat us down at Elvis' table. There wasn't a soul in the room yet, but Joe said people would start arriving soon. So we ordered a drink, and sure enough, the room filled to capacity in no time.

Then in walked Linda Thompson. She was not pleased, to say the least, to see Kathy and me sitting in her booth. When she sat down, I tried to introduce us, but she could not have cared less. I tried again to tell her Elvis had been on my flight, how nice he was, and that Joe was so kind to let us sit there. Linda acted even colder than on my first attempt. I thought to myself, "Screw you, lady. You are not going to ruin my trip to Tahoe. I am going to enjoy this moment whether you like it or not."

Elvis came out on the stage, and the place went nuts. I could have almost reached out and touched him. It was so wonderful to be that close. He actually looked over at the booth where we were sitting and seemed surprised to see anyone there besides Linda. I bet Elvis felt how pissed off she was too. Several times he looked my way and smiled. I must say, I was loving it! It was worth the trip just to see him smile again, especially at me. Kathy was enjoying herself too, but she really wasn't as big a fan as I was. We stayed for the next show too, but during intermission, Linda had asked for us to be moved to another table. Poor Joe had to come in and ask us to move, but we didn't care. After Joe told us Linda had asked that we be moved, I looked at Kathy and asked, "A little insecure, are we?" I was being a jerk, but I thought to myself, my gosh, Linda was the one sharing his bed not us. Damn her!

J. D. Sumner saw us the next night and asked if we would like to come up to his room for a visit. He said he would try to get Elvis away from Linda so we could meet him. We were gullible, so we went to J. D.'s room; I don't know if he ever really asked Elvis to come meet us or not, but he told us Linda said Elvis wasn't going out that night.

So Kathy and I talked with J. D., and he decided to share with us that he was married but in love with another woman. He had written her some poems and wanted to know if Kathy and I wanted to hear them. We told him we did, especially since Kathy liked poetry. J.D. read them to us, and they were quite beautiful but filled with a lot of pain.

J.D. must have taken a shine to us because when he found out we were leaving the next day, he said he would get a limo to take us to Reno. We weren't really sure if we could believe him, so we made a backup plan, but sure enough, early the next morning the phone rang, and it was J.D. telling us what time the limo would be there. Boy, did we feel special.

We had planned to take a flight out of Reno on Holiday again and then to San Fran and back to Dallas. When we got to Reno, we saw the tail of a parked American Airlines plane. Normally, American didn't fly there, so that was a big surprise. As we walked through the terminal, Kathy spotted Captain Dan Ketchum, and we went to talk to him. We told him we had been in Tahoe to see Elvis, and we were working our way back to Dallas. He told us he had flown a charter into Reno and was flying one back home and since it wasn't full, we could hitch a ride as long as we didn't say anything to anyone on the plane. He figured half the people didn't know each other anyway so no one would even notice us. The plan worked until I opened the Braunschweiger and Swiss cheese sandwich I had bought for the trip home, since there wouldn't be any food for us. The smell of the sandwich went across three rows of seats. Kathy looked over in disgust, "Bev, couldn't you have bought a different kind of sandwich; one that didn't draw so much attention to us?"

I put my head down and softly said, "Sorry," and she burst out laughing. We ate and fell asleep and didn't know a thing until we hit Dallas. Thank you, Captain Dan.

I spent the night at Kathy's because I couldn't get on the next flight to Tulsa. When I called Derek, he knew I would be delayed already. It was because Tulsa is American Airlines' maintenance base, and there had been some big meeting in Dallas so the flights were full of supervisors and a bunch of mechanics.

I was sleeping like a log when Kathy came into any room and told me James was on the phone and wanted to talk to me. James told me Tommy wanted me to call him in Houston. I told James, no way. He insisted on giving me Tommy's number and even made me repeat it back.

When I hung up the phone, Kathy asked me what James had wanted. I looked at her like I thought James was nuts and reluctantly said Tommy told James to tell me to call him in Houston. Kathy said, "Do it." I asked her why in the world she thought I would want to call Tommy after the disastrous evening we had together in Cincinnati. She said, "I want you to call him and see what he wants." I told her it was silly, but she insisted. I had absolutely no idea why this man would be calling me, especially when we didn't seem to care too much for each other.

When I called, Tommy sounded surprised to hear from me. He apologized for our evening together and asked me if I would give him another chance. I could not believe my ears and didn't want Kathy to know what he was saying to me. He went on to ask me to come to Houston to watch him play and spend the weekend with him. I thought, Oh, my God, I cannot believe he's asking me to do this! I didn't know how to reply with Kathy standing right there in the room with me. So I said, "I accept your apology, Tommy, and I am sorry that we got off on the wrong foot. I hope you win your game, and thanks for calling."

I handed Kathy the phone. She said hi to him, and then he asked to talk to me again. I was getting more and more uncomfortable by the second. Tommy asked me, "So are you coming to Houston?"

I said, "Thanks for the invitation to come watch you play, but Kathy and I have to fly tomorrow." He then asked if he could call me sometime. I told him I would be in touch and thanks again for the invite, then I hung up. Tommy was nuts! I had been so rude and mean to him - why in the world would he want me to come to Houston and spend the weekend with him? Men - who can understand them?

I flew my trip to Boston, where I called Bob Bernhardt, and we went out to dinner. We laughed so hard over our first meeting and the hell I put him through. He said, "Bev-a-lee, it's a miracle that I'm still speaking to you." I told him I agreed but that he was a really great friend and I hoped we would always feel this way with each other. (And to this day we do. We still keep in touch by email, Christmas cards, and an occasional phone call. He is one of my all-time favorite people.)

I got to JFK and was getting ready to catch my flight to Tulsa. When I heard someone say, "Oh miss," I turned around, and there was Derek. I was so surprised to see him. He had flown to JFK so he could fly home with me. Mercy, what was getting into him? I was glad to see him, but when we got to the gate, he turned into the monster from hell. He was acting funny, very standoffish. The flight was very tight, the load had picked up, and there weren't going to be as many available seats as there had been when he checked it that morning in reservations. Derek became irate. We managed to get on the flight, and there were two Flight Attendant Supervisors sitting across from us. They had overheard Derek giving the agent a bad time in the boarding area, telling the agent he was already listed in reservations ahead of a lot of these other pass riders and that he had better get on before them, because he would check the boarding of non-revenue passengers and there had better not be any out of line. I wanted to die - this wonderful surprise was quickly turning into a humiliating incident.

One of the Supervisors had gone to the bathroom. I got up to wait outside the lav when one of the Flight Attendants said to me, "I see you are one of us (I had my uniform on) and because you are, I won't report what the agent shared with me about how your husband acted in the boarding lounge, but hear this, if he ever does it again, I will report him."

I was mortified. The Supervisor had walked out of the lavatory when I was listening to the Flight Attendant, and she knew me from when I was in New York. She said, "Bev, you had better get a hold on your husband because he is getting ready to get himself in a lot of trouble for his behavior."

I could feel tears burning in my eyes as I said, "I am so sorry. I don't know what came over him. He is not normally like this. Please don't report him. I will talk to him as soon as we get home." The Supervisor told me she wouldn't, but she had better never hear of him repeating these antics again or he would lose all of his pass privileges.

When we got home, I asked Derek why he had gotten so loud and given the agent such a hard time. He offered no excuse other than he was tired and wanted to get home. I felt like saying, "Now you know how I feel every fourth day whenever I have to go off on a three-day trip and then come home again." But I didn't want to say anything that might cause Derek to ask me to quit flying. I needed my job more than anything now. I asked him to please not ever cause a scene like that again because one of the Supervisors said she would report him, and I didn't want that to happen because then we wouldn't be able to go on trips together again.

Derek was really angry. He didn't feel like it was the Supervisor's place to interfere with what had gone on between him and the boarding agent. I wanted to tell him that just about every person in the boarding area had heard him, but I could tell I wasn't going to get anywhere with this conversation, so I just gave up. I didn't understand what got into Derek sometimes. I knew he didn't like his job, but he didn't have to act like an ass when he was in my arena and embarrass us both in front of people I had to work with.

I had a horrible habit of sunbathing nearly every day in Tulsa. I would get up, do my house chores, iron or wash, plan dinner, and then I would. head for my chaise lounge and bake myself in the sun for hours. I never felt better than when I was lying there basking in the rays. I had always been a sun goddess. On one of my flights, a gentleman who worked for Hawaiian

Tropic Sun Tanning Lotion told me he had never seen a more beautiful tan on all the women he had seen on beaches and by swimming pools. He gave me his card and actually asked me if I would like to be one of his Hawaiian Tropic Girls. I mentioned it to Derek, but he said, "Absolutely not!" I was not going to parade around in front of a bunch of guys in a bikini, no way. So I gave up on that idea.

I was starting to get the feeling things weren't going as well with Derek and me as I had hoped they would.

I broke down and called Wendell. He asked me if it was really true that I was dating Tommy Branch. I told him no and asked where he got that idea. Although he never told me, I had the feeling Kathy had called and told him. In a way, I was glad he sounded jealous, but I reminded him the reason I wasn't seeing him anymore was because I wanted desperately to make my marriage work. Wendell asked me how that was going, and I told him not very well. I didn't want to get into details with him about it, but I told him I really didn't know if Derek and I were going to be together much longer. Wendell told me that after the last time we had talked, he had decided to try and work things out with Bessie and that it was a catastrophe. He said he didn't love her, so he was really going to go ahead with the divorce. I said I wasn't sure I was there yet, but after a few incidents, it was looking more and more feasible.

Wendell said he really missed talking to me and that whenever I was ready, he wanted to see me again. I could feel the tears welling in my eyes. I really missed him too! Not just the sex but also the laughter. I always had a joke to tell him, and I seemed to have a knack for putting him in his place. Even though he acted like he resented it, I think he actually got a kick out of me doing that. I told Wendell I would call him soon and to take care of himself. I felt so sad when we hung up. Still our good-bye was the same as it had always been.

Right before my trip, Derek and I got into it over money. He felt like I had spent way too much on my trip to Lake Tahoe, and I told him it was worth it because I had had a great time. He accused me of being on an ego trip, which really got to me. For the first time in my life, I was feeling confident, attractive and secure, and now here Derek goes trying to take me down. I screamed at him that it wasn't my fault if other men found me attractive. My land, how had we gotten so far apart? He had just come to Phoenix for my birthday only ten days ago. I had felt so close to him, and now I couldn't wait to get away from him. What the hell?

By the time I got to Phoenix, I was down and out. I had a temperature, was dizzy and light- headed, and felt miserable. I went out by the pool for a little while, and then decided to go to my room and try and sleep off this illness.

When the crew called to see if we wanted to go eat, Sue Hanson, the gal I was sharing a room with on this trip, insisted on staying to "babysit" me. Sue was a sweetie, and although she hadn't been flying very long, I enjoyed flying with her. She wrote me a two-page letter while I slept thanking me for being so kind to her and telling me how much she admired me. In the letter, Sue said, "Perhaps what makes you so very exceptional is a kind of exuberance yet sensitivity and gentleness that come from deep within you. I must admit it is not often that I do irrational things such as this, but unfortunately, I fear, not nearly often enough do people remind you just how very special you are and how easy it is to care about you. I want to thank you, Beverly Schoenmann, for a month of 3-day misadventures to remember and for an opportunity to learn about an incredibly funny, sensitive, beautiful lady." She gave me the letter after we had gotten back to Dallas while I was waiting for my trip to Tulsa. "Here's something for you to read before your trip leaves. Thanks for everything. You are one incredible lady." Her letter touched me so much that I still have it today. Thanks, Sue, for taking the time to bless me with your thoughts and accolades.

I was sick for the next week. Derek cancelled a trip he had planned so he could take me to the doctor, where I got lots of meds to try and kick this thing, but I was still burning up with fever. I missed EPT's and had to miss my trip too. Doc said I had some sort of virus, and about the only thing that would get rid of it was rest and sleep. Derek had rescheduled his trip and had to leave for two days. It was awful feeling sick and being by myself, although Muskogee tried her best to give me TLC. I even let her sleep on the foot of our bed, something I had never allowed her to do before, but it was good to have her there with me.

A few days later, Derek answered the phone and someone hung up on him. He spun around and yelled at me, "So, who the hell was that! One of your boyfriends?" I asked him what he was talking about, and he told me someone had just hung up on him after he answered the phone. I said, "Did you ever think it might have been a wrong number? Boyfriends? Derek, what are you talking about?" He just turned his back to me.

I felt like I didn't deserve this because I was trying so hard to put my marriage back together. Yes, I had done some things I wasn't proud of but at times I felt like Derek drove me to it. I never would have run into Wendell's arms if Derek hadn't told me to get myself a lover and to basically quit bugging him for so much attention and affection. He had hurt me deep down to my very core. I never planned to become an adulterer, but I had, and now I was trying desperately to be a wife and save our marriage. I knew in my heart this wasn't working, and I didn't want to face it.

When I flew to Cincy the next month, I called Tommy and asked him for some tickets to the ballgame for me and some of the cockpit crew. He was so sweet and asked how many I needed, then left them for us at the window. It was fun watching him play. We had actually made our "peace," and I thought he turned out to be a really nice guy.

Derek was dealing with some issues and started seeing Dr. Turner more frequently. He never shared with me what his visits were about, but after one office trip he came home in a terrible mood, and we really got into it. He got so angry with me he cursed at me. I nearly fell on the floor. We had never talked to each other that way before, and he was in one of his "walls up" moods where he didn't want to let me into his world. I ran into the bedroom and threw myself on the bed. I was beginning to realize we were on a one-way trip to divorce. I left and walked around the complex for over an hour. When I got back, Derek apologized. I asked him what was wrong, and he said he didn't want to talk about it, so we got absolutely nothing resolved.

I called Wendell when Derek went to work and told him I would be in Cincinnati on Tuesday and would love to see him. "It isn't working, is it?" he asked me, referring to my attempt to fix my broken marriage.

"No, Wendell, I don't think it is fixable. Can you come to Cincy?"

He said, "I'll see you Tuesday if you don't have plans with Tommy Branch." I laughed and told him I had already cancelled those plans in hopes that Wendell could be there, but if not, I was sure Tommy was waiting by the phone for my call. Wendell didn't think that was very cute.

I was an absolute nervous wreck when I got to the Netherland Hilton. There was a message from Wendell saying he would be there around 2:00 p.m. I couldn't get to my room fast enough. I jumped in the shower and got ready for his arrival. When Wendell called my room, I let it ring a few times so he didn't get the idea I was sitting there waiting by the phone, even though I was. I answered, and he said, "Baby, I'm on my way up and you had better be ready."

I stupidly asked, "Ready for what, sir?"

He immediately answered, "For the loving of your life."

I felt my face turn crimson. "Bring it on, big guy," I told him.

When he knocked on the door, I opened it to see him dressed in a black, orange, tan, and white multi-striped shirt and orange pants. The words just flew out of my mouth, "My God, Ladner, who dressed you? Artis Gilmore?"

Wendell put his hand on my shoulder as he entered the room and said, "Get your smart-ass in here!"

I couldn't stop staring at his clothes. Then he started to unbutton his shirt and unzip his slacks. "I swear, Wendell Ladner, if you have on orange box..." I couldn't finish the sentence because he was standing there in orange boxers. Not cotton ones, but some kind of silky material. I couldn't control myself; I went into hysterics. "I know where you can get a part-time job if you ever get tired of basketball. You could work on a road-side construction crew in those. They won't even have to put up signs to alert traffic. They'll be able to see you for miles."

"Get over here, you smart-ass," he said grinning from ear to ear. (Somehow profanity sounds so much cuter when it is spoken with a Southern Accent.)

I didn't laugh very long. The very sight of that gorgeous body drove me crazy. I just couldn't understand why he didn't have more hair on his chest. I used to tease him about it, until he finally said, "I used to have a lot of hair on my chest until I discovered girls." Needless to say, I decided not to tease him about that anymore.

Since we were together like that so infrequently, I couldn't help but think we would feel a little uncomfortable with each other, but we never did. It was just like we had been together yesterday, and the only thing that mattered was us, here and now. I will say, if the sex had been any better, I don't think either one of us could have stood it. It was sublime! We made love so many times - hot, passionate, sweaty love. Yet he was so tender with me. He would put his hand under my chin and stare into my eyes. He made me feel like the most beautiful and important woman in the world and taught me so much about lovemaking.

"You are the most amazing teacher in the world, Wendell."

"I just hope I never run out of things to teach you," he replied.

"Don't worry, when you think you have taught me everything there is to know, then we can start all over again." He smiled and said that was fine with him.

We wore each other out, just like we always did, then fell asleep in each other's arms. It was so wonderful that neither one of us had to leave, that we could actually spend the whole night together. This man was so incredible! I hadn't realized how much I had missed him and the way he made me feel. I knew I never wanted for him not to be a part of my life. I didn't know how we were going to manage that, but I knew it was what I wanted more than anything else. I was sorry I was sneaking around seeing him, but I made up my mind that I would do whatever it took, and do it forever, if he would have me.

We were deep into some heavy lovemaking the next morning when suddenly there was a noise at the door, and it opened. Talk about being embarrassed! I don't know who felt worse, us or the maid. She opened the door, looked at us and then blinked, looked again, and said, "I'm so sorry," as she backed out of the door. I had nearly fallen on the floor because I was on top of Wendell. He almost threw me there because he was so startled too. The maid slammed the door. "Well she'll have something to talk about with the other maids at lunch!" Wendell said.

"Yeah, but she missed the best view 'cause I was on top," I stated.

"You are getting terrible. What have I created here, some kind of a monster?"

"That you have, Dr. Ladner, that you have."

"Come here, monster?' he said as he pulled me down beside him. "Let's do what I created you to do!" He laughed.

"Let's do that," I told him.

We never seemed to take time to go eat. It's a miracle either one of us could walk after one of these sessions. I was feeling so sad because he had to go back to Louisville for a meeting, and I didn't have too much time before I had to start getting ready for my pickup. I didn't want to let go of him. I smelled his hair as I held him. I took in all of the odors that were part of him. I didn't ever want to forget how he smelled or felt. I loved being with him, in his arms, sleeping next to him, making mad, passionate love, laughing and learning. I just couldn't believe I had contemplated giving him up. Was I crazy?

Wendell looked over at me and asked what I was thinking. I told him I had this problem. He looked at me so seriously. "What's wrong?" he asked almost hesitantly.

"I can't stop smiling after we have been together."

He laughed, "What am I going to do with you, woman?"

"I've got a couple of ideas, big fella, but I don't think you have the time."

Wendell said, "I'll make the time." We made love again, one more time before he had to leave. The separating was always the hardest part I did not want to ever let him go!

We got dressed, and I walked with him to the basement to get his car. We were standing there kissing when the parking lot attendant drove up with Wendell's Toronado. I had to laugh, for as the old fella was about to get out of the car, Wendell and I parted, giving the attendant a direct view of Wendell's crotch. He was an elderly black man, and I'm here to tell you his eyes were as big as fifty-cent pieces as he handed Wendell the keys. "Thank you," said Wendell as he handed him some money, "This is for you."

"I'm glad that's all you got for me," the attendant mumbled. I turned beet red. The old black man grinned a toothless grin and said, "Sir, I'll be glad to take your car back to the lot if there's somethin' you need to take care of."

"I sure wish I had the time, Buddy. I sure do." Wendell replied. The old man heehawed all the way back to his position in the little booth.

"Wendell, what am I going to do with you?" I asked.

"Whatever you have in mind will have to wait until next time, so hold onto that thought," he said with a big, beautiful grin.

There never were enough "next times" to suit me. It seemed our schedules always had us in different parts of the United States at different times. Probably one of the craziest things I ever did to see Wendell was when he was in Tulsa playing at ORU on September 26, 1973. What made it even crazier was that my mother-in-law was visiting when he called. Somehow I had gotten the date confused and was taken aback when I picked up the phone and heard Wendell's voice. I excused myself and went into the other room, telling Claire it was Crew Schedule, and I could barely hear them on the phone in the kitchen. Wendell told me he was at the Camelot and asked if I would come over. I wanted to die because there was no way I could get out of the house and leave my mother-in-law sitting there, but I had to at least see him. I came up with this insane plan and told Claire I was planning a surprise birthday party for Derek (which was true) and that I needed her help to get me out of the house once he got home, so I could put the finishing touches on the party with a friend of mine. I told Claire that Derek probably wouldn't want me to leave since she was there, but would she mind encouraging him to let me leave so I could finish the party plans? She went along with my deception, unknowingly of course, telling Derek she would enjoy spending some mother-son time with him.

There was just one problem - the sky opened up and started pouring barrels. I had told Derek I was going to the hospital to visit a friend from my art class. He offered to drive me, which was exactly what I was afraid he would do, so I turned to Claire for help. "Oh, Derek, I'm sure Bev can manage." She winked at me.

Derek was worried about me driving in the storm which made me feel even guiltier, but I was determined to see Wendell even if it was from afar. "If it gets too bad, I'll turn around and come back home. Okay?" I asked him. He finally gave in. Damn, I was terrible!

The weather was worse outside than I had imagined. I prayed all the way over to ORU; of all places for me to be going to see my lover, Oral Roberts University. If I got in a wreck, I would surely know why. I felt like it was a miracle I got there safely. I hated driving at night anyway, and especially in what appeared to be a monsoon.

I made it to the Maybee Center. By the time I got inside, I found, to my dismay, I had gone in the wrong door, so I was at the wrong counter to get the tickets Wendell had left for me. I must have looked pretty forlorn because one of the Coaches from ORU approached and asked me if I had a problem. I explained my dilemma to him, and he said, "No problem, just follow me," as he reached for my hand. He led me across the basketball court in front of both teams. The game hadn't started yet, but the players were warming up. Wendell caught a glimpse of me out of the corner of his eye and nearly got hit in the head with the basketball. He stopped and stared. "I came in the wrong door," I mouthed to him. He just shook his head and smiled from ear-to-ear. The Coach took me through the locker room to the front of the ticket counter. I picked up what I thought was my one ticket and was puzzled to see two in the envelope. The Coach escorted me to my seat. I smiled, thanked him and he winked at me saying, "My pleasure."

The more I sat there though, the more guilt I felt; guilty because I lied to Derek and even guiltier because I brought Claire into my little deception. I couldn't seem to help myself because Wendell was so important to me! In spite of that, I started to get scared of driving back in the thunderstorm. I could hear the thunder in the coliseum and knew the storm wasn't letting up at all. I hated to leave but only stayed until half-time. It was such a fruitless trip; I wasn't even able to speak to Wendell. All I could do was sit there in the stands and watch him, although he was constantly turning around looking up at me and smiling. I wanted to touch him, to hold him, to be with him, and I couldn't. I had to leave.

The drive home was just as bad as it had been going over. I did have a picture of Wendell from the program to keep me company on the way back. I tore his picture out, put it in my wallet and threw the program in the trash. What if I had a wreck and someone found that picture of Wendell in my wallet? I didn't care. I made it home, but I still felt bad; bad because I knew Derek worried and bad because I didn't get to be with Wendell.

When Wendell called the next day, he asked me why I had left so early. He said he was so disappointed when he came back onto the court and looked up at my empty seat. I told him why I left and hoped he understood.

Then I asked him why he had left two tickets in the envelope. "I thought maybe you couldn't get away without bringing your husband, so I left two tickets."

"Wendell Ladner, did you honestly think I would bring Derek to watch you play?"

"No, not really, but I wanted you to be there so much. It meant a lot to me for you to come even if I didn't get to spend any time with you. It felt so good to see you in the stands." He left Tulsa that day, and I ached because I couldn't be with him. He told me we would be together really soon if he had anything to say about it, and I hoped that would turn out to be true.

Wendell called me a couple of days later and asked me how soon I could get to Louisville I told him I would have to try and pick up a trip because I wasn't flying there, and there weren't all that many layovers in Louisville. "Call them and get yourself here. I want to see you. I was so sad that I couldn't be with you in Tulsa."

"Well that makes two of us, Wendell. I wanted to be with you so much too." I called and Crew Schedule just happened to have one trip because a girl had just called in sick. When I told them I would take it off their hands, they were overjoyed.

A few days later, I called Wendell as soon as I got into my hotel room in Louisville, and he said he'd be right over. I was so nervous I dropped one of my false eyelashes, and Wanda, the gal I was flying with, helped me find it just in time. There was a tremendous knock on the room door, and I flew across the room to answer it. I was never so glad to see anyone in my life.

After we left the room, Wendell threw that long arm around me and kissed me softly on the lips, "I'm so glad to see you!" he said, smiling from ear to ear.

"I guess I'm pretty glad to see you too." I said, being a smart-ass.

He just squeezed me, "You guess?"

"Oh, okay, so I'm so happy to see you too."

"That's more like it," he said looking deep into my eyes; God, how I could get lost in those brown eyes!

As Wendell drove, I couldn't keep myself from staring at him in the rearview mirror. I loved looking at that handsome face. He seemed, as I mentioned before, to be a combination of so many souls. He was a grown man, but he still had so much little boy in him. I often thought about how cute he must have been growing up. (I found out later Wendell was not especially that cute when he was younger, but as he matured he become the gorgeous hunk I knew.)

I wasn't sure how I felt about him deep down inside of me. I felt at times like I genuinely loved Wendell, but I would never, ever tell him because I didn't want him to think I was trying to put any kind of hold on him. After our little incident over the telegram, I just never felt like I could tell him what he meant to me, yet I think he knew, and not just because of the incredible sexual attraction we had for each other. It went way beyond just chemistry - it was volatile! Every time we were together, it was like we had just been together the day before. Our time together was so precious, we had to make the most of every minute.

For some reason, we were both a little nervous being together that night, almost like we were shy with each other. When we got to his apartment, I looked for something to break the tension, and then I spotted his carpet. "Wendell!! Where in the world did you get this carpet? There can't be that many tigers in this world. Aren't they an endangered species?" The carpet was yellow, orange, black, brown and white. "Artis again?" I asked him.

"He's my decorator, didn't I tell you that?" he said laughing. We both chuckled out loud, and the nervousness between us was gone.

Wendell took me by the hand and led me into the bedroom. I noticed the mug I bought for him in Mexico sitting on his bureau with pencils in it. I was just happy to see it there.

He laid on the bed and pulled me down on top of him. It was time for the joking to end. It was time to be together, time for loving. When he kissed me, I felt that sinking feeling in the pit of my stomach. I had really missed him so much but didn't have the nerve to tell him. I guess I always knew there would come a day when I wished I had. Tonight was different. Our lovemaking was so tender. He would lay there and stare at me and run his hands all over my body in such a loving way. It felt so wonderful! I just wanted to stay there forever, but sadly I had a really early pickup the next morning, so I told him I had better get back to the hotel. He leaned over me and held me so close in his arms. I wanted to hold him forever.

On the next layover a week later, we weren't the least bit nervous with each other. We went to a little drive-in place for a hamburger but had to make a hasty retreat when a car full of girls spotted Wendell and ran over to the car asking for autographs. They were young, cute, and giggly. He signed a napkin, looked at me, and mouthed, "Let's get out of here," I definitely agreed. He had other things on his mind than being sought after by a bunch of giddy teenagers. I had trip-traded with another Flight Attendant, who thought I was nuts to give up a Los Angeles layover for a flight to Louisville. If she only knew what was waiting for me in Louisville, she would have been jealous, I'm sure. I was so incredibly happy to be there with Wendell!

Wendell was in the mood to tease me. He went directly into the living room and turned on the television. He sat on the couch, and I lay down with my head in his lap. "Gonna watch a little television, Wendell?" I asked with an attitude in my voice.

"Yeah, I thought I would. There's a game on I want to see. You don't mind, do you?"

"Oh, me, mind? Of course not, I came halfway across the U.S. to be with you so that I could watch you watch a basketball game. Why would you think I would mind? Do you have something I could read? After all, once you've seen a bunch of men in shorts, you've pretty much seen them all." His head turned quickly in my direction, and he was trying so hard not to break character and laugh. He handed me a basketball program from his last game, with an article about him inside and four different pictures of him gracing the cover. "Oh, how modest; I bet you just happened to have one or two dozen of these lying around this place, don't you?" He was proud of the program, and so was I, but I was having too much fun bruising his ego. The article was titled "From Mizzipi With Love" by John Hamilton and told a little about Wendell, his Coach, and how all the girls loved him. (Oh yeah, I loved that part.) It even mentioned the collision with the water cooler at Freedom Hall.

The part I was surprised to read, something Wendell hadn't shared with me, was the Colonels' office did a promotional poster featuring Wendell as a spoof on the Burt Reynolds centerfold in *Cosmopolitan*, except Wendell wasn't naked. He was lying across several stools with his shirt off, his basketball shorts on, and a basketball placed strategically in front of him. Mr. Hamilton said, "On December 21, full color posters of Wendell reclined in the locker room dressed only in his basketball shorts were put on sale. And, to quote one member of the front office, the poster just might save this Franchise single-handedly." Oh, my stars, just what he needed. I looked up from the article to see Wendell staring sheepishly at me. "Oh, brother, little did they know they covered up the best part," I stated.

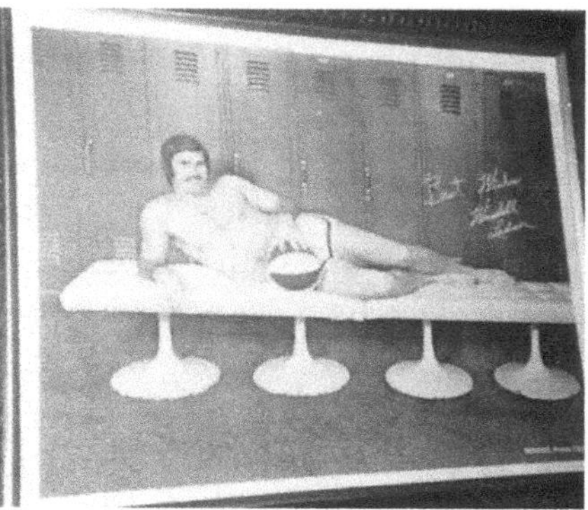

Wendell's Poster

"Now you don't really want everyone to see that, do you?" he asked me, grinning from ear to ear. I put down the article, leaned myself across his lap, and started unbuttoning his shirt. Wendell grabbed my hand and looked at me with those big, soft brown eyes. I noticed his breathing had changed.

"Don't mind me; just watch your ball game," I said. He must have thought this was fun because he let go of my hand and returned his glance towards the television while trying to pretend he was concentrating on the game. But I knew Wendell all too well. After I unbuttoned his shirt halfway down, I started to tickle his tummy with my fingers. He began to squirm and breathe a little heavier than before. Finally, I leaned down and licked his stomach. "That does it, girl!" He jumped to his feet nearly dumping me on the "tiger-striped" floor.

"Something I can do for you, sir?" I asked with a total look of innocence in my eyes.

"You bet your sweet ass there is."

"I was hoping you'd say that!" I replied as I raced him to the bedroom.

I had taken great pains to select the clothes I wore that night. I had on a white sweater with tiny pink flowers on just the front of it. It had short sleeves and crisscrossed buttoning under my bust. I had decided to be daring and not wear a bra. The slacks I selected were a very pale grey. All in all, I felt awfully sexy. I think Wendell liked my sweater too, but he seemed a little surprised I had the nerve to wear it without a bra. Honestly, so was I.

In the bedroom, he decided to continue playing games. Those long slender fingers managed to find their way to the buttons beneath my bust. He was so good at this that I loved him and hated him all at the same time. I didn't even want to know how many times he'd repeated this scene in his bedroom. Wendell slowly unbuttoned my sweater. He knew I was going crazy because he often told me he may have seen girls with bigger breasts but none were quite as sensitive as mine. It happened every time; he put his hand on my breast, and I gasped. He probably loved having that much control over my feelings.

Wendell started kissing my neck and running his hands across my breasts. I felt him push my sweater back and down my arms. It fell to the floor. I reached over and finished unbuttoning the remaining two buttons on his shirt, pulling it out from his slacks and pushing it back over his shoulders so it dropped onto the floor beside my sweater. (Oh, how cute, I thought to myself, our clothes are lying together too. How silly of me.) I slid my arms around his neck and pressed our half-naked bodies against each other as hard as I could. That was all he needed since he was already aroused from my little antics in the front room. Wendell gently, but forcefully, leaned me backwards onto the bed, then unzipped my slacks, ever so slowly. (Sometimes I thought the anticipation of our lovemaking was almost as exciting as the real thing.) He pulled my slacks down off my legs onto the floor, then placed his hand on my tummy and started to rub my stomach. The more gently he rubbed, the more passionate I felt. I reached for the hook on his slacks and then slowly unzipped his slacks, which wasn't the easiest thing I have ever done because he was so turned on I was scared I'd hurt him with the zipper. (Can you stand all of this, folks? I am just about to die myself.) I managed to pull his pants off. He was like quicksilver and had my panties off before I knew it. He pushed me back on the bed again, kissing me so hard I thought my lips were going to bleed. Wendell entered me with such force I thought he was going to hurt me, but I was more than ready for him. I put my arms around his neck tightly and held on. We went crazy! We always sweated so much when we got into our lovemaking, and I would be so turned on by it. He felt so good inside me, so strong and so passionate. I wished I could stay right there for the rest of my life.

Wendell wasn't exactly the quietest lover in the world, and he taught me it was more than okay to be verbal when you were making love. He encouraged me to let him know how he was making me feel. For some reason that night, we were both really loud and expressive with our feelings and got carried away. The guy in the next apartment started beating on the wall. Wendell went nuts! He slammed his big fist against the wall with such force I expected us to be covered in plaster. He scared me half to death as he yelled, "Go to hell, you bastard! You're just jealous."

I cracked up laughing. "That's an awful thing to say, Wendell."

"Well, he is. He's a squirrelly little wimp with glasses and zits all over his face. He probably has to sneak up on himself to masturbate."

"Oh, my Lord, you are terrible." I started laughing so hard I could barely catch my breath.

Somehow I found myself thinking back to our "sex-a-thon" in Dallas, grinning to myself when I thought of how I must have looked when Wendell told me to bring him a little bottle out of his coat pocket. When I did, he told me to open it and smell. The liquid inside smelled like bananas. I must have had a funny look on my face because he laughed. "You put it on your body and the hotter your body temperature gets, the stronger the scent becomes," he told me.

"This would be just great if one of us were a monkey," I smarted off.

He just rolled his eyes and asked, "You mean you don't want me to put this on you, Bev?"

"I didn't say that, Wendell. Just next time, for your information, I love strawberries." To this day I can't smell bananas without thinking of him.

In Louisville, we laid there quietly in each other's arms for what seemed like a long time. ("Spent from our passion" is how it was expressed in a Mac Davis song. Another Mac Davis song that made me think of Wendell was titled "Baby, Don't Get Hooked On Me," but it was much too late for that to apply because I was already hooked!)

I looked up at Wendell and kissed him on the eyes, the nose, and then I started to run my tongue across his cheeks toward his ears. This usually got an immediate response from him, but he just laid there, not moving. I turned and glanced into his eyes, "Having an energy crisis, Mr. Ladner?"

"A what?" he said in a rather annoyed way.

"An energy crisis?" I repeated.

"That'll be the day. I'll show you energy!" This time the wimp next door had even more reason to bang on the wall because we got really loud! But he didn't complain again.

For the next two years, Wendell and I would see each other whenever our schedules permitted. I knew in my heart I really loved this man so much, and I regret that I never told him. I was always afraid if I told him he would feel smothered or turn and run. I remember one time after he took me back to the hotel, he stood outside my room and acted like he didn't want to leave me. We had enjoyed our usual evening of lovemaking, laughing, and holding each other, but tonight he seemed so serious.

Wendell told me he had something he wanted to talk to me about that was very important to him. I was scared he was going to say something that might break my heart. He looked directly into my eyes and waited until I was looking into his, and he said "Bev, you are so special to me! You may never realize how special. I know that you know that I see a lot of women, some once and never again and I am fine with that. Things are different between us. I never want there to be a time in my life when you aren't a part of it."

I was so very surprised by what he was sharing with me, but I felt so good to know I meant more to him than just an occasional sexual partner. Wendell said he always wanted me to keep in touch with him no matter what happened in our lives and made me promise I would always contact him and try to see him whenever we could manage. This was so unlike Wendell. In my heart, I felt so happy to hear what he was saying, but it kind of scared me a little too.

The only thing missing in all of this was for Wendell to say he loved me. I think in his way that was exactly what he was trying to say without using those three little words. I put my arms around his neck and his long arms encircled my waist as I told him I would always be there for him no matter what. He leaned even closer to me and actually put his head on my shoulder. (He must have looked so adorable doing that. I wished I could have seen us from afar.)

Wendell held onto me like there was no tomorrow.

Sadly, there was no tomorrow for Wendell and me.

TRYING TO FIGURE THINGS OUT

Flight 209 Uniform

In 1973, I decided to do something I had always wanted to do – sign up for a few courses at Oral Roberts University. I felt inferior because I hadn't had the opportunity to go to college and now I would get to go. I could hardly wait for classes to start, and then the weather was so bad I didn't even get to go to class the very first day.

To give me something to do when I wasn't flying, I joined a group of ladies called Flight 209, who worked conventions and showrooms. Some of the gals were absolutely beautiful, and I felt good that they had accepted me to work with them.

I wanted to work the American Airlines Golf Tournament in Arizona and actually had an interview set up in New York. Due to the weather, the airport had to be shut down, and the flights were cancelled so I didn't get to interview for that very special assignment. Derek was glad my flight had cancelled because he really didn't think the American Airlines Golf Tournament was a place for a married woman, since the Flight Attendants working the event would be mingling with professional football and baseball players. Mr. Peak, the man in charge for selecting Flight Attendants for this prestigious assignment, wasn't too pleased with me for missing my interview because he had recommended me, but there was nothing I could so about the weather.

On January 28, 1974, I called Wendell to see how he was doing. When we had been together in Louisville just a few days earlier, he had acted really strange. On the call, I found out why – he had been traded to the New York Nets and was not happy about it. He couldn't imagine himself in New York. Wendell loved being in Kentucky and did not want to have to leave.

Walt Simon, another professional basketball player, had been on my flight in the fall and hinted that Wendell was having some problems with the owner of the Colonels, John Y. Brown. Supposedly, there was a rumor going around that John's wife, Ellie Brown, was smitten with Wendell, and she made no bones about it. Although I couldn't blame her, it would have been suicide for Wendell's career if he had let himself get into that situation with her. I didn't want to believe it, but he was definitely traded.

Poor baby, I knew Wendell was scared of the whole thought of New York. A Mississippi boy might not have a problem relocating to Kentucky, but New York was a different story. I would have to start bidding New York layovers to see him. I tried to encourage him, telling him how I had adjusted to New York although I was terrified when I got sent there; I knew he would be able to manage it also. He thanked me for my support and told me I always understood and made him feel better. "You'll do fine, Wendell. I know you will."

"Thanks, Bev, that means a lot to me." I would have done anything for Wendell. Encouraging him was just a small thing I could do to make him feel better. This time he said, "Miss me." I smiled and replied, "Always."

I met a guy on one of my flights named Bernie Talley, who was a former P.O.W. coming to Dallas for an interview with American to be a pilot. He was worried because he was already in his thirties and afraid the Chief Pilot would hold that against him. One of the stupid girls I was flying with actually had the nerve to ask him about his time as a P.O.W. She asked if he had really been tortured and what the Vietnamese had done to him. I was so angry I confronted her in the galley, accusing her of being insensitive to what this man had gone through. I told her she was nuts to ask him to relive those horrible memories by talking about them. She thought I was overreacting. When I apologized to Bernie, he assured me she had not been the first person to ask him something like that, and he was sure she wouldn't be the last. Still, I felt terrible because it was so insensitive. The poor man had suffered enough for heaven's sake. Needless to say, she and I didn't exactly enjoy each other's company for the rest of the month.

Bernie asked me if I would share a pizza with him if I ever got a San Antonio layover. I told him I would be delighted. Then I shared with him about watching television with my husband the night the news showed some of the P.O.W.s returning. I remembered the announcer saying, "Little does Major Talley know, but his parents have been flown in from Baltimore to surprise him." I cried like a baby when I saw Bernie (he preferred being called by the nickname "Bunny") grab hold of his Mom and Dad.

He also asked if I would mind calling his folks to say "Hi" if I ever went through Baltimore. I found that request unusual, but hey, after what this man had gone through, it seemed so little to ask of me. So I took Mr. and Mrs. Talley's number, and I did call them several times when I went through their city.

Bernie became a pilot with American, and we would go out together on layovers, enjoying each other's company as friends. One of the stories he told me was that after returning to freedom, Bernie had written a letter to the manufacturer of his jet's ejection seat telling them it had worked perfectly. Then he told me he had sent some film to be developed and wrote to find out how much he owed Kodak after six years for the film he never got to pay for. They sent him a letter telling him it was their pleasure to develop all of his film free for the rest of his life. Kodak jumped up a notch on my admiration scale.

He told me one of the things he did to keep his sanity in the "Hanoi Hilton" was to plan his wedding. Everything was to be in white. So when he married Florence, everything was. It was a beautiful wedding, and I was doing great until they played the song "Born Free." I never heard so many people boo-hooing at a wedding. They had a daughter, but the marriage didn't last. Bernie remarried, and we lost contact with each other after several years. (Now, thanks to my book, we have reconnected. Bernie told me he and Florence have remained in contact because of their daughter, and they are looking forward to becoming grandparents soon.)

Even though I was keeping busy with a lot of convention work for Flight 209, one day I decided I wanted to do some modeling. I'm not sure where I got the confidence to do this, but I found a photographer named Phillip Lowry who had a studio around the corner from our house. I went to see him about taking some pictures, and we had a wonderful rapport. He took such stunning pictures of me - I couldn't believe how good I looked. Phillip kept telling me how photogenic I was, and I found myself totally at ease with him. We spent one whole afternoon taking multiple poses in different types of clothing. The pictures came out so well we put together different looks into a printed brochure. I never felt more attractive or proud. Although Derek didn't seem to feel too comfortable with me spending all of this time with Phillip, it was completely a professional relationship. Phillip and his wife, Jane, came to our home a few times for parties and dinner, and Derek finally grew to trust him.

I contacted some modeling agencies to see if I could stir up some interest, but I wasn't too successful, so I just went out to find modeling jobs on my own. I think someone from Flight 209 recommended a commercial producer named Bob Calloway, who was auditioning models for a television commercial for a local jewelry store named Peacocks with branches in Tennessee and Louisiana. I met with him, and we hit it off right away. He told me about the commercial audition and said right then and there I had the job if I wanted it, that I didn't even have to go to the audition unless I wanted to, so I went.

Bob told me I could help pick the guy who was going to be my fiancé in the commercial. It was so exciting. There were so many people there, all shapes, sizes, and nationalities. I spotted one young man who walked in a little later than the others, with a great smile and very thick wavy brown hair. He was about 6' tall and slender, and I liked him instantly. When he spoke to Bob, he had this tremendous speaking voice. (I used to tell him that James Earl Jones couldn't possibly get every role; that he ought to do voiceovers for a living. He was flattered.) Bob took Bill McCright's name and number and told him he would get back to him. He was the one.

I went home excited to share this news with Derek. He didn't seem very enthusiastic about me filming a commercial where I had to kiss a guy. I told him it was just for the commercial, that it wasn't like I would be going home with Bill. Derek acted miffed when I smarted off to him, but he wasn't going to quench my eagerness to do something different with my life.

Bill came to the house to pick me up for the shoot, so I introduced him to Derek. Derek was cordial but very standoffish, wanting to know how soon we thought the commercial shooting would be over. Bill told Derek he figured about two or three hours, depending on how well things came together.

It was already dark but not late because we were shooting at a drive-in movie. Bill was supposed to be a college guy, I was his girlfriend, and we were going to get engaged in a convertible. When we first got there, the makeup people took us aside and put on heavy-duty stage makeup. I didn't really see Bill's finished product until we got in the car. When I looked at him, I was surprised to see all the eyeliner they had put on him. He almost looked Asian. When I snickered, Bill asked what was so funny, and I told him I thought we were doing a jewelry commercial, not a Chinese takeout advertisement. He looked into the rearview mirror and laughed. He said, "You know, Bev, you're right, I do look Chinese." There was a sound guy in the back seat of the car, and a guy with a light on the floorboard in front. It felt so odd to have all those people around when it was supposed to be just the two of us. (I remembered what Elvis had shared with me about his love scenes and smiled. Now I understood how difficult this must have been for him.)

Bill and I would say a few lines, and then it would rain. We had to wait for the rain to stop, and then wait for the car to get wiped down. We climbed back in, said our lines and then a bunch of crickets would chirp so you couldn't make out our words. Because the rain was intermittent all evening, we were there for hours. It was kind of funny because Bill and I barely knew each other, yet we had to kiss a bunch because of all of the retakes. One of the cameramen said to Bill, "Hey buddy, I can see you're getting kind of tired there. Do you need a stand-in?"

Bill assured the guy he could handle it. I asked, "Hey, what about me?"

The fellow grinned and said "No, you don't get one; just the guy." Bill and I cracked up. We had so much fun, but it took much longer than either of us expected.

Bill drove me to the house, and as he was getting out of the car to walk me to the door, the porch light came on. I told Bill I was fine and that he should go home since it was so late. Derek was on the porch before Bill backed out of the driveway. "What took so damn long?" he yelled.

"Derek, it was raining, and they had to wait for the rain to stop, wipe down the car, and reshoot the scene. Honest!" He turned around and walked into the house. He was pissed!

No matter what I said to him, he wasn't believing a word of it. I tried to explain again once I was inside the house, but Derek just went to bed. I was so excited and wanted to share with him about my first commercial, but I could tell that was the last thing in the world he wanted to hear about. Derek did listen to me the next day but still didn't act too happy about this whole new career I wanted to pursue.

AA Newspaper Article
Photo by Phillip Lowry

American Airlines had a company newspaper, so I decided to send in a story about my modeling assignment with one of Philip's splendid photos accompanying the article. To my delight, they accepted my story and printed it. It read: it took eight hours for Beverly J. Schoenmann to accept the diamond ring and then she had to give it back. Not just because her husband insisted, but so did the stores whose television commercials Mrs. Schoenmann was filming.

Mrs. Schoenmann, a flight attendant based in Dallas-Fort Worth is known in modeling circles as "Beau," and the engagement ring was given to her by a college lad who also does modeling. The setting was an outdoor drive-in movie with a whole crew of video technicians looking on. It took eight hours to shoot the commercial because of intermittent rain.

Mrs. Schoenmann and her television fiancé, who in real life is engaged to someone else, did the advertisement for jewelry stores in Oklahoma, Tennessee and Louisiana.

Mrs. Schoenmann said her AA career comes first, but she'd like to do more commercials in the future."

I was so proud, and the picture of me was gorgeous! Don Johnson in Los Angeles cut the article from the paper in Operations and mailed it to me in case I wanted another copy. That was so like Don. It meant so much to me to receive a note from him telling me how proud of me he was and how beautiful I looked in the photo. He was truly one of the nicest men I had ever met in my life. I do believe Mom had been rooting for me to choose Don when I was dating him, Joe, and Derek — one of the few times in my life when I didn't listen to my mom's advice.

When I got back to Tulsa after my next trip, Derek had printed a little sign that said "Welcome home Celebrity" and left it inside the door leading to our den. I was tickled to pieces over his acknowledgement of my accomplishment. It was so special coming from him, especially after he had been so upset with me and Bill after the shoot. After we spent several evenings with Bill and his real fiancée Amy, Derek didn't seem to resent Bill any longer.

Phillip got a call from Miss Jackson's bridal department saying they needed someone to model a gown for their new bridal collection. He was excited when he took me over to the bridal consultant, Mrs. Gerri Cochran, to see if I'd do for the ad. She was delighted and chose the perfect dress for my figure. It was so beautiful, and I wished I had been able to wear a gown like that for my wedding. Phillip and I had a ball taking photos at the Phillbrook Planetarium, which was a perfect location for the bridal pictures. Miss Jackson's published the photo on November 10, 1974.

I called Wendell to touch base and see how he was doing in New York. He told me he hated it there, but he had no choice. He was rooming with a black player named Mike Gale and folks were making a big deal about it.

It didn"t matter to Wendell — even though he was from Mississippi, he had a lot of friends who were black. He was excited to be playing ball with Julius Irving, also known as ""Dr. J."

My Favorite Picture of Wendell Photo by Ann Chwatsky

Wendell told me the program titled *Of Nassau* had written a story about a few of the players, titled "Sexy Nets," and he and five other guys were on the cover. (Wendell was playing for the New York Nets ABA team by now.) There was even a full-page picture of Wendell lacing up his size fifteen sneakers. (This photo is absolutely one of my all-time favorite pictures of Wendell. He was just so adorable in this pose. I think it showed the little boy that was still in him, and I found myself wishing I had a son that looked like that. I loved his smile in this shot). There was a six-paragraph story about Wendell. Although I knew it had been a challenge, hopefully he was adjusting and starting to enjoy his popularity in New York.

I told Wendell I had been doing some fun things too, and I shared with him about my modeling career. I said I would send him one of my brochures to put up on his bulletin board to let all of his other women know what the competition looked like. I hated saying things like that, but I didn't want him to think I was trying to be exclusive with him. Wendell laughed and said I had no competition. Even though I knew he was lying, I loved hearing it. He said I had better call him when I got back to New York because he really missed me, and I was starting to believe him after our conversation in Louisville. He knew I cared for him as a person, not necessarily just as a basketball player. I wasn't trying to hook Wendell, even though I would have loved to have had him all to myself, because I knew that would never be.

During this same time, Derek and I would have some really good days together, and then we would get into some ridiculous fight over money or something I did he didn't like. He even reached a point where he actually wanted to help me do my bids, which meant choose the trips I would be flying in the next month. He wanted me to fly the trips with high time and the most expense money, but I put my foot down and told Derek I would fly where I wanted to fly, and he never mentioned it to me again.

I just never understood Derek's obsession with money, especially since he had been raised in an affluent home where I doubt he wanted for much. He acted like there was never enough money, and yet we had a brand new home, two cars, two dogs, and just about everything any couple could ever want.

Whenever we would talk about starting a family, Derek would say it was not economically feasible to start one yet. I knew Dr. Turner had discouraged Derek from thinking about starting a family when I was sick, but this was two years after the fact. I had always had a fear of having children, although I had no idea where that came from. Even my little sis had already had a child. Maybe seeing those stupid fortune tellers in my past and having every one of them tell me I'd never have a child had left a lasting impression on me. I loved kids and babies, but I was a little afraid to pursue having a baby when Derek and I weren't getting along. I sure didn't want to have a baby and then end up in a divorce. Besides, I was enjoying my life, and I had plenty of time to have babies later. Or so I thought.

My parents came for a visit, so we took them to Phoenix and Los Angeles. We had such a good time, and Derek was on his most social behavior. We went to some of the places with Mom and Dad that Derek and I always visited with his parents when they were in Phoenix. Mom and Dad were so proud of me and were in awe of the trips that they were able to go on to places they had never seen before. It made me feel so good to be able to share these trips with them because they had worked hard all of their lives and didn't have an opportunity to see things outside Port Clinton, Ohio.

We had a really good time until Mom and Derek got into an intense discussion about work ethics that quickly heated up. While Dad and I had been talking about where we wanted to go eat, Mom and Derek got into it. I looked at Dad and said, "You go get Mom, and I'll get Derek." Mom said they were just talking, but Dad and I could tell they were both getting angry.

After eating dinner, Mom and I decided we wanted some dessert, but Derek told me we didn't need any. Well, that made me angry, and I was bound and determined to eat some sweets whether he liked it or not. "You want some dessert, don't you, Mom?" I asked her.

She looked at Derek and said, "You bet I do." We ordered the most disgustingly dry cheesecake I had ever put in my mouth. It was horrible!!

I had no idea how many days, weeks, or months it had been sitting there, but it was gross! Mom and I looked at each and tried not to choke on it. We were so glad we had decided to share one piece because we weren't sure we could even get that one down, but we made it, smiling all the while as if it were the best cheesecake ever. I guess Mom and I learned it doesn't always pay to be vindictive.

We went to Los Angeles and to Disneyland. Dad loved the Country Bears, I loved *America Sings*, and Mom just enjoyed everything. I remembered having watched Walt Disney as a kid and when Jiminy Cricket would come on at the end of the show, I would wish that one day I would be able to take my family to Disneyland. I had already taken my sister, and now I was getting to take Mom and Dad.

All was right with the world. Derek and Mom actually had fun together. Daddy was so excited to be able to ride on a DC-10 back from Los Angeles to Dallas. He couldn't get over how big that airplane was and especially liked watching the camera in the cockpit as we took off. (That didn't last very long on the flights for obvious reasons, but it was pretty overwhelming when it first came out.)

We enjoyed having family come to see us. Derek's parents came for several visits, as did his sister Pam and her husband Jeramie. Even Aunt Dori and Uncle Gary came for a few days. To the outside world, Derek and I were the perfect couple, and we had it all. But sadly, we weren't getting along, and I had no idea how to fix what was wrong with us.

We called Dr. Turner, and each of us met with him separately and then we met with him together. I don't think Dr. Turner was really in this line of work, but he knew Derek and me pretty well and had a good idea what we had been through, so he thought he might be able to help us. In one of my sessions, I told him about Wendell. Dr. Turner didn't seem too pleased but tried not to be judgmental. He asked how I felt about Wendell, and I told him that, in my own way, I loved Wendell but knew there was no future with him, and I didn't really want to leave Derek. I truly wanted us to be able to work things out. Dr. Turner visited with Derek too, but of course I didn't know what he and Derek talked about. Dr. Turner made some suggestions for each of us and thought it might be a good idea if Derek thought about returning to Passenger Service where he had seemed to be happier than he was in Sabre. I wasn't sure what that would mean, but I didn't want to go back to New York, not now.

We continued to visit with Dr. Turner every few weeks or so, but nothing seemed to change. Derek still appeared to want to control me. I didn't know how to regain control of my life because we had been this way for over six years.

We tried going out with other couples, bowling, going to movies and parties, but we still came home to the fact that we were having issues of compatibility. I'm not saying all of our problems were based on sex, but we would go months without being together. I never understood this. I felt undesirable, and I couldn't understand why my husband didn't want to be with me.

At times we would get so frustrated we would lash out at one another, saying things we didn't actually mean. I know I said some things to Derek I wished I had never said because I never wanted to hurt him. Derek also hurt me many times. It broke my heart to think of some of the things we had done or said. I told Dr. Turner I thought we should separate for a while to see if we would realize what we had and be able to put our lives back together, or if not, at least we wouldn't continue to cause each other so much pain. Dr. Turner felt like we could still work things out together there in Tulsa.

Occasionally, Derek would show up on my layovers and surprise me, but I was very fortunate he never came to Cincinnati or Louisville. As I mentioned earlier, he had come to Phoenix that time on my birthday when he had been drinking and acting weird. One minute he was meek and quiet, and then he would act all cocky and loud. I worried that somehow I was at fault for Derek's mood swings.

Of course, I was always quick to blame myself for our marriage falling apart. I really wanted it to work, but I knew we weren't compatible in the physical aspect of our married life, and I didn't know what to do about it. I often thought it might have saved us some grief if we had been more experienced. If I had had some experience, I would have known Derek and I weren't pleasing each other. If I ever had children, I wondered how I would feel about telling them not to have sex before marriage. It was such a difficult situation with Wendell because he was the only man I had been with besides Derek and being with him was incredible.

I was miserable and so was Derek, I was sure of it.

I started holding my feelings inside and ended up with a hiatal hernia and a peptic esophagus. My stomach would get such incredibly sharp pains that I would get nauseous. Then I would get a headache. I lost a lot of weight. I went to the doctor and had some tests done and ended up having to take antacids and some other meds to quiet down my stomach. I knew a lot of it was guilt and frustration because of our situation.

I was feeling so bad and afraid of getting depressed again that I went to Ohio for a week to spend time with my parents. Mom and Dad had a fit at how much weight I had lost. I am almost 5'11" and only weighed 125. (Hey, I would have made a great super model.) I didn't look well at all. Daddy always had a silly habit of pushing his fingers onto my hip joints to check my weight, but that time he got so upset with me when he did his little weight measurement that he told Mom he was really worried about me. Honestly, I was worried too.

I told Mom things were getting really bad with Derek and me and that I just didn't know what to do about it. I was so unhappy, and I knew he was too. We were starting to do and say things that really hurt each other. I wasn't a spiteful person, but I was acting like one. Mom said she had always felt Derek and I were mismatched, but she had hoped that somehow we would be able to make a go of it. I informed her I didn't want us to go on hurting each other and that I was thinking of moving to Dallas for a trial separation. Mom knew about Wendell (well, not the details - you just didn't discuss that with anyone, much less your mother, for heaven's sake!), and she didn't judge me, but I don't think she was too happy about our involvement either. She never told me to stop seeing Wendell because she knew I wouldn't have.

I had played a little joke on her and Dad and sent them a picture I tore out of *Sports Illustrated* magazine. It was of Artis Gilmore jumping for a basketball, and Wendell was to the left in the photo under the net. I told Mom Wendell had dark hair and dark eyes. When she received the clipping, I called to ask her what she thought of my true love. She asked me again what Wendell looked like, and I only described his dark hair and eyes. Daddy was looking at the picture when he yelled into the phone, "You had better not be serious, young lady!" He thought I was in love with Artis, who happened to be black. I laughed and laughed before I told them Wendell's jersey number, four, and that he was in the lower left side of the picture. Mom told me I shouldn't have done that to Daddy because he nearly had a heart attack.

Wendell called me at my folk's house to see how I was feeling. I had already shared with him about my stomach problems. My Mom was feeling silly and asked to talk to him. She told him what a good-looking man he was and that he could put his sneakers under her bed any day. Wendell roared! He thought it was hysterical and that my Mom had such a great sense of humor. I was mortified. Then she told him she was sorry and was just trying to get a rise out of me.

I told Wendell I was so miserable with Derek, but I didn't know how to get out of our marriage. The most hurtful part of our situation was what we were doing and saying to each other. I told Wendell I was thinking of moving to Dallas for a while to see if I could make it on my own. I had gone from my parents to roommates to a husband, and I had never been by myself. I said I was a little scared. He told me he knew I could do it (I guess it was his turn to encourage and support me), but more than anything, he wanted to have a place to stay in Dallas. Wendell burst out laughing, and I could have choked him. "Wendell, you turkey!"

"Bab-....er Bev, I just want you to be happy; and if you're not happy with this guy, get the hell out." I asked him if he would pay half of the rent on my apartment. He was taken aback, but then I told him I was only being a smart-ass too.

We chatted a little longer, and I told him I needed to go visit with Mom and Dad, so I'd call him in the next day or so. I said, "Miss me."

As usual he replied, "Always."

When I called Derek, he informed me he had shared with his mother we were having trouble, and she was more than unhappy with me. I got defensive and told him to tell her it wasn't entirely my fault I guessed that my leaving Derek brought back memories of when Derek, Sr. had left her that time. Derek said Pam and Jeramie were more understanding about our situation than his Mom, but Claire felt like I needed to get my butt back to Tulsa and work this marriage out. I told him I needed a few days with my family, and I would be back by the weekend.

Mom, Dad, and I just ate out, cooked out, went to visit Mrs. Roth, and basically just spent time together. Daddy told me I had better get some weight on before the next time he saw me. I started feeling guilty about Derek, so I asked him to come to Columbus for a few days. Derek told me he was on his way to Lexington, Kentucky where his folks had moved a few years back, and would let me know. The next day, he called and told me he wasn't coming.

When I had called Crew Schedule a week earlier, I had been crying hysterically saying I absolutely had to have a leave that very minute because I was losing it and wanted permission to go to Ohio to be with my folks. I was surprised because they were unbelievably understanding. I must have sounded pretty desperate, since they appeared to actually be worried about me. That was not the usual response from Crew Schedule, but some of the guys were wonderful. Every once in a while, you would lock horns with one of them, but they had a difficult job to do, and I always tried not to give them any problems. I never missed a trip, was never late in spite of my commuting, and I always tried to give them as much notice as I could when I was sick. But that Friday night, I just lost it, and they were great.

I stayed with my parents a couple more days, then returned to Tulsa, stopping in Dallas to talk to Crew Schedule. I told them I would be able to go on my next trip and thanked them for being so good to me when I really needed their help.

Derek and I went to Ohio for my ten-year class reunion. I had saved up to purchase a very expensive dark chocolate-brown knit dress. It was one of the sexiest dresses I had ever tried on. With a turtleneck and the back cut out, it formed to every curve I had, and I felt so attractive. Derek and I drove to the reunion because TWA was on strike, and all of the flights were full.

Dori and Gary

We stopped in St. Louis on the way and had a great visit with Aunt Dori and Uncle Gary.

When we finally got to Ohio, we stayed with Mom and Dad. I could have choked Derek because he took his sweet, sweet time getting ready, which made us late, and I missed getting in the class picture. Before we left for the reunion, Derek asked Mom if there was anyone in particular he needed to be aware of, someone I might have had a special place in my life for. Of course, Mom said, "Oh, be sure and check out Terry Kneisely," so I was ready to choke her too.

When we got there, Derek kept asking everyone which guy was Terry I guess word got around because Terry kept his distance from me all evening. I was angry with Mom and Derek because I had wanted to talk with Terry at least for a few minutes and maybe even dance with him once, but it wasn't going to happen that night.

It was good to see some of my classmates. Some of them had aged so much it was hard to imagine they were only ten years older than the last time I had seen them; they looked more like my parents' generation. I danced with a few of the guys, none of whom I really cared about, except for my good buddy Bill Van Gieson. He had dated Karen Roth for a while, and then the three of us became really close friends.

I had surprised several people with how much I had changed, but what surprised them the most was what I was doing for a living. I doubt if any of them ever imagined I would be a Stewardess (or of late, a Flight Attendant). I felt justified knowing some of those girls who had been so mean to me were definitely jealous.

Earlier, Derek and I had gotten into a terrible argument. I had bought myself a mink coat for this special occasion. He freaked out because he thought some guy had bought it for me until I showed him the receipt. Then he really went crazy to think I would spend that kind of money without consulting him first. He was livid! At the reunion, one of the girls mentioned how beautiful the mink was and Derek smarted off by saying, "One of her boyfriends bought it for her." I was so embarrassed I told her Elvis had bought it for me, which Derek didn't like one bit. My tenth High School reunion didn't turn out as great as I had hoped.

Derek and I were so good together in other ways. We always threw the best parties. We hosted a "Remember When" or fifties party, where everyone was told to dress like a teenager. I decorated the den and family room, and we played silly games and danced and danced. I had sewn the names of a bunch of oldies records on one of Derek's old shirts. For "Teen Angel," I drew an angel and embroidered it. I must have had about thirty songs on the shirt, and across the back, in great big letters, I embroidered "Elvis the Pelvis" in bright orange thread. Derek had his hair slicked back, his jean pant legs rolled up and a t-shirt with a pack of cigarettes rolled up in the sleeve. Everyone always seemed to have such fun at our parties.

Derek and I worked on our front and back yards, enjoyed taking Muskogee out for long walks, and had fun bowling in a league. I was so sad when we would get into fights over the stupidest damn things, like towels or sheets. I never understood Derek's tight grip on anything and everything I wanted to buy. I was actually shocked he didn't throw me out the door when I bought that mink coat. I had decided I worked hard for my salary, and I was ready for the fight that didn't happen. He took it relatively well, all things considered.

We went to visit Derek's sister Pam. We went to the mall to get Derek some shirts, and he threw such a fit at the poor salesman because he had to go to a Big Man's shop and pay extra for his shirts. Derek was talking so loudly and taking it out on the poor guy. Pam was with us, so I looked at her, then turned and walked outside because Derek had started bitching about the cost of his shoes. I think Pam understood how I felt, but it was her brother.

When we got back to Pam's house, Derek and I got into a screaming fight. We talked about getting a divorce, and I am sure Pam and Jeramie could hear us downstairs - heck, the people who lived next door probably heard us. I was just sick and tired of Derek's penny-pinching ways. We finally calmed down and went downstairs to apologize to Pam and Jeramie, but they sensed things were not going well for us. Now we were starting to show it in front of other people.

I was enjoying ORU because it was fun to see what kids were thinking about in those days. I showed up in my uniform one day because I had to fly to Dallas right after class, and I didn't have time to change before leaving. The girls in the class all asked me a lot of questions about flying, and the guys all looked at me with a little more admiration than they had before. I was very proud they knew I was a Flight Attendant.

Derek and I both went to see Dr. Turner again, and he suggested we try once more to see if we couldn't salvage our marriage. I didn't want to give up on us, but I didn't know how to fix the things that were tearing us apart.

We went on what was supposed to be a loving second honeymoon to Maui, Hawaii, but it didn't work either. I had taken tennis lessons in an attempt to play tennis with Derek, but I wasn't very good and he had played for a long time. The only thing I had going for me was a killer backhand, but you couldn't do that the entire game. I tried to play with him, but I was no challenge. We laid on the beach, but Derek wasn't into that. We would walk along the beach hand-in-hand and appear to be a happy couple, but when we got back to the room, we were worlds apart. I felt so hopeless.

My "saving grace" was always my job. I loved being a Flight Attendant. I always did a fantastic job, and I was proud of how my passengers always responded to me. I could make them laugh, and they would tell me things they probably wouldn't normally confide to anyone else.

On occasion, I put myself in some embarrassing situations listening to folks. I was sitting on the jump seat reading during an all-night flight when this nice looking guy in his late twenties or early thirties came out of the lavatory and asked if he could chat with me for a few minutes. I was happy to, since one of the reasons I was there was to make conversation with the traveling public. He told me he and his girlfriend had just ended their engagement I felt sad for him, but then he went on to tell me she had told him she had better sex with her water pick shower massage than with him. I nearly fell off the jump seat. That was way too much information! I was speechless. What could I say to a guy after he'd had the nerve to share something that intimate with me? I just told him how sorry I was about what had happened, and I hoped he could find someone who would appreciate him. I excused myself and went into the galley hoping against hope he wouldn't follow me. Thank goodness, he didn't.

Another time, I was walking through the cabin and by a window on the left side of the aircraft, I saw a lady bawling. She was about fifty or so. My heart ached every time I went by her, but I hesitated to stop because I knew that whatever she was crying about had to be awful. Finally, I did stop and ask her if she was okay and if I could do anything for her. She told me she was accompanying her son's remains. He was a Marine participating in an undercover drug project, and apparently, he and his new wife were having dinner in their apartment and some guys came in and killed them both. She was devastated. I certainly understood and put my arms around her to let her cry on my shoulder. She said her husband had died over a year ago, and the boy was all that was left of her family. One of the other Flight Attendants walked by and saw me sitting there holding the poor lady. She practically ran past me because I could tell she didn't want to stop and get involved. I finally had to go back to work, but she thanked me for my kindness. My heart broke for her, and I hoped I had given her some comfort even if it was for such a short time.

On a happier note, once with I was flying with a Flight Attendant named Faith Ann Monahan, she handed me a piece of paper that cracked me up. It was entitled "You Know You're a Flight Attendant if…":

1. You never unpack
2. You look to the ceiling if your doorbell rings.
3. You wish you had jet engines mounted in your bedroom so you could fall asleep faster.

4. All of your pens have different hotel names on them.
5. You can recognize pilots by the backs of their heads but not by their faces.
6. You have two sets of uniforms: fat and thin.
7. You always point using two fingers.
8. You wish your supervisor had really been a flight attendant because then he/she could talk with some authority about what you are actually going through.
9. Your thighs are covered in bruises from armrests and elbows.
10. You secretly cheer when another flight attendant has to deal with a medical emergency.
11. You don't want passengers talking to you when you are pass-riding.
12. You remember the passengers with great manners (that's sad).
13. You love foreigners because they can't adequately complain in English.
14. You hate early morning departures; who in the hell needs to fly at 6:00 a.m. anyway?
15. (My all-time favorite) You stand at your front door and politely say "Buh-bye, thanks, and have a nice day," when someone leaves your home.

Carol, Barbie, and Me

Late in 1973, I flew with two wonderful girls, Barbara Alexander and Carol Hegener, and we were quite the trio. I was the tallest, followed by Carol at 5'9", then Barb at about 5'8". We immediately developed a tight bond. Carol, with sandy blonde hair and hazel eyes, was from Beardstown, Illinois and had a similar upbringing to mine. Barbie was from Ethyl, Mississippi, with only a slight southern drawl unlike Wendell's, and she was the epitome of a Southern Belle. Barbie had darker brown hair and brown eyes and the most beautiful complexion. Carol was single, and Barbie was married to J. Michael, an attorney. We had the best month of flying I had had in months.

Barbie and I had fun with the F/O, Tom Long, and the Flight Engineer named Ralph Cox. Since there was never anything the slightest bit romantic between the four of us, we just enjoyed harassing each other constantly. It was a "good friend" thing. We ate together with Carol when she didn't have a date, and we all went out dancing. One of my most favorite things in the entire world is dancing, and those two nuts were willing to take us anywhere to dance. It was one of the best months of my flying career to that point. I loved those gals and really enjoyed their company. The next month, Carol was on vacation so Barbie and I "Buddy Bid" like Bette and I used to do. It was so great to know at least one person would be familiar every trip instead of constantly having to meet new people.

Barbie and J. Michael

Barbie and I complemented each other. She liked to do galley, and I enjoyed being in the cabin with the passengers. At one point, a passenger was complaining about not being able to make his connection, so I went to talk to him. I finally calmed him down and assured him he would be accommodated on the very next available flight. When I returned to the galley, Barb said, "Bev, I swear you could tell someone to go to hell, and they would look forward to the trip." We both cracked up. What was funny too, was that Barb would walk through the cabin and not one passenger would ask for a thing, and then I would walk through, and it seemed everyone wanted something. Barb told me I needed to learn how to scowl. I guess she was right, but we had a great time flying together!

This one trip was particularly bad, and we were both exhausted. Barb had to go visit with her in-laws, so I bought us a bottle of sangria to have when she got back from their house. It was iced down in the sink ready for when she got back. Barb came through the door with an outstretched hand holding a brown paper bag. She had her father-in-law stop at a liquor store, and she was holding a big bottle of sangria. We both laughed because neither one of us had mentioned that we liked sangria before that night.

Barb and I both liked liver too, which is incredible. You just don't find many people who eat liver. On occasions we would stay in our room and order it from room service. It was one thing for one person to order that disgusting stuff, but two! Since the poor person who delivered our meal almost always acted like they were about to gag at the smell of our entrees, we would just look at each other and lose it.

I confided in Barbie I wasn't doing so well in my marriage. We talked about her marriage and that she had been engaged to someone else before Michael. I told her I had been too. She told me about Frank, and I shared about Alphie. We became very close throughout the month and ended up Buddy Bidding several months in a row, unless one of us had vacation. Carol came back and bid with us too. She was the most senior, so she had to bid some yucky trips to be able to fly with us, but we had such a good time together it was worth it. We could pretty much make a good month out of almost any bad trip. Some of these three-day, fifteen-stop trips were a challenge, but we had fun. We might have been tired at the end of the day, but we were never too tired to spend some time together.

It seemed all I ever did at home in Tulsa was clean the house. After every trip, I cleaned, ironed, cooked, and did all of the wifely duties, and then I would go off on my trips and feel like a single woman. I was beginning to wonder if I didn't have a split personality. I liked being married, but I also enjoyed flirting and having fun with the crews or my passengers. I never took it to the level I did with Wendell because I didn't want to. I didn't go out with any of my passengers.

I was starting to wonder if something wasn't quire right in my head, and the thought of that scared me. I don't think doctors know how EST works or what it actually does to one's brain. I sometimes thought maybe I should have just stayed in Columbus and raised a bunch of kids with Alphie. Life would have been so simple. I wouldn't have liked for Alphie to be a policeman which is what he and his two brothers ended up doing. Gary worked undercover for the DEA, Jim worked as a detective in the Robbery Division, and Alphie was a patrolman. I would have worried myself sick. Fortunately, the DiGuilio brothers didn't get hurt in their careers of choice. Thank heavens!

I had a lot of celebrities on my flights when I flew out of New York, especially to the West Coast, but I didn't get as many celebrities flying in and out of Dallas. I had met Johnny Cash, Rex Allen, Alex Karras, Roman Gabriel, Steve Kanally, Eddie Arnold, and Shirley Cothran, one of the

Miss Americas. I usually got along really well with most of the high-profile folks.

The only one I didn't have a good rapport with was Jerry Lewis. I found him to be really rude, but maybe he was having a bad day. Flight Attendants like to share celeb stories, and I think one of the celebrities that just about nobody got along with was Lucille Ball, though I never met her myself. There was a rumor she refused to talk to Flight Attendants and even said, "I don't speak to the servants." I couldn't swear if that was the truth or not, but I heard it from several different sources. Most of the celebrities I had on board were really nice folks, but of course, my favorite was Elvis Aaron.

It seemed most of my life I'd had better luck with men friends than with women. I was flying a trip with a Chicago crew, and the Flight Engineer had come on the plane earlier than the other guys. He came into the galley to introduce himself to me. I was busy checking out catering, but when I turned around and saw his face, I was glad I had stopped. His name was Jim Henderson, and he was tall with light brown hair and an adorable smile. We chit-chatted for a few minutes before he headed for the cockpit to do some checking before the F/O and Captain arrived. I just smiled to myself and thought he sure was "easy on the eyes."

After we boarded our passengers, Jim came back to the galley for something and the lady in the front row of First Class caught sight of him. As I was taking her beverage request, I asked, "What may I get for you, mam?"

She pointed at Jim as he returned to the cockpit and answered me bluntly, "Him!" I smiled and told her I understood. I went into the cockpit and told Jim there was a lady who needed to talk to him, that she thought maybe they had gone to school together or something. Jim looked a little puzzled, but we had a few minutes, so the Captain told him to go ahead but to be quick about it. I don't know what she said to Jim, but he turned cherry red and almost ran back to the cockpit. When I served the lady, I asked her if she got what she was looking for. She laughed and said, "I think I shocked him. I don't think he's interested."

I looked at her and said, "Oh well, his loss." When I took the crew up their meals and beverages, Jim scolded me for doing that to him. I told him he just shouldn't be so darn cute. He laughed and said, "Gee, thanks." We talked off and on during the trip, and he asked me if I would mind having dinner with him on our layover. I enjoyed talking to him and thought that would be okay because we were both wearing wedding rings. We had a great time at dinner just talking. He was a perfect gentleman and walked me back to my room.

The next time Jim and I flew together, I was flying with a precious black girl also named Bev. She and I hit it off right away, and she mentioned how cute our Flight Engineer was. Of course I had to go to the cockpit to see this cute Flight Engineer - it was Jim. Bev and I decided to play a joke on him, so before we boarded, she went into the cockpit and asked Jim, "Where are we going to dinner tonight, Baby?"

I put my head in the door and said, "Wait a minute, girl, he has already asked me out for dinner and there won't be three of us."

She was further in the cockpit than me and she leaned over to Jim and said, "You better make up your mind, Honey, which one of us you want because you ain't getting both of us." Poor Jim was so embarrassed. The Captain and F/O were looking at him like he was some kind of a wild man. Jim just sat there dumbfounded, not knowing what to say.

I said, "You'd better get out here, woman. We need to have a talk. That is my man."

Bev turned and stomped out the door saying, "We'll see about that, girl." We both burst out laughing once we were in the cabin because we knew we had really gotten Jim good.

Jim and I became good buddies and would drop each other a note as to where we were flying each month to see if we could hook up for dinner. He teased me about what Bev and I had done to him and said the guys in the cockpit really thought he was a "rounder." (Definition: a guy with a girl in every port, like a sailor.) We enjoyed each other's company and had a lot of fun together. We didn't want to broadcast that we liked to eat together so when the crew mentioned getting together for dinner, we both made up excuses not to go. We got caught one time on a layover in Memphis. Jim had told the guys he had to do some revisions in his manual because he was having a check ride, and he didn't want to wait until the last minute to do them. I told the guys and girls I had to meet a friend. We waited until long past the time the crew had said they would meet before we headed towards the elevator. The doors opened and there stood the rest of our crew. The F/O looked at the Captain and asked, "Wonder where I can get a manual that looks like that." The Captain replied, "If you find one, I want one too." The girls burst out laughing as Jim and I got on the elevator with our cherry-red faces to go downstairs to eat with the crew.

Anytime Jim had a layover in Tulsa, he would call, and I would go over to the Camelot Hotel and have lunch with him. He was always so easy to talk to and told me he was starting to have some marital problems too. I was beginning to think no one had a happy marriage. I did see Don Johnson for dinner in New York one trip, and he seemed to be happy with Sally, so maybe that was one for the books.

Whenever I had a BOS (Boston) layover, I would have dinner with Bobby Bernhardt. He made me laugh, and I sincerely enjoyed talking to him. We really became great friends, which was funny because we sure had a terrible start. It was always fun to be seen with Bobby. He was so cute and several of my flying partners wanted to know the scoop on me and Bob. I told them we were only friends, but I don't think they believed me. I ended up playing cupid, hoping he would have a romance with one of my flying partners, but I think Bobby was only interested in me.

I had a crazy month of laughs with a gal named Colleen and two guys named Lou and Al. We flew to MEX (Mexico, City) where Al got chased by a bunch of Mexican girls who thought he was Ryan O'Neal. We laughed until our sides ached. They were chasing him down the street yelling, "It's Ryan O'Neal! It's Ryan O'Neal!" Lou was our Spanish speaker and told everyone I was his pregnant girlfriend but that he would fix them up with me for the right amount of money. Since I didn't understand what he was saying, I just stood there looking stupid and smiling. I could have killed him when he told me what he had done.

I flew with this nut named Jo Ann Garfield, and we just made each other laugh so much. We had gone into Mabley and Carue, a department store in Cleveland, Ohio to do some shopping. I do not know what came over me, but I started to talk as if I had a harelip. (Sorry, I wouldn't normally do something like this; I was just feeling crazy.) I have no excuse, I just did it, so Jo Ann started doing it too. We were trying on hats and conversing with each other rather loudly. The saleslady came over to me when I put on a huge, navy blue straw hat with a wide brim and daisies clustered on the ribbon at the base of the hat. She told me how cute I looked in that hat. I was embarrassed, but I knew she had heard Jo Ann and me talking like that, so we had to continue doing it. Because she had complimented me on the hat, I asked her how much it cost, and she told me $15.00. I took it off rather quickly and told her that was more than I could afford. She told me to wait right there and ran to get the manager. I wanted to bolt, but she could see us. The manager came over and told me I could have the hat for

$10.00. I was so embarrassed I said, "I'll take it and thank you very much for your kindness." She put the hat in a bag, and we left. Jo Ann was dying laughing when we got outside. I never did anything like that again.

I found out Derek had become interested in one of my flying partners. I didn't actually fly with her, but I found out from the "ole American rumor mill" that he had a crush on this particular girl. I was insulted; she wasn't even cute. I suspected something was going on, so when he left the house to do an errand, I got into his briefcase and found all sorts of suggestive cards. (Guess he learned from the best - me.) I got a pair of scissors and cut up every single one of them. There must have been six or eight cards. I cut them into little bitty pieces, and I strew them all throughout his briefcase in every nook and cranny I could find. I went back to doing our ironing, and when he got home, I told him some girl had called for him but wouldn't leave her name. He acted very funny. He went into his office and opened his briefcase, and then I heard him burst out laughing. I came to the doorway and said, "Something funny, Derek?" He just looked at me as the pieces fell to the floor. I hated we were doing this stuff to each other.

Her name was Sandy Rotherman, and she was supposed to be engaged to another guy. I got her phone number from Crew Schedule, telling them I was calling her for a trip trade. When her fiancé answered the phone, I told him who I was and asked for Sandy to give me a call as soon as she could. He asked if it was something he could help me with, and I told him it might be a good idea if he informed his fiancée to leave my husband alone. I could tell by the sound in his voice this news was a big shock to him. He said he would have her call me, but she didn't.

I went to the hockey game with Derek that night, and we were being pissy with each other. He finally looked at me and asked me what the hell was wrong with me. I looked back into his eyes and merely said her name, "Sandy Rotherman," in a seriously smart-ass tone. He stared at me for a split second and then looked away, informing me we would discuss this after the game. Well, we did discuss it later, and we got into it pretty bad. The silly part of it all was I almost wished he had found out about Wendell and reacted the same way over him as I had over finding out about Sandy. But then Derek seldom reacted the same way I did to anything.

In spite of it all, we spent Christmas with the Schoenmanns in Louisville, Kentucky. It was not the best experience since everyone knew Derek and I weren't getting along. I had called my parents to wish them a Merry Christmas and asked Claire if she wanted to extend season's greetings to my family. She pointed to her throat and said she really had a very sore throat. Would I mind telling them happy holidays for her? Okay, so I did. Then Janet's boyfriend Tom called, and Claire couldn't get to the phone fast enough to wish him and his family a Merry Christmas. I just glared at her as I left the room.

I had just about made up my mind that I had to move to Dallas. I couldn't understand why I stayed in Tulsa; I suppose it was because I had been raised to think marriage lasted forever; you might have some bad times, but you hung in there and got through them. I didn't want to get a divorce, but there was just no sense in Derek and I continuing to hurt one another, and I was feeling resentment towards his family. I didn't want that to happen either because I had grown fond of Derek's parents and sisters. I felt really ashamed of myself for all the crap that was happening, but it wasn't all my fault.

I was having trouble sleeping now. I would fall fast asleep and then wake suddenly to be up for hours on end, both at home and on my layovers. I had been fighting the stomach problems for months, and now I couldn't sleep. I got into a wreck and smashed my beautiful "Rosie,", and fortunately, they were able to fix her. I don't know even now if I got in the wreck because I was over-tired, but I certainly didn't volunteer that information to the police. I did get a ticket, my one and only, even though I didn't feel like I deserved it.

For our seventh anniversary, I had taken my engagement ring and had a necklace, wedding band, and wedding ring made for Derek and me. I had always wanted a marquise diamond, but Derek said I already had a diamond and if I didn't like it the way it was, I should change it. He never dreamed I would do just that. I made a band for him and a gorgeous, or so I thought, ring that was more to my liking.

We were on our way to Miami, Florida to visit my old roommate Joyce and her husband for a few days. I gave Derek a beautiful card with the ring inside and asked if we could try to start over. Instead of having the "seven-year itch" where everyone breaks up, I asked him if we could really try together to get our marriage back on track. When he opened the card, the ring fell out, and he asked me what it was for. I told him it was for new beginnings. Derek told me he didn't like the ring and that he would just keep the one that he had always worn.

I felt my heart hit the floor. I put his ring back in my purse and put on the ring I had made for myself, not caring if he liked it or not. I loved it! The center stone showed up so much better with just a few diamonds around it instead of the fifty-two that were originally surrounding it, and the star necklace had come out really neat too. Derek didn't say a word about either one of them.

We had a nice visit with Joyce and Frank, but Derek had to get back to Tulsa. When Joyce and I talked about Derek and me, she said she was frankly shocked we had made it this far. I knew she was right but still I didn't want to admit it.

But I knew.

Citizen-Journal
Wednesday, June 25,1975

109 dead in jet crash
Short of JFK runway

MY WHOLE WORLD'S BEEN TURNED UP SIDE DOWN

The phone call came from Kathy Winslow on June 26, 1975. I was in Tulsa on leave with a back injury. She asked me if I had read the newspapers or heard the news on TV. I said, "No, why? Did something happen to Tommy?"

Kathy asked me if I was sitting down. I said rather irritably, "Yes, but what is wrong? Why are you asking me if I'm sitting down? Tell me Kathy, what's up?"

She asked me if I knew there had been a plane crash at JFK. I said it was weird she should ask because when Derek had told me about it the night before, I had a terrible gut feeling something really awful had happened. "Did something happen to Tommy, Kathy?" I almost yelled at her.

"No, Bev, it's not Tommy. It's Wendell."

"Wendell?" I screamed. "What about Wendell?"

She told me he was in the plane crash.

"Oh, my God!! NO! Where is he? Did the article say? I've got to call him. I'll have to go see him!"

"Bev, Bev, listen to me. God, I hate to tell you this, but he didn't survive the crash."

I screamed right into her ear. "NO! NO! I don't believe that. It can't be true. Kathy, tell me it's not true!" Tears started streaming down my face, they were burning my cheeks. "Oh, my God, Kathy. this can't be true!"

Kathy tried to console me with the details she knew, but I refused to believe it.

I called a radio station, and they told me it was true. I jumped into my Mustang and drove to the local grocery to get a newspaper. It was a miracle I didn't get in a wreck getting there because I was crying so hard I couldn't see the road. I grabbed a newspaper, and there was a picture of the airplane in pieces. I turned the pages until I came across the sports section where there was a picture of Wendell.

I screamed at the top of my lungs. A lady from the grocery came running over to me and grabbed me before I hit the floor. She helped me sit down. She kept asking me what was wrong and if could she do anything. I just kept sobbing and shaking my head. I told her someone I loved very much had died in the plane crash in New York. She stayed with me for a few minutes and asked if I needed a ride home, but I told her no, that I could make it.

I had just talked to Wendell less than a week ago. He was at home visiting his family. We had a crazy, silly conversation with him telling me he wanted me to come to Mississippi to meet his family, and I made him promise to go to the Ohio State Fair with me in August. Were we both nuts for asking this of each other? It was nice to know he wanted me to meet his family. He was going back to New York for a few days, then back home, and he wanted me to come visit. I had told Wendell I would get away somehow and asked him if he thought his family would like me. He told me he knew they would love me. We talked sexy to each other, and he teased me about having a party line. Wendell said things wouldn't be the same around there if anyone he knew heard our conversation. We both laughed and had so much fun acting silly on the phone.

I felt so close to him. I told him to behave himself down there in Mississippi, and he lied and said, "Of course I will."

I told him, "Yeah, that will be the day."

I had suppressed the urge to tell him I loved him on that call. There were times before when I had wanted to say it but never allowed myself to actually do it. I didn't know why, but the feeling was especially strong that time. I guess now I understood it would have been my last chance to ever tell him how I really felt about him. "Miss me!" I said to him instead.

"Always," he replied.

I never got tired of hearing that. We hung up.

I called Wendell's sister, Shirley, who confirmed Wendell's death. I screamed in her ear and bawled until she could barely make out what I was trying to say to her. She asked me if I would come to the funeral, and I told her I would try.

I called Dr. Timer and will never know how I got to his office. He tried to get me to calm down by talking while I sobbed. He gave me a shot then sent me home.

When Derek called from Chicago, I was still hysterical. I told him a "friend" of mine was on the Eastern plane that crashed at JFK. When I told him I was going to his funeral, Derek must have suspected the person was more than a friend and forbid me to go. I was going no matter what.

I made my reservations and called Shirley to see if someone could pick me up at the airport in Gulfport. I told her what I looked like and what I would be wearing. Even though we had talked on the phone before, we had never met in person. I was hoping to meet her that summer, but not like this.

I called Mom who had been trying to call me because she thought she recognized Wendell's name on the news report. I told her what I knew about the crash, and while she tried to comfort me, all I could do was wail. I could not get control of myself. This just wasn't real; it was a nightmare, and I was going to wake up and talk to Wendell on the phone and hear him laugh. This just couldn't have happened and especially not an airplane, where we had met.

I told Mom Derek had forbidden me from going to the funeral. She said, "Go anyway. If you need me to come and go with you, I will."

I said, "Mom, I have to go. I have to be with Wendell one more time. Do you understand what I am saying? He can't leave here without me having a chance to say good-bye. I know he can't see me but I have to be there. I have to, Mom."

She told me to try and calm down a little bit so I would be able to get myself to the airport and down to Mississippi. Mom said she would feel better if she were going with me, but I told her I wouldn't have time to set her up on a flight to get here and go with me because the funeral was the day after tomorrow. "Please be careful," she pleaded.

When I got off the plane in Gulfport, I suddenly realized I had no idea how I had gotten there. As I walked through the doors of the airport,

I saw a young man standing to the left of the doorway. I know I gasped when I saw him because he was the spitting image of a younger Wendell. He took my breath away. He looked right into my eyes and asked if I was Bev. Instead of answering him, I just burst into tears. He said he was there to take me to his mom's house and to just hold on to him. He introduced his Aunt Dorella and said he was Randy Cuevas, Wendell's nephew.

Randy Cuevas

I was so nervous I talked all the way to Necaise. I couldn't get over how beautiful Mississippi was with the pine trees so tall and green. It was so peaceful. Randy's family lived way back in the woods, and I jokingly asked if I would have to use an Indian scout to find my way back to their house. No wonder Wendell loved to escape the rat race of New York to come here. I only wished I had been able to come here with him just once.

When I got out of the car, a tall woman with dark hair came towards me with her arms stretched out. "Why? Why did Wendell have to die?" she asked me.

For a few seconds, I had put the reason for my trip in the back of my mind and now...smack! The reality hit me once again. I burst out bawling, holding her in my arms as we cried and cried on each other's shoulders. She was Shirley, Wendell's sister, and she somewhat resembled Wendell. They both had those high cheek bones from their Indian heritage. I was still in shock at how much her son, Randy, looked like a younger, smaller version of Wendell. It was uncanny.

I met hundreds of people: relatives, friends, school chums, teachers, co-workers. Even Dr. J had come to be a pallbearer along with Jay Bauer, his friend from Louisville. I'd never seen so many flowers, but then this was my first funeral. I had not lost a family member or friend so I had never been to a funeral, especially a Catholic one that had a wake. There were so many people in various stages of shock wandering around in disbelief. This just wasn't happening, this couldn't be real.

It took me forever to get myself ready to go into the house to see the casket Shirley took me in and introduced me to Bernell, Janell, and Berlin. Glen, the oldest brother, just couldn't bring himself to come. Then I met

Wendell's Dad, Aaron, who was such a handsome man, I assumed it must be where Wendell got his good looks. I was told Ollie Mae had suffered a heart seizure and wasn't strong enough to leave her room.

Aaron, Ollie Mae Ladner and Randy Cuevas

Wendell's parents were much older than I had expected, and I remembered that horrible telegram I had sent him. I felt pangs of guilt, but I tried to make myself forget that. Wendell was the baby, and Ollie Mae's heart had been broken in two when she found out about the crash. Aaron had been watching a television broadcast when the cameraman zoomed in on a piece of luggage. It was Wendell's luggage with his Nets insignia on a tag. Aaron nearly lost it right then and there, but knew he had to be strong for Ollie Mae.

My eyes kept avoiding the casket, thinking this was a nightmare, and begging God to let me wake up. I'm going to be able to call Wendell when I'm in New York and see those dancing brown eyes and that incredible smile. This just wasn't happening.

Oh God, there it was.

The casket was closed because Wendell had been severely burned in the crash, but I couldn't think about that. I felt so sorry for Wendell's brother, Berlin, who had to go to New York to identify his brother's body like that. Would he ever be able to get that out of his mind? I just stood there staring at the bronze-colored casket.

Berlin came up to me. "Thank you for coming. I know it would have meant a lot to Wendell," he said as he choked back the tears. I turned to look at him with tears pouring down my face. I leaned into Berlin's chest and sobbed until I couldn't get my breath. He was big and broad like Wendell. I almost wanted to pull myself away, but at the same time I wanted to get lost in the feel of him.

I don't remember much about the rest of the evening except it seemed to last forever, and I couldn't stop crying. I would stop for a few minutes, then I would lose it all over again. No matter how hard I tried to keep from crying, there was no end to my tears.

Wendell was procrastinating as much as I was. He hadn't gotten a divorce from his wife Bessie, so she was there. He told me Bessie had a figure like Raquel Welch. Honestly, I couldn't tell if she did, and I don't think she was dressed appropriately because she had on jeans. I couldn't believe she would wear jeans to her husband's funeral. Bessie looked the least upset of anyone there. They had been separated for over two years, and Wendell kept telling me he was going to get around to getting a divorce, but obviously he hadn't. He had told me the last time they talked, they had agreed on proceeding with the divorce.

Then I met Camme. She was an 18-year-old girl from Mississippi who Wendell had dated when he was home. She was attractive, but oh, so young, and she acted like she was lost. I liked her and resented her both at the same time. I knew Camme had been the last woman with Wendell, and I was jealous, but I couldn't hold that against her.

Later, some of the New York Nets arrived. Although Wendell still didn't like being in New York, he had had his revenge in a way because the Nets had won the ABA Championship the year he got traded to them. He told me he was going to go back to Kentucky and give them the finger. I jokingly asked him, "The one with the championship ring on it?

"No, Baby, the one right in the middle." He was just acting tough; I knew he was still hurt from being traded but just hated to admit how much.

With the players sat a dark-haired beauty named Jill. For some strange reason, I went over and asked her if she wanted to take a walk. It dawned on me how much Camme, Jill, and I resembled each other. All tall, all with long hair, brown, brunette, and blonde. Wendell, you stinker! Jill was from Kentucky, and I believe she was one of the nurses who took care of Wendell when he had his water cooler accident (I knew Wendell wouldn't have any old nurses taking care of him. Not Wendell!) She told me Wendell had given her a cross for Christmas and that she would never take it off, ever. I felt jealous again because Wendell and I never exchanged Christmas presents. But then, how would I have explained his gift to Derek?

At 2:00 a.m. I could barely keep my swollen eyes open. Randy offered to take me to his house. Oh, my God, Randy, I thought, you look so much like Wendell. I couldn't stand to be near him, but at the same time, I wanted to hold him and never let him go. I was losing it. My emotions were going crazy! I insisted on sleeping on the floor because my back was killing me. Randy got me a pillow and blanket, then leaned over and kissed me, right smack on the mouth. I could not believe he did that. I was shocked, but too exhausted to say anything to him. I just stared at him and couldn't speak. We didn't say another word to one another. He went into his room, and I laid there staring at the ceiling feeling the hot tears pour down my cheeks.

I couldn't believe it when I heard Shirley telling me to get up. I was supposed to wake up, and this was going to be all over, just a dream, a nightmare, but it was supposed to be over. It wasn't! I found myself dressed and in the car before I knew what had happened.

The funeral was that day. They were going to bury my Wendell. Dear God, I don't ever want to put my loved ones through this. When I die, I want them to burn me to ashes and throw me out of an airplane. No casket, no funeral, no flowers, and I don't want anyone to see me after I am dead.

That day was, without a doubt, the worst, most heartbreaking day of my life. I kept remembering all our good times. Even the bad times didn't seem as bad. I had learned to love Wendell for who and what he was. He loved the ladies, and they loved him. He had told me I was special, and I chose to hang on to those words forever. I loved Wendell so much, but I never, ever told him, because I was always afraid he'd think I wanted some sort of commitment from him. I still wish I had told him I loved him, but I had to believe he knew how I felt about him.

Wendell had taught me how wonderful it felt to be a woman; to make love and return that love to a man. It was okay to laugh and act silly in bed. Sex could be fun. He showed me the importance of pleasing someone and letting him please me. When we were together, no one else mattered. It was such an awesome experience, one that had changed my life forever. Yes, Lord, I loved Wendell in my own special way; then and forever for the rest of my life. I'd never forget him. Never!!!!!

Everybody was standing outside the house waiting for the casket to be taken to the church. Why was Wendell's brother, Berlin, calling my name? Oh, dear God, it was my turn to go back inside that house. I was being given only a few moments in front of a cold bronze casket to say good-bye to a man who had come to mean so much to me. Wendell Larry Ladner, what can I say? What could I convey to you in death that I never could bring myself to say to you when you were alive? There was a picture of Wendell sitting on top of the casket. I picked it up and said to it, "I love you Wendell! Even though you can't hear me: no trap, no commitment, just I love you! May God bless you and keep you in His care. I'll always love you, Wendell, for the rest of my life."

When I stood up to leave the house, I suddenly felt weak. I had not eaten in three days and hadn't slept much either. As I left the house, I felt my knees give, and I fainted. When I came to, I remember a hand reaching out to help me up. It was Randy. Oh, how could two men resemble each other so much?

On the way to the funeral, I was in the back seat of Berlin's car with Camme on my right and Jill on my left. They clung to me and cried on my shoulders. I couldn't control myself, and Berlin's wife, Carolyn, asked me to please stop crying so hard. She said we had to be strong and not upset Aaron any more than he was already.

But I just couldn't stop. Couldn't Carolyn see my heart was broken? Did they want to see it? Would that prove how much I was hurting?

I must have gone into shock. The church, The Infant of Prague Catholic Church, was so small that half the folks attending had to be outside. It was reported that over 5,000 people were in and out of Aaron and Ollie Mae's home from dawn on Friday to dawn on Saturday before the funeral. Camme, Jill, and I sat right behind Wendell's brothers, sisters, and his Dad. Carolyn kept turning around tapping me on the knee trying to comfort me and to get the three of us to quit crying so hard and so loud, but none of us could.

I didn't want to upset Aaron, but I couldn't hold my heartbreak inside. I had no idea what the priest said about Wendell. I just couldn't get over the song they played - something about "a time to live, a time to die," the rest was a blur - it tore me up.

At the gravesite, I wanted to choke Bessie because she was putting on an Academy Award performance. She hadn't told anyone she and Wendell were getting a divorce and was playing the grieving wife, the one most people didn't even know existed.

The next thing I remember, I was removing my topaz ring from my finger, the one I had bought in Mexico on the same day I purchased the mug for Wendell. I leaned toward the casket and dropped the ring on the ground underneath his casket. It was a stupid thing to do, but I just wanted a piece of me to be with him forever.

I found myself back at Wendell's parents' home after his burial, and Randy was trying to convince me to eat something. Eat? How can people eat at a time like this? But there sat Bessie stuffing her face.

Before the funeral, I had accidentally opened the door to the bathroom to find Bessie putting on mascara. Mascara! How could she do that? I had cried nearly nonstop for three days, looked like a damn frog, and there she was tearless and putting on mascara. She spun around and glared at me, and I just stared back at her. She had obviously heard there were going to be photographers and reporters from various newspapers, and Bessie wanted to look her best. Even if nobody knew she even existed. "You make me sick at my stomach!" I heard myself saying to her. I could not believe I had said that. She yelled at me to get the hell out of there, and I slammed the door. How could Wendell have ever let her trick him into marrying her? The bitch!

Bessie couldn't get away from Necaise fast enough after the funeral. A place she knew she wasn't really welcome in the first place. Ollie Mae and the rest of Wendell's family never did have much use for her. I had heard the only reason she married Wendell was to show her ex-husband, a professional baseball player, that she could marry another professional athlete. Randy said Wendell had told him that both he and Bessie knew their marriage was a big mistake right after they had gotten married. Randy asked me to go with him to take Bessie and her friend to the airport. Although I didn't really want to be near Bessie, I went so I could talk to Randy.

I kept staring at Randy in the rearview mirror, like I used to when I was with Wendell. The eyes were different, but his hands were very similar to Wendell's, only smaller. He chatted with Bessie. She never said a word to me, and I was very glad. I am sure she really didn't want me to be there, but she heard Randy ask me to go with him and there was nothing she could do about it.

It was a long ride to New Orleans. After they got out at the airport, I stayed in the car. When Randy came back, the tears had started again. "Are you okay?" he asked in his southern drawl.

"I was just remembering a time in Louisville with Wendell," I replied.

"Want to tell me about it?" he asked.

"Sure, I do." We exchanged stories all the way back to his house.

I felt the emptiness in Randy. Wendell, alias "Unc," was Randy's whole world. Randy had wanted to live with Wendell after he finished school, and they had great plans. There wouldn't be a woman alive who would be safe. I believed Randy when he told me that. They were both determined to score with every woman that they met. At first, what he said hurt a little, but after a while, I understood they were having guy talk and I was okay with it.

It was hard to say good-bye to Wendell's family, and I was sad I didn't get to meet Ollie Mae. They had all opened their arms and hearts to me, and I never felt more like part of a family in all of my life. I felt a closeness to each and every one of them. Camme and Jill hugged me and thanked me for being there for them. I was surprised because all I did was let them cry on my shoulders. Shirley asked me to please come back again and not to lose touch. I promised her I would. When Randy walked me to my gate at the airport, he held onto me for a very long time. I started crying again and didn't want to let go of him either.

I walked onto the Braniff flight, and the boarding Flight Attendant took one look at me and asked what in the world was wrong. I told her about the Eastern crash, and then I got brave and asked her for a favor. I had a Coach ticket, but I really didn't want to be squeezed into a seat with two other people, and the flight was nearly full in the back. I asked her if I promised not to ask her for anything or bother her in any way, could I please sit in a First Class seat and try to sleep since I hadn't slept eight hours in days. She looked at me, put her arms around my shoulders, walked me to a First Class seat, and sat me down. She gave me a blanket and pillow and said if I wanted anything to eat or drink during the flight, just to let her know. I thanked her and told her I wouldn't need anything. She was so sweet to do that for me. I would have done the same for her if she had been in my shoes. I guess it was like a sorority - the particular airline didn't matter, we were all Stewardesses, Hostesses, or Flight Attendants.

I walked in the door of our house in Tulsa, and Derek was sitting at the kitchen table. I told him I was moving to Dallas for a trial separation, and I didn't want to talk about my trip. He was fine with that and went back to doing whatever it was he had been doing at the table.

I called my friend Barbara Jean to see if the apartment next door to her was still for rent and if I could move in after my next trip. I had already told Barbara Jean about Wendell's death, and she sort of expected me to call. She had mentioned the possibility of me moving to Dallas, and Mrs. Wallace said she would hold the apartment for me until the first of the month. I told Barb to tell her I wanted it.

The night before I was to go to Dallas, I went into the den and asked Derek to hold me. He put his arm around me and said, "Well, thanks for seven years." I burst out bawling. He apologized, but I think he was just trying to cover up how he was really feeling inside. This was hurting so much!

Much to my surprise, Derek offered to drive me to Dallas after my next trip. I had packed up a few things I would need right away, and he drove my Rosie down with me. When we were getting close to Dallas, he said to me, "You'll be back. You can't make it without me."

I just glared at him and wanted to say something horribly ugly, but instead I just said, "We shall see, Derek. We shall see." I took him to the airport to fly back to Tulsa and found I was numb as I watched him go through the jetbridge to the airplane.

I felt so empty. I wasn't sure I could ever feel anything again.

When I walked into the door of what was now my apartment, I was terrified. Was I really doing this? Could I actually make it on my own? I had no idea, but I had to try. I had to see if there was anything left between me and Derek or if it was time for us to move on in our lives. I hated the thought of being a divorced woman, but I despised more the thought of Derek and me continuing to hurt each other forever. I sat down in the middle of the front room floor, with no couch or chairs, nowhere to sit, and I started bawling. I cried until I finally fell asleep on the floor, too drained to walk upstairs to the bed.

I kept in touch with Shirley, as I had promised, and went back to Mississippi several times. On one occasion, she had received some of Wendell's personal possessions from his apartment in New York. There was an address book she handed me to look at. It was full of girl's names, but better than half of them were scratched out or had big "Xs" over them. My hands started trembling as I worked my way back to the "Ss." I saw my name - with no scratches or Xs over it. I breathed a sigh of relief. I raised my eyes in Shirley's direction, "You don't think I would have let you see it if your name had been scratched out now, do you?" I smiled at her, and she smiled back.

Shirley handed me a small pouch with three rings in it. As I removed them, I thought I just might throw up. There was dark black soot all over the rings. Oh, my God. I knew what that was. I felt sick.

Randy walked into the room. He looked at me as I sat there white as chalk holding Wendell's rings. Shirley had left the room to help her youngest son, Deron, find his sneakers. My eyes welled with tears. "Randy, please ask your Mom if I can clean these rings. It's awful to leave them like this."

"Do you think you feel up to it?" he asked me.

"I'd feel much better if they were cleaned before the rest of the family sees them, especially Wendell's Mom and Dad," I answered.

We convinced Shirley to let me clean the ring. She was reluctant at first because she was afraid something might happen to them. I assured her I had cleaned a lot of jewelry in my day and that they would be fine. Randy and Shirley gasped when I selected a cup out of the cabinet to put the ammonia in to soak the rings. It was Wendell's favorite cup. I stared at it for a few minutes, then took a deep breath and set it on the counter. I cleaned his ABA Championship ring, Randy cleaned the tiger's eye, and then I finished cleaning a gold and silver ring with small diamonds on it. While I cleaned the soot off the rings, I closed my eyes as the tears started down my face. I didn't want to think about it. All I wanted to do was spare Wendell's family from seeing them the way I had just seen them.

While I was there, Shirley showed me the inscription written by the priest to put on Wendell's headstone. I read it, then blurted out, "I don't mean to be sacrilegious, but this doesn't seem quite right to be on Wendell's headstone. It just doesn't say what I feel everyone would expect it to say to remember him and his life."

Shirley told me she agreed but that she wasn't a writer and none of the other family members wanted to take on the challenge of writing something. I told her I'd like to try to write something if it was okay with her and her family. She said she would talk to everyone, then called to tell me they all agreed to give me a chance to write something, so I did. It was very difficult. I wrote several versions, but most of them seemed too personal, and I knew it had to say something that would apply to family and anyone else who had been touched by Wendell. Suddenly the words just came to me like a flood:

ALWAYS REMEMBER WENDELL
THE 110% HE GAVE TO LIFE
THE GAME OF BASKETBALL HE LOVED SO MUCH
AND THE HAPPINESS HE GAVE TO ALL OF US

The family was so pleased with what I had written. They had a meeting, and everyone agreed it was perfect. It was placed on his headstone with a picture of him in his Net's basketball uniform in Necaise Crossing, Mississippi.

I became very close to Wendell's family and went to visit them several times. I grew to love Aaron and Ollie Mae who cried whenever I had to leave. One time when I was visiting them, I gave Ollie Mae a necklace with a carved bird made out of Mother of Pearl on it. To me it looked like a dove from Heaven. We were standing outside of their home, and she put her hand on my arm, looked into my eyes and said, "I wish Wendell had brought you home with him. Aaron and I just love you." I was so touched she would share with me that they felt that way about me. Needless to say, that would have been my fondest wish too.

I missed Wendell with all of my heart too. I could not imagine that I would never get to see him, hold him, and love him ever again. I missed our passion and chemistry, but most of all I missed his laughter and looking into those deep, dark brown eyes. I'd never known eyes like those, and I probably never will again, I don't know that I'd really want to. He changed my life forever, and I will never forget him.

CLOSE ENCOUNTER WITH "THE KING"

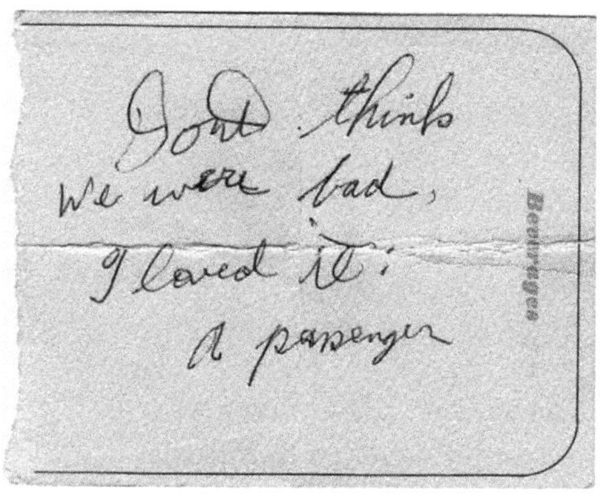
Dont think
We were bad,
I loved it:
A passenger

Beverages

Elvis's Note To Me

I collected several copies of different papers covering the plane crash and stories about Wendell. I went on a one-woman campaign writing letters to different publications regarding how they reported the accident. I wrote a blistering letter to *Newsweek* because I felt their article was way too graphic for the families of those who died. I didn't feel they needed to go into such explicit details about what had happened to the passengers on the airplane. Madeline Edmundson, writing for the editors, responded to my letter saying, "We feel there is a vast difference between the idle curiosity of a crowd and the professional investigation of a reporter. As a newsweekly, it is our sometimes unpleasant job to present the facts of any major news story fully and exactly as they have happened. Of course, the particulars of a plane crash are gruesome; however, we feel the best reporting is the kind that offers an eyewitness account of events, even at the risk of offending some readers." I was so angry, and it didn't change the article one bit but at least I had given her my two cents.

Some of the sports publications were cruel in writing things about Wendell. I wrote a few poison pen letters to those authors, accusing one guy named Jim O'Brien of just being plain jealous of Wendell's appeal to women and his fans. I think he wrote for *Sporting News* newspaper.

One article I loved was written by Dick Schaap for *Sport Magazine*. The article was titled "The One and Only Wendell," and was accompanied by a fabulous picture of Wendell jumping from the announcer's table onto the basketball court. The caption stated, "No picture ever captured more clearly the spirit of Wendell Ladner: he'd leap tall buildings to get into the action." Schaap wrote:

> Statistics never did justice to Wendell Ladner. He spent five seasons in the American Basketball Association playing for four different teams and he never produced much of a shooting percent or scoring average or anything else that could be reduced to fractions or decimals. But Wendell Ladner led the league in enthusiasm.
>
> If anyone had kept track of the number of times each ABA player crashed onto the floor, chasing after a loose basketball, Wendell could have set the world's record. Six-foot-five and 220 pounds, Ladner often said that someday he'd like to take a crack at pro football; he'd already played it on the basketball court.
>
> Wendell was unusual, in many ways. He came out of Necaise Crossing, Miss., played his college basketball at Southern Mississippi and his professional basketball in Tennessee, North Carolina, and Kentucky. Yet when he was traded to the New York Nets; he chose as his roommate Mike Gale, a black man. This was surprising to a lot of people, a white man from rural Mississippi rooming with a black man from urban Pennsylvania. Wendell was sophisticated in that way, and naive in so many others. One of his favorite magazines along with *Playboy* and *Penthouse*, was *Oui*, which he pronounced "Oh" which was as close to proper French as anyone ever got in Necaise Crossing. No one ever accused Wendell of being an intellectual, but young women with Phi Beta Kappa keys fought to meet him.
>
> Wendell died this summer. He was killed returning from Necaise Crossing to New York City, killed in the airplane crash that claimed over 110 lives aboard a 727 cruising from New Orleans into John F. Kennedy Airport Ladner was 26 years old; another statistic that didn't do him justice.

I wrote a letter to one of the surviving Flight Attendants, Mary Eileen Mooney, who answered pretty quickly considering all she had been through.

In my letter, I tried to express my grief without causing her pain, but I wanted to know what Wendell might have done on his flight. I attempted to be flippant by saying to her I was sure she had noticed Wendell on her flight unless, of course, she preferred blondes. She responded the way I had hoped she would:

> I am very sorry about your loss. I lost a lot of good friends on flight 66 also. My only consolation is no one suffered, it happened so fast. Thank God for that.
>
> I did notice Wendell, he was so big although I do prefer blondes. I figured he was a basketball player but did not know who he was or played for. I was working the back galley that day and he was sitting in the last row of seats, across from the galley. He had a look of bored detachment on his face you see so often in people who have to fly a lot He was watching us trip over each other and me drop things on the floor. I think he was amazed that such a klutz ever got a job as a Flight Attendant. The rest of the flight he either read or napped, never saying anything.
>
> When the accident happened, I was in my jump seat and could not see him or his reaction, but I am sure it was minimal since it happened so fast. He was sitting in an aisle or middle seat, I am not sure, but he was not by a window so I am sure he did not know what happened.
>
> Just try to see it this way if you can. This is my philosophy, granted it is sad that in his prime of life, he was killed. When he died, there was no suffering. Who knows what difficulties and sadness would have been in store for him if he had lived. Maybe some time in a game he would have had an injury which would have prevented him from playing a game he loved so much.
>
> I know you and his parents loved him very much. Try to remember the happy times and the things he did to make your life full. Don't look back. There are no

> regrets, cause you can't change anything. But be glad he did not suffer. I am sure you are finding my outlook a little strange but this is my way of thinking. When it is your time to go, you can't do anything about it. Everyone's time comes, sooner or later.
>
> Well Bev, I don't know what else to say. Try to be happy and live your life to the fullest. The past is past and I hope you have a lot of happy memories to carry through life with you.

Mary Eileen asked me to call her whenever I was in New York. She nearly fainted when I walked into her apartment because I was so tall. She said, "Oh my gosh, girl, if you and Wendell had had kids, they would have been giants." We both laughed. We had dinner together a few times in New York and wrote to each other for years, only losing contact after she moved to Kunkle, Pennsylvania. (If you read this, Mary Eileen, please get in touch. It would be great to hear from you again.)

A few of the articles referred to Wendell as "Wondrous Wendell." That nickname I could live, with but one article called him "Winnie." I have no idea where or how that nickname got started, but if there was one thing Wendell was not, it was "Winnie." Most of the articles were kind in saying one of the most important things in Wendell's life was his friends, which I knew to be true. Several of Wendell's friends shared their stories with me at his funeral. I laughed and cried over and over again.

One of the saddest stories I read referred to Wendell as having a black cloud over his head. I never looked at him like that Yes, he got traded, but one thing I never understood was the fact that although he was such a crowd draw, he was let go three times. He took it in stride, though and every time he got traded, he tried that much harder to do a better job for the next team. No, of course he would never rank up there with Dr. J, but then I think Wendell never cared as much about being the star as he did about being able to play the game. We'll never know what he would have been able to accomplish that season in New York because his life ended way too soon.

I was trying to settle into my Dallas apartment as best I could. I had to go back and forth to Tulsa to bring stuff to Dallas, and that was always a difficult time. Derek would either be unbelievably wonderful or a total ass, and I never knew which Derek would meet me. I often wished he had asked me to come back home, but then I decided we really did need this time apart to find out what we were going to do.

Carol and Barbie tried to keep me busy. Barb and Mike were so kind to ask me to come for dinner or to join them when they went out to eat. I ran around with Carol a bunch, going to clubs or out to restaurant,. Since she wasn't involved with any particular guy, it made it more fun for us just to hang together.

Wendell's nephew Randy started writing to me. He would send the most beautiful letters sharing what was going on in Mississippi and how everyone was doing. I could tell by his letters he had a really big crush on me. When I would go there for visits, we would sit and talk for hours on end and had become really close. His letters were always a joy.

I couldn't wait to go to work, where I could forget all my cares and woes and just enjoy my job. I was usually flying with Barbie or Carol, sometimes both.

Out of the blue, Derek called and asked me to come up to Tulsa. I wasn't exactly sure why he wanted me to come until I got there and the house was a disaster. I guess he wanted me to come home and clean. My plants were dead, and the place was a mess. How could he live like that? I couldn't stand the house another minute so I cleaned it, did Derek's laundry, and ironed him some shirts for work.

Had I lost my mind? I wanted to do these things for Derek though. I felt guilty for leaving him. I felt guilty about my relationship with Wendell. I was afraid I was getting depressed again because I was right back where I was when we moved to Tulsa — living in two worlds.

Randy at Barbie's

I saw Dr. Turner and told him I was worried about getting depressed again. He said I was stronger than I thought I was, but he was there if I needed him. I thanked him for helping save my life back in 1972, saying that I might not be here if he hadn't taken such drastic steps to make me well. Dr. Turner did tell me I was going to be alright with or without Derek, that I had changed a great deal since he had started treating me, and he was proud of how far I had come. I told him I was just so exhausted, and I didn't know what to do anymore. He asked me not to make any important decisions without giving them a great deal of thought.

Wendell's nephew, Randy, came to Dallas to visit, and I jokingly told Barb I didn't know whether to take him to Six Flags or take him to bed. I was teasing, but at the same time I knew how he made me feel because of his resemblance to Wendell, which wasn't fair to him. So I took him to Six Flags. Besides, dear Lord, he was only nineteen, and I was thirty.

Randy brought the mug I had given Wendell, and it was covered with Wendell's fingerprints. My heart sank, and I started crying. Randy held me and told me he understood. We shopped for clothes for Randy and souvenirs for him to take back to everyone. I took him to his first Mexican restaurant, and although he didn't care for it very much, at least he tried it.

Although we had a great time together, I knew Randy had a crush on me, and I wanted to keep my distance. He told me I just blew him away whenever I walked off that plane in Gulfport. Then he told me Wendell and he used to lie on the beach, and Wendell would tell him about different girls he had been dating. I asked Randy if Wendell told him about me, but before Randy could answer, I told him I didn't want to know what Wendell said about me. Randy said Wendell had told him how special I was to him. I hoped Randy didn't know about our sex life, but I kind of figured he did.

I hated for Randy to leave, but I had to fly the next day and told him I would be coming to Mississippi soon and we'd spend some time together then. I did let him kiss me good-bye, which felt strange.

I needed to do something besides fly so I didn't have so much time on my hands alone. One of the girls I was flying with named Cindy Bell asked me if I had ever worked at the Apparel Market on Stemmons. Since I had only been in Dallas a few months, she explained that clothing manufacturers would bring their lines of clothing for the approaching season to show in a showroom. The manufacturers hired people to "go through the line" (which meant show the buyers all the clothes that had been made for that season) with prospective buyers. We would write orders, and the clothes would be sent to their stores before the next season started. It sounded like fun, and I was kind of excited about filling those empty hours. And why not make a little extra money doing it? I worked for a line called Jerrell. Although it was fun, it was a lot of hard work too. The lines had about fifty or sixty pieces you had to hang in front of the customer, and then if they wanted to see a certain portion of that group, you had to start over. Sometimes you wanted to choke the people because they would talk among themselves and not pay attention until you started to remove that group, and then they would want to see it all over again. I worked at the Market for about four days, and I was beat before it was time for me to go on my next flight. Thank goodness this only happened about four times a year, so I would have time to rest up before the next one.

Derek and I called each other off and on. Some days we would really connect and then others we were at each other's throats. I just couldn't figure out what we were going to do. At times, I would turn around to tell him something and realize he wasn't there. I missed our doggies too. Muskogee, who I considered my child, and Talley (the Irish setter I fought with Derek over buying) were both good company. I wanted Derek to want me to come home because at times I desperately wanted to. Then he or I would say something, and we'd get into a fight and end up getting angry with each other. How in the world did we ever get so far apart?

I was still seeing Aunt Dori whenever I had a STL (St. Louis) layover. I finally told her about Wendell. I didn't tell her about the sex stuff, but I told her Derek and I had some serious issues and that I had befriended this man who had been killed in a plane crash. She never judged me and just said she hoped that Derek and I could work things out because she loved both of us a bunch and wanted us to be happy.

Randy picked me up when I went to Mississippi for All Saints Day. As we were driving to Randy's house, Berlin and Aaron, Wendell's brother and Dad, drove past us. I waved at them, and then Aaron started to cry. It broke my heart! I guessed he must associate me with Wendell, and it hurt too much when he saw me. That visit was the first time I had seen Wendell's grave with my words written on the headstone. I broke down, and Berlin put his arm around me and thanked me for writing it. Randy and Shirley were there also, both crying as much as I was. Shirley had so much guilt over Wendell's death because they had gotten into a fight on the way to the airport right before he left for flight #66. She never, ever forgave herself.

I was flying MEM (Memphis, Tennessee) and SAN (San Diego, California) in September with Barbie. We were in the limo headed for our hotel when I remembered I had been given that phone number for Elvis, so I decided to give him a call. "Bev, you are crazy! You're not really gonna call that number, are you?" asked Barb. "You bet I am, Barbara Jean, why not?" I asked her.

"You won't get to talk to Elvis; that Passenger Service Manager was just jerking your chain. It is probably a number for Dial-A-Prayer."

I knew it really was Elvis's number because I had talked to his Dad that time I went through the airport, but I was having fun teasing Barbie. "Oh well, what else is there to do in Memphis but call Elvis Presley? After all it could turn out to be the answer to a dream."

"That's what you are, Beverly Jane, a dreamer. Why in the world do you think that PSM gave you Elvis's 'real' phone number?"

I winked at her and replied, "Well, Miss Barbara Jean, because that PSM wants to get in my britches; that's why!"

She burst out laughing, "You are absolutely awful! Unfortunately, that is probably the truth, but how could he expect to make time with you if you manage to get in touch with Elvis?"

"I guess he figures I'll owe him. I don't know. He fancies himself such a ladies' man. Perhaps I'll just be so grateful to him that I'll be obligated to make him happy since he helped me in becoming the next Mrs. Elvis Presley."

"I can't stand it! You have truly lost all touch with reality," stated Barb.

"Could it possibly be because I have been buddy bidding with you for too long? We've even started to finish each other's sentences. Now that is pitiful!"

"We're just compatible, Beverly Jane, that's all." (We got a kick out of calling each other by our first and middle names.)

"Either that or no one else can stand to fly with us!" We started laughing out loud.

"What are you two laughing about?" asked Fred Teal, our F/O who was in the front seat of our limo.

Barb replied., "You wouldn't understand, Fred. Bev is just in a hurry to get to her room to call Dial-a-Prayer." Fred gave me the oddest look while Barbie and I giggled like teenagers.

We got out of our stinky uniforms, and I put on Wendell's jersey Randy had given me. I loved that big shirt because it was so comfortable to sleep in, and I felt close to Wendell when I wore it. I jumped on the bed and grabbed the phone. "Here goes nothing, Barbie."

Barb just shook her head and grabbed a pear out of her suitcase. She always had more snacks in her suitcase than a local snack shop - she needed to have them if her sugar felt like it was down. She sank onto the other bed with a sigh. "Let me know what verse is on the Dial-A-Prayer today."

A man answered after the second ring; I was so startled I almost couldn't get my words out. "Uh, er, uh, hello, may I speak to Elvis please?"

"Who's calling?" he asked in a rather curt voice.

I had mustered up a little confidence and announced my name, "Bev Schoenmann. I'm a Flight Attendant for American Airlines. Elvis was on my flight, so I thought I'd call him and say hi."

I heard him turn to someone else in the room and say, "Hey guys, this girl's name is show and tell." I heard a lot of laughter.

"No, no, I said Schoenmann, not show and tell!" I wanted to call him an idiot, but I didn't.

When Barb heard what I said to the guy, she perked up then burst out laughing. "Who is it?" she asked.

I shrugged my shoulders, put my hand over the mouthpiece and said, "Probably one of Elvis's gofers."

"Hold the phone," he commanded.

Barb was on the edge of the bed now. "What's going on?"

"I'm not sure, but he told me to hold the phone."

"You don't suppose he went to get Elvis, do you?"

"Nah, I..." Before I could finish, there was another man's voice on the other end of the phone.

"This is Vernon Presley. Can I help you?"

My eyes nearly bugged out of my head. I mouthed to Barbie "It's his Daddy." This really got her attention. "Hello Mr. Presley, I spoke to you once before when Elvis was at Lake Tahoe. My name is Bev Schoenmann; your son was on one of my flights, and we had a great rapport. I thought I would just give him a call and say hi since I was here in Memphis."

Mr. Presley shocked me by responding, "Are you going to make him an offer he can't refuse?" I was a little taken aback by his question and imagined he was grinning from ear to ear. "Yes sir, I do believe that's exactly what I had in mind." He roared.

I looked over at Barb in complete amazement.

"What is going on? I am dying over here!" she said.

I smiled and whispered, "I think he likes me."

She slipped her hand against her forehead, falling back onto the bed, "Spare me, spare me; only you would think that...you crazy woman!"

I couldn't hear what else she was saying because Mr. Presley was talking. "Well let me tell you, Bev, Elvis hates to talk on the phone. He really doesn't like it and would much rather talk to you in person, I'm sure." (Oh, be still my heart!!!)

"I think that could be arranged, sir," I replied.

"Well he just got out of the hospital a couple of days ago, and he's not quite himself yet. Why don't you give him a call next time you're in town? I'll let him know you phoned."

"I appreciate that so much, Mr. Presley. Please tell Elvis I hope he feels better real soon. And thank you for talking with me." I hung up the phone and stared at it for a second before Barb's voice distracted my train of thought.

She was sitting on the edge of her bed, "My God, Bev, tell me about it. What happened?" I told her Mr. Presley's part of the conversation, and she was beside herself. "That PSM must really, really want in your britches!" We both fell backwards on our beds in gales of laughter.

On my next trip, Elvis was out of town, so I talked to Joe Esposito. I reminded him of the flight that he, Alan, and Elvis had been on and about my trip to Lake Tahoe when I had last seen him. I told Joe I was very tall and had been wearing a hot pink dress the night he sat my friend and me at Elvis's table with Linda. He said, "I remember you, Bev, but I'm not sure Elvis would. He meets so many people." It was my turn to be surprised. I was sure Joe was just being kind and he could not possibly have remembered me, but it sounded good to my ego.

To make a long story short Joe told me to send him a picture of myself, and he would deliver it to Elvis. If Elvis wanted to hook up with me, then he would take it from there. Joe asked, "You will be in Memphis another time, won't you?" I told him I had one more trip that month. I took the address so I could send a picture when I got back to Dallas. Joe told me to call and ask for him when I got back to Memphis.

Barb asked, "You are going to send a picture, aren't you?"

"Well hell yes, I'm going to send the most gorgeous picture I can find of myself, and you are going to help me pick it out"

"Deal," said Barb. We decided to send him a copy of my modeling portfolio I used in Tulsa. I still looked the same, my hair was just a lot longer.

Barbie and I were spastic waiting for our next flight. We both tried not to talk about the inevitable phone call I was to make. We were unpacking at the hotel, and she blurted out, When are you going to call?

I was very nervous, "In a minute. What if he didn't like my pictures, Barb?" "Are you kidding? Those were beautiful. What was not to like?"

"I just feel really insecure, Barbie."

"You'll hate yourself if you don't call, forever!"

"Okay, okay, I'll call."

I called Joe about 4:00 p.m. Maggie, the housekeeper I had talked to a couple of times before, told me he would be back at 5:00. I asked her to leave a message for Joe to please return my call. We chatted briefly, and I was flattered when she said she remembered I was a Stewardess for American Airlines.

After I hung up, I turned to Barb and told her Joe wasn't there, unless it was an excuse to avoid me. "He'll call back, Bev, I just know he will."

"I am not waiting in this room. I am calling Bob (a fellow I had met a long time ago who worked at a local television station. We were just friends and had dinner occasionally), and I'm going out for some ribs. Want to join me?"

"No, Bev, of course not! I'm going to stay in my room and wait for Elvis to call."

Me, Marcus and Barbie

"You just might have a very long wait, Miss Barbie." I smartly said to her. Bob said he would be glad to take me and Barb out for ribs, so I decided to wash my hair.

We'd had a male Flight Attendant on this trip names Marcus Mussett who was gorgeous. He was almost too pretty to be a guy with his blonde hair, blue eyes, and a killer smile. We enjoyed flying with him but felt we had to fend off all the passes made at him from both guys and girls. He was fun, taking it all in stride and letting us "mother" him. There was a knock at the door, followed by a male voice. I wasn't too surprised because we assumed it was Marcus. "Who is it?" I asked.

"My name is Dick Groeb. I'm Elvis Presley's bodyguard. Is there a girl there named Bev?"

I started laughing hysterically. "Sure, Marcus, and I'm, Raquel Welch too."

"I beg your pardon. What did you say?" asked the gent outside my door.

"This is cute, Marcus, really cute. But I'm not falling for it."

"I don't understand. I said my name is Dick Groeb, not Marcus. Is there a Bev in there?"

"Oh, please. Yes, Dick, I'm Bev," I flippantly replied still playing along as if it were Marcus. I opened the door with a silly grin on my face only to be shocked not to find Marcus but some guy with dark hair and a moustache. I don"t know who was more startled, me or Dick.

I had my makeup on, but I had just washed my hair and put it up in a towel. I was wearing Wendell's big jersey, which was at least two or three sizes too big for me and came down to my knees. I felt so silly standing there like that.

"Are you Bev?" he asked.

"Uh, yes, yes I am." I told him.

He grinned at my outfit and tried not to laugh, "Elvis is out in the car, and he'd like for you to come out and see him."

About this time Barbie had come out of the bathroom. "Who are you talking to, Beverly Jane?"

I was standing there staring at Dick trying to comprehend what he had just said to me. "This is Dick Groeb, he's Elvis's bodyguard and says Elvis is out in the car and wants to see me."

Barb marched across the room to the sliding door and opened the drapes, "Oh shit, oh damn, oh fuck, he's really out there! He just waved at me. I don't believe this!"

I don't know what shocked me more: what she was telling me or what she had just said. Barbie didn't usually talk like that. Dick was laughing. I stood there in utter disbelief.

Dick brought me back to reality by saying, "Bev, do you think that you could get dressed and come on out to the car? Elvis wants to talk to you."

"Uh, yes, it'll take me a few minutes, but I'll be there." He snickered a little at my statement that it would only take me a few minutes because he could tell I had obviously just washed my hair, and it was probably soaking wet. He said he'd tell Elvis and proceeded down the hall.

I closed the door as Barb closed the drapes. She had tears streaming down her face. I'm not sure if it was the surprise of seeing Elvis or the feeling of satisfaction for me having actually made it happen. I hugged her and told her to give me the hairdryer quick!

I was getting dressed when I heard a knock at the door again. As I headed towards the door, the phone rang. I grabbed it up in such a hurry I nearly hit myself in the side of the head. "Hello, hello," I practically yelled into the phone.

"Well hello, you, this is Joe Esposito calling."

"Oh Joe, I'm sorry. I didn't mean to sound so rude."

"That's okay, Bev, have you heard from Elvis?" he asked with a smile in his voice.

"Heard from him? He's sitting outside my window!"

Joe laughed and said, "Well have fun, baby."

"Thanks, Joe" I muttered. I hung up the phone as there was another knock on the door. I asked, "Who is it?"

This voice asked, "Are you going to make me stay in the hall all night?"

My mouth flew open. I looked at Barb in disbelief as she blurted out, "That's Elvis! I would recognize that voice anywhere."

I couldn't help myself. I squealed, "Oh no! It can't be."

"Bev, I don't like standing in the hall like this," Elvis sounded a little irritated.

Barb made a mad dash for the bathroom. I pulled open the door and thought I was going to faint right there in the doorway. I didn't and somehow gained my composure and said, "Do come in, Elvis." (I could not believe this; Elvis Presley outside my door!! Dear Lord, this can't be true.) He had on a khaki-colored, caped coat trimmed in chocolate brown, with khaki slacks and a yellow silk-looking shirt. Elvis smiled as he came into the room. He was probably somewhat relieved to no longer be standing in the hallway.

Elvis walked across the room and sat down in a chair by the table. As he passed my bed, he threw a small black pouch onto the bed. I was surprised and curious as to what it might be. I apologized about taking so long, but I told him I had just washed my hair and it was taking much longer to get ready than I had originally thought. He also removed his sunglasses and tossed them into my suitcase that lay open on a table by my bed. That morning Barbie had stuck the cover of *People* on the side of my suitcase with a picture of Elvis when he turned 40. I was so glad I had pulled it off when we came into the room. I mean, how like a teeny bopper that would have looked! The picture was still in my suitcase, just not taped to the side of it. Thank God!

I started to sit on the bed, forgetting about the little black pouch and nearly sitting on it. "Heck of a way to lose weight, Hon, get your ass shot off." I nearly missed the bed and ended up on the floor, fortunately, I caught myself with my arm and didn't fall. I picked up the pouch and handed it to him. It was obviously a handgun. "I can't be too careful," he said so matter-of-factly. "Tell me about this flight of yours I was on."

I told Elvis it was from Memphis to Los Angeles and that we'd had a terrific time together. I reminded him he had written me a note, which I then handed to him. "Don't think we were bad; I loved it. A passenger." I am sure this sounded a little peculiar out of context as to when he had written it. He cast those gorgeous eyes my way and asked, "What did we do?"

"You men are all alike. One night, and you forget all about it," I jokingly responded.

His comment astonished me, "Believe me, I wouldn't have forgotten you." I was so embarrassed and pleased at the same time; partly by my flippant remark but also by his statement. I told him he had kissed me. "Is that all?" he grinned as he asked.

"I mean, Elvis, we were on an airplane with passengers," I replied smiling. He was just enjoying this too much.

Barbie finally came into the room looking like a contestant in the Miss America Pageant. Every hair was curled perfectly and in place and her makeup was gorgeous. She looked great, and I hated her. There I sat with my hair still damp, looking like a drowned rat. Seriously, Barb did look beautiful.

We three talked about Mississippi and this and that. Elvis talked about his new airplane, and I asked if he would have trouble getting fuel. (There was a fuel crisis at the time. Duh, I am a blonde!) Barb said "Bev, he could probably buy American Airlines if he wanted to." Oh what a dumb thing I had just said, and how I wished I could take it back.

I asked him if he had a Stewardess, and he said he did. Then he mentioned he needed one for his other plane, so I suggested he hire me. Elvis said, "No way, Honey. I'd never get off the airplane; I could see it all now - 15,000 people waiting and me getting off the airplane with a big ole hard-on." You could have knocked me to the floor when he said that. I was totally caught off guard. I didn't know whether to be flattered or shocked or both.

Elvis didn't seem to be the same man I had had on my flight seven years ago, but then of course, he wasn't. I thought I preferred the shy, somewhat insecure man I had met in 1968 to this guy. I realized his life had changed a bunch for him too, getting a divorce and all. Still I was so surprised he said that to me.

We kept telling Elvis we couldn't believe he was really there. I told him I had seen him at Lake Tahoe, and then I did the most embarrassing thing I had ever done in my entire life, something I will never forget. I told Elvis my friend and I had gone to see a young performer across the hall from Elvis one night, and this performer mentioned we were all probably there because we hadn't been able to get into see "the man across the hall," meaning Elvis. So this performer said he was going to give us his impersonation of Elvis. I told Elvis and Barb they turned the lights down, and the young guy pulled his collar up and turned his back to the audience. When the lights came back on, he raised his left arm in the air and made a funny "Uh, huh" noise before he started to sing.

I was mocking the whole scene, and Elvis burst out laughing. I wanted to die for the third time that night. Elvis asked me if I could repeat that "Uh, huh" thing for him. I put my head down and said, "Dear Lord, I still can't believe I did it the first time." What was wrong with me? He grinned from ear to ear, and I could tell he was having so much fun at my expense.

The phone rang, and it was Bob calling to tell me they were a little behind at the TV station. I said, "Guess who is here, Bob?" (He had taken me by Elvis's house earlier in the month, and I had gotten a big kick out of telling him that one day I would drive up to the gates of Graceland, and they would open and Elvis would be inside with open arms waiting just for me. Bob, of course, shook his head and said, "Yeah, right Bev.")

"Oh, I guess Elvis is there with you, huh?" Bob said.

"Well, actually he is" I said with a gigantic smile on my face.

"Bev, I swear I knew if anyone could get to Elvis, you could. Have fun and call me next time you're in Memphis."

"Will do," I replied.

Elvis looked at me kind of funny, and then he asked, "So what do you do? Call and make dates with guys and whoever shows up, that's who you go out with?"

"Excuse me, Mr. Presley, I have been trying to get a hold of you all month and couldn't. I was not about to sit in my room waiting for you to call." Barbie nearly fell off her perch on top of the dresser beside Elvis. She couldn't believe I was talking to him like that.

Elvis laughed and threw a grin my way, "Well it so happens that a bunch of us are going to go see a movie tonight..." and then he stopped mid-sentence. I sat there with baited breath, and the room got very quiet as I sat there waiting to hear what he would say next.

He looked over at me and said, "About that movie..." But he stopped again.

I finally told him, "If you're going to ask me to the movies, you had better ask me to go." He winked at Barbie, and I told him his time was up.

"Do you want to go to the movie with me?" Elvis asked.

I said, "No thanks, I'm busy," and burst out laughing. He looked so surprised by my response. I said, "Gotcha! Yes, I would like to go to the movie with you."

Elvis told me he planned to go back to his house to do a workout, and then would have someone pick me up. (The ornery side of me wanted so much to tell him if we spent time together, he wouldn't need a workout. But I controlled myself and didn't say what I wanted to say because I didn't want to give him the wrong idea.)

Barbie asked him if we could take a picture with him. He said any other time he would be glad to, but he hadn't been feeling too good, and he would rather not. But he would be glad to write her a note if she would get him a piece of paper So she did, and he wrote, "To Barb, Love Elvis Presley." She still has it.

I asked Elvis where my souvenir was. He leaned forward and started to kiss me as he was walking towards the door, but he missed my mouth and caught me half on the mouth and half on the cheek. I looked at him and said, "I sure hope your aim improves."

Elvis burst out laughing and said, "I'll work on that." He started out the door when I realized he had left his sunglasses in my suitcase. I grabbed them and gave them to him. (A tragic mistake my older son, Josh, has reminded me of for years. I read that a pair of his sunglasses sold for $35,000 at an auction. Silly me, but I never would have sold them anyway.) Elvis thanked me and left.

I turned around, and Barb was standing there shaking her head. "I don't believe you. I do not believe the way you talk to him," she said. I raised my arms up and ran around the room singing "If they could see me now." It felt so good to know I had actually been able to get Elvis Presley to come to my room, and I was going to go out with him. "I hate you, Beverly Jane, I hate you with all of my heart!" Barbie said, half laughing.

"You can come too, Barbie," I told her.

"Oh, no, he didn't say would you like to go to the movies with me, Barbara, or with me and Bev? No, hell no, he didn't." she stated.

"Are you sure you don't want to come? This is your last chance," I half-heartedly asked her; hoping she would say no.

"No way, but you had better tell me all the details, or we aren't friends anymore," she demanded.

"All of them?" I smartly asked.

"All of them!" she said.

"We'll see, Barbie Jean, we'll see. They just might be x-rated."

She laughed out loud. "Well I sincerely hope they are for your sake."

"Why, Barbara Jean, whatever are you saying?" We both cracked up laughing.

Barbie and I went out so she could grab a bite to eat. I couldn't eat because I was way too nervous. As we came into our room, the phone was ringing, and it was Elvis. He asked me if I minded coming to his home earlier than we had planned because he had decided he didn't want to go to the gym after all. I looked at Barbie and jumped up and down as I tried to act all cool by telling Elvis that would be fine with me.

Dick arrived at 10:15 and drove me to Graceland. There were all sorts of people around the gates trying for a glimpse of Elvis. I couldn't resist my "fifteen minutes of fame" and started waving at everyone. I am sure Dick thought I was some kind of a nut, but it was fun with the fans trying to get a glimpse of me and wondering who I was. We drove around to the back of the house. Inside, I met Charlie Hodge and his date, and some other guy and his date. I'm usually very good with names, but I was so nervous. I could not believe all of the different women waiting there - tall, short, blonde, brunette, old and young - to go to the movie with Elvis and his "Memphis Mafia."

Dick took me up the stairs to a room with two huge leather-covered doors. When he opened the doors, Elvis Presley was sitting in the middle of a king size bed in black silk pajamas. Uh oh, I thought to myself, I really gave him the wrong idea. Elvis patted the edge of the bed, and I sat down, feeling uncomfortable. He told Dick to tell him when the movie theater was ready, and Dick left the room closing the double doors behind him.

Elvis motioned for me to sit on the bed beside him, so I took off my shoes and climbed in. He told me he hoped I didn't feel uncomfortable (no, not much!) being in his bed but that he really wasn't up to par yet from his latest trip to the hospital. He thought we could watch this show on television titled *The Sex Symbol.*

I grinned and asked, "Is it about you?"

Elvis laughed and said, "No BABY, I'm the KING! How would you like to go through life being called the KING?"

I looked right into his eyes and said, "I'd much prefer to be called the Queen." He burst out laughing, and I didn't feel quite as nervous anymore.

I got under the covers, and he turned on the TV. It was supposed to be about Marilyn Monroe, and Connie Stevens was playing the part. Elvis said he had met her and told me she was pretty but had a huge butt. I snickered, then asked him, "Who was the one person you didn't enjoy kissing in your movies?" He told me it was Mary Tyler Moore. He said they just didn't do well together in that department. I didn't ask who he preferred to kiss most because I figured it was Ann Margaret, considering their relationship.

We talked about some of his movies. He shared with me how much he hated making them because they all had the same exact plot: Elvis meets the girl, Elvis gets the girl, they break up and then Elvis has to get the girl back. In the meantime, sing twelve songs. He told me he was so unhappy with some of his movies that the studio had actually hired a shrink to come and follow him around while he was filming. Elvis said this little, bitty, squirrelly guy with dark thick glasses turned up behind him everywhere ringing some stupid bell. At one point, Elvis said he had had it with the shrink, so he jumped up out of his seat, raised his arms, threw them about, and started growling at the guy. Elvis said the shrink never came back. The movie was *Harem Scarem*. He looked over at me, and I kind of rolled my eyes. "Yeah, I know it was bad," he stated.

I told Elvis it was a shame he never got to do a serious movie because I imagined he was a fine actor. He told me he was being considered for Kris Kristofferson's role in *A Star Is Born* with Barbra Streisand. But when he and Barbra met, they didn't hit it off at all. She made some reference to him about being an aging rock 'n' roll star, and Elvis ended up telling her he didn't want to work with some Jewish princess. Based on his tone in talking about her, I would really be surprised if he actually had slept with her as she is claiming in her book.

Elvis also said he had been offered the role of Sonny Corleone in *The Godfather*, but Colonel Parker wouldn't hear of that.

We talked about family, mostly mine. I told him I had called my Mom to tell her I was going to Graceland. Then I said, "Oh, Mom said to tell you Hi." Elvis smiled and told me to tell her "Hi" back. That was just too cute. I also told him about my brother and sister.

Then we got on the subject of him not being able to go anywhere like a normal person. Elvis said he wished he could just go to a football game or a restaurant and have a dinner without being mobbed. He told me not to get him wrong, that he was so grateful for the blessings he had in his life, but he had had to turn nocturnal to be able to have any kind of a life. I said I understood because it was close to 10:30 p.m. at night, and the sidewalk was packed with fans hoping for a glimpse of him.

Elvis grinned and told me he wanted to show me something. I looked at him with the dumbest face possible, and he laughed and said, "No, not that." I snickered. He pushed a button and showed me the surveillance system he had that could view any spot on Graceland. Elvis said, "I saw you drive in." Yet another opportunity to be embarrassed that night. I put my head in my hands and turned a shade of crimson. Then I defended my actions by saying, "Hey, mister, you get to do that all of the time. It was a totally unique experience for me and I had a ball doing it."

"I could tell," Elvis said. (All I had done all night was do and say embarrassing things in front of him. I bet he wished he had asked Barbie instead of me to come over here. But I am glad he didn't. Maybe it was refreshing to see a grown woman make a total fool of herself; although I was sure a lot of women did just that when it came to E.P.)

I tried not to get caught as I looked around his bedroom. There were several pictures on shelves, which I think were mostly of Lisa Marie and maybe some of Linda Thompson. There was a sign on the television that read, "Yeah, though I walk through the valley of death, I fear no evil, for I am the meanest son of a bitch in the valley." I was kind of surprised by that, but maybe Elvis was having a "tough guy" day when he ordered it. To my right was a dresser or cabinet with a jewelry box on top of it. All sorts of chains were hanging out of it, and it was so full it couldn't be closed. I thought how I would LOVE to look in that box, but I didn't want to do anything to make Elvis think I wanted anything from him like so many people did. Elvis had told Barbie and me about people asking him for cars, medical payments, donations, and jobs. He said there were a lot of folks he was able to help, but he received requests daily for monetary help in one way or the other. As much as I would have loved to have seen his jewelry, I was not about to ask. I could see into what seemed to be a closet, and there were tons of clothes in there.

I started to get a headache because I hadn't eaten all day, but I hated to say anything. Still I didn't want to ruin my evening with Elvis either, so I asked him for an Excedrin. He got on the phone and called his housekeeper who brought me the biggest bottle of Excedrin I had ever seen with a glass of milk. I was a little uncomfortable with her seeing me in Elvis's bed, but I was sure I wasn't the first, nor would I be the last. (At least I had all my clothes on.)

Elvis and I just talked and talked. We didn't seem to run out of things to say. He seemed interested in me, which made me feel good. I told him about my marriage and how hard it was to leave. I didn't feel like telling him about Wendell because I didn't want to admit I had had an affair, and I sure didn't want to start crying.

When the phone rang, I nearly jumped out of my skin. It was Dick, and Elvis put his hand over the mouthpiece and said, "Bev, I invited you over here to see a movie, and I will be glad to take you to the movie. I would prefer to just stay here and spend the evening with you if that is okay with you, but I will take you to the movie if you want to go."

I had an immediate vision of all of those women downstairs waiting for Elvis to make his grand entrance, and I thought, I'm not an idiot, why in the world would I share him with all of those women when I can have him all to myself? No Brainer "Elvis, that is fine with me. I really didn't want to see a movie tonight anyway."

He told Dick we wouldn't be joining them, so to go ahead. Elvis put the phone in the cradle and grinned the most wicked grin imaginable. "Don't you think they're all going nuts wondering what we are doing up here?"

I laughed and laughed. "I bet they are, Elvis, I just bet they are."

He asked me if I wanted to slip into something more comfortable. I kind of gave him that "Uh, huh" look and he said, "Well, you have all of your clothes on, and I'm sitting here in my pajamas."

"Okay, but you gotta promise to be good," I said to him. A mischievous grin came over his face once again, but he didn't promise. Thank goodness!

Elvis pointed to a dresser. I got out of his bed and picked out a pair of powder blue silk pajamas. I went into the adjoining bathroom, which was obviously Priscilla's because it was so feminine. When I put on Elvis's PJs, I realized I wasn't quite sure I could keep the bottoms up because they were so large. I didn't want to embarrass him by saying anything, so I twisted the waistband around a couple of times and stuffed them into the elastic band at my waist.

I came back into the bedroom and noticed my modeling brochure on his nightstand. I asked him if he liked the brochure. He told me, "If I hadn't liked it, you wouldn't be here."

"Cute, Elvis, real cute; do you have a favorite picture?" I asked him. He told me he was especially fond of the one of me lying on the floor in a two-piece dress. I crawled into bed. I didn't know why I hadn't noticed before, but there were two televisions on the ceiling. I was a little surprised, and when I pointed up at them, Elvis said they were for when he just wanted to lie in bed and watch TV That way he didn't have to sit up.

Elvi's Favorite Picture
Photo by Philip Lowry

Elvis told me he wanted to show me something, and I immediately asked, "Are you trying that again?" He shook his head, laughing to himself, and got a different remote.

For whatever reason, I'll never know, Elvis showed me the Zapruder film of the day JFK was killed. I was shocked. He got out of bed and sat on the floor, telling me to watch how the policemen pulled back their motorcycles as they turned onto Commerce Street. "It was to allow for all of those shooters to get good aim," he told me. When I asked if he didn't think Lee Harvey Oswald had killed JFK by himself, Elvis told me he really knew who had killed JFK but he couldn't tell me, because, "if I tell you who really did it, I'd have to kill ya," he said smiling. Then he was grabbing his throat the way JFK had done in the film.

I suddenly felt sick at my stomach and had this overwhelming feeling of fear. It dawned on me that one day Elvis would be gone too, just like JFK. I don't know what came over me, but tears started to roll down my face. Elvis looked at me rather oddly and asked if the film was upsetting me. I told him I had been a real big JFK supporter so it was kind of upsetting. That wasn't the real truth, but I didn't want to tell Elvis I had a bad feeling he wouldn't be on this earth much longer himself. He apologized and turned it off. I told him maybe I was just a little overly emotional and tired since we had started our trip early that morning and had had multiple stops all day.

Then Elvis tossed a leather-bound badge onto my lap. It was a DEA badge with his name on it. I do believe it is the one President Nixon had given him. A picture of them with the badge showed up on the news and in a lot of papers. Elvis seemed so proud of it. Apparently he collected police, sheriff, and other law enforcement badges from all over the country.

Elvis got back into bed. He put his head down on the pillow and closed his eyes. I wasn't sure what I was supposed to do. I had told him I absolutely had to leave by 6:00 a.m. in order to get back to the hotel to get ready for my trip. There was a clock on his nightstand, but I couldn't see it so I put my head on the pillow next to his, facing him, and closed my eyes. We had laid there for a few minutes when I felt him move. Elvis put his hand on my cheek and kissed me gently on the lips. Although I wanted to smart off and say I was glad his aim had improved, I didn't want to ruin the tenderness of the moment. I kissed him back, and then we kept kissing each other for what seemed like forever, although I wasn't sure because I don't think I was really in my body at that time.

This was just too unreal! I loved that Elvis Presley was kissing me. Although I knew he had kissed thousands of other women, right now it didn't matter because he was kissing ME. His kisses got a little more passionate, and I wasn't sure where we were going with this. I wasn't sure I really wanted to have sex with him: I did and I didn't. I was afraid if I did, I would never see him again, and if I didn't, I might never get a second chance.

Elvis made the decision for both of us as I could feel my temperature rising (just like the lyrics in his song "Burning Love" - okay, I know that's corny but it was appropriate!) We were both getting turned on, our breathing had definitely intensified, and the next thing I knew he had removed my pajama bottoms and panties. I made up my mind I was going for it, so I removed his pajama bottoms too. Elvis pulled me on top of him and kissed me deeply. When my long blonde hair fell onto his face, he caught it in his hands and pushed it back as he leaned forward kissing me passionately, and then suddenly we became one.

We made love. Actually, we really weren't making love because we weren't two people in love, but saying we had sex just didn't seem appropriate for the tenderness of the moment. It was so wonderful! After seeing Elvis perform and projecting more sex appeal than any other man on the face of the earth, I had expected our lovemaking to be more like with Wendell - consumed with passion, sweat, and heavy-breathing - but it wasn't. Elvis was so gentle, so warm and tender. ("Love Me Tender" came to mind. Ok, ok, so maybe that is pushing it a little, but it was what I was thinking.)

I really enjoyed this gentle side of Elvis. We held each other afterwards, and I put my head on his shoulder. It was very quiet, and then he looked down at me, held my chin in his hand and sang a portion of "The First Time Ever I Saw Your Face." I was so deeply touched. Elvis had the most gorgeous voice in the world! I snuggled up next to him, his arms encircled me, and I held on tight. "We're going to have to get you a barrette next time for that long hair of yours," he said ever so softly. (Next time? I was overjoyed hearing what he had just said to me. I hoped there would be a next time.)

That was one of the best days, oops, nights of my life! We kissed and kissed, and then the phone rang. It was time for me to get ready to go. Oh, damn it, where's a magic time machine when you need one? I wanted so much to relive this night over and over again.

I had to go into the bathroom to put my clothes on before Dick got there because I didn't want him to see me in Elvis's pajamas. I had laid my clothes beside a television in the bathroom, and as I took off the pajamas, I placed them on top of the TV. When I went to lift the pajamas off the television after I dressed, a small, gold-colored plaque fell onto the floor. On it were the words "Owner Elvis Presley" I thought it odd, but since it had come loose, I just put it in my shoe and went back into Elvis's room. I knew I should be ashamed, but I took it anyway. My main fear was that one of the sharp edges would cut into my foot and I'd start bleeding into my shoe. Thank goodness that didn't happen.

Elvis was sitting up in bed. He opened his arms, so I leaned in for him to hold me one last time, and he gently kissed me on the forehead.

Seconds later, it wasn't Dick but Charlie Hodge who showed up. I thought I had to act flippant because I didn't really want to leave, but I didn't want to cry in front of Elvis. I said something stupid like, "Thanks for the souvenir."

Elvis looked at me and quietly said, "You've got the best souvenir I have to offer; my seal of approval. And I'm really picky about my women." I just squeezed him, gave him a peck on those soft lips, and told him to get some rest and take care of himself. He said he would, and then he smiled, and hugged and kissed me back.

Charlie took me downstairs and through the kitchen. An older lady in a nurse's uniform was making coffee. She smiled warmly, introduced herself as Marion Cocke, and asked if I wanted a cup of coffee. I told her no thanks and started to walk away. I stopped in my tracks, walked back to her, and asked if she would do me a favor. Marion was obviously puzzled but said she would if she could. "Take good care of Elvis for me," I said.

I actually had to choke back the tears as the words stuck in my throat because I had that funny feeling again. I learned a long time ago that when

I had one of those overwhelming feelings, I really needed to pay heed to it. If I didn't, something usually ended up turning out badly. I was scared this feeling was not a good one, that this time it was even stronger than the one I had earlier in the evening about Elvis not being here much longer.

"Of course I will" she replied, looking at me rather oddly.

"Thanks, Marion," I told her as I walked out the door with Charlie.

I walked into my hotel room and Barbie yelled, "Smile if you got some!" I burst out laughing then told her I didn't have time for her foolishness because I had to get ready for pickup. On the ride to the airport, the driver was all abuzz with the fact that someone had spotted Elvis Presley's Stutz Bearcat parked in the hotel parking lot, and rumor had it he was there to pick up some stewardess.

Barbie chirped up, "Oh yeah, buddy, that is the truth. He was there to get my best friend sitting right here. Right, Bev?" The driver turned around for a look and the co-pilot told him to keep his eyes on the road.

I looked over at our F/O named Rex and asked him if the crew thought I was nuts. He looked at me and said, "Bev, we all have dreams."

I sort of lowered my eyes and then looked back at him and replied, "Yes, but Lordy, mine just came true."

I was the talk of the Dallas base. Barbie told someone, Marcus told some of his friends, the pilots told their version, and word traveled everywhere. I was tickled in a way. A couple of the pilots asked me to ask Elvis to get cars for them. Yeah right, you bet I was going to do that - never in a million years! One Captain even took to calling me Mrs. Presley, which I loved. I was so surprised that some of my flying partners asked me horribly personal questions about Elvis, none of which I dignified with answers. That was a personal night for me, and I never told anyone the details about my night with Elvis until I wrote this. Yes, I know he spent many nights with lots of women, but no one can ever take those memories of that incredible man and our night together away from me.

I only talked to Elvis one more time. He told me he was getting ready to go on tour, and he would call me when he returned. He called me late one night when I was out with friends, but I couldn't find my keys and just heard the phone ringing and ringing. When I spoke to Marion a few days later, she told me it was Elvis who called me that night, and he wanted me to go to Vegas with him. I could have screamed!!!! (I did not have a voice message system, and caller ID had not been invented yet. Damn!)

I am sad to say, sometime thereafter, he met Ginger Alden. (If you read her book ELVIS AND GINGER you will read parts of her story that are just like mine. But I assure you, everything I wrote happened just the way I wrote it long before he met her.)

Marion and I developed a friendship, so when I called, I'd talk to her to see how Elvis was doing. Occasionally, I would send him a card or letter and she would tell me what he said about it. Elvis would come into her room to read what I had sent him and told her he loved the way I treated him like other people and made him laugh. He said I had the best sense of humor.

I had mentioned to Marion I doubted if he even remembered what I looked like. Marion tested him by saying, "It's been so long since I've seen, Bev. I don't really remember what she looks like." She said Elvis turned to face her, smiled, and described me to a "t," although he added he wished I hadn't reminded him so much of Linda Thompson. Marion agreed that Linda and I did resemble each other, but only in stature, not in personality. I felt sad that I reminded Elvis of someone he had already had a long-standing affair with, and I wished it could have been me. But having a long-lasting relationship with someone like Elvis was just about as impossible as me ever hoping to have been the only woman in Wendell's life. It was never going to happen. Marion said Elvis had taken a trip to Dallas to look at some exercise equipment and tried to reach me. I checked my schedule to see what day he had been in Dallas and found I was off flying somewhere. It would have been awesome to have been there for him, but I think having been with Elvis all by myself that one night was one of the greatest things that ever happened to me.

On my flight that night back in 1968, I had fulfilled a dream of meeting Elvis and having him kiss me like he had kissed Juliet Prowse in *G. I. Blues*. I was doubly fortunate enough to have spent an evening with him alone, which I am sure was something women all over the world would have loved to have done. I was so happy and felt blessed by having been with Elvis twice. He was a wonderful man, and I will always get a warm feeling when I see some of the facial expressions in his movies that were reserved for me alone that one night. His kisses were all mine, and for that magical evening from September 24 into September 25, no one else mattered to him but me. What more could a girl ask for?

I wrote this in my diary at the end of 1975:

This will be remembered as one of the worst years of my life. Wendell's death was so tragic! Why did it have to end on an airplane? He was so young, and I miss him with all of my heart!!!! I miss his voice, his laugh, his kiss, his hugs; I miss everything about him. I doubt if I will ever have a relationship like that again with any other man. I loved him, but I couldn't tell him because I was afraid I would lose him. And then I lost him anyway, without ever telling him how much he meant to me."

I guess my marriage officially ended this year too. I moved out of our beautiful home away from the man I thought I would spend the rest of my life with. Leaving Derek was so difficult. Wendell's death made me realize just how short life was and that I didn't want to go on living a lie. Derek and I were just hurting each other too much!!! He wasn't happy with me, and I wasn't content with my life with him. I had hoped our lives would straighten out, and I guess they did, but separately. Our marriage had some wonderful times with such hope for our future, but we hadn't been close for over two years. I'd always love Derek, maybe because I left him. I just didn't want us to hurt each other anymore.

The highlight of the year was spending time with Elvis Aron Presley. It was a dream come true! Me. Beverly Golden Schoenmann, tallest girl in the class, hillbilly, High School graduate, was able to meet Elvis the man, not the superstar. I made him laugh and was fortunate to share his tenderness, even for only one night. He was someone so beyond my reach, but somehow I was able to touch him, if only for a short time. I regret I didn't have the opportunity to get to know him better, but I will always be thankful for the memories we shared that evening.

Lord, help me grow from these experiences. I want to do your will. I have regrets, let me learn from them and go forward. Let me become a better person and follow the path you have planned for me. Please, Lord, I feel so lost.

I'm glad 1975 will never be again.

DEAR LORD, WHERE DO I GO FROM HERE?

The family of
Elvis Aron Presley
acknowledges with grateful
appreciation your kind expression
of sympathy.

Sympathy Notes

On January 1, 1976, I got a call from Derek. "I called to tell my separated wife that I'm filing for a divorce."

No "Happy New Year" greeting, just those words. I was expecting it, and I was sure he delivered them with a little encouragement from his parents. I honestly didn't blame them.

It was time to face facts that we were no longer going forward together in this life. I couldn't help myself though and felt numb after listening to him read the divorce papers. I just never dreamed I would ever be a divorced woman. My parents had been together for over thirty-one years. I thought I would be like them and be with Derek forever.

I went downstairs to the kitchen, got a glass of milk, then sat in the front room bawling so loudly my landlady came over to see if I was hurt. I told her I wasn't hurt physically, just emotionally. I shared with her that I was so confused. I would always love Derek, but we had been doing nothing but hurting each other for quite some time now, and I didn't want to go on living like that. I didn't want us to end up hating each other. I didn't tell her about Wendell; she was in her late sixties and I couldn't expect her to understand I had had an affair and lost someone I loved very much. She fixed me some tea and sat with me for about an hour. I thanked her and went next door to tell Barbie and Mike about Derek's call.

I moped around for days. I thought what Derek and I were about to do was the right thing, but still I wasn't sure what had happened and how we had grown so far apart. I called my folks and told them, but they weren't surprised. I know that in some ways, they hoped we would stay married, but in others, they thought it was best for both of us. I felt pretty sure Derek's Mom wouldn't miss me, but maybe Derek, Sr. would - but I wasn't even sure of that.

I felt depression creeping back inside me. I didn't want to go there, but there were many nights I cried myself to sleep. Barbie and Carol tried to keep me busy doing stuff with them, shopping, running around and eating dinner, but they knew I was pretty miserable and feeling like a complete failure.

Maybe I was a complete failure. I knew our breakup wasn't entirely my fault; it was both of ours. We just grew apart and obviously decided we wanted different things out of life.

Again my saving grace was flying. I was able to leave most of my heartaches at the apartment and just enjoy being a Flight Attendant.

I truly loved my job! There were so many different types of people to meet. I had been flying ten years, and there were still places I wanted to see. While I had imagined I would be seeing them with Derek, like our great trips to New Zealand and Switzerland, I realized I would more than likely be going to these places alone.

I kept hoping something would trigger in Derek and me to restart the flame, and we might somehow get things back on track. It didn't happen. I just couldn't get back the feelings I had for him when we first met. We had hurt each other way too much, too many times.

Derek called and asked me to come to Tulsa. Although I was reluctant, there was the matter of selling our home and packing up my personal things from the house. It felt so weird to go to our home after he had officially filed for the divorce.

I found it rather odd that Derek never asked me why I moved to Dallas. About a year before Wendell died, I came home from a trip and Derek was livid! He was so angry with me he couldn't even talk. I took one look at Derek and asked him if he had read my diary. When he didn't answer, I knew he had. While I wasn't sure exactly what he had read, I knew it must have been pretty awful for Derek to have had that much rage towards me. I honestly didn't blame him, especially if he had read something I had written about Wendell. Although I never got really descriptive in what I put in my diary, I definitely talked about how much Wendell had meant to me for those three years. I almost wished Derek had told me what he had read, but we had so many issues we never even talked about.

Derek and I talked to a friend about listing our home for sale. It was strange sleeping in the same bed with Derek and yet feeling like two strangers. When I thought of that Frank Sinatra song, "Strangers in the Night," I thought of Derek and me. I would feel like an empty shell when it was time to go back to Dallas because we never resolved anything while I was in Tulsa. We talked, but only at each other, not really with each other. We had a strange link – we had trouble letting go, but we both knew we had to.

Bobby Bernhardt

I kept in touch with my buddy, Bob Bernhardt. I went to Boston quite a few times, and we went out to eat and chat. He really was a great friend. We even showed up together at my former roommate, Jeannie and Richard's house one evening. (Yes, she chose Richard the hairdresser over Jerry, the other guy.) I don't think they realized Bob and I had kept in touch all of these years. It was fun for Bob and me to have this secret.

I told Bob about my impending divorce. He said, "Bev-a-lee, why do you think I never married? It would be just too painful to get divorced. So why not just have relationships?" I guessed in his own way of thinking, Bob was right. (Even though he did marry, but that was years later.)

Derek and I continued to talk to one another - he would come to Dallas at times, and I would go to Tulsa - but we never talked about stopping the divorce. At times when I would see him, I wanted to grab him and hold him and tell him we shouldn't do this thing, but I couldn't. I wanted Derek to tell me he didn't want to live without me, but he didn't.

I was pleased Mom had gotten on my flight in San Diego; she had been visiting my sister Charmaine, whose husband Randy had joined the Navy. Several times when I had layovers, I would spend the day with my sis and my nephew. He was such a beautiful little boy with blonde hair and blue eyes. I imagined he looked like what my children with Derek would have looked like.

On this particular flight, Mom was seated by Paul Schoelen, the owner of a company called Strawberry Plant Mom told him he needed to hire me to work for his showroom at the Dallas Apparel Market. Their clothes were so much nicer than Jarrell. Paul was the husband of the designer and gave me Eddie Nelson's number to call at Market and tell him to hire me. Paul laughed and said he would put in a good word for me, especially since I had the nerve to have my Mom "pimping" for me on flights.

Lee Majors

All Mom could really do on that flight was swoon over Lee Majors who was on board. I asked Mr. Majors if Barbie and I could take a picture with him, and he agreed. Mom went over and told Lee's traveling partner to get up because she wanted a good picture with Lee too. Then she grabbed Lee's arm and put it around her shoulders and asked me to take the picture. She told him "I'm old. I don't have as much time as these girls do, and I want a good picture." Lee laughed and so did Paul. Mom was really something because she had no fear, and I loved that about her.

I met Eddie Nelson when I got back to Dallas, and he hired me. I worked hard for Eddie, who was a real taskmaster and couldn't stand for anyone to sit. We had to be constantly doing something. We would be straightening the line of clothes, cleaning the tables, or rechecking the order forms, as long as we were doing something. I could have made a lot more money flying overtime, but this was a change and it was fun to play dress up for five days.

I kept in touch with Shirley and Randy almost weekly. I just felt such closeness to them that I almost felt I needed to call. Maybe I was afraid they would forget me, but I didn't really think they would.

Shirley told me the Kentucky Colonels were retiring Wendell's jersey on February 15 in Louisville and asked me if I wanted to go with the family to the event. Of course I did. I met Shirley, Janell, Berlin, Bernell, and Glen in Louisville, and it was such a sad, sad evening! I kept expecting to see Wendell come down the court. It was so empty there without him.

The owner, John Y. Brown, gave Shirley and the family a beautiful framed picture of Wendell in his Colonel's uniform. If only he hadn't traded Wendell, he wouldn't have been in New York, and he might not have died in that plane crash. Part of me wanted to sock Mr. Brown right in the kisser, but of course I didn't. Good Lord, Wendell was so gorgeous!!! We all shed buckets of tears.

My friend Jim Henderson came to Dallas to see me. We had a great time out at dinner where he told me he was single. I told him about me and Derek He said he wasn't surprised to hear that but was sorry because he wanted me to be happy. He really was a good friend and someone I enjoyed being with. But I didn't really figure we would have any kind of a future together judging by the way other Flight Attendants swooned over him. I guess I'm just a sucker for good-looking men.

Randy and his friend, Randy Becknell, drove up to Dallas to surprise me for a few days, which I wasn't very happy about. There are some surprises I don't like, and this was one of them, but I was glad to see Randy.

I fixed Randy and Randy breakfast, then we just sat around and talked. Later that evening we all went to the Easy Way restaurant for some chicken fried steak. (That always sounded so weird to me. It really wasn't chicken, it was actually ground meat. So why did they call it chicken fried steak? That never made any sense to me, but it is a very popular Texas dinner.)

Carol and Rog

I had to fly the next day, and they had interviews on Monday for jobs in Dallas. I felt a little uneasy about the thought of Randy moving to Dallas on a full-time basis. I did feel sad when Randy left but asked him not to surprise me again. If he had told me they were coming, I could have trip traded and gottn some time off to spend with them.

Carol had met a guy she really cared for named Roger Simonds. He was a nut and so funny! I loved being around him because he would say the craziest things just to make you laugh. He was so cute, and they made the most adorable couple.

Carol had a party, and for the life of me I don't know why, but I asked Derek to go with me. Sadly the party bombed, so the four of us just hung out together and had a great time. I started doubting if I really did want to go through with this divorce. What had happened? What did we do wrong? Where did we fail each other and ourselves?

I wanted to go to Tulsa to be sure I really wanted to get divorced, but I had promised Shirley I would come to Mississippi, so I put all these questions out of my mind and hopped on an airplane. Randy was there to meet me. He was so wonderful, truly a sweetheart and so honest. He didn't play silly dating games, he told you what he felt. He wasn't ashamed to cry or to let you into his heart.

I thought I had lost my very last marble, but Randy was the most wonderful man I had met in ages. I thought I was smitten with this nineteen year old guy, but that couldn't be happening. I wouldn't let it.

La Risa, Thermon, Randy
Shirley, Tammy & Deron

I was always so at peace in Mississippi and felt like I belonged there. All of Wendell's family accepted me and actually acted like they loved me right away. His Mom Ollie Mae was so loving and sweet and such a pretty lady. His Dad Aaron was so gentle and kind. I felt close to Shirley, and her husband Thermon was so kind to me. Janell and Bernell acted like I had known them my whole life. Glen and his wife Mary were so quiet, but they always welcomed me with open arms. Berlin and Carolyn treated me so well and made me feel like part of their family. It was a feeling I hadn't really experienced since Kaki and Mary (Alphie's folks). We had so much fun cooking out and just being together. It was wonderful to catch up with everybody.

I just adored Randy. We talked about everything. but he scared the stuffing out of me. He was just a boy, and I was a grown woman, so I couldn't let myself have feelings for him. Yes, he reminded me of Wendell, but he wasn't Wendell and he wasn't like him. With no pretense about him, he was just Randy! Take him or leave him. He was going to be completely honest with you, so you had better not ask him something if you didn't want to know exactly how he felt about it because he was going to tell you.

I enjoyed spending time with Randy's little sisters, Tammy and La Risa, and with his younger brother Deron. I adored Thermon, Randy's Dad, who was so good to me from the very first time we met. This family just didn't play games. If they liked you, you knew it, and if they didn't, I was pretty sure you would have known that too.

I felt so guilty the next time I saw Derek because he looked terrible! I think he had been drinking too much. When I was in Tulsa, he actually had a fainting spell, so I was worried about him.

He had changed so many things in the house I no longer felt like I belonged there. I used to have a "Wall of Fame" in the den with my pictures with different celebrities around the fireplace. Derek had removed all of those, but I didn't blame him. I'm sure if he had a woman friend over, it would have been hard to explain to her who that woman in the pictures was. It hurt for those pictures not to be there, but Derek was moving on.

Derek was interviewing for a job in New York. Claire called me to say Derek had been there for me when I needed him (meaning, of course, my bout with depression), but now that he needed me, I wasn't there for him. I felt awful, but I couldn't go with him to New York. It just wouldn't work. We would end up hating each other, and I didn't want that to happen. She didn't like my answer, but I told her Derek would probably be better off without me.

Barbie agreed to go to Tulsa with me for a garage sale Derek and I had planned on having. It was much worse than I had ever imagined! Derek and I both took turns crying. It was so painful to sell our things to strangers and know our life together was over. When Derek went for pizza, Barb told me she had never seen two people care so much for each other and not be able to communicate. She was almost as upset as Derek and I were and asked me if we were sure we were doing the right thing. I told her I was so messed up I didn't know anything anymore. She couldn't wait to get back to Dallas, and I didn't blame her.

When it came time to leave, I felt ill. I didn't want to say good-bye to Derek because it hurt too much! I had cried buckets that weekend and he had too, but neither one of us would or could say, "Let's try again. Let's just see if we are doing the right thing."

Derek hid a note in my purse. When I read it on the plane, I broke down completely. It said "Bev, thank you from the bottom of my heart for helping me get through this weekend. It hasn't been & won't be easy for me (or you) but it certainly helps having someone. Your garage sale was a success and now cleaning & selling the house. I'm trying to keep the faith and ask God for help. You too. I love you, no matter what. Thanks Hon. We're quite a team sometimes. Derek."

Dear God, what were we doing to each other? I felt awful again. Derek had gotten the job in New York and was moving back east. I knew it was going to be hard for him to go alone. but I didn't know what I could do to help him; I just couldn't make myself go back there. I felt like I had to stay in Dallas and continue on without him. But was that the right decision for both of us?

After I got back from my trip to Tulsa, Carol and I flew a three-day trip. I told her about my horrendous weekend of unending hurt with Derek. She also asked me if I was sure I was doing the right thing, and I told her I didn't know anything anymore.

I felt like I was on an emotional roller coaster. The last time this sort of thing happened to me, I had ended up in the hospital, but I believed what Dr. Turner told me. He had said I was stronger than I thought I was and that I could handle whatever came my way, just not to make any major decisions right then. But now it was the hour of decision-making, and it looked like neither Derek nor I were stopping the divorce proceedings.

I was feeling pretty sorry for myself when one of the other flight attendants came on board. Her name was Alice Stanton, and she was similar to my former roommate Bette: petite, cute, usually bubbly, and a lot of fun. That day she looked like hell. I had flown with her before and had never, ever seen her like that. She had obviously been crying all night long. I didn't know whether to ask her what was wrong or to try and ignore the whole thing. I opted for, "What's wrong, Alice?"

She looked up at me and told me she had gone to a club in Dallas and run into her former husband. They had been married for a shorter time than Derek and me but still a fairly long time. They started talking, then dancing, drinking, and the next thing she knew he was talking like he wanted to get back together with her again. They went back to her apartment and made love. That morning when she woke up, she rolled over to find him gone and a note lying on the pillow where he had slept. She opened It, and it said, "Fooled you again, didn't I?"

I was stunned! What a total and complete jerk! My heart went out to her. Yes, Derek and I had hurt each other, but I don't think either one of us had been that cruel. I put my arms around her and told her she needed to stay in the galley this trip, and Carol and I would cover for her. Even though Carol was senior to me, I was working in First Class because Carol preferred Coach. It wasn't an easy task, but I knew how much Alice was hurting; she didn't need to be out there doing "Chins and Grins" for American Airlines when her heart was shattered. We made it through the trip and tried to be there for Alice, but she was just broken in two. I called her a couple of times to check on her..

Our job was odd because you would fly with pretty much the same crew for one whole month and usually, get pretty close, and then you might not see those people again for months or even years. There were almost

16,000 flight attendants in the system and usually a few thousand at every base. So it was not unusual to fly with so many different people. I was so thankful to have met Barbie and Carol. I don't know what I would have done without them.

When we got back from our trip, Carol asked me to go to San Francisco with her and Rog, but as much as I would have loved laughing with Rog, I just didn't feel like it.

The only time I felt really good and completely happy with someone was with Randy. I loved being with him, but didn't want to pursue a romance with him because he was so young. That was nuts, and the last time I checked the name on my driver's license, it wasn't Mrs. Robinson. Even though he was "legal," I wasn't supposed to be doing something so crazy. I was already messed up enough over losing Wendell, divorcing Derek, and not knowing which end was up.

Randy found a job with NASA and was living in an apartment in Slidell, Louisiana with his crazy friend Bill Oakley he had known for years. Every time I went to Mississippi, they would pick me up in New Orleans and take me to Shirley's house. We laughed and carried on like (I hate to say this — it's embarrassing) teenagers because we thought everything was funny.

I visited with Shirley and all of Wendell's family for a few days. When it was time to go back to Dallas, I still had a couple of days before I had to fly again, so Randy and Bill asked me to stay with them and go see the sights of New Orleans. I didn't see a problem with it. We played tourist with Bill and a gal he was dating, even going to Pat O' Brien's Club for a Hurricane; a drink that was supposed to "knock your socks off." Well, I had one, and it didn't seem to faze me, which I thought was strange since I drank infrequently. So I had another one. Well, as Randy would say on occasion, "Katy, bar the door." I got snookered!

We all went back to the apartment, and Bill's date made some screwdriver drinks. I had one and was absolutely giddy. When I went into Randy's room and fell across his bed, he jumped in right beside me and started kissing me. Next thing I knew, things went way further than I had ever thought I would allow. We had sex, and I couldn't believe how good it was. It was a wonderful experience, and for such a young guy, he sure knew what he was doing, but I was eaten up inside, to the very core of me, with guilt.

Dear God, what was I doing? I was so messed up in my own life, and now I had gone and had sex with the nephew of the man I loved with all of my heart. I desperately felt like I needed a shrink. I just loved the honesty between me and Randy - we could tell each other how we felt about just about everything. He knew all about Derek and what I was going through. He understood I was ending a part of my life that had been eight and a half years, and he knew I wasn't the type of woman who just wanted to sleep around. In spite of the feelings he knew I had for his uncle, he said he couldn't help how he felt about me from the first moment he laid eyes on me. I was flattered, but now I definitely felt like Mrs. Robinson from *The Graduate*. I was ashamed of myself. What had I done?

I returned to Dallas to fly with Carol. I couldn't bring myself to share with her or Barbie what had happened between me and Randy. I was torn up inside something terrible and never should have allowed that to happen. I could blame it on the alcohol, but to me, that was no excuse for my behavior.

Shirley called and invited me to come back to Mississippi for a giant cookout they were planning and asked me to bring my folks. It sounded like so much fun, and we all needed something fun. Dad had not been feeling very well, and all you had to do was say "Go" to Mom and she was on her way! They came to Dallas, and we all flew into New Orleans together. Randy was there to take us to his house where Shirley and Thermon were anxiously awaiting our arrival. We had the most wonderful time of our lives! Mom and Dad talked with Shirley and Thermon in the swing sets in front of the house. Aaron and Ollie Mae showed up, and everyone had a great time visiting. They knew Mom's birthday was August 4, and they even had a cake for her. I was so happy my folks seemed to feel as at home there with Wendell's family as I had. I thought how wonderful it would have been if Wendell had been there to see our families having fun and getting to know each other.

Mom and Dad met the rest of Wendell's family at the cookout the next day and loved them. Everyone had cooked, baked, and grilled for days in preparation for this gigantic event; I had never seen so much food: shrimp, fish, goat, pork, all kinds of salads and vegetables. Desserts were abundant on every table. We ate so much we were miserable! After eating, several of Wendell's brothers and kids decided to go to the river and for a swim. I was shocked when my Daddy jumped into the truck with them. Randy said Dad was the first one into the river and had a ball!!! Everyone was laughing and having such a good time, which was a wonderful change from the last time I was with all of Wendell's family.

It was so sad when it came time to leave. Ollie Mae and Aaron had stopped by to tell us good-bye and both started crying. It broke my heart! Randy drove us to New Orleans, and we had a difficult time saying good-bye too. When Mom got on the plane, she asked, "What exactly is your relationship with Randy? You two seem awfully close." I told her we were, that we had developed a really close friendship. "It looks like more than that to me," she stated. I couldn't look at Dad, but I could feel him staring a hole through me. They both knew Randy was only nineteen, and I am sure they felt like I had lost my mind. So did I!

Derek sent me papers to sign for the house to be sold. Oh, wow, it seemed so unreal, and I felt so empty.

Derek called and asked me if I still wanted the divorce because he was going to a final hearing and wanted to know if I wanted to be there. I was heartbroken at what I was hearing. Still, I told him I guessed it was for the best for both of us because I didn't see myself moving to New York again, and I knew he had accepted that job there and our house had already been sold. I was still hurting over Wendell's death, and now I had done the most unbelievable thing I had ever done in my whole life with Randy. I was an emotional mess! I told Derek to go ahead with the divorce. He got very quiet but didn't try to change my mind. He just told me he would send me the paperwork when it was final and send me my half of the money from the sale of the house.

On October 6, 1976, I was officially single again. I felt deadened. I cried and cried. I felt just completely empty inside. I never dreamed this would ever happen to me.

Randy had moved to Dallas and was living with me and my brother Mike in Mrs. Wallace's duplex until I bought my own house in Dallas and moved in November of '76. I was afraid if I didn't invest the money, it would somehow slip through my fingers, and I didn't want to have nothing to show for all the years of work I had put in at American.

Derek came to visit me and see the house I had purchased. He told me he was proud of me, which meant an awful lot. I told him Randy was staying with Mike and me until he could find a place of his own. He never asked about my relationship with Randy, and I never volunteered.

Derek had met Randy when he, Mike, and I drove with a U-Haul to get some of the furniture out of the house before it sold. I recalled that last time in our house in Tulsa. I was standing in our old bedroom when Derek walked in and put his arms around me and said, "I hope that we aren't making the biggest mistake of our lives." He caught me so off guard that I burst into tears and ran out the front door to the truck to drive back to Dallas. I couldn't talk for several hours. All I could think was that this really was the end.

Randy had ideas that we were going to spend every waking moment together, and I was guilty of making him think that way because that's what we had done every time I went to Mississippi. I was feeling closed in by both my brother and Randy. They were constantly under my feet every time I came home from a trip, and I felt like I was smothering. The last thing in the world I wanted right now was a commitment, and I knew that was exactly what Randy expected out of me. I had to get really forceful with him one time when I got home from a trip. Mike told me some guy had called for me, but Randy told him the caller he was my fiancé. No way, I did not want to jump out of a marriage straight into another one, and I told him so. Besides, I honestly believed Randy would get tired of me and start dating girls his own age. He and Rog, Carol's fella, enjoyed each other's company and running the roads together, so I figured they would end up with an apartment or something soon.

Mike was living with me because he and Bernie had moved to Hawaii, but things didn't work out for them. He and Bernie weren't getting along, and her family had started treating him like an outsider. Mike was miserable and had fallen for another women he met at a hospital in Hilo. They had started spending time together and having an affair. He got scared and decided he needed to get back to the mainland for a while to try and figure things out, but he didn't want to go back to Columbus, Ohio. Of course I understood, as I had been there and knew what he was going through. I told him he could stay with me until he figured out what he wanted to do. He stayed about two months.

I got very upset with my brother when I came in from a trip one day to find out Mike had flown back to Hawaii but couldn't face me to tell me in person. He had taken my car and left it at the airport, and I had no earthly idea where it was. I was livid! It took Randy and Rog nearly a half a day to find my car at the Braniff terminal. Mike also took a whole jar of Kennedy fifty-cent pieces I had saved for years. I could have choked the very breath out of my brother. If only he had waited until I got home, I could have driven him. Or why didn't he ask Randy to take him to the airport? Mike and I ended up in a really big fight over his decision not to tell me he was leaving and going back to Hawaii.

Christmas was really weird. Mom and Dad came down to spend it with me, and Derek actually called and stopped by on his way to Lexington to be with his family. He left a gift for me under the tree. When I unwrapped it, it was a wallet. I had to leave the room because I was sobbing. It was so strange. I had all these bottled-up emotions that I felt were going to implode any minute causing me to end up back in the hospital. I never got over the fear of that happening to me again.

New Year's Eve was also weird. Barbie and Mike had a party, which was the last thing in the world I wanted to do, but they had invited Mom and Dad too, and I thought they might have a good time. It was Daddy's birthday, so there was a cake for him and we sang Happy Birthday. I excused myself and went to call Derek to wish him a good New Year. He was very cold, understandably, and I wished I hadn't called. It was just so hard to accept the reality of being divorced and that everything was so final.

One good thing about the holiday was that Randy helped make one of Dad's greatest dreams come true. Dad had always wanted to go to the Cotton Bowl or the Rose Bowl. Randy got tickets for Dad, his ex-roommate Bill, Rog, and himself to go to the Cotton Bowl. They nearly froze to death. They even bought a bottle of peppermint schnapps and drank the entire bottle at the game trying to keep warm. Randy reported that Daddy had his share of the schnapps. They had a great time together and went to a bar after the game and ate some kind of black-eyed peas, drank too much beer, and got to feeling really sick. But they said it was all worth it.

I felt so sad when I learned Ollie Mae had passed away on June 9, 1977. I don't think she ever got over Wendell's death. I believe she died of a broken heart. She grieved so much for Wendell that the Lord was merciful in taking her to join him. In a way, I felt so much better knowing he wasn't alone anymore.

Going to her funeral was painful, since she and I had become really close. Aaron grabbed me by the arm and took me to her casket. (Something I chose never to do was look at people who had passed. I wanted to remember them the way they were when they were here on earth.) I went with him, but I never looked at Ollie Mae. Aaron asked me to look at his beautiful wife, but I couldn't. I just looked at the end of the casket and told him she did look beautiful. And now Wendell would have her there with him.

I really needed something happy in my life, and fortunately, speaking of dreams coming true, Mr. Peak, the Flight Service manager, called and told me I was being considered as one of the Flight Attendants going to the American Airlines Golf Tournament in Scottsdale, Arizona. I was so elated, but wished more than anything it would be anywhere but the city where Derek and I had vacationed with his family nearly every year.

I went into the office to talk to Mr. Peak and asked him when I had to go for an interview and if he had any pointers to share with me. He stood up and said, "You won't be interviewing." I felt my heart sink. "You are going to the Golf Tournament, period!" I was so surprised because I knew my supervisor had questioned whether or not I should go since I had too many sick days. I thought she would stand in my way of being able to go, but Mr. Peak said he made up his mind and didn't care what Kathy Schroeder or Eileen Hearne said. I was going!

Yeah!!! This was something 1 had wanted to do for years, and now I was going to be able to do it. It was the "creme de la crème" of Special Assignments, and I couldn't wait to share the news with Randy, but he wasn't happy; he had a fit. I told him no one was stopping me from doing this and that it had been a dream of mine for a very long time. I was going whether he or anyone else liked it or not. Randy didn't say another word. I didn't mean to sound ugly, but no one was going to tell me what to do ever again.

Joe Namath

When I got to Scottsdale, they immediately put all of us to work. We had to unpack golf accessories to give to the VIPs and the athletes. Mercy, AA, gave them a bunch of freebies: shoes, pants, jackets, hats, balls, and towels. What a haul!

The other Flight Attendants were all talking about which athlete they wanted to meet most. I told them I'd like to meet Joe Namath. We had to fill out invitations to a dinner, and I wrote on Joe's that I hoped to meet him and have a picture together. Later that evening, one of the Sales Representatives for AA took me by the hand, walked me into the bar at the resort, and introduced me to Joe. Joe was almost shy, and very sweet when he mentioned he would be happy to take a picture with me. He suggested I go upstairs and get into something more comfortable than my uniform and then come back. But one of the girls, Lane Redman, had already hit on Joe and had no intention of sitting still long enough for me to come back and join them. Instead, she suggested they all go out and get some Mexican food. I told Joe I would get a picture another time. He seemed surprised I didn't take him up on his offer, but Lane had already grabbed his arm and was hanging on for dear life.

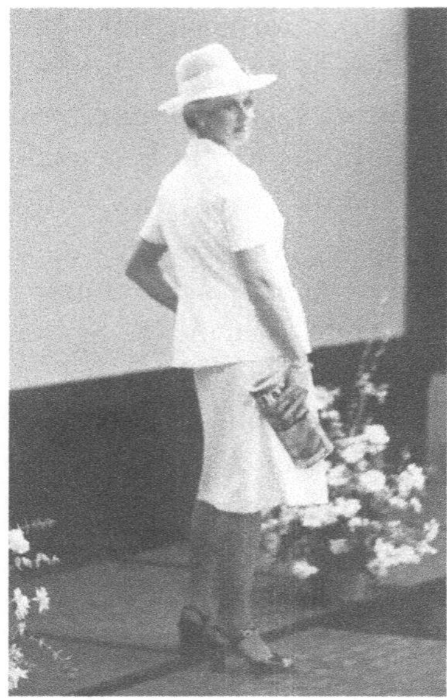

Modeling For Koret

I got fitted for three outfits to wear in the fashion show. I was so excited because I had never been in a real fashion show before. As a Girl Scout in Ohio, I had taken lessons at Lazarus, a big department store, and we had a little fashion show but nothing on the scale of this one. All the wives of the VIPs and athletes would be coming to the fashion show after a luncheon AA sponsored for them. There were only two girls who had any kind of modeling experience. One was a gorgeous black woman named Deborah Pillow; yes, that was her real name. And the other gal was Pat Madison; she was based in San Francisco. She looked like a model and sure knew how to make it look easy as she strutted down the runway. I was nervous, but I gave it my all, and it was fun. Koret of California let each of us pick out an outfit we had worn in the show to keep. I kept a beautiful white two-piece suit. I was so proud and knew Mom would have loved to have seen me walk that runway. She always thought I should have tried to become a professional model, but it wasn't meant to be.

We had a bunch of activities where we had to get all gussied up. I loved that part. The majority of the time we had to be at different stands throughout the course to hand stuff out to the players. I got tons of pictures and couldn't wait to get back to show them to Daddy. He was going to have a fit.

Some of the athletes were a little disappointed that all the Flight Attendants didn't want to sleep with them. There was one Flight Attendant who was engaged and decided this was her last fling, so she was going to bed every athlete she wanted, and by golly, she did too. One of the football players, whose name I won't mention, went down the barstools asking every girl in the club if they wanted to "fuck" him. I could not believe my ears or eyes, but sure enough, one of the girls got up from her seat and left with him. Dear Lord, all of the girls ahead of her knew what he had asked her, and they had all turned him down. I guess she didn't care.

Some of the athletes thought we were snobs, and we thought the majority of them were shallow. Merlin Olsen, Ray Nitsche, and Dan Pastorini were all very, very nice, as were Dan Fouts and Joe Di Maggio. But a few of the guys were such losers. I thought Tommy Branch was coming, but he had another commitment. Too bad because I was looking forward to saying hello.

One of the Flight Attendants, Marcie, and I didn't exactly hit it off. I never understood what her problem was, but she wanted to be the center of attention at every turn. I couldn't be bothered with her or her ego. I struck up a conversation with Dan Pastorini's wife at the time, a former playboy centerfold, and we were having the best conversation when Marcie came over and asked what we were talking about. Mrs. Pastorini didn't care much for her either, I guess, because she said, "If we wanted to tell you what we were talking about, we would have invited you into our conversation. Enough said?" I wanted to crack up right there, but I controlled myself as Marcie did an about-face and left. I wanted to hug Mrs. Pastorini's neck, but of course I didn't.

I was so glad I had been able to do the Golf Tournament. I had told Derek I was going to do it, and he said, "Good for you. I know this is something that you have wanted to do for a long time and I hope it turns out to be everything you hoped it would be." I think it was. It had been fun being stopped in clubs by people when a bunch of us were there and watching the guys sign autographs. It made me think of how much fun Wendell had when he had to do that. I smiled at the thought of him.

When I got home, Mom called and told me Daddy had had a heart attack and was in the hospital, so I took off for Columbus. I called Derek, and he came too. I do not know why I called him, but I guess it was because he had been a part of our family for almost ten years. Perhaps I was just having trouble letting go. I was surprised Derek came, but he was so sweet to all of us.

It was so difficult to see my Daddy lying in that hospital bed with all those wires hooked up to him. He had always been so strong, invincible, and hardly ever sick. I stayed with Daddy when Mom and Derek went to eat. I sat there and prayed and prayed for his total recovery. I just couldn't believe Daddy had felt so good in December, and now here he was, two months later, in the hospital. It was especially scary since Uncle Ed had died of a heart attack.

The second morning Derek woke up with a pulled muscle in his neck. When we went to the hospital, Derek went to the Emergency Room while we visited Dad. When Derek joined us, he was wearing a huge cloth collar around his neck. I felt so bad for him - here Derek came to be with me when my Dad was ill, and he ends up in a neck brace. He did make Dad laugh when he saw him. Dad asked, "Did she hit you, Derek?" (Meaning me.) "Cause if she did, you ought to hit her back." Derek laughed, and so did Dad. Daddy stayed there for a few days in intensive care before he was moved into a regular room.

When Derek had to head back to work, I thanked him for coming, and he said he was glad I had called. I probably shouldn't have, but I did and he wanted to come so, of course I let him.

I called my old buddy from High School, Terry Kneisley, and he came over to visit with me and Mom. We all sat around and talked until well after 11:00 p.m. Then Terry did the strangest thing. After Mom went to bed, he scooted closer to me and starting kissing me passionately. I was so surprised because he had never done that before. I loved it! We "necked" for a long time, and then he asked me to go out with him on Saturday. I told him I would. When he left, I sat there for quite a while and couldn't get over how affectionate Terry had acted towards me.

Charmaine and her husband Randy arrived from San Diego. They had driven all night and day to get there and were exhausted. They had two boys by then, both blonde-haired, blue-eyed dolls. Sis, Randy, and I went to the hospital to see Dad. He was pleased we all were there with him, but he did lecture them about driving all day and night.

Dad went home the next day, and I was a little worried because there were so many of us in that little house. I was especially worried about the kids and hoped Dad could handle the noise. I was very disappointed that he smoked two cigarettes just after he got home. When I started to say something to him, Mom stopped me. I just couldn't believe he was doing that after what he had just gone through.

Terry Kneisley

Terry came and got me for our date. We were supposed to go to a movie, but I just wanted to be with him and have a glass of wine in a quiet place. We ended up having a lot of wine – I guess the "let down" from worrying about Daddy was overwhelming. We both were giddy when he suggested we go back to his apartment. I was curious to see if he still had that passion locked up inside him. We had barely gotten inside his apartment when I found the answer to that question. We started kissing passionately, and he took me by the hand and led me into his bedroom. I could not believe this was happening. Here was a man I had had a crush on since I was thirteen years old. I would have given anything to date him and have a relationship, but somehow it never came about — his fault not mine.

We were about to get into his bed and make love, and I found myself admiring his physique. Terry always had a great build. He used to remind me of the letter "T" with broad shoulders and slender hips. I had seen him in his swimsuit but never without any clothes on. He helped me remove all of my clothes, and I took off the rest of his. We slid into his bed and kissed for what seemed like forever. He had always been such a good kisser. I was tickled he had given me my very first kiss, and he had certainly improved with age.

We both really got into turning each other on, and it was wonderful. I know I must have nearly lost my breath when he first made love to me. He was so hot and strong. We made beautiful love together, and then I laid my head on his shoulder. I pushed myself up on my elbows, looked at him and said, "Terry, do you know I have loved you since I was thirteen years old?" He was surprised by my question. "No, I didn't."

"Well, I have. I have dreamed of being with you over half of my life. I want you to know you have always had a special place in my heart, and you always will." He leaned forward and kissed me deeply, which started those rushing emotions all over again. He never told me he cared about me, but it didn't matter. I hadn't told Wendell what he meant to me, and I regretted it, so I wasn't going to let this chance to tell Terry how I felt go by. Again we made love.

He got up and got some sort of lotion that I rubbed all over his back, arms, chest, and legs, Terry reacted by getting turned on all over again -for the third time. I could not believe this. This was awesome! He held me and said, half laughing and half serious, "You sure weren't anything like this in High School."

"Terry, I was a virgin then. A lot has happened since High School."

"I, for one, am glad you changed," he said with a smile. He put his arms around me and held me close to him. I rested in his arms for a bit, but then I got very aggressive with him. I started to kiss his neck and his chest, and I took my sweet time doing it. I decided I was going to share some of that education Wendell gave me with Terry. Well, it worked, and we made love for the fourth time. I think Terry was as surprised as I was.

We talked and drank more wine. I guess the warmth of his bed, the taste of the wine, and the view of the snowflakes falling outside his window was just too romantic for us. For the fifth time in about six hours, we made love a final time. This time it was slow and gentle and lasted forever. I felt so happy! It wasn't the passionate, sweaty, zealous love Wendell and I made, but it was extraordinary.

Terry never said much, which I found kind of sad, but I guess I really didn't know what I expected him to say. We walked down the snow-covered steps from his apartment to the car, and he drove me back to my parent's house. It was nearly 5:00 a.m., and like a teenager, I hoped my parents weren't awake. Thank goodness they weren't. Terry walked me to the door, kissed me, and told me to take care, and then off he drove into the snow.

How could two people have had such a connection for as many years as we had known each other and not ever been able to build on it? This only made things that much more difficult for me to comprehend. Why didn't Terry ever take the initiative to see me again or come to Dallas?

I am sad to report that my beloved Terry Kneisley passed away on March 22, 2014, two months after his sixty-ninth birthday. It was so strange, but after the 50th reunion, I had planned to send him his yearly birthday card, but I hesitated because I was a little angry with him for not coming. Then I had an overwhelming feeling, like I had once with Elvis, that Terry wouldn't live much longer. I sent that birthday card to Terry on January 22, two months to the date his neighbor found Terry on the couch, already passed away.

NO MORE TOMORROWS WITH TERRY

I saw Terry walking down the hall.
Oh, so handsome and so tall.
Dressed in his khakis and madras plaid.
He smiled my way and I felt so glad.
Finally a boy taller than me.
Would our lives entwine? I had to see.

A party to celebrate turning thirteen was
made extra special because of him.
Daddy filmed us standing side by side.
I was filled with "Puppy Love" and so much pride.
His heart.... I desperately wanted to win.
I hoped our future together was about to begin.
It would have if I had my way.
Sadly he was in and out of my life
......but chose never to stay.

I went off to my career in the sky.
To college he went to give it a try.
I tried to see him when I was in town.
I was always hopeful he'd want me around.

Vietnam called and he went to serve.
I wrote him at least once a week, happy
thoughts and pictures to share.
He joked that the guys with him wanted to go
AWOL after seeing my photos there.
I was never happier when I heard he
was safe, back home in the USA.
I remember saying "Thank you Lord
for that good news today."

Finally I married. I couldn't wait for him forever.
But the ties between us I just couldn't sever.
I got divorced and lost my Dad.
I turned to see him standing there, looking so sad.

He held me in his arms as I continued to cry.
Oh dear Lord, how I love this guy!

I once again married and had two sons.
I enjoyed being a Mom. It was so much fun!
Life went on but he was always there.
I saw Terry when I could; we'd talk and share.

They say you never get over your first
love and I know that's true.
Because now he's gone and I don't know what to do.
There' s a hole in my heart because
of a boy named Terry.
The man I hoped one day to marry.

Terry and Me at the 30th Class Reunion

I went back to Dallas after Daddy's doctor assured me Daddy was going to be okay. I told Mom and Dad I would come back soon, but I had to get back to work. Randy met me at the airport, and we went home to have a long talk. I told him he meant the world to me but that I was in no way ready for a committed relationship. He knew Derek and I had just divorced and that it was probably the second most painful thing I had ever experienced, second to losing Wendell. I told Randy he was welcome to stay with me, but I had no intentions of getting married any time soon. I cared deeply for Randy and loved having him there with me. However, I always thought he would get tired of me and move on to women his age, and I was not about to go through another heartbreak like the end of my marriage. He didn't like what I was saying to him because I honestly believe he thought he would move to Dallas and marry me. But I had no intentions of that happening any time soon.

August 19, 1977 I was about to board my flight for PHX when I ran into a goofy Captain named Jack Anderson. He was the one who would call me Mrs. Presley every time we flew together, and I secretly loved it. We discovered he was flying that night with Carol and me.

Half way through the trip, Captain Anderson rang and told me to send Carol to the cockpit for a minute. I was very puzzled by this, but who was I to question the Captain's request. I told Carol her presence was needed in the cockpit. She looked at me funny but went up there to see what Jack wanted. I was finishing my meal service as she came out of the cockpit looking rather pale. I asked Carol what was wrong, and she said she would tell me later. I was persistent and asked her again what was wrong. She got stern with me and said she had to get back to Coach, but we would talk about it later.

We had a turnaround which brought us back to Dallas before continuing on to Phoenix. As we were taking a break in the First Class cabin, Carol said she hated to have such bad timing, but she had to tell me something. She was afraid if she didn't tell me right then I would hear it from someone else and be caught completely off guard.

I was so puzzled by what she was saying to me. "Carol, what in the world are you talking about?" I asked her. "Bev, I hate to tell you this, but Elvis died. He had a heart attack."

I could not believe my ears. I said, "No, no this can't be true, Carol. Where did you hear this?" She told me Jack had been told by the control tower or some other means of communication during the flight, and he felt like he had to tell Carol so she could prepare me.

I refused to believe what Carol had just told me. I ran off the plane to call Mrs. Marion Cocke who answered on the first ring. I told her it was Bev and asked her if what I had just been told was true. She was crying and told me it was. Then she asked me if I would be coming to the funeral.

I was flabbergasted! This just couldn't be true! Yes, I had a horrible feeling about Elvis that night I left him in 1975, but I never imagined it would be so soon, not even two years from the time I had that awful feeling. I asked Marion if it was true about the heart attack, and she said it was. Again, she asked me if I wanted her to pick me up to attend the funeral. I told her no, that I didn't want to go. I just wanted to remember him the way I had seen him when I left Graceland that morning. I didn't want to attend what I feared would turn out to be a circus. She said she understood. I told Marion I was in between flights, and I would have to call her when I got back to Dallas in two days. I told her to be strong.

I went back onto the plane and stood there staring at Carol. I told her I had just spoken to Marion, Elvis's nurse, and she had confirmed he had indeed passed away. For some reason, I couldn't cry. I just sat down in the seat and looked out the window. I still had a flight to Phoenix I had to work, therefore, I could not let go until I was in the quietness of my room. I don't know how I made it through the trip because passengers were talking about Elvis's death at every seat.

But I made it until I got to my room. I opened the door and was barely inside when the flood of tears poured down my face. It had only been two years since I was in his company. Yes, I know I was a one-night stand, but I loved that my letters and cards Marion had read to him had brought him joy. Elvis had done so much for everyone else with the great gift of his beautiful voice. I was tickled he had enjoyed my company for at least two nights and that my small gesture of friendship, maybe, made him feel better when he wasn't doing so well health-wise or when he might have had the blues. Needless to say, the entire night I spent with him went through my head, so I would switch between smiling, laughing, and then crying some more.

I cried myself to sleep that night. The world would never be the same! Not just for me but for millions and millions of people. Elvis was such a gift from God to the whole world. His movies may have been hokey, but they were wholesome. His music was initially controversial, but then everyone seemed to accept the fact he had one of the most beautiful voices that had ever sang a song.

When I got home, there were calls from other Flight Attendants who knew I had "dated" Elvis. (I never felt that was the true way to describe my time with Elvis. We didn't actually date, darn it. I would say I was fortunate to spend "private time" with him. Still, I didn't want to have to explain all that to everyone.) They called to check on me, and I even got a few sympathy cards from some folks. This was kind of strange, but I don't think people knew what to say to me.

Barbie was sad and called to make sure I was okay. We laughed about some of the things Elvis had said that night or something stupid I had done in front of him. Barbie asked if I was going to the funeral too. I told her the same thing I told Marion - I wanted to remember Elvis the way he was when I left him. I knew it would be a mob scene, and I didn't want any part of it. I was flattered Marion even asked me to go, but I wasn't going to do that to myself.

I hated some of the horrible books that had come out about Elvis. I was ashamed of the book his bodyguards had written, *Elvis, What Happened?* I knew, as did everyone else, that all sorts of bad and ugly things would be written about Elvis, and it was so sad. I was sure Elvis had some things in his past he wasn't particularly proud of, but why did everyone have to try to make a buck on ruining his reputation? I'm sure he had some weaknesses, but who doesn't? I didn't feel like it was necessary to tell the whole world. I don't have any respect for most of these people who took advantage of their relationship with Elvis. If only they would take a moment to think about it, what would their sorry lives have been without him?

I admired Joe Esposito for all of the sacrifices he made to stick with Elvis through thick and thin; to even have his family break up because of his loyalty to Elvis. Joe and I had dinner in Los Angeles one evening, and he shared a few special stories with me about Elvis. I am sure there were a lot of things Joe would have liked to help Elvis change if he could, but his influence was limited. Joe was the one thing Elvis had too few of — real friends. If anyone knew Elvis Aaron Presley, it was Joe, and I'm glad Elvis had him in his life.

My life from now on would be about adjusting. Adjusting to being single, having Randy living with me, and trying to figure out who I was now and what I wanted out of life. One thing I knew for sure was that I didn't want to stop flying. I enjoyed flying so much with either Barbie or Carol. They were the best flying partners and the greatest friends anyone could ask for. They still are.

This is not the end of my story. This is probably half of it. I continued flying until December 1, 2001. But in the meantime, I had a lot more experiences that ultimately led me to the Lord. I'm hoping you will be intrigued to learn about my International flying episodes, the wonderful rumor that I was having Tom Selleck's baby (got ya there didn't I? - that ought to sell my next book if nothing else does), and going against all odds to marry a second time and have two incredibly awesome sons named Joshua Aaron and Kaleb Micah. Hopefully, you will want to read about our seven-year walk in Job's shoes. I want to share with you how faith truly can pull you through the most challenging times of your life. I look forward to sharing the second part of my life with you when I finish that next book. God bless you, and I hope you have enjoyed your flight with me thus far.

THE END

ABOUT THE AUTHOR

Beverly Golden Cuevas was born Beverly Jane Golden in Ironton, Ohio in 1945. She spent the first 10 years of her life in Parkersburg, West Virginia with her family. Her father had a job opportunity in Columbus, Ohio in 1955 so away they went. Beverly started working at the age of 14 to contribute to her family finances. She graduated Columbus North High School in 1963. She moved on to work at the Ohio Bell Telephone Company after graduation. In 1965, on the dare of her best friend she went to an interview to be a Stewardess for American Airlines. American hired her and she started her flying career in New York, then commuting from Tulsa, Oklahoma to her Dallas base. She flew both domestic and international. During her career, she never received a bad passenger letter. In 1977, she was 1 of 12 Flight Attendants selected out of 16,000 to participate in a highly coveted special assignment to work at the prestigious American Airlines Golf Classic. Her flying career ended on December 1, 2001 after 35 years.

Beverly now lives in Dallas, Texas. She has been married to her wonderful husband Randy for 43 years. She has two sons, Joshua and Kaleb. She is a loving wife and mother, never missing a baseball game or school talent show, in spite of her flying schedule! Mimi is blessed to pass on her knowledge and love of life to her grandchildren Eden, Elijah, Ellie, Logan and Holly.

Milton Keynes UK
Ingram Content Group UK Ltd.
UKHW021836151223
434457UK00004B/14